D0214970

A Mickey Spillane
Companion

A MICKEY SPILLANE
COMPANION

Robert L. Gale

GREENWOOD PRESS
Westport, Connecticut · London

HOUSTON PUBLIC LIBRARY

R01298 55029

Library of Congress Cataloging-in-Publication Data

Gale, Robert L., 1919-
    A Mickey Spillane companion / Robert L. Gale.
        p. cm.
    Includes bibliographical references and index.
    ISBN 0-313-32334-8 (alk. paper)
      1. Spillane, Mickey, 1918—Dictionaries.   2. Detective and mystery stories,
American—Dictionaries.   3. Hammer, Mike (Fictitious character)—
Dictionaries.   4. Private investigators in literature—Dictionaries.   I. Title.
PS3537.P652 Z67 2003
813'54—dc21   2002035339

British Library Cataloguing in Publication Data is available.

Copyright © 2003 by Robert L. Gale

All rights reserved. No portion of this book may be
reproduced, by any process or technique, without the
express written consent of the publisher.

Library of Congress Catalog Card Number: 2002035339
ISBN: 0-313-32334-8

First published in 2003

Greenwood Press, 88 Post Road West, Westport, CT 06881
An imprint of Greenwood Publishing Group, Inc.
www.greenwood.com

Printed in the United States of America

The paper used in this book complies with the
Permanent Paper Standard issued by the National
Information Standards Organization (Z39.48-1984).

10 9 8 7 6 5 4 3 2 1

For Maureen and Our Family

Contents

Preface

Frank Morrison Spillane, universally known as Mickey Spillane, may well be the most widely read author in the world. At one point, he wrote seven of the ten best-sellers of all time. He is allegedly the most widely translated author America ever produced and fifth in world competition, below only Vladimir Illyich Lenin, Maxim Gorky, Count Leo Tolstoy, and Jules Verne.

So why have so many respectable critics reviled Spillane? Before Anthony Boucher repented, he dismissed Spillane's time-worn formula as "sex cum sadism." John G. Cawelti labeled Spillane's writing "atrocious"; Malcolm Cowley diagnosed Mike Hammer, Spillane's main hero, as "a homicidal paranoiac"; Julian Symons labeled an early Spillane novel "nauseating." Have upwards of two hundred million book buyers been wrong?

No, and the simple explanation is twofold. First, Spillane is a master storyteller. His works are page-turners. He grabs his readers with his first paragraph and points them spellbound toward his climax—often revealed in the final paragraph, twice at least in the final word.

Second, Spillane appeals to innumerable men's—and many women's—primitive, Jungian lust for gore, hidden though it may be these days, especially in the arcadian groves of pale academicians and under the lamps of effete book reviewers. Many of Spillane's first million readers were veterans returning to civilian life after World War II. Most had known violence up close and were freed by it, and by boredom and loneliness in faraway places, from homegrown 1930s hypocrisies concerning sex and chivalry. They found Hammer's guns, fists, and lusts exciting, even enviable. True, many readers deplore Spillane's often shoddy, too-fast handling of the English language; but better it is to repeat that the subject of this *Companion* is a master storyteller.

Spillane should be considered by self-respecting critics of mystery and detective fiction as deserving of membership in a four-horsemen cadre also mustering Dashiell Hammett, Raymond Chandler, and Ross Macdonald: Hammett is more of a pioneer, his Sam Spade leading directly to Mike Hammer; Chandler is more subtle, more cosmopolitan; Macdonald, more profoundly cerebral. But Spillane outsold all three together and will live in the hearts of his readers as long.

Spillane's most famous hero reveals himself in his signature speech, delivered to a police captain of homicide: "I don't underrate the cops. But cops can't break a guy's arm to make him talk, and they can't shove his teeth in with the muzzle of a .45." Ominously, since what has come to be known simply as 9/11, that horrific blow to America's inadequate body armor, many so-called conservative Americans have come out of the closet of naïveté shared by liberals and are advocating a kind of Mike Hammer-like, Tiger Mann-like style of retaliation. Spillane alone, among the big four pop novelists just named, features in several novels many problems and villainies arising in the Middle East, insufficiently addressed by the United Nations, and requiring a unique reply to evil. Is our Constitution a suicide pact? Is high-pressure interrogation of one justified if it saves a thousand?

Also, corruption seen in America at every level of religious, political, juridical, commercial, educational, entertainment, and sports activities makes fist-clenching, muscle-flexing Americans frustrated almost beyond endurance and has them wondering whether Spillane-style responses are ever warranted. Vigilantism, in groups or—as in Spillane—alone, no. But yes, Mike Hammer, toned down, becomes a metaphor for Americans dismayed by political correctness, time's delay, and established pusillanimity.

Welcome indeed would be a rollicking autobiography in which the colorful Mickey Spillane would detail his pleasures, perils, pitfalls, and accomplishments over the decades. Even better, perhaps, would be a full-length, conscientiously documented biography.

A Mickey Spillane Companion is designed to augment, not replace, the zestful reading of Spillane's fictional works. It should appeal to those who have read some of them, have forgotten details, and wish to refresh their memories; perhaps it will encourage them to dust off an old copy, or replace one discarded long ago, and read it again. High school, undergraduate, and graduate students, teachers and scholars, and general readers in the field of pop fiction cannot possibly retain details of plot and characterization in Spillane's twenty-four novels and nineteen short stories. I invite readers to use this *Companion* as a mini-refresher course. Additionally, a brief look at my write-ups of unfamiliar Spillane titles may entice readers to have a go at the originals.

While preparing this book, I joyfully became indebted to several friends at the University of Pittsburgh, at Pitt's Hillman Library, and at Carnegie Public Library across the street, including H. David Brumble III, Patricia Duff, Lois Kepes, Lawrence Tomikel, Thomas M. Twiss, Vicki Redcay, and Donald Wentworth; and to freelance researcher Annette M. Krupper. I am also grateful to

Sue Laslie Kimball, of Methodist College, Fayetteville, North Carolina, for her expert thoughts regarding Spillane. Hearty thanks are also due to Dr. George F. Butler and Betty C. Pessagno of Greenwood Press for their wise suggestions and unfailing cooperation. My love to my wife, Maureen, and to our family— John, Jim, Christine, Bill, and Lisette. Special thanks to Jim for his computer expertise.

Chronology

1918 Frank Morrison Spillane born March 9 in Brooklyn, New York, the only child of John Joseph Spillane, an Irish-Catholic bartender, and Catherine Anne Spillane, a Presbyterian. The family soon moved to Elizabeth, New Jersey. Nicknamed Mickey by his father, Spillane moved back to Brooklyn.

1929 Says he has read all of Alexandre Dumas and Herman Melville by age eleven.

1935–1939 Attends Erasmus High School; does winter odd jobs, is summer lifeguard.

1939–1940 Attends Kansas State Teachers College (now Fort Hays State University), in Kansas, intending to become a lawyer.

1940 Is part-time salesman for Gimbel's in New York City during Christmas season; meets fellow employee Joe Gill, through him meets Joe's brother Ray Gill, an editor of Funnies, Inc.; is hired by Ray, becomes script-writer and assistant editor, writes Captain Marvel stories at rate of one per day.

1942–1945 Enlists in U.S. Army, May 1942, becomes aviation cadet, Florida, Mississippi; is honorably discharged October 1945 with rank of first lieutenant.

1945 Marries Mary Ann Pierce (1924–), in Greenwood, Mississippi: children—Kathy, Mark, Mike, Carolyn.

1945 With Ray and Joe Gill, establishes and operates comic-book factory in Brooklyn.

1946   Decides with wife to buy four acres of land near Newburgh, New York; writes *I, the Jury,* in nine (or perhaps nineteen) days.

1947   Early royalties of $1,000 provide down payment for land; soon builds Little Bohemia, a four-room cinder-block house and nearby one-room studio; *I, the Jury* becomes best-seller, as do next five Mike Hammer novels: *My Gun Is Quick* (1950), *Vengeance Is Mine!* (1950), *The Big Kill* (1951), *One Lonely Night* (1951), and *Kiss Me, Deadly* (1952).

1950   Is denied request to go on active duty in Korean War.

1951   *The Long Wait,* first non–Mike Hammer novel.

1952   Becomes a Jehovah's Witness; is earning about $50,000 per novel.

1953   Sells movie rights for his novels to Victor Saville, British producer, for $250,000; productions are *I, the Jury* (1953), *The Long Wait* (1954), *Kiss Me, Deadly* (1955), and *My Gun Is Quick* (1957).

1953–1954   Writes Mike Hammer comic strips for newspapers.

1953–1960   Writes numerous short stories, beginning with "Everybody's Watching Me," four-part serial in *Manhunt,* and continuing in *Manhunt, Male,* and *Cavalier.*

1954   With family begins permanent onshore residence at Murrell's Inlet, south of Myrtle Beach, South Carolina.

1956   Skids and overturns Jaguar car outside Newburgh, bruises ribs, and injures shoulder (April).

1962   Flies own P-51 Mustang to and from South Carolina to New York and Florida to visit movie sets filming some of his novels; divorced.

1963   Returns to Hammer with *The Girl Hunters,* writes screenplay for it, stars in it as Hammer (1963); Corgi, British publishing company, issues Spillane short stories in collections, beginning with *Me, Hood!,* followed by *The Return of the Hood* (1964), *The Flier* (1964), and *Killer Mine* (1965).

1964   Marries Sherri (Selma) Molinou; *The Snake,* next Hammer novel, followed by *The Twisted Thing* (1966), *The Body Lovers* (1967), *Survival . . . Zero!* (1970), *The Killing Man* (1989, for payment of $1,500,000), and *Black Alley* (1996, for another $1,500,000); *Day of the Guns,* first Tiger Mann novel, followed by *Bloody Sunrise* (1965), *The Death Dealers* (1965) and *The By-Pass Control* (1967).

1969   *The Delta Factor,* first of three non-Hammer, non-Mann adult novels, others being *The Erection Set* (1972) and *The Last Cop Out* (1973); establishes Spillane-Fellows Productions, independent film company, with producer Robert Fellows.

1973   Begins appearing on TV in Miller Lite beer ads (until 1989).

1979   *The Day the Sea Rolled Back,* children's book, earns Junior Literary Guild Award; is followed by second children's book, *The Ship That Never Was* (1982).

1980   Writing book for *Oh, Mike!,* musical, to feature Mike Hammer (evidently never produced).

1982   *Mike Hammer: The Comic Strip 1;* divorced.

1983   Marries Jane Rodgers Johnson (1946–), a former Miss South Carolina twenty-eight years his junior: stepchildren—Britt, Lisa; receives Private Eye Writers of America's Lifetime Achievement Award.

1984–1987   Creates *Mike Hammer,* television series.

1985   *Mike Hammer: The Comic Strip 2.*

1990   Receives Private Eye Writers of America's Short Story Award.

1995   Receives Mystery Writers of America's Grand Master Award.

1998   Is associated with *Golden Age of Marvel Comics.*

Abbreviations

Collins   Max Allan Collins, "Mickey Spillane," in *Mystery and Suspense Writers: The Literature of Crime, Detection, and Espionage,* eds. Robin W. Winks and Maureen Corrigan, 2 vols. (New York: Charles Scribner's Sons, 1998).

Collins and Traylor   Max Allan Collins and James L. Traylor, *One Lonely Knight: Mickey Spillane's Mike Hammer* (Bowling Green, Ohio: Bowling Green State University Popular Press, 1984).

Johnston   Richard W. Johnston, "Death's Fair-Haired Boy," *Life* 32 (June 23, 1952): 79–80, 82, 85–86, 89–90, 92, 95.

Sifakis   Carl Sifakis, *The Mafia Encyclopedia,* 2nd ed. (New York: Facts on File, 1999).

A

AARON. In *The Last Cop Out,* he is a callow Jew whom Papa Menes would not mind letting make love to Sylvia Menes, his dull wife.

ABBERNICHE, NOTO. In *The Killing Man,* this is the name of the man who impersonated a policeman in the gang's effort to kidnap Velda from the hospital. Mike wounds and Captain Pat Chambers kills him. Abberniche, a killer, began his career with the Costello gang.

ABLES, PADDY. In "The Gold Fever Tapes," he is a bartender whom Fallon knows.

ABOUT. In "Me, Hood!," this is the name of the Brooklyn firm for which Harry Peeler worked. Peeler accidentally struck and killed Henry Billings.

ADAMS, CINDY. In *The Snake,* she is Joey Adams's wife and is a *TV Guide* columnist. She and Joey gets information about Sally Devon Torrence for Mike.

ADAMS, JOEY. In *The Snake,* he is Cindy Adams's husband and is a nightclub entertainer. He and Cindy tell Mike about Sally Devon Torrence's past.

ADAMS, VIRGIL. In *Bloody Sunrise,* he is a Newark Central agent who provides Tiger Mann with information. Adams mentions the Valcheck Project to him. In *The Death Dealers,* Adams, called Virg, aids Tiger, notably by providing photos of Malcolm Turos. In *The By-Pass Control,* Adams is a steady source of information by phone for Tiger.

ADLER, JAKE. In "Kick It or Kill!," he is a Pinewood citizen whom Simpson's thugs beat up for interfering.

ADRANO, HARRY. In "Kick It or Kill!," he is an ex-convict working for Simpson. Kelly Smith kills him in Simpson's mansion.

ADRIANNE. In "The Girl Behind the Hedge," she was Chester Duncan's fiancée.

"THE AFFAIR WITH THE DRAGON LADY" (1962). Short story. (Characters: Blakenship, Vic Cabot, Waldo Casey, Arnie Castle, Charlie Cross, Fred Halloway, Elaine Hood, Jonesy, Irene Kubitsky, Lou Kubitsky, Henry Lucerne, Curly Mason, Ed Percy, George Poe, Tiny Sinkwich, Henry Stamph, Stephano, Pappy Thompson, Vern Tice.)

After the war, the eleven crewmembers of a B-17, named the Dragon Lady and mothballed, disperse to various civilian jobs. The narrator was first pilot; Vic Cabot was radioman; Charlie Cross, engineer; Lou Kubitsky, left waist gunner; Henry Lucerne, navigator; Ed Percy, tail gunner; Tiny Sinkwich, right waist gunner; Vern Tice, copilot; Arnie Castle, Fred Halloway, and George Poe complete the crew. All but Tice have married. Tice made a fortune in the stock market. Elaine Hood, a Broadway actress, is his girlfriend. When Tice tells them he has bought the Dragon Lady, reconditioned her, and trucked her to a secret hangar in a swamp, the old buddies rendezvous there, drink, reminisce, and fish and hunt nearby. So what if their wives object? One day an F-100 pilot from a nearby base has to parachute into the swamp. The old gang gets the Dragon Lady near, generates power to light the scene as she partially sinks, rescues the pilot, returns triumphantly to the hangar, and is photographed by *Life* photographers. The secret out, the Dragon Lady is hauled to safety. Tice marries Elaine. In this story, Spillane uses too much imagery derived from air force lingo.

AFFIA, AL. In *Kiss Me, Deadly,* he is a criminal associate of Carl Evello. He was a waterfront boss. William Mist kills him. Affia called himself Tony Todd.

AGROUNSKY, LOUIS ("LOU"). In *The By-Pass Control,* he is the brilliant, drug-addicted Polish inventor of the by-pass control, which can immobilize missiles. Uncertain whether to use it to stymie American ICBMs because of his political uncertainties, he leaves Eau Gallie, Florida, near Cape Kennedy, and holes up in Leesville, North Carolina, with his by-pass control. Niger Hoppes, a Soviet agent, seeks him there. When Tiger Mann finds him, Agrounsky is dead of an overdose.

AL. In *The Deep,* he is one of Lenny Sobel's gunmen. Deep shoots him in the arm. Al tortures Helen Tate and is shot to death during the final attack on the Knights Owl Club.

ALBO, LOUIS. In *The Erection Set,* he is a man The Turk destroyed some time ago.

ALDRIDGE. In "The Seven Year Kill," he is a policeman, along with Garcia, under Johnny's command in Phoenix.

ALEX. In "Return of the Hood," he is a Soviet agent Ryan slugs viciously.

ALIET. In *The Girl Hunters,* this is the name of an insurance company, which hired Mike. He recalls this, his first job, as involving "a lousy heist" in which he was hit and nearly burned to death.

ALLEN. In "Tomorrow I Die," he is one of Auger's thugs. He slugs Richard Thurber but is presumably killed by the police.

ALLEN, DR. VANCE. In *Survival . . . Zero!,* he is experienced in narcotic rehabilitation and helps Heidi Anders.

ALLEN, HELEN. In "Kick It or Kill!," she is a Pinewood girl whom Simpson employed as a sex slave and rewarded with a new car.

ALLEN, JOE. In *The Erection Set,* Dog Kelly tells Charmaine he located her through Joe Allen, of Belgium.

ALLERTON. In *The Big Kill,* this is the name of a movie company for which Marsha Lee worked ten years ago.

ALVADA, MANUEL. In "The Flier," he provided Tucker Stacy with evidence about the Russian nuclear warheads. Both men were blown up when Stacy was flying back to Celeda.

ALVEREZ. In *The Deep,* he converted Constantino's business, located close to where Bennett was fatally shot, into a grocery store.

AMEGA, CARLOS. In "Return of the Hood," it is said that he was killed in Madrid by Manos Dekker.

AMES, CARL. In *The Last Cop Out,* he is one of Papa Menes's henchmen, in Florida. His partner, George Space, kids Ames because he was recently kicked in the genitals by an air force soldier.

AMES, LENNIE. In "Return of the Hood," he is a hotel clerk who reluctantly gives Ryan a key to his spare room. Ames's fellow clerk is a homosexual, unnamed, who turns out to be an aide to Manos Dekker.

AMORY, CANDACE. In *The Killing Man,* she is an assistant D.A., with experience in law and FBI work. This gorgeous woman, who sports a Phi Beta Kappa key, has an apartment near the U.N., and is ambitious to be governor of New York and then president of the United States. She helps Mike in sundry ways, both professional and intimate. She is inaccurately nicknamed "the Iceberg Lady," "the Icicle Lady," and "the Ice Lady."

ANDERS, DR. ("DOC"). In *The Deep,* he is a disreputable physician who tends the wounded Lew James.

ANDERS, HEIDI. In *Survival . . . Zero!,* she is a beautiful, heroin-addicted actress and companion of Woodring Ballinger. She likes Mike Hammer, who helps her even as he resists her charms, which include a navel painted to resemble a human eye.

ANDERSON. In *Bloody Sunrise,* he is a Newark Central agent who tells Tiger Mann at one point to get in touch with Ernie Bentley. Anderson also tells Tiger that an unsuccessful attempt on Gabin Martrel's life was made with Monger poison.

ANDERSON, SERGEANT. In *The Death Dealers,* he has the idea of having television coverage of Teish El Abin.

ANDRA, BILL. In *The Day the Sea Rolled Back,* he runs a radio shop on Peolla Island.

ANDRÉ. In *The Delta Factor,* it is at his bar that Morgan locates Bernice Case.

ANDREW. In *Vengeance Is Mine!,* he is a rich man seeking thrills at the Bowery Inn. He says he has known better times.

ANDREWS, DOUG. In *The Day the Sea Rolled Back,* he is Captain Stephen Morelli's first mate.

ANDY. In *Kiss Me, Deadly,* he is a fat bartender and worries because thugs are after Mike.

ANDY. In *The Last Cop Out,* he was Ted Proctor's wino friend, deceased.

ANDY. In "Return of the Hood," Ryan asks Pete-the-Dog to call him at Andy's place.

ANDY. In *The Twisted Thing,* he is the bartender at a Bayview honky-tonk where Mike Hammer stops. Mike notices that Andy has Ruston York's pajama bottoms.

ANGELO. In *The Delta Factor,* he is the loyal, "jockey-sized" bell captain at the Regis Hotel. A university graduate, he provides Morgan invaluable information and assistance.

ANGELO. In *The Snake,* he is a person reputedly killed by Marv Kania.

ANGIE. In *The Body Lovers* and "Man Alone," she is a waitress at the Blue Ribbon.

ANN. In *One Lonely Night,* she is Lee Deamer's secretary.

ANNA. In *Bloody Sunrise,* her name is inscribed on a ring owned by Spaak Helo. This reference could be a red herring to make the reader think Helo knows Ann Lighter.

ANNIE. In "The Bastard Bannerman," she is the Bannerman family's old servant. She likes and aids Cat Cay Bannerman.

ANTON, MAURICE. In "The Veiled Woman," he was an associate of Sergi Porkov until Anton died of cancer.

ARANDO, PASI. In *The Last Cop Out,* he is a member of a newly established crime family.

ARANDO, STEVE. In *The Last Cop Out,* he is Pasi Arando's cousin.

ARANDO, VITALE. In *The Last Cop Out,* he is Steve Arando's uncle, on the crime syndicate's Big Board.

ARBATUR, COMMISSIONER. In "Killer Mine," he is the New York police commissioner who puts pressure on Lieutenant Joe Scanlon for quick action.

ARCHIE. In *One Lonely Night,* he drives Mike Hammer and Lee Deamer to the George Washington Bridge. He will keep Mike's secrets because Mike knows about Archie's having committed a murder, "justified" though it was.

ARDMORE, WALTER HEAD. In "The Gold Fever Tapes," he was a prisoner whom Squeaky Williams kept from knifing Fallon.

ARGENIO, AL. In "Man Alone," he is a crooked policeman. His partner is Sergeant Jerry Nolan. Argenio participated in framing Patrick Regan for Leo Marcus, a mobster, by planting $5,000 in a supposed bribe in Regan's apartment. When Argenio kidnaps Madaline Stumper, Regan tracks him down and kills him.

ARGROPOLIS, CHARLIE. In *The Last Cop Out,* he was a criminal who choked Papa Menes, when Menes was age twelve, to make him talk. Menes seized Argopolis's icepick and stabbed him to death.

ARLENE. In *The Big Kill,* she is Harry Bailen's secretary and works occasionally with Cookie Harkin, whom she helped when he sought Georgia Lucas.

ARMSTRONG, CAMMIE. In *The Last Cop Out,* she is Willie Armstrong's wife and happily cooks grits and gravy for Gill Burke when he visits.

ARMSTRONG, MASON. In *The By-Pass Control,* he is a loyal agent who flies Tiger Mann from New York to Florida, then up to Leesville, North Carolina, to help him track Louis Agrounsky, and is wounded by Niger Hoppes.

ARMSTRONG, WILLIE ("JUNIOR"). In *The Last Cop Out,* he is an army buddy of Gill Burke's, lives in Harlem with his wife, Cammie, and helps Gill locate Henry Campbell.

ARNIE. In *The Body Lovers,* he is the owner of a liquor store near where Orslo Bucher lived. Bucher may have robbed Arnie's store.

ARNOLD, SIR HARRY. In *The Ship That Never Was,* he is the British naval archivist who is delighted to see the *Tiger* longboat, accepts it, and sends it home to England.

ART. In *One Lonely Night,* he is Captain Pat Chambers's ballistics expert.

ARTIE. In "Kick It or Kill!," he is Kelly Smith's New York City contact who provides Smith with necessary information about criminals gathering in Pinewood.

ARTIE. In *Vengeance Is Mine!,* he is Rainey's skinny henchman. Mike shoots him in the leg after shooting Rainey in the leg.

ASPEN. In *Survival . . . Zero!,* Little Joe finds shelter in Aspen's Snack Bar when it rains.

AUDIOCASSETTES AND SPILLANE. Stacy Keach made abridged recordings of *The Big Kill* (1990), *Kiss Me, Deadly* (1990), *My Gun Is Quick* (1990), and *Black Alley* (1996).

AUGER. In "Tomorrow I Die," he is the leader, small, fat, and conceited, of the bank robbers. Richard Thurber foils him by sending him for the hidden loot. He is presumably killed by the police.

AUGIE. In *The Death Dealers,* he is a chef at the Blue Ribbon on 44th Street.

AUGIE. In *The Deep,* he is a criminal who rose from "the sewer slums" to work for Wilson Batten. He moves on to Deep, hopes to inherit the organization if Deep is killed, but is shot to death by Morrie Reeves.

AVALARD, TROY. In *The Long Wait,* she is an ex-girlfriend of Lenny Servo, hides out, receives evidence from Gracie Harlan, and is brought by Lobin to Servo, who mortally wounds her even as she shoots him dead.

B

BABCOCK. In "Me, Hood!," he is a hood named by Stan Etching.

BAGGERT. In *The Last Cop Out,* he was a loyal member of Mark Shelby's criminal organization, recently killed by an unknown gunman.

BAILEN, HARRY. In *The Big Kill,* he is a syndicated newspaper columnist for whom Cook Harkin is a legman.

BAILEY, HERM. In *The Delta Factor,* he is Joey Jolley's contact and provides Joey with information about Whitey Tass.

BAINES, JOHNNY. In *Survival . . . Zero!,* he is mentioned as a Philadelphia pickpocket. Could Spillane have had Lyndon Baines Johnson in mind when he named this punk?

BALCO. In "Everybody's Watching Me," he is a Mark Renzo man, killed.

BALFOUR, HENRY. In *The Death Dealers,* he is the State Department official who is murdered after escorting Teish El Abin to the basement of the Stacy Hotel.

BALLANCA, CASEY. In *The Death Dealers,* he is a Midwestern oil engineer. Malcolm Turos tried to kill him in Paris. He briefs Tiger Mann on technical details of the oil industry.

BALLINGER, WOODRING ("WOODY"). In *Survival . . . Zero!,* he is a rich, old-time gangster, whose underlings include Larry Beers, Carl, and Sammy.

Ballinger likes Heidi Anders. His losing his wallet is the indirect cause of his being knifed to death by Stanley, William Dorn's hired killer.

BANGER, AUSTIN. In *Black Alley,* he is a politician who holds a courthouse hearing during which Mike insults him.

BANNERMAN. In "The Bastard Bannerman," he was Cat Cay Bannerman's grandfather. He "piled up the loot during the gold rush trade" and willed Cat a fortune.

BANNERMAN, ANITA. In "The Bastard Bannerman," she is Cat Cay Bannerman's "distant cousin," is engaged to Vance Colby, but marries Cat.

BANNERMAN, CAT CAY. In The Bastard Bannerman," he is Max Bannerman's illegitimate son. After a checkered career, he becomes a police officer. While on vacation, he chances to visit his Bannerman relatives in Culver City, exposes the criminal conduct of Vance Colby, Popeye Gage, Carl Matteau, and others, and marries Anita Bannerman. When seeking information from Irish Maloney's neighbors, Cat Cay calls himself Mr. Wells.

BANNERMAN, MAX. In "The Bastard Bannerman," he was Miles Bannerman's brother and Cat Cay Bannerman's colorful father.

BANNERMAN, MILES. In "The Bastard Bannerman," he is Cat Cay Bannerman's uncle and the father of Rudy Bannerman and Theodore Bannerman. The three abused Cat when he was little; but when they conspire with Vance Colby, Cat exposes them all.

BANNERMAN, RUDY. In "The Bastard Bannerman," he is Miles Bannerman's fat, alcoholic son, Theodore Bannerman's brother, and the would-be but impotent lover of Irish Maloney. Cat Cay Bannerman, his cousin, exposes him.

BANNERMAN, THEODORE ("TED," "TEDDY"). In "The Bastard Bannerman," he is Miles Bannerman's son and Rudy Bannerman's brother. Cat Cay Bannerman, his cousin, exposes him.

BARNER, LIEUTENANT. In *One Lonely Night,* he is an official at the scene of Harvey Robinson Jenkins's alleged suicide.

BARNES, CARLO. In *Kiss Me, Deadly,* he makes a duplicate of William Mist's apartment key for Velda.

BARNEY. In *The Erection Set,* he plays the piano at Hiram Tod's place.

BARNEY. In *The Long Wait,* he is an ex-con bartender who will not identify Wilson to Captain Lindsey's circular-circulating cop.

BARNEY. In *My Gun Is Quick,* this is the bar where Mike Hammer first meets Lola Bergan.

BARNEY. In "The Pickpocket," he is a bartender Willie knows.

BARNEY. In *Survival . . . Zero!,* he is a doorman at Heidi Anders's apartment building.

BARRETT. In "The Flier," Lois Hays says she writes for the Barrett Syndicated Features.

BARRIN. In *The Erection Set,* he was Dog Kelly's great-grandfather. He was responsible for having Leyland Ross Hunter educated and placed in law work.

BARRIN, ALFRED ("AL," "ALF," "ALFIE"). In *The Erection Set.* he is Dog Kelly's homosexual, woman-abusing cousin. Dog makes it his business to exact revenge on him.

BARRIN, CAMERON ("CAM," "GRAMPS"). In *The Erection Set,* he was Dog Kelly's maternal grandfather and willed Dog $10,000 because his conscience troubled him for abusing Dog.

BARRIN, DENNISON ("DENNIE"). In *The Erection Set,* he is Dog Kelly's cousin. As a youth, Dennison got a girl pregnant, put the blame on Dog, and forced the girl to have an abortion. Dog, bent on revenge, had Dennison, now a homosexual, photographed compromisingly with Rose Porter.

BARRIN, MRS. In *The Erection Set,* she married Cameron Barrin's son but was pregnant by Kelly, Dog's father, and soon died.

BARRIN, VEDA. In *The Erection Set,* she is Dog Kelly's cousin. Ruined by gambling, she became a prostitute for a while.

BARTEL, HARVEY. In *The Last Cop Out,* he is a bartender who lets Papa Menes and Artie Meeker in to use cottages in the Keys for sexual meetings.

BARTOLDI, VITO. In *The Last Cop Out,* he and Baldie Foreman work for Leon Bray, check on Bray, find his corpse and seven other dead men, and are soon blown up themselves.

BASIL, ARNOLD. In *The Big Kill,* he was a criminal with an arrest record. He worked for Charlie Fallon, went to Los Angeles, returned to New York, and worked for Ed Teen and Toady Link. Basil shot Charlie Decker, after which Toady ran over him and killed him.

BASSO, MOUSIE. In *Kiss Me, Deadly,* he is a minor Mafia figure whom Mike forces to talk.

"THE BASTARD BANNERMAN" (1964). Short story. (Characters: Annie, Bannerman, Anita Bannerman, Cat Cay Bannerman, Max Bannerman, Miles Bannerman, Rudy Bannerman, Theodore Bannerman, Vance Colby, Leslie Douglas, Hank Feathers, Forbes, Fred, Popeye Gage, Simon Helm, Jack Jenner, Sidney LaMont, MacCauley, Chuck Maloney, Irish Maloney, Carl Matteau, Sam Reed, Mrs. Petey Salvo, Petey Salvo, Guy Sanders, Marty Sinclair, Lieutenant Travers, Dr. Anthony Wember, George P. Wilkenson.)

Cat Cay Bannerman, named for the place where he was conceived and born, is the illegitimate son of deceased Max Bannerman. Cat was raised by his uncle, Miles Bannerman, who inherited the Bannerman estate and abused Cat, as did his spoiled sons, Theodore and Rudy. Cat liked Anita Bannerman, his "distant cousin," but ran away when he was twelve and she was ten, joined migrant workers, ranched and schooled in Texas, and served in the army. Thirty-five and scarred, Cat, having some free time, drives to the Bannerman residence in Culver City, meets and demoralizes Miles, cousins Teddy and Rudy, and Carl Matteau and Popeye Gage, both of whom he recognizes as Syndicate men. He also meets Vance Colby, a newcomer in real estate and engaged to Anita, who rushes up and hugs Cat. He learns about the Bannermans by reading newspaper files and talking with Sidney LaMont, a gambler, with Hank Feathers, Max's old friend and now a reporter, and by phone with Sam Reed, a Chicago horse-parlor operator. Miles has influence; his sons are wastrels who bribe their way out of frequent trouble. Cat picks up Anita for a pleasant drink-and-dance evening at the Cherokee. Stripper Irish Maloney, widow of Chuck Maloney, a recently murdered parking attendant, entertains. Cat reminisces with the bouncer, Petey Salvo, known from high-school days.

Next morning Reed informs Cat that Matteau and Gage are in Culver City with $100,000 in mob money to broker something huge. Cat asks Feathers to check into Rudy's relationship with Irish. Cat learns from Simon Helm, a real-estate local, that Colby has options on lush seafront properties. In his room, Cat is jumped, kicked by Gage, and warned to get out by Matteau, who thinks he is a small-time, unwanted Bannerman. Salvo ministers to Cat and takes him to Irish's house. Far from grieving, Irish flirts with Cat over drinks. Cat sneaks into the Bannerman kitchen. Annie, the Bannermans' old servant, tells him she heard that Rudy killed Maloney but was too drunk to remember, Matteau has the stiletto used, and the family is being extorted. Cat startles the clan with his knowledge and learns Matteau wants $1,000,000 for silence. Cat says he'll help and when Colby postures punches him. Back at the motel, Cat hears a radio flash: Guy Sanders, framed as Maloney's killer, is being brought in.

Next day Cat blandishes Helm for details about Colby's options, tells an honest cop named Lieutenant Travers to shadow Matteau and Gage, visits cowering Rudy in his office, and phones Anita and learns the crooks want their money soon. Returning to his room, he finds Irish; she names Arthur Sears as another of her lovers; her sinewy nakedness proves irresistible.

Cat leaves early, gets the police physician to admit that any Cherokee Club kitchen knife could be the murder weapon, and goes with Feathers to where he has located Matteau and Gage. They batter both; Matteau won't talk; they stash Gage in the Bannerman smokehouse until, missing his heroin fix, he'll sing. Cat drives Anita with him to call on a woman whose friend wrote down the license-plate number of one of Irish's male visitors. Near his motel, Cal and Anita are shot at but missed. Lieutenant Travers detains both. Anita phones Colby and is soon allowed to leave. Cat phones George P. Wilkenson, who, Petey said, wanted to see him. At ninety-three, Wilkenson is a respected attorney and was a friend of Cat's rich grandfather. Wilkenson tells Cat he is to inherit several million. Cat confers with Travers, who determines that randy Colby was "Sears," Irish's mysterious visitor by car. Travers will follow Cat to the Bannermans' estate. Petey will bring Matteau and Gage. The family gathers. Cat explains: Colby planned a coastal gambling resort with Syndicate money, also killed Maloney; Matteau and Gage followed as enforcers, per-suaded Rudy he killed Maloney; Miles, Rudy, and Theodore, low on money, cooperated with Colby. Cat persuades Colby to prefer surrendering to Travers not the Syndicate, tells the male Bannermans to work for a change, marries Anita, and tells her he is soon due in New York on official police duty. "The Bastard Bannerman" was a rehearsal for aspects in *The Erection Set.*

BATTEN, WILSON ("BATTY," "WILSE"). In *The Deep,* he is an unprincipled lawyer who holds Bennett's will, which is in Deep's favor. Batten hopes, unavailingly, to survive probable carnage and inherit Bennett's criminal or-ganization.

BAXTER, MRS. In *The Twisted Thing,* she is Miss Cook's old landlady. She lets Mike Hammer examine the girl's room.

BAY, TONY. In "Return of the Hood," he owns a deli where Ryan meets Pete-the-Dog.

BEAMISH. In "Killer Mine," he is a gunman killed by Larry Scanlon.

BEANSEY. In *The Erection Set,* he was an air force buddy of Dog Kelly's and had something to do with British Spitfires.

BEANSY, HELLER. In "Stand Up and Die!," he was one of the Harts' unfor-tunate neighbors.

BEAVER. In *Day of the Guns,* he is a tall, thin British embassy worker in New York.

BEAVER. In *Survival . . . Zero!,* he is the elusive, red-vested pickpocket, up from Miami to New York. Befriended by Lipton Sullivan, Beaver stole wallets, took a secret map from the wallet of William Dorn, and was thereafter sought and eventually killed by Stanley, Dorn's hired killer.

BECKHAUS, DR. In *The Snake,* he is a dentist who cares for Nicholas Beckhaus, his injured brother.

BECKHAUS, NICHOLAS. In *The Snake,* he was prosecuted by Simpson Torrence, was imprisoned, and vowed to kill Torrence upon his release. However, he was crippled and brain-damaged in a prison fight, and is now supported and cared for by his brother, Dr. Beckhaus.

BEERS, LARRY. In *Survival . . . Zero!,* he is one of Woodring Ballinger's punks, with a long criminal history. He was a *pistolero* with the Gomez Swan gang. When Beers ransacks Mike Hammer's office and lies in wait for him, Mike outshoots and kills him.

BELCHEY. In "Stand Up and Die!," he was a neighbor killed by the Harts.

BELHANDER, LOUISE. In *The Last Cop Out,* she is a cute blond prostitute who pleases Papa Menes so much in Florida (he crudely calls her a "three-way woman") that he takes her to his Long Island hideaway. Because she was tortured by Francois Verdun, Menes's associate, Louise shoots Menes to death and takes a bus to freedom. Her manual dexterity with males makes Spillane's choice of her last name onomastically subtle.

BELL, ARNOLD. In *The Erection Set,* he is an experienced killer sent by The Turk to kill Dog Kelly. Bell tries to drown Lee Shay, kills Bridey-the-Greek and also (calling himself Peterson) Markham, stalks Dog, finds him in bed with Sharon Cass, and is killed by Dog.

BELLEMY. In *I, the Jury,* he was a Southern textile-mill owner and the father of Esther and Mary Bellemy, to whom he willed an estate of twenty-two rooms and a substantial income.

BELLEMY, ESTHER. In *I, the Jury,* she is Mary Bellemy's twin sister, age twenty-nine, reputedly a big shopper. The twins are rich, beautiful, and athletic.

BELLEMY, MARY. In *I, the Jury,* she is Esther Bellemy's rich, beautiful, athletic, ragingly nymphomaniacal twin sister, age twenty-nine. She goes after Mike Hammer, successfully after she invites him to attend a huge dinner party followed by a tennis match featuring two fine players. What was Hammer to do? After all, her "kiss was like molten lava."

BELLEW, SERGEANT. In *The Big Kill,* he is an uptown police officer who tells Mike he vaguely remembers a man named Nocky. *See* Cole, Arthur.

BELLO. In *The Deep,* this is the name of gang-bangers whom Deep long ago prevented from raping Helen Tate.

BELLOTICA, CARMEN. In *Day of the Guns,* according to Mann, she underwent successful plastic surgery to resemble her younger sister, aided the Allies in Norway, and was killed.

BELTOV. In *Bloody Sunrise,* Gabin Martrel is said to have run the Beltov Project.

BENDER, HERBIE. In *Bloody Sunrise,* he, according to Ernie Bentley, could get little information about Gabin Martrel aside from news-release material.

BENDER, LESTER. In *The Girl Hunters,* he served with Alex Bird and Richie Cole, and was killed shortly before the war ended.

BENDER, PAT. In *The Girl Hunters,* she was a Craig House manicurist whom Richie Cole knew.

BENNETT ("BEN"). In *The Deep,* he was Deep's juvenile partner, who amiably took over the gang from him, and twenty-five years later was murdered. Deep returns to seek justice.

BENNETT, COBBIE. In *My Gun Is Quick,* he is a pimp from whom Mike Hammer gains information. Mike uses him as a would-be sacrificial goat to draw gunmen into the open. Bennett escapes from the city permanently.

BENNIE. In *The Last Cop Out,* he calls George Spacer and Carl Ames to report Teddy Shu's murder in Chicago.

BENNIE. In *The Last Cop Out,* Mark Shelby recalls that Gill Burke killed both Bennie and Colfaco by tossing them from a rooftop eight years earlier.

BENNY. In *The Deep,* either of two fellows who years ago stole a car, crashed it, and died.

BENNY. In "Me, Hood!," he has a grocery store near Ryan's apartment. In "Return of the Hood," Benny runs an errand for Pete-the-Dog.

BENSON, PETEY. In *The Killing Man,* he is a knowledgeable reporter with overseas connections of use to Mike. He puts Mike in touch with Russell Graves of Manchester, England.

BENSON, TEDDY. In *The Ship That Never Was,* he is a British Member of Parliament who confers with Sir Harry Arnold.

BENTLEY, ERNIE. In *Day of the Guns,* he is a technician expert in ballistics and weaponry. He aids Tiger Mann, who jokes with him about sex. In *Bloody Sunrise,* it is revealed that Bentley worked on the Manhattan Project and then specialized for Martin Grady in chemicals. Bentley provides Tiger with information and also an all-important explosive-loaded pen. In *The Death Dealers,* Bentley helps disguise Tiger, Tom, Dick, and Harry, and also provides Tiger with miniature recorders. In *The By-Pass Control,* Bentley helps Tiger again, this time by providing him an inhaler booby-trapped with cyanide gas.

BENTLEY, MRS. ERNIE. In *Bloody Sunrise,* Tiger Mann crudely tells Ernie he is too old to need to go home to his wife for sex. Mann (or, rather, Spillane) has sex on his mind excessively. In *The By-Pass Control,* Mrs. Bentley is mentioned.

BERGAN, LOLA. In *My Gun Is Quick,* she is a former prostitute, originally from Byeville, Mississippi, and a nurse's aid during the war. Her knowledge of city vice and corruption helps Mike Hammer. Lola falls in love with Mike, feels inferior to him, but manages to attract him into one night of fervent lovemaking. Lola finds a camera her friend Nancy Sanford pawned, with Nancy's address. Feeney Last gets to Lola ahead of Mike and stabs her to death. Mike's attitude toward women is indicated by his calling Lola the following: "babe," "girl," "honey," "kid," "little chum," "sugar," and "sugarpuss." In *Vengeance Is Mine!,* Mike recalls Lola's murder with sorrow.

BERIN-GROTIN, ARTHUR. In *My Gun Is Quick,* he is a rich philanthropist, now eighty, who says he is making up for a misspent youth by generosity. When Mike Hammer learns that Feeney Last is his bodyguard, Last leaves. Mr. Berin, as he prefers to be called, tells Mike he has outlived his wife, only son, and that son's granddaughter. He hires Mike to get information about Nancy Sanford, who turns out to be Berin's granddaughter. When Mike learns that Berin is profiteering from city vice and corruption, Mike kills him.

BERKOWITZ. In *The Last Cop Out,* he and his friend Manute were photographers. They took pictures for Mark Shelby. When they sought to blackmail him, Shelby killed both of them.

BERKOWITZ, CYNTHIA. In *The Last Cop Out,* she is the photographer's widow. She provides Gill Burke with information and refers him to Myron Berkowitz.

BERKOWITZ, MYRON. In *The Last Cop Out,* he is a lawyer and leads Gill Burke to conclude that Berkowitz and Manute, the photographers, planned to blackmail Mark Shelby. Although Myron's last name is the same as her late husband's, Cynthia calls Myron her cousin.

BERN, HARRY. In *The Killing Man,* he and Gary Fells are ex–CIA agents turned rogue and working for Libya. They seize Mike, who knocks Bern's partial plate loose. It becomes a clue to his identity. Either Bern or Fells kills Richard Smiley in their effort to kill Penta, who is stalling on his assignment to kill the vice president. But Penta kills them.

BERNIE. In *The Girl Hunters,* Nat Drutman gratefully recalls Mike's help in connection with "Bernie and those men."

BERNIE. In "Tomorrow I Die," he is one of Auger's gang. He and Carmen die when their getaway car rolls down a gully.

BERNSTEIN. In *Kiss Me, Deadly,* Mike reads this name written in place of "Carver" and "Torn" by the mailbox by the door of the apartment where Lily Carver lives.

BERT. In *The By-Pass Control,* he and Herman are mentioned as living near Edith Caine.

BERT. In *The Last Cop Out,* he is a desk clerk at the fleabag hotel where Shatzi Heinkle stays briefly.

BERTRAM. In *The Erection Set,* in reminiscing about the war, Dog Kelly recalls that Helgurt shot down Bertram and then Dog shot down Helgurt.

BESHIP, CARMEN. In *The Death Dealers,* he was invited to Teish El Abin's party, but Malcolm Turos murdered him, took his invitation, and attended in his place.

BESSER, F. I. In *Bloody Sunrise,* he is a bookie with an office in the Tomlinson Building. Is Spillane using Besser's initials (F.I.B.) to make a comment on betting?

BEST. In "The Seven Year Kill," he is evidently a newspaperman with whom Gates, Phil Rocca's spineless boss, later worked. Best is named along with Hines.

BEST-SELLERS BY SPILLANE. The following novels by Spillane, in descending order of commercial success, have sold in excess of five million copies each: *I, the Jury; The Big Kill; My Gun Is Quick; One Lonely Night; Kiss Me, Deadly; The Long Wait; Vengeance Is Mine!*

Bibliography: Alice Payne Hackett and James Henry Burke, *Eighty Years of Best Sellers, 1895–1975* (New York: R. R. Bowker, 1977).

BETH. In *The Erection Set,* she was the midwife when Sharon Cass was born, is now the towel girl in Lucy Longstreet's brothel, and helps Dog Kelly with information.

BETS. In "Me, Hood!," she is that "tall, raven-haired doll" Jake McGaffney dances with at the Spanish shindig.

BETTERTON. In *The Erection Set,* he and Strauss in London are agents that Dog Kelly tells the manager at Weller-Fabray to phone for instructions.

BETTS, MRS. In *The Day the Sea Rolled Back,* she runs a grocery store on Ara Island and is evidently Petey Betts's mother.

BETTS, PETEY. In *The Day the Sea Rolled Back,* he and Jake Skiddo rent Oliver Creighton's dune buggy to explore the sea bed.

BETTY. In *I, the Jury,* Charlotte Manning helps her by babysitting her baby in Central Park.

BIFF. In *The Body Lovers,* he is an old newsman in charge of the newspaper morgue. He helps Mike and Al Casey locate information generated by Mitch Temple.

"THE BIG BANG." *See* "Return of the Hood."

BIG BENNY. In *The Erection Set,* he was an RAF pilot from Brussels. Lee Shay tells Dog Kelly that one of the thugs who attacked him had an accent like Big Benny's.

THE BIG KILL (1951). Novel. (Characters: Allerton, Arlene, Harry Bailen, Arnold Basil, Sergeant Bellew, Binnaggio, Captain Pat Chambers, Arthur Cole, Dixie Cooper, Kay Cutler, Mrs. William Decker, William Decker, William Decker Jr., Devoe, Charlie Fallon, Glenn Fisher, Lou Grindle, Mike Hammer, Cookie Harkin, Harvey, Bernie Herman, Marvin Holmes, Mel Hooker, Joan, Johnny, Lake, Marsha Lee, Toady Link, Louie, Georgia Lucas, Sergeant McMillan, Martin, Mertig, Nelson, Jerry O'Neill, Helen O'Roark, Patty, Roberts, Mrs. Roberts, Mrs. Ross, Scobie, Ellen Scobie, Scottoriggio, Ed Teen, Tolly, Tucker, Velda, John Vileck.)

It is now 1950. After being away for six months, Mike is drinking in an East Side bar one rainy night. A man enters with a baby boy, kisses him, sobs, and exits. Mike chases after him. A Buick speeds by. The man is shot dead and frisked by one from the car. Mike shoots him in the legs, but the driver runs over him and kills him. The police, including Captain Pat Chambers, arrive. Mike silently recognizes the dead thug as one of crime-king Lou Grindle's men, tells Pat about the baby, and is allowed to take the kid home, for now. Mike taxis to the Hop Scotch, finds Grindle gambling, and warns him viciously; meets Velda at Penn Station, shows her the kid, sends her to Florida on a case; then taxis home with the kid.

Next morning Mike sends out for clothes and food for the kid, puts his tattered overalls in a trash can, stops him from a constant desire to play with Mike's .45, hires a retired nurse to baby-sit, and checks with Pat. He reveals this: William Decker, the father of the kid, also named William, was a safe-cracker gone straight until his wife died of cancer; his prints were found on the safe in a Riverside Avenue apartment; only minor items were taken; his lookout cohorts figured he stashed a real take; the run-over gunman was Arnold Basil. Pat reveals Decker's address and that of Marsha Lee, the Riverside robbery victim. Mike visits Decker's superintendent, John Vileck, who is with a priest. They tell Mike this: Decker attempted to go straight and support his kid, had an insurance policy with the boy as beneficiary; and worked on the docks with Mel Hooker. Mike visits Marsha and learns she is a wealthy, sexy, retired movie actress. The two believe Decker was aiming for the apartment of wealthy playboy Marvin Holmes, one floor above, but hit her place by mistake. When she returned home, she was slugged by the intruder. After a close embrace with Marsha, Mike leaves for his office. By phone, Vileck reports that Decker owed $3,000 to his wife's physician. From the dock paymaster, Mike learns Hooker's address and the location of a bar he frequents. At a ratty bar he finds Hooker, who is scared and says little, sends two thugs shadowing him to follow Mike, and escapes. Mike batters both thugs and goes to Hooker's rooming house, terrifies Hooker, and gets him to admit Decker gambled at the track, borrowed from a loan shark named Dixie Cooper, and lost. Mike finds Pat in his office, learns that someone in the frustrated D.A.'s office reports his surprise raids to the well-organized gamblers. Ellen Scobie, a gorgeous police secretary, flirts with Mike, and they drive to Dixie's favorite bar. On the way they wonder who's the leak. Mike finds Dixie, waves his .45, and says Dixie probably squeezed Decker until he had to crack a safe but targeted the wrong apartment. Dixie counters that Decker paid him back in full. Where did he get that money? Dixie doesn't know. On the way out, Mike finds Grindle at a booth with smooth Ed Teen, the city's "biggest bookie." Mike's threatening both of them terrifies Ellen. Mike takes Ellen to her lavish apartment, shared with two other girls. Ellen undresses; Mike resists, goes to his apartment, is sapped from behind, but kicks his assailant down the stairs before losing consciousness.

Mike recovers in the morning as the nurse enters with the kid. Marsha sends clothes for him. The nurse will continue babysitting. Mike reports to Pat, who says Hooker has been shot dead. The D.A. snarls at Mike, who gets Ellen to confirm his alibi and calls attention to the D.A.'s ineffectiveness.

Alone, Pat tells Mike he will get Teen for bookmaking and Grindle for sending killers after Decker; Mike counters that he wants their higher-up. Mike goes to the Greenwich Village theater where Marsha is rehearsing neophyte actors and togaed actresses. He tells her about Hooker's death, mentions the late Charlie Fallon, and is introduced to Kay Cutler, an actress there who says she and Marsha knew Fallon in Hollywood. Mike agrees to dine with Marsha at her place, returns to the bar where he met Hooker, and asks the bartender to identify the thugs he beat up. He can name only "Nocky." Mike phones Pat about that name and learns the department leaker may soon be identified. Mike turns to a womanizing informant of his named Cookie Harkin, meets him at a bar with Joan and Tolly, two floozies, and learns Nocky is one of big-shot Toady Link's two bodyguards. Resisting Tolly's blandishments, Mike drives to the Bronx, finds bloated Toady alone in his mansion, and with his .45 makes him talk: Decker, sure, lost "a few grand"; Toady refinanced him; Nocky, really Arthur Cole, argued with but didn't kill Hooker; Cole's pal is Glenn Fisher; they live above the Rialto Restaurant. Mike phones the place. The thugs have packed and disappeared. Mike leaves. When Toady rushes away in his Packard, Mike re-enters the mansion, searches its sterile accoutrements, but finds nothing relevant. He proceeds to Riverside Drive and apologizes to Marsha for being late. She offers to baby-sit the kid. They theorize about the case and then make dreamy love. He returns to his apartment.

Next morning Velda phones Mike that the Miami police have taken over. Feeling "like a heel," he stalls by ordering her to go to Cuba for more evidence. The papers are full of the D.A.'s antiracketeering actions. An editorial links Teen and Grindle. After checking on the kid, Mike reports to Pat and learns that only low-level gangsters have been caught, that evidence against Teen is nonexistent, that Hooker regularly banked big sums. Mike says Hooker didn't win at the track but was being bribed, and asks Pat to check on Cole and Fisher, now out of town, says they are linked to Toady, whom he visited and thus learned their names. Mike believes the loaded safe of Marsh's upper neighbor, rich, womanizing Marvin Holmes, was Decker's target. Pat phones Holmes, only to learn he has just skipped to South America. When Pat says he was about to arrest Toady, Mike bets Toady drove the Buick when Decker was murdered. Pat says he will give Mike three-days' leeway. Mike finds Ellen at lunch and persuades her to borrow Toady's secret police file. Ellen agrees to have her roommate Patty grab it at closing time but on condition Mike sleeps with Ellen. First, they go to the races. Ellen, whose father's horses she knows well, wins and so does Mike—$4,000, in fact. They drive to an East Side settlement, where Ellen donates her winnings; Mike contributes $1,000. After a Broadway dinner, they go to Ellen's apartment to examine the files—containing nothing relevant. Ellen gets a kiss and a rain check, and Mike plans further immediate moves against Toady, whose part in the action he begins to doubt. Pat awaits Mike at his place, demands his .45, and says Toady has been shot dead. Hoping to establish a dishonest alibi,

Mike asks Pat to phone Marsha, who blithely says Mike spent last night with her. Mike accompanies Pat to Toady's mansion, thoroughly ransacked by his assailant, evidently without finding anything. Toady collected photos of actresses, many autographed for Fallon.

Mike taxis to his apartment but is grabbed by two gunmen, Johnny and Martin, who force him to drive them in his car to a cottage at Islip, on Long Island. Grindle is there. When he slugs Mike, Mike swings back and breaks Grindle's front teeth. Mike is sapped unconscious and revives confronted by dapper Teen, who, convinced Mike shot Toady, suavely supervises Mike's being battered to reveal something Mike denies knowing about. Teen tires; Martin drives him home to establish an alibi for the time Mike is to be killed; Grindle rests; and Mike is forced to drive Johnny to a place where Teen wants Mike killed. Mike has a .32 near his seat, kills and dumps Johnny, returns to the cottage, and attacks in dark confusion: Grindle shoots Martin, back from the city; Mike shoots Grindle.

Mike drives to police headquarters, happens to see again a man outside curiously pretending to fiddle with a hearing aid, and gets to Pat, who arrests him for conspiring with Ellen and Patty to rifle Toady's file. Mike forces the D.A. to drop all charges in return for his revealing that the "deaf" man was a lip-reader conspiring with the cop who leaked raid targets to him. Mike tells Pat about Johnny, Martin, and Grindle. Pat reveals this: Teen said he was playing cards all night with friends; Philadelphia cops killed Cole and Fisher in a shootout; dying, Cole fingered Teen; Toady drove the car and after Basil killed Decker ran over Basil; Toady ordered Hooker's rub-out. Mike gets home to a crowd of well-wishers, including Marsha, the kid, and his nurse. He sleeps and dreams about a mysterious woman.

Pat phones in the afternoon: Teen has an alibi; the D.A. wants a meeting; Ellen wants Mike to phone her; Holmes, Marsha's rich neighbor, is back. The nurse will stay in Mike's apartment with the kid, since her place is being repainted. Mike goes with Marsha to her place. He grins at her when the radio reports Grindle's murder. Jerry O'Neill, a love-struck young actor with a broken arm in a cast, visits Marsha, worried about her absence from their rehearsal. He glares jealously at Mike when Marsha shoos him out. Marsha slinks to bed; but Mike merely sits, smokes, drinks, and thinks. Remembering Ellen's wish, he drives to her place. She has material from former D.A. Roberts's rejected files; it shows that Fallon hired Toady as a photographer and that after Fallon died Toady rose to prominence as one of Teen's bookies. Ellen says she loved dangerous Mike, realized he would never be permanent in her life, then beds down with him just this once. Suspecting the dream woman is significant, Mike asks Cookie to get a bead on Fallon's last girlfriend. Awaiting Cookie's report, Mike returns to Marsha. They kiss but nothing more. Cookie phones: Fallon's mistress was Georgia Lucas, a has-been singer at Harvey's in Greenwich Village; Cookie will wait there.

Mike and Marsha rush to Harvey's and spot Teen and two goons in the audience. Mike has Cookie phone Pat, sends Marsha home, and goes backstage for Georgia. She says this: Teen and Grindle aided Fallon, who had a weak heart; fearing a rub-out, Fallon had Toady microfilm documents incriminating Teen and Grindle to file with Roberts; Toady made a spare copy, told Teen so as to curry favor and gain power; Grindle forced Georgia to hide Fallon's nitroglycerin tablets; Fallon died. Mike concludes Teen thought Mike stole Toady's set of films. Mike gets Georgia outside. Teen's gunnies jump him. He fights and breaks free. Georgia hides. Pat brings aid, arrests the gunnies, collars Georgia for her information, and agrees to give Cookie the scoop. Mike phones Roberts and learns that, yes, Fallon sent him something ten years ago, but it was of no significance.

Mike hurries home, finds the nurse unconscious with a head wound, the kid pulling at things, and Marsha with a knife cutting his furniture in search of her missing films. Mike pulls his .45 and summarizes: Fallon wrote a fan letter to Marsha when she was a Hollywood starlet, but sent it to Roberts and the films to Marsha in error; Marsha came to New York and persistently blackmailed Teen and Grindle; Toady had Hooker cause Decker to lose and have to crack Marsha's safe; Holmes's cash was never any target; Decker got Marsha's films; Marsha played sex kitten to Mike thinking he lifted them from Decker. Suddenly Jerry, back to see Marsha and hiding to do her bidding, decks Mike with his cast. Marsha takes Mike's .45, shoots Jerry with it, and puts it on a table. Mike sees she found the films in the kid's overalls, discarded in the trash can. She gloats she'll shoot Mike with her own revolver and put it in Jerry's dead hand, then tell the police the two men quarreled for love of her. But the kid, still eager for Mike's .45, grabs it and by accident shoots Marsha in the head.

The title of *The Big Kill* has two meanings: Decker hoped for a big killing at the tracks but was the victim of such a kill. Spillane achieves structural symmetry by having the action start in a street-smearing rain and end during a cleansing rain. The sequence of days is nicely indicated by numerous references to precise times. The reader benefits when Mike pauses three or four times to summarize events and to theorize (often incorrectly). The novel is punctuated by the most "goddamns" thus far in the narratives of Mike's career. In this novel, he lights twenty-eight cigarettes and enjoys nineteen (or more) drinks. Up to and including this novel, forty-eight people have died, thirty-four of whom, innocent of initial involvement in crimes, would have survived.

Bibliography: Collins and Traylor; Johnston.

BIG MAN. In "Me, Hood!," he is the tough, reluctantly cooperative police official who assigns Ryan to find Lodo. Even as he gives Ryan information, Big Man also informs Ryan's opposition.

BILL. In "The Pickpocket," he is Willie's and Sally's small son.

BILLINGS, HENRY. In "Me, Hood!," he was Ryan's enemy. He was involved in a heroin shipment, tried to implicate Ryan, and was murdered.

BILLY. In *The Body Lovers,* he owns Billy's Cave, where Mike meets Roberta Slade.

BIMMY. In *The Deep,* this big three-hundred pounder owns the White Rose Tavern.

BINAGGIO, CHARLES (1907–1950). Kansas City political boss and Cosa Nostra figure. His gangland-style assassination helped to spur the formation of the Kefauver Committee (May 1950–May 1951) in the U.S. Senate, to investigate organized crime. In *The Big Kill,* Mike names "Binaggio" to Captain Pat Chambers as a person whose murder in Kansas City remains unsolved.

Bibliography: Sifakis.

BING. In *The Killing Man,* he owns a gymnasium where Mike works out.

BIRD, ALEX. In *The Girl Hunters,* he served in the war with Lester Bender and Richie Cole, then bought a chicken farm in Marlboro, New York. Mike correctly concludes that Cole sought to have Velda taken to Bird's farm. Mike goes there and finds Bird dead of a heart attack caused by Gorlin.

BIZZ, CHARLIE. In *The Deep,* he was a member of the Knights Owl Club and helps Cat trace the whereabouts of Lew James.

BLACK ALLEY **(1996).** Novel. (Characters: Austin Banger, James Bledsoe, Marshall Brotorrio, Casey, Captain Pat Chambers, Dan Coulter, Marty Diamond, Marcos Dooley, Marvin Dooley, Howie Drago, Gaetano, Gerrity, Mike Hammer, Harris, Slipped Disk Harris, Jackie, Miss Florence Lake, Bud Langston, Johnny Leeds, McClain, Sergeant Peppy Marlow, Dr. Ralph Morgan, Leonard Patterson, Angelo Ponti, Azi Ponti, Lorenzo Ponti, Mrs. Lorenzo Ponti, Ugo Ponti, Bill Raabe, Andy Reevo, Richmond, Sammy, Slateman, Teddy, Velda, Homer Watson, Willie-the-Actor.)

Eight months ago Mike Hammer was trying to warn Lorenzo Ponti, a Mafia don, of danger when Mike was severely wounded in a New York waterfront crossfire initiated by the Gaetanos, a rival family. Mike killed Azi Ponti and wounded Ugo Ponti—Lorenzo's sons. A derelict alcoholic physician, Roger Morgan, found Mike, secretly nursed him to health, got him to his place in Florida, and now pronounces Mike—and himself—better. Captain Pat Chambers thought Mike was washed to sea and had a memorial service for him. Velda kept her private-investigator license and Mike's office open. Pat learns Mike is alive and calls him to fly to New York, because Marcos Dooley, their old army buddy, was shot, is dying, and will talk only with Mike. Pat and Velda greet Mike at the airport.

The two get Mike to his apartment, kept by Velda. He tells her they will be married—soon. Mike visits Dooley, who calls Mike the nasty snake needed now. Dooley worked for old Angelo Ponti, the deceased don of the Pontis, now jeopardized by impatient underlings. These hoods skim money, launder it, and invest in legitimate businesses. But Dooley hid $59 billion from Lorenzo, and Mike must find it from hints Dolley mutters before dying. Pat tells Mike this: Dooley took three .357 slugs from an unknown assailant; younger criminals are attacking their parents; Dooley oddly owed Marty Diamond, a loan shark, $5,500. Mike returns to his office, which Velda has too tastefully renovated. When Mike tells Pat, there drinking beer—Mike can no longer drink—that he shot Azi Ponti, he is advised to keep mum. Pat says Ugo Ponti was fired at repeatedly, survived, and boasts he is bulletproof. The two men theorize that Ugo, back from vacations in Mexico and Canada, has access to expensive new body armor.

When Miss Florence Lake, the D.A., calls Velda to order Mike to her office, Velda demands that Lake come instead to Mike's office. Journalists and a television crew have a field day, but Mike equivocates and Lake learns little concerning the waterfront shootout and Mike's slow recovery. Back in his apartment, Mike showers, pockets some .45 cartridges but is too weak to carry a weapon, feels dizzy because of his medication, hails a cab, picks up Velda, and takes her to Le Cirque for a fancy dinner. They drink iced tea. When Howie Drago and Leonard Patterson, two of Lorenzo's gunnies, follow and dine there too, Mike stuns them by dropping a .45 bullet at their table and grinning wolfishly. Afterwards, Mike rebukes himself for being stupid.

Mike and Pat stop at Mike's office. Velda tells them she found a bug in their phone. Mike tells her to put it into the other office phone. Mike gets Pat to estimate what it would take to hide $80 billion in hundreds. A warehouse, he answers. Mike and Pat attend Dooley's funeral service. Mike sees and insults Ugo Ponti there, accepts Dooley's urn of cremated ashes, and notes the urn is engraved with Dooley's serial number and record of duty aboard the U.S. destroyer *Latille* but nothing concerning army duty. The funeral director tells Mike that Dooley had a son named Marvin—Mike didn't know this—to whom Mike should deliver Dooley's ashes. Mike goes to his apartment, finds Velda rearranging it, and learns she too spotted a little fat man at the funeral. She says he was at a trial she attended and is a Treasury or IRS agent. Mike tells her to locate him and also Marvin Dooley. Mike and Pat put Dooley's ashes in a Queens repository managed by Marshall Brotorrio. Velda soon tells Mike this: Homer Watson is the name of the fat fellow, who is a government tax-dodge investigator; Marvin has an address in New Brunswick, New Jersey. Mike tells Velda he believes Dooley knew the location of the missing $89 billion. Watson calls on Mike and says that Washington, D.C., alerted him when Velda phoned the V.A. about Dooley. After verbal fencing, they discuss gigantic sums of hidden drug money, rival mob families, and the need for cooperation. Mike goes to the office of an old buddy named Bud

Langston, an inventor and a computer programmer, who tells him this: Dan Coulter invented a metal-mesh body armor the government declined to buy; he peddled it elsewhere; he died in a factory explosion; two suppliers were killed in separate car accidents; he can show Mike a sample of the armor.

Mike and Velda plan to go see Marvin Dooley. First, Mike finds and disarms an explosive under his car hood, and keeps it in his car. Did Ugo have it planted? Mike finds Marvin and tells him where his father's ashes are. Queried, Marvin says little of value aside from the fact that Marcos Dooley had a boat, went up and down the Hudson River, often stopped at a marina north of Newburgh, New York, run by Slipped Disk Harris. Velda recalls reading about Harris, a liquor supplier during and after Prohibition. Mike warns Marvin that the mob may think he knows something of value. Alone, Mike brazenly visits Lorenzo Ponti, says, yes, he killed Azi, who shot him twice first. Mike says all he wants is the name of Dooley's killer and adds he suspects Lorenzo's other son, Ugo, did it. Home again and tired, Mike has a voice-mail message: Velda says Dr. Ralph Morgan will see him tomorrow at the Waldorf.

Mike and Velda find Morgan fit, well dressed, and solvent. He read about Mike and the Pontis and met some of Lorenzo's friends at his health club, including Slipped Disk Harris, who probably distributed fine Canadian whiskey in the old days. When Velda leaves to probe the Harris-Ponti relationship, Morgan examines Mike's still-open wounds, cautions against exertion, and gives him some former medication and a renewal prescription. Pat brings Watson to Mike's office, and Watson reveals this: In 1986, mob money started disappearing; ever since John Gotti was imprisoned [in 1992] there has been a scramble for control and power; mob coffers seem depleted. Watson checked Dooley's background, found nothing. Mike says he wants only Dooley's murderer. Pat worries about Mike's evasiveness and the missing billions. Velda reports these discoveries to Mike in his apartment: Lorenzo has hilly property in his wife's name in the Adirondacks, with slate now being mined; Harris left his daughter property five miles from Lorenzo's. While Mike and Velda are wondering if a foreign government could have embezzled the billions and how safe Lorenzo is from hot-headed Ugo, the phone rings. Brotorrio reports that last night someone scattered and kicked Dooley's ashes all over the floor, robbed nothing, and left. Mike suspects Ugo followed Mike from the funeral, saw where the urn was placed, and rifled it in search of something. Although Mike hid nothing in it, maybe Ugo thought otherwise. Mike is still physically weak; but regardless, he also believes in no sex with Velda until marriage.

Next morning the security guard warns Mike about men outside in cars (one with a license plate reading, in part, 411) and helps him leave the apartment from the rear. Mike breakfasts with a retired cop who remembers prohibition days and tells him that Harris used to off-load trucked-in illegal Canadian whiskey in upstate New York, and that Lorenzo got his start by bootlegging. With Pat, who received a report about Dooley's disturbed ashes,

Mike visits Marvin, already ensconced in his father's Brooklyn apartment. The place was recently ransacked—by Ugo, Mike guesses. Expecting Ugo to attack him, Mike gets a sample of body armor that Langston has handy. Mike finds Velda at the office, takes some medicine for the shakes, ponders their evidence, and asks Velda to hire researchers to dig into news reports concerning recent Mafia feuds. Next morning Florence Lake, the D.A., and Watson call on Mike. They reveal that some years ago Dooley rented trucks and bought several cartons. Mike fibs that he figures Dooley was helping Lorenzo furnish his upstate place. Over lunch, Pat tells Mike that the police have a warrant to raid an office where the Pontis have high-level mobsters working batteries of computers but that Mike must stay out. So Mike hires an actor he knows to phone Ugo with a tip that his computer office is being cased. When Ugo drives there, Mike follows. Ugo finds no strangers nearby and leaves. Mike picks some locks, finds the computer room, takes sample printouts, but hears Ugo returning, this time with Drago. He hides, disarms Ugo, knocks Drago unconscious, and forces Ugo to reveal this: Azi and a New Jersey gunman named Andy Reevo planned the waterfront murder of Lorenzo that Mike helped go awry; Ugo didn't warn his father, because he wouldn't have been believed. Mike knocks Ugo out, takes both men's guns, leaves, and checks Ugo's license plate. Part reads 411.

Mike gets home, sends the weapons to Pat, collapses, and is aided for two days by Ralph and Velda. Velda offers details from the researchers that a hundred billion could have been the Mafia's years-long take. She adds Pat confirmed that Dooley used rented trucks around his place north of Newburgh. Mike drives up with Velda to the pier where Dooley docked his boat and finds a boat proprietor who has been caring for Dooley's boat. On its mahogany dashboard Mike finds the same numbers inscribed that Dooley ordered put on his urn. Figuring they are latitude and longitude numbers, he and Velda visit a surveyor in Albany; he pinpoints the location on Harris's slate-filled property. Its caretaker, calling himself Slateman, shows them a hidden cave on it. Velda photographs its interior, which contains only empty liquor boxes, discarded tools, and junk. While eating at a diner, they puzzle over events. Velda says Lorenzo awaits Mike's next move. They sleep in a motel, coolly.

In the morning they case Lorenzo's fortresslike estate, hide and see Patterson and others arrive in several cars, return to the motel, spot Drago, check out unseen, and get to another motel for another sexless night. While breakfasting, Mike and Velda are approached by Watson, who boasts that federal agents have kept track of Velda's research and Mike's movements, ever since he visited old Dooley. Mike goads Watson, who says Lorenzo also has a cave, devoted to legitimate mushroom farming. Keeping in cell-phone contact with Velda, Mike boldly drives to Lorenzo's estate, is allowed in, and converses frankly with the old don. Lorenzo says he trusted Dooley, who didn't lust for money and was merely his gardener. Mike says Dooley didn't betray Lorenzo, only hid the money because he saw the post–World War II world turning rotten. Lorenzo, tired and cynical, opines that crime will continue in the otherwise changing world. He says he will spare Mike's life, instead hoping he will eventually lead the mob to the money. Once outside in his car, Mike hears a weapon cocked, careens through would-be assailants, and breaks free.

Mike returns to Velda, who says she called the state troopers and Pat. Mike and Velda move to another motel. Morning television programs report this: Lorenzo Ponti shot Patterson but was executed gangland fashion; four New York hoodlums were critically injured; a missing mystery car (Mike's) is mentioned. Mike and Velda drive to Albany, get a marriage license, and submit to blood tests. Velda produces developed photos of the cave. They return to Harris's place. Mike has bad vibes when they find no signs of Slateman. They enter the cave with flashlights, see evidence of drilling in its roof, but are accosted by Ugo with a shotgun. He boasts of killing his father, killing old Dooley, and bribing Dooley's son Marvin to tell about Dooley's boat—with its latitude and longitude numbers. On signal, Mike and Velda douse their flashlights and evade Ugo's shotgun blasts; Mike's .45 slug slams Ugo's shotgun breech into his face, disabling him. Watson and reinforcements appear and take over, joyfully accepting Velda's recording machine, which caught Ugo's fatal boasts. But—no one finds the billions. Released, Mike and Velda receive their blood-test clearances. Mike succumbs to stress, awakens days later, ministered to by Velda and Morgan, and feels better. Mike appears at a courthouse hearing, rebukes his main federal questioner, and explains that the Mafia can regroup, deal with narcotics cartels worldwide, and replace lost billions quickly.

Mike and Velda return to Harris's place, find Slateman slugged by Ugo and dumped down a cistern, but alive. They get him to a hospital in Albany, where Mike finds a jeweler and buys Velda a two-carat diamond engagement ring for $15,000 by credit card. He responds to a call from Watson, who soon appears and says this: Ugo was sprung from prison by eight Mafia gunmen; he thinks Mike knows where the billions are—as does Watson—and aims to nail Mike. Authorities escort Mike to his New York apartment, where Ralph treats him again, for four days. Pat visits him with this news: Albany hoodlums just learned that Ugo killed his own father and want to kill him for family disloyalty. Mike and Velda evade tails, drive back to Harris's place, and rent a backhoe and a digger. They return to Harris's cave, where Mike finally realizes the billions are hidden under a man-made, deceptive roof cave-in. He scoops the rocks away, digs, and opens the tomb-like burial place, fifty feet wide, containing carton after carton of currency. He extracts only enough money for Velda's ring, their salaries and expenses, and IRS taxes, then uses the explosive, saved from the failed car booby-trap, to tumble the rubble back over the billions. They drive down rainy roads, unhitch the digging equipment, check into a grimy motel, and rest. Mike is awakened from his chair by Ugo, who entered by a window, slugged and tied Velda, and has a gun at Mike's head. They chat a while; Ugo tortures Mike with a chest shot, but his body armor protects him; Mike slips out his snub-nosed .38, and wounds Ugo twice in the chest. Velda persuades him to spare Ugo; so he offers to deliver Ugo either to the mob or to what will be life imprisonment. Your call. Ugo chooses prison. Mike phones Pat with sufficient details, and the engaged couple, having avoided the black alley of death, head for home.

Black Alley is yet another thriller, with its plot and sundry hints stressing its hero's—and its author's—tough-man antigovernment bravado. The two express their continued love-hate relationship with New York City. Much action takes place north of Newburgh, where Spillane lived with his first wife and their family. Appearing when Spillane was seventy-eight years old, *Black Alley* has plenty of predictable derring-do but betrays careless haste. Ponti family relationships are awkwardly revealed. Velda's formerly black hair turns auburn. She doesn't know where Mike hides his weaponry, then does. Ralph Morgan is renamed Frank. Marcos Dooley's eight serial numbers become six. Mob-code betrayers like Ugo get killed in jail, but he's going to rot in one for decades. Joyfully, Mike and Velda are heading for inexpressibly delayed but indubitably furnace-hot conjugal bliss. Perhaps because Spillane had this happy ending in mind, he sanitizes his prose; the most vulgar word in *Black Alley* is "crap," used sparingly, once further denatured when Mike comments, "Finally the stuff had hit the fan."

BLAKE, WINSTON. In "The Veiled Woman," he is a federal agent who dislikes Karl Terris.

BLAKENSHIP. In "The Affair with the Dragon Lady," Vern Tice bought an airfield from the Blakenship family to house the Dragon Lady.

BLEDSOE, JAMES. In *Black Alley,* he owns a boat shop past Newburgh, knew Marcos Dooley, and gives Mike useful information.

BLOODY MARY. In "Killer Mine," Lieutenant Joe Scanlon remembers that she ran an abortion room one floor up from his family's apartment.

BLOODY SUNRISE **(1965).** Novel. (Characters: Virgil Adams, Anderson, Anna, Beltov, Herbie Bender, Eric Bentley, Mrs. Ernie Bentley, F. I. Besser, Henry Buckman, Edith Caine, Sonny Carter, Chobeay, William Copely, Charlie Corbinet, Albert Cutter, Donovan, Sonia Dutko, Fat John, Clement Fletcher, Flo, Fountain, Wally Gibbons, George, Hopkins, Roberts, Martin Grady, Spaad Helo, Hooker, James, Johnson, Jones, Ann Lighter, Judge Long, Oscar McDowell, Steve Mango, Tiger Mann, Gabin Martrel, Billy Mendes, Messner, Hal Randolph, Mrs. Hal Randolph, Ron, Klim Rosser, Burton Selwick, Dave Severn, Smith, Stanton, Thomas Watford, Raymond Watts, Wells, Bing Willis.)

Tiger Mann, the narrator, plans to marry Edith Caine today. He calls her Rondine *(see Day of the Guns)*. Free in the morning, he chats with Clement

Fletcher, a sailor whom he rescued during a Panama mission, who was conned into buying a Geiger counter to use hunting uranium in South America, and who has disembarked off the *Maitland.* Its cargo includes Keipleitz printing presses destined for Washington, D.C. When Fletcher says his counter clicked near them, Tiger explains that their luminous dials caused the sound. Suddenly Martin Grady, his intelligence-network boss, orders Tiger to delay his wedding and investigate Gabin Martrel, a knowledgeable Soviet spy who has defected. When Tiger tells Rondine she must wait a while, she says she may not. Anyway, Tiger leaves their Chester Hotel, registers as H. Talbot at the King Leopold Hotel and confers with Wally Gibbons, war veteran turned Broadway columnist, who introduces him to a political legman named Dave Severn. He will dig into Martrel's past. Tiger checks with Ernie Bentley, a Manhattan Project worker, expert chemist, and Grady agent. He remembers Martrel fell in love with a beautiful Communist skier during the 1956 Olympics; since she also defected, Martrel may be defecting only to seek her somehow. Tiger, as Talbot, obtains press privileges, crashes a news conference featuring Martrel and guarded by U.S. intelligence-agent Hal Randolph, gets close to Martrel, and scares him by whispering, "Have you found her yet?"

At breakfast the next morning, Severn tells Tiger that the beauty is Sonia Dutko, who defected in 1956, became a skiing instructor in New England, then Sun Valley, but has since disappeared. Tiger has Newark Central, an intelligence switchboard, assign three agents—Hook, James, and Ann Lighter—to find where Martrel is stashed. Tiger phones Raymond Watts, head of a Los Angeles agency expert at finding missing persons, to seek Sonia. Ann soon tells Tiger that Martrel is in the Chamberlain Hotel, offers herself sexually to Tiger—bridegroom manqué, she adds—but gets told he doesn't "like duty-bound sex." Through a hotel bell captain and then Bentley at his laboratory, Tiger gets a copy of Martrel's key, has a diversion pull Martrel's guards away, braces Martrel with a .45, and makes him promise to spill Soviet secrets if Sonia can be saved for him. Tiger returns to his hotel and soon is visited by Rondine. They ready themselves for some pre-nuptial sex but are interrupted when Watts phones: Sonia became a movie adviser in Los Angeles, is now vacationing in New York City; William Copely, a Watts operative in New York, has found her here. Tiger phones Copely's place, is told he has just committed suicide, and abandons Rondine again. Tiger goes to the "suicide" scene, voices his belief that Copely was murdered, orders Ann, James, and Hooker to backtrack Copely, and returns to his hotel. Intelligence agent Thomas Watford is there, with Randolph and a new man named Albert Cutter. Tiger silences their criticism of his handling of Martrel, tells them to check into Copely's death, registers at the Brigham Hotel, phones Watts about Copely, and sleeps until noon.

Ann pops in, reports that Sonia taxied from the airport to the all-women's Shrevesport Hotel, but evidently didn't check in. Ann disrobes and hops into

Tiger's bed, alone. But he proceeds at once to the Shrevesport, forces two biddies at the desk to give him the numbers of any of the rooms where Sonia, undoubtedly having entered disguised, might be, and leaves. Shot at outside but missed, he calls in a false fire alarm so that authorities will rush up and seal the building. He orders Ann to case the relevant rooms and find Sonia. The newspaper reports Martrel's being hospitalized for a possible poisoning. Tiger follows Ann, only to find her dead, of a viciously broken neck, in a room where Sonia, registered as L. Grace, was.

The morning papers report Ann, called Mrs. Romero from Paterson, New Jersey, murdered and L. Grace missing; also, Clement Fletcher, a drunken sailor, who accidentally drowned. Sonia calls Tiger. She says Ann sent her to Fat John's sleazy hotel and gave her Tiger's phone number. James warns Tiger the cops have identified him at the Shrevesport and seek him. Tiger goes to Bentley, who disguises his face and arms him with a fountain pen containing an explosive. Tiger phones and meets Charlie Corbinet, his wartime espionage boss, and asks him to check the Shrevesport for clues and also to guard Rondine. Tiger makes his way to Fat John, learns Sonia is upstairs, and finds her. She is sad to learn of Ann's death, says she has no love for Martrel now, defected without his help, simply wants a new life in America, loves American lingerie, will help Tiger keep Martrel out of Communist hands. Hearing noises outside, Tiger gets Sonia to the roof, returns from a higher room, shoots two thugs in the hall below with his .45, finds Fat John knifed dead, and gets Sonia to Bentley's lab. Bentley rebarrels Tiger's .45 and prepares a photograph of Tiger with Sonia. The two hide in a fleabag hotel and in the morning make torrid love. Tiger phones Rondine and orders her to bring Sonia a disguising wardrobe to the Bristol End, a fishhouse started by a Brit. Tiger phones Corbinet and learns that one of the dead assailants was a hit man out of Mexico. At the Bristol, Tiger orders Rondine to rent a car and stash and provision Sonia, now disguised, in the Connecticut summer home of Burton Selwick, a Britisher now in England. To evade the cops, Tiger goes by the docks, happens to see the *Maitland,* and queries crewmembers about Fletcher. They reveal that Treasury agents sought something aboard, and someone stole and pawned Fletcher's Geiger counter. By phone Tiger alerts Gibbons of a possible scoop concerning agents aboard the *Maitland* and Fletcher's death. Mike meets Rondine, back again and submissive, at the Blue Ribbon, and tells her to get to Martrel in the hospital and reassure him about Sonia by showing him Tiger's photo with her.

Wondering how Ann's killer got into an all-women's hotel, Tiger checks its adjacent buildings and finds women's clothes, obviously a disguise, discarded under a grating. He phones Corbinet the news, to pass on to Randolph, and phones Severn, who can cover the finding for a scoop. Back in his room, Tiger gets a message from a London colleague that Spaad Helo, a Red killer, has been traced from Mexico into the United States and may attack Martrel. Tiger's hotel phones that a female wants to visit. Tiger thinks Rondine is coming with news concerning Martrel, answers the door, is shot at, grabs his assailant, and breaks his neck. Dying, the fellow says he followed after Tiger found the clothes. Tiger camps with Gibbons and beseeches him to sneak Rondine into Martrel's hospital room. Corbinet informs Tiger that Helo, while in Mexico advising documentary filmmakers, was phoned by someone in the Tomlinson's building on Broadway who mentioned a ring Helo had with the name "Anna" inscribed. Tiger takes a much-needed nap.

In the morning Gibbons phones bad news: Rondine, posing as a nurse, has been arrested by Randolph; Mortrel narrowly escaped being poisoned by cyanide in a flower pot. Visiting Corbinet personally, Tiger has him arrange a meeting with Randolph out of town in the evening. Meanwhile, Tiger checks three offices in the Tomlinson building—those of F. I. Besser (bookie), Fountain (lingerie-catalog salesman), and Prado (film company)—but notes nothing useful. He picks up a car via Newark Central, drives to Corbinet's New Jersey hideout early in the evening, and meets with Corbinet, Randolph, and two terse Washington men. Only Tiger's bluff that he can dump Project Valchek (a name Newark Central mentioned earlier) in his lap persuades Randolph to imply that, if so, he will void all charges against Rondine.

Tiger goes to the building where Rondine is held, waits in a taxi, grabs her as she is escorted out, and evades two would-be killers in another taxi. He stashes her with Gibbons. Tiger rents a car, drives to Selwick's house in Connecticut, reunites with Sonia there, and the two make love again to the accompaniment of lightning and thunder. Outside, he spots two would-be killers and grabs one, whom the other, firing at Tiger, kills. The killer drives off. The dead man has U.S. Treasury identification. Tiger phones Gibbons and learns that the same Treasury men who inspected the *Maitland* found Selwick's address in Rondine's purse later. Tiger drives Sonia into Manhattan and stashes her in a warehouse Grady owns. Newark Central tells Tiger to check with Bentley, who has just been wired Helo's long-sought photo. Obtaining copies, Tiger recognizes Helo as one of the thugs in the taxi.

Tiger lunches with Corbinet, gives him a photo of Helo, says he prefers his secret mission assignments to Rodine even, and sleeps all day in a movie house. That night he subways to Martrel's hospital, slugs an intern and dons his clothes, gets to Martrel's room, slugs a cop there, dresses Martrel in the cop's uniform, and spirits him away with the help of a garbage-truck driver, prepositioned at the hospital by Bentley. Tiger and Martrel rest overnight in the driver's Riverside Drive apartment. Martrel, aging and calling the Communist world "a vile mess," hopes he and Sonia can share a future.

The morning papers report, with pictures, Martrel's kidnapping by Tiger. Tiger dresses Martrel in the garbageman's coveralls and takes him on a dozen subways until darkness falls, then phones Gibbons to bring Rondine to Stanton's bar. He sends the two to Grady's warehouse, where Sonia is. The Tomlinson elevator man happens to see Tiger's photo of Helo and says the man made deliveries to Fountain. Martrel identifies Helo as involved in the Valchek project. Tiger sends Martrel in a taxi to Sonia, at last, and taxis himself to the *Maitland,* gets Corbinet there to hold the ship, and the two learn from the captain that Helo and another, with Treasury credentials evidently forged, boarded the ship in search of drugs. Tiger concludes that Helo was planting a uranium bomb in a press to blow up a Washington building. Tiger, accompanied by Corbinet, alerts Randolph, tells him Fountain's office is Helo's communication center, and they rush there, kill a Soviet operative when he fires at them, and retrieve boxes of evidence. Corbinet forces Randolph to give Tiger a running head start. The scales falling from his eyes, Tiger taxis to the warehouse, bursts in, kills Helo, but is wounded by Sonia and handcuffed to a pipe. Tied up are Rondine, Gibbons, and Martrel, whom Sonia busily curses as a "[f]ilthy swine" traitorous to their glorious country. Gloating, she explains she was a double agent waiting to nail defectors like Martrel, who became a target of opportunity. Over Rondine's patriotic objections, Tiger agrees to write a confession that he was hired by the Communists to get Martrel. He uses his special pen, twists it to explode in one minute, clips it to his signed papers, and hands everything to Sonia, who places near her victims a time bomb Helo brought, and departs—figuring to embarrass America thoroughly. Tiger releases himself from the pipe, drags Rondine and Gibbons to safety outside, and hears not only the building erupt but also a deadly bang converting Sonia into "a wet splash," just as the sun rises.

Published in 1965, at the height of the Cold War, *Bloody Sunrise* includes Tiger Mann's colorful definition of the Soviet Union as "that goddamn stupid country" to which "do-gooders . . . [are] giving our country away." Tiger pragmatically asseverates that we need both "Right and Might" to win. Spillane continues mucho macho, first by having Tiger browbeat Rondine into apologizing in the face of his rude infidelity, and then, more generally, by having Tiger explain that Sonia quit training as a muscular athlete "to become a woman." By this time, Spillane's hero can use "Balls!" as an elevated expletive (four times here).

BOCK, CALVIN. In "Kick It or Kill!," he is a criminal hired by Simpson. Kelly Smith shoots him in Simpson's mansion.

THE BODY LOVERS **(1967).** Novel. (Characters: Angie, Arnie, Biff, Billy, Orslo Bucher, Bud, Al Casey, Captain Pat Chambers, Clendenning, Cleo, Corning, Bobby Dale, Davis, Lucy Delacort, Maxine Delaney, Lucy Digs, Dolly, Ali Duval, Ed, Charlie Forbes, Hy Gardner, Theodore Gates, George, Greenie, Paul Gregory, Mike Hammer, Walt Hanley, Richard Hardy, Donald Harney, Norman Harrison, Virginia Howell, Max Hughes, Lorenzo Jones, Lakland, James Lusong, Dulcie McInnes, Marsha, Ronald Miller, Lew Mitchi, Naku Em Abor, Julie Pelham, Helen Poston, Matt Prince, Sol Renner, Tim Riley, Belar Ris, Rosie, Bob Sabre, Richard Salisbury, Greta Service, Harry Service, Phil Silvester, Jean Singleton, Roberta Slade, Miss Tabor, Teddy, Mitch Temple,

Tillman, Ray Tucker, Gerald Ute, Mrs. Gerald Ute, Velda, Vernie, Miss Wald, Ed Walker.)

While driving in New York City one evening, Mike Hammer hears a little boy crying in a region of demolished buildings. He investigates and finds him and also the body, clad flimsily in green, of a young female redhead, who had obviously been strung up and whipped to death. He calls the police, and Captain Pat Chambers and medics arrive and take charge. The boy is uninvolved. Mike and Pat recall a blonde school teacher from Nebraska, similarly clad though in black, and identically killed a month ago.

In the morning, Mike and Velda in their office read the journalist Mitch Temple's account in *The News* of the redhead's murder; Temple also mentions Mike's presence at the scene and compares the two murders. Mike gives a report to an assistant D.A., avoids the press, and learns that the blonde died of a slow, painful poison, and that the whip used on the redhead was from Australia and of the sort featured in circuses and stage shows. Mike calls on Temple, who will try to trace the similar negligees worn by the victims. Mike persuades Temple to delay follow-up reports for a week. A case takes Mike out of town for that period.

When Mike returns, Velda tells him the redhead was Maxine Delaney, a stripper from the West Coast, arrested as a call girl, released, and last seen in Chicago. A package from Harry Service, whom Mike caused to be imprisoned upstate for robbery, contains a handmade wallet. Chambers tells Mike that Temple has been murdered. Mike and Velda visit the murder scene: Temple was stabbed at his door, evidently reached for a white handkerchief, and died. At dinner with Velda, Mike examines the wallet. In a secret compartment is a letter saying Harry's sister (later named Greta Service) knew the redhead and the blonde (later identified as Helen Poston); Harry asks Mike to find his sister, recently out of touch.

Mike obtains a photograph of her from Hy Gardner, a journalist friend, goes to the Greenwich Village apartment where Greta once roomed, but finds only Cleo, a sexy commercial artist. She knew Greta, doesn't know her present whereabouts, and attempts unsuccessfully to interest Mike in sexual dalliance. At the office, Velda reports that by phoning people in Nebraska she learned that Helen Poston was a beauty and bought a car for a good time out of her small town. Velda also phoned Los Angeles contacts and learned that Maxine Delaney tried for a movie career, failed, tried to become a model in Chicago, but failed. While Velda checks Greta's credit-card purchases, Mike learns from Service's lawyer that Greta vowed to help Service with money should he get paroled. Mike finds a gossipy bartender in Greenwich Village, from whom he learns Greta was seen escorted by a rich "gook." Mike walks out to catch a cab but happens to see Cleo. The two decide to seek information about Greta at some gin mills. In the first one, Mike talks with a man who doesn't know Greta but who introduces him to Sol Renner, who writes ads for women's trade magazines and who did know Greta. He tells Mike that

Greta was his friend but recently snubbed him when, decked out in furs and diamonds, she appeared at a restaurant with "a Charlie Chan type." Mike again resists Cleo's sinuous approach.

In the office, Velda tells Mike that Gardner is preparing columns on Temple, whose leads to the women's negligee purchases Chambers is pursuing. Mike barges into the office of Dulcie McInnes, a distinguished fashion editor Cleo told Mike she sent Greta to. Dulcie, maturely attractive, encourages Mike's macho talk, tells him Greta was "too stacked" to be photographed for dress catalogs, gives him a photo of Greta, and urges him to return some time. Over lunch, Gardner agrees with Mike that the murders of Helen and Maxine are connected, fears for Greta's safety, and says someone filched Temple's notes concerning negligee sales. Gardner promises to circulate duplicates of Greta's photo. Mike reports to Chambers, who shows him negligees—black, red, green, blue, and yellow—that Temple bought and the police took from his apartment. He says that vice cops a month ago raided a porno-film ring, identified Maxine in a stag reel, located the hotel room used, and have descriptions of the criminals involved. He adds that the medical examiners are trying to identify the poison used on Helen. Mike briefs Chambers on his interest in locating Greta and says he would like to visit Harry, her brother, in prison. Mike visits the newspaper morgue and learns that Temple was seen checking into files from *P* to *T*, also that crime reporter Al Casey looked into them after Temple's death. Mike returns to his office, sees that it has been broken into and searched by someone, is alerted by sudden silence in the corridor, and trades shots with and kills an assailant.

Mike breaks office doors nearby to make it seem that he surprised a robber not targeting him alone. Pat arrives, half-accepts Mike's account, and gives Mike a pass to visit Service in prison. Service provides one clue: Greta, when she last visited him, had a letter postmarked "Bradbury." Velda and Hy are at Mike's office. Hy says Temple had an assortment of photographs. Velda reports gossip she gleaned from Greta's neighbors: Greta suddenly seemed to have money, spent weekends away with Helen, once just before Helen was killed. Pat tells Mike the man he killed was Otto Bucher, an Algerian citizen, an army deserter, and a criminal wanted by Interpol. Bucher roomed in the Bronx and regularly visited one prostitute. Pat also says the police exhumed the body of a beautiful but tawdry woman killed in a car crash four months ago and discovered evidence of murder—by torture on a rack. She and Greta modeled together for garment-industry photographs. Mike goes to Bucher's neighborhood and learns from a bartender he knows that Bucher's prostitute was Rosie and that Bucher was once seen getting into what a boozy witness named Greenie called "a dipple car." Hy calls Mike to come to a lower Manhattan restaurant, where he introduces him to Casey. It seems that Temple bribed a salesgirl and learned that another negligee buyer evidently sought to buy a white negligee. Temple may have followed him out of the store. Velda theorizes that white would go nicely on Greta, a brunette.

Mike agrees to go with Hy and a political reporter to a party thrown by an influential, wealthy businessman named Gerald Ute for U.N. personnel honoring some African diplomats, including Naku Em Abor. Mike meets Ute, a widower, and is surprised that Dulcie McInnes is acting as Ute's hostess and has brought several Proctor models along for their vivacity. He agrees to meet Dulcie at her office building, where, she says, she just remembered that Teddy Gates, who photographed Greta, has an office and may have Greta's address. Meanwhile, Hy gets a call from Casey, who has just learned of Temple's unsuccessful attempt to follow a man who made a purchase in a department store and delivered it by taxi to someone in a recklessly speeding private car. Mike gets Tim Riley, a reporter he bumps into, to let him read carbon copies of Temple's old columns. In several, mention is made of Ute, Dulcie, the U.N., Belar Ris, a "part-Arab complex headed by Naku Em Abor," the Mafia, and corrupt labor unions. Mike meets Dulcie, and they check Gates's address cards. The one for Greta has an alternate name—Howell— and a fleabag called the Sandelor Hotel as her address. They go there by taxi, find and confront Greta, get nowhere by questioning her, but scare her into packing. Mike bribes a taxi driver, nearby, to tell him Greta's destination should he drive her somewhere. Then Mike and Dulcie proceed to her lush apartment, where she becomes an irresistible "writhing masterpiece of sensuality."

Mike sacks out in his hotel room next to Velda's room, awakens midafternoon, sees Velda's note telling him to meet her at the Blue Ribbon at 6:00 P.M., and learns through Dulcie's office that Dulcie has gone to a fashion show in Washington, D.C. The taxi driver that followed Greta calls with this information: Greta was driving a new Chevy with a dented rear fender, but he lost her as she headed out of town. Mike returns to the Sandelor, barges into the room Greta used, and decks a pimp who is slapping one of his girls. She tells Mike this: Virginia Howell is her name; Lorenzo Jones, her pimp, assigned her to a customer on Eighth Avenue last night; she doesn't know Greta. Two young punks suddenly enter and try to attack Mike, who, however, soon renders both of them unconscious. Jones vanishes. Mike summons Pat, who arrests the punks. Mike wangles his way into Gates's office, notices that Greta's file is missing, locates Gates's studio apartment in the Fifties, picks the lock, and finds folders of photographs of Greta, Helen, and Maxine—all with "too much breast and thigh" to qualify as skinny Proctor models. Velda, at the Blue Ribbon, tells Mike this: Pat is pursuing Jones's "other women"; Hy says Casey has leads; Velda located Greta's rented Chevy, its mileage indicating she drove sixty-odd miles to a location and back, twice. By drawing a circle on a map, Mike discovers Greta probably drove out on Long Island to Bradbury, the town Harry saw named on Greta's letter. Velda will get a room in Bradbury and nose around. Mike visits Pat's office and is told this: Greta and Gates are still missing; Dulcie is in Washington; the poison (later called C-130) used on Helen was popular with now-defunct Oriental royalty, is currently used in Turkish vendettas. Startled when Mike mentions Bradbury, Pat reveals this: Ute has financed jazz festivals there; U.N. personnel flock there; French and Middle Eastern embassies have located there.

Mike joins Hy, Casey, and two old journalists as they examine sixty-eight photographs Temple seemed interested in. Belar Ris, whom Mike saw at Ute's party, is in one. Ris is a politically vicious U.N. representative. In one of Biff's files, Mike finds a photograph secretly taken, in which Ris is arguing with Naku Em Abor. Mike leaves, intent on finding Lorenzo Jones. Three of his girls can reveal nothing, but the fourth, Roberta Slade, sipping a martini in a bar, is pay dirt. Abused by Jones but with a police record, she feels trapped. She gives Mike the name of a hotel Jones holes up in. They go there. Mike disarms him and forces him at gunpoint to name Ali, a heroin-smuggling steward on the *Pinella;* this demented "gook" enjoys torturing girls handed to him by Jones for high pay. Mike delights Roberta by battering Jones horribly, taking $3,000 from his wallet, and asking her to use it as escape money for herself and other girls Jones has controlled.

Through a friend, Mike learns that the *Pinella* is a Panamanian freighter accommodating ten passengers, with Ali Duval as steward. A wharf watchman tells Mike that Ali has money, has been seen in a limousine, and wears a fez. Mike visits Pat at his bachelor apartment, reports on Jones and Ali, and brainstorms with him about negligees and "gooks." Mike gets some sleep, until disturbed when Velda phones him from Bradbury to say she found a prostitute named Julie Pelham, lured from New York City by a guy who drove her to Bradbury, said he wanted her for a local embassy party, but scared her when he began to threaten her. When he stopped for gas, she escaped but without her purse, and Velda gave her some money for a motel room.

The next morning, Casey tells Mike this: Ute bought land at Bradbury ten years ago, recently donated it as a tax write-off for embassy use; Ris is a ruthless "modern day pirate" in business and politics. Mike phones Dulcie, back from Washington, and asks how he can meet Ris. She says she'll take him tonight to a hotel reception where he will be an honored guest. At the Blue Ribbon, Pat tells Mike that the C-130 poison, fatal through skin contact and perhaps used to kill Helen, was shipped aboard the *Pinella* from Marseilles. Ali, now known to be of French-Arabian parentage, is being sought.

Mike gets into a tuxedo, meets Dulcie at a Park Avenue hotel, learns Gates is still missing, proceeds with Dulcie to the party, and meets Ris, a hardhanded, cocksure criminal type. The two fence verbally about the U.N., which Mike despises for its inability to foster world peace. Mike returns Dulcie to her apartment and goes to his when she says she is busy. Cleo calls, desperate to see him. He takes a taxi to her Greenwich Village digs. She promises to give him vital information, but only if he lets her preserve her hold on him by letting her paint him nude. He does. The painting of Mike—raw, vicious, combative—is a revelation. The two make love. In the morning, Cleo is gone. A note from her reveals that Greta's companion was Ris.

Mike freshens up and tries but fails to phone Hy and Dulcie. He gets a call from Pat: Gates was found, a suicide; Mike must meet Pat at the Blue Ribbon at 6:30 P.M. Pat, late, brings the D.A.'s lawyer, who says that Ris owns the *Pinella* and that Ali Duval, a former Algerian terrorist, is one of Ris's enforcers. Pat adds this: Dulcie, according to a phone tap, is to be with Ris at a party this evening at Bradbury; if Ali shows up there, he will be arrested; Ris, a "dipple," is immune. When Mike is puzzled, Pat says "dipple" stands for "DPL plates. Diplomatic immunity." That explains both why Temple failed to catch a safely speeding car and Bucher's connection with Ris. Mike gets a message from Velda: Julie, whom she found, and she are going to the Ris party, to be held at G-14. Mike borrows the Blue Ribbon bartender's car, drives to Bradbury, gets a local road map, locates a mansion at its *G* and *14* coordinates, knocks out one guard, evades other guards, hears voices, and spies through a door crack on a shocking scene. Greta is caged, with two rattlesnakes ready to bite once she falls. Ris is there, having bet she will fall before a certain time, and if not, she wins $50,000. Dulcie is there, fascinated, as are other depraved guests, mostly U.N. delegates from emerging countries. Mike instantly makes sense of his evidence: Ris saw Temple observe him at the store, had him killed; Ali knew his smuggling had been spotted, used Jones; Ris hired Bucher; Dulcie tampered with Gates's address files, scared him; Helen, Maxine, Greta, and Julie were attractive to Ris and other sadists. Mike barges in on Ris's show, slugs a guard, shoots the heads off the snakes, kills two more guards, wounds another, but then suffers a head wound rendering him groggy. As he is tied and dumped in an empty basement kitchen, he hears Ris and Dulcie discuss their escape plans, including hushing their guests and later disposing of all the evidence. Greta, also tied, and the dead guards are there too, as well as Julie, murdered, and the guy, murdered, who failed to deliver Julie to Ris promptly. Velda is there, also, locked in the kitchen but having easily slipped her ropes. She frees Mike, Greta, and Julie. Mike rigs an old-fashioned phone so that its buzzer will spark a light bulb when the phone is rung, opens the gas lines on the old stove, breaks a crumbling window frame, and leads Velda and Greta to his car. They drive to a gas station. Mike phones Hy for the phone number of the Bradbury mansion Ris has been using, gets it, and dials it. Mike, Velda, and Greta are gratified to see and hear an enormous orange explosion in the distance.

The Body Lovers is an intricately plotted, jumpy narrative involving many taxis and even more telephones. Spillane continues his love-hate affair with rainy Manhattan and expresses his hatred of modern Greenwich Village by calling it "a sore throat and coughed-up phlegm." In a worse image, Mike tries to sift out the evidentiary pieces of his puzzle that gnaw the corners of his mind. Spillane predictably pens in Mike Hammer's snide remarks about the U.N., "gooks" (defined as "native help," who "toted" and washed for you, begged, killed, stole, and called being caught "kismet"), women (often "stuffy animals" endowed with wily "ways"), and homosexuals. Mike's work here is akin to that of Tiger Mann in his U.N.-based challenges. The blurb on the back cover of the New American Library paperback reprint of *The Body Lovers* stupidly gives away the central crime of the novel.

BOLIDY, CHIGGER. In "Stand Up and Die!," he handles the local mail and reluctantly provides Mitch Valler with information.

BONES, SMITTY. In "The Flier," he ran games in Havana and, according to George Clinton's report to Cat Fallon, was murdered, along with Dertelli, by Andro Marcel.

BORDEN, HENRY. In "The Gold Fever Tapes," he was an expert, age fifty-nine, at hiding metal by working it into harmless-looking shapes. His job done, he is murdered.

BORLEY, PHIL. In "Killer Mine," he is a criminal from "Chi" who muffed an extortion plot in New York.

BORLIG, MARTA ("GIGGIE," "LITTLE GIGGIE," "MARTY"). In "Killer Mine," she is a beautiful policewoman, of Irish extraction, assigned to work with Lieutenant Joe Scanlon on the multiple-murder case. They knew each other as youngsters, work well together, and make love. Spillane continues to have his macho heroes call their ladies by demeaning names. Joe calls Marty "baby," "chicken," "kid," "kitten," and "sugar."

BORLIG, SED. In "Killer Mine," he is mentioned as Marta Borlig's brother, in dental school.

BOSTER, CLAUDE. In *The By-Pass Control,* he is a friend of Louis Agrounsky and lives in Eau Gallie, Florida. Tiger seeks information from him concerning Agrounsky. Niger Hoppes tortures Boster into telling him that Agrounsky is living in Leesville, North Carolina.

BOTENKO. In *The By-Pass Control,* Tiger Mann mentions the 1964 Soviet trial involving Botenko and Sokolov.

BOWEN, RUSS. In *My Gun Is Quick,* he was a West Coast procurer of girls, whom he sent via Feeney Last to New York City call-girl houses. When he bucked higher-ups, he was shot to death. Nancy Sanford took incriminating photographs of him. Bowen was also known as Paul Miller.

BOYLE. In "Everybody's Watching Me," Joe Boyle says his brother was killed at Anzio in the war. Since Joe Boyle is a fictitious name, there may not have been such a brother.

BOYLE, FRANKIE. In *The Snake,* Mike remembers Boyle as a criminal patient enough to keep $70,000 in his mattress for sixteen years, only to have the rooming house he lived in burn down.

BOYLE, JOE ("JOEY"). In "Everybody's Watching Me." *See* Vetter.

BRADDOCK, AL. In "Kick It or Kill!" *See* Smith, Kelly.

BRADLEY. In *The Death Dealers,* he was an agent whom Tiger Mann instructed and who then instructed Lennie Byrnes.

BRADLEY, BENNETT. In *The Killing Man,* he is a duplicitous State Department killer, in reality the elusive Penta. He is assigned (perhaps by Libya) to assassinate the vice president, but stalls first to get Mike for causing the death of Bradley's murderous twin brother (*see* DuValle, Francisco) and second to find a cocaine shipment. He fools all of the authorities until Mike discovers his identity and kills him. When Bradley phones Velda to make an appointment to see Mike, he calls himself Bruce Lewison.

BRANT, JACK. In *The Death Dealers,* he was a commercial developer in Israel and Arabia, was attacked in Arabia, became anti-Arab, and returned to Brooklyn. He provides Tiger Mann with Tom, Dick, and Harry.

BRAY, LEON. In *The Last Cop Out,* he is a skillful accountant, fifty, for Mark Shelby's criminal organization. Although he is protected by seven men, he and they are killed by a man in a gas mask. In naming Bray, Spillane probably had in mind the name of Robert Bray, the actor starring as Mike Hammer in the 1957 movie version of *My Gun Is Quick.*

BRENT, MRS. SAMMY. In *Survival . . . Zero!,* she is mentioned as the jealous type.

BRENT, SAMMY. In *Survival . . . Zero!,* he sells theater tickets and indirectly helps Mike Hammer locate Beaver.

BRIAN. In *Day of the Guns,* he is bartender at P. T. Moriarty's. Mann is friendly with him.

BRIDEY-THE-GREEK. In *The Erection Set,* he is a killer who murdered Brown and Voorhies, and made Bud Healey a paralytic, with his favorite weapon, an ice pick. Bridey is sent by The Turk with Markham to kill Dog Kelly. Dog puts both men in the hospital. Bridey is later killed because he did not accomplish his mission.

BRIGGS, TONY. In "Everybody's Watching Me," he was a Chicago criminal, allegedly killed by Vetter.

BRIGHTON. In *One Lonely Night*, he is Ethel Brighton's wealthy father. His preventing her marriage caused a rupture in their relationship. But he visits her in the hospital after she is wounded.

BRIGHTON, ETHEL. In *One Lonely Night*, she is a beautiful, naive woman, age about thirty. Mike Hammer meets her at a Communist meeting, sleeps with her, and disabuses her of her faith in Communism. When he is shot at by a Soviet thug, Ethel is wounded but will recover.

BRILL, JOHN. In *The Last Cop Out. See* Meeker, Artie.

BRISSOM, SERGEANT MACK. In "Killer Mine," he is a helpful policeman working with Lieutenant Joe Scanlon.

BRISSON. In "I'll Die Tomorrow," his is the name by which Buddy Riley's secretary misidentifies Rudolph Lees.

BRODERICK, ANTHONY. In *The Last Cop Out*, he is mentioned as a shy-locking boss working for Mark Shelby.

BROGAN. In *The Deep*, he owns a market on 103rd Street, over which Tally Lee lives. Deep is knocked unconscious at its entrance. (In the badly proofed New American Library edition, Brogan is later spelled "Grogan.")

BROTHERS, HARMONY. In *The Snake*, he is a criminal who, Mike Hammer recalls, hid $1.5 million for forty-one years and revealed its location only when dying.

BROTORRIO, MARSHALL. In *Black Alley*, he works at the place in Queens where ashes of the deceased are deposited. He calls Mike to report that Marcos Dooley's ashes were disturbed.

BROWN. In *The Erection Set*, Dog Kelly recalls that Bridey-the-Greek killed Brown with an ice pick.

BRYAN, INSPECTOR. In "Killer Mine," he is a tough police officer who pressures Lieutenant Joe Scanlon to solve the murder cases.

BUCHER, ORSLO. In *The Body Lovers*, he is an internationally known crim-inal whom Belar Ris hires to pursue Mike. Mike catches Bucher outside his office and kills him.

BUCK. In *My Gun Is Quick,* he cares for Mike Hammer's car.

BUCKMAN, HENRY. In *Bloody Sunrise,* this is the false name a Soviet agent working for Spaad Helo uses when he is posing as a U.S. Treasury inspector. When Spaad shoots at Tiger Mann, he kills "Buckman."

BUCKS, LEW. In *The Deep,* he owns or frequents the Pelican bar.

BUCKY. In *My Gun Is Quick,* he manages the Zero Zero Club when Murray Candid is away. Spillane carelessly names two characters Buck and Bucky in this novel.

BUD. In *The Body Lovers,* he is a john Lorenzo Jones orders Virginia Howell to meet.

BUDDY. In *The Death Dealer,* an East Side bar girl tells Tiger Mann that Buddy pulled a gun on Gretch and hopes he is not a policeman investigating. Tiger says he isn't.

BUFF, SHERMAN. In *The Snake,* he was a two-time loser prosecuted by Simpson Torrence and vowing revenge when he gets out. Mike determines, however, that Buff is successful in electronics and is considered by his parole officer to be rehabilitated.

BUNNY. In "Killer Mine," he runs what is called "a fag joint." Lieutenant Joe Scanlon goes there for information about suspects.

BURKE, GILLIAN ("GILL"). In *The Last Cop Out,* he is an ex–police sergeant persuaded to return to the New York police department to investigate criminal activity controlled by Papa Menes in New York and contested by Mark Shelby there. Gill works with Captain Bill Long, insults assistant D.A. Robert Lederer, falls in love with Helen Scanlon, and is responsible for multiple quick murders on his road to success. Helen questions him timidly but then accepts the love of the man she knows was a do-it-yourself killer. Spillane was surely thinking of Joe Gill and his brother Ray Gill when he provided Burke's nickname. Spillane met Joe, a fellow employee at Gimble's during the 1940 Christmas season. Joe introduced Spillane to Ray, a Funnies, Inc., editor, who soon hired Spillane to write scripts and help him edit.

Bibliography: Collins and Traylor.

BUSSY, BILLY. In "Stand Up and Die!," he is engaged to Caroline Hart, who soon prefers Mitch Valler. When Bussy offers to fight Mitch, he gets one ear shot off and his teeth kicked out. Bussy later tries but fails to hang Valler.

BUSTER. In "The Pickpocket," he is an armed thug Marty sends to scare Willie.

BYERS. In *The Killing Man,* he called Velda for information Mike wanted. She fortunately placed a tape recording of his voice and Penta's in Byers's file.

BYLE. In *My Gun Is Quick,* this is the name of a place in Greenwich Village where Murray Candid has a hangout.

THE BY-PASS CONTROL (1966). Novel. (Characters: Virgil Adams, Louis Agrounsky, Mason Armstrong, Ernie Bentley, Mrs. Ernie Bentley, Bert, Claude Boster, Botenko, Diana Caine, Edith Caine, Dr. George Carlson, Caswell, John Clark, Charlie Corbinet, Courtney, Daniels, Delaney, General Ortega Diaz, Dave Elroy, Henri Frank, Wally Gibbons, Martin Grady, Doug Hamilton, Captain Hardecker, Miss Hays, Herman, Niger Hoppes, Camille Hunt, Johnson, Henry Jordan, Sonny Kipton, Dr. Kirkland, Don Lavois, Linda, Lisa McCall, Beezo McCauley, Tiger Mann, Marge, James Miller, Earl Mossky, Pecky, Pete, Marcus Pietri, Hal Randolph, Ron, Vito Salvi, Shigley, Vincent Small, Sokolov, Henry Stanton, Talbot, Wax, Tony Williams.)

Tiger Mann, the narrator, has just fought Vito Salvi in Salvi's secret rooms. Tiger, shot in the side and knifed, has badly wounded Salvi. Salvi, Soviet agent, has just tortured three Americans to death, including Don Hamilton. Hoping to be arrested, not killed, Salvi reveals much of his mission to Tiger, who then shoots him dead and phones Hal Randolph, the federal security chief. He and an agent come and grill Tiger, learn only that Hamilton was a private investigator whom Martin Grady, Tiger's wealthy, free-wheeling supervisor, asked to look into Belt-Aire Electronics, a Grady company. Tiger taxis to the apartment of his fiancée, Edith Caine, called Rondine, has her summon a doctor to treat his wounds and prescribe sedatives, phones Grady to have Don Lavois assigned to him, and phones Charlie Corbinet, his ex–O.S.S. commanding officer, to come over. Corbinet explains that Salvi was seeking Louis Agrounsky, a Polish electronics expert working for American ICBM projects until he disappeared last year. Two of the three men Salvi murdered were American agents also seeking Agrounsky. It seems the Russians could launch missiles at the United States safely, because Agrounsky has installed a by-pass control capable of halting America's ability to counterstrike. Tiger is too woozy to say more than that he thinks he can find Agrounsky.

Tiger awakens next afternoon, silences Rondine's complaints by macho talk, and reports as ordered to Randolph's office. Randolph fails to discomfit Tiger, who agrees to cooperate provided Grady's organization has free rein. Tiger meets Don Lavois, tough and experienced, in the laboratory of Ernie Bentley, a weapons inventor, and asks Don to backtrack Salvi while he investigates Hamilton. Something was awry with Hamilton. Tiger learns that he was of modest means from 1946 until recently, then moved into a lavish apartment-office. The police cased it but found little. Tiger checks and notes only that the folder labeled Belt-Aire Electronics, once obviously jam-packed, is empty.

Tiger goes to the Belt-Aire factory and meets Camille Hunt, Hamilton's suave, beautiful personnel director. The two squabble briefly; then she loans him the files on employees Hamilton approved and hired. Tiger checks with Corbinet, who says this: Agrounsky overworked as a student, bought a house in Eau Gallie, Florida, near Cape Kennedy, was in a minor car accident, sold his car in Myrtle Beach, and vanished; the two dead federal agents sought Salvi, because Salvi sought Agrounsky. Tiger checks into the Salem hotel as T. Martin, learns by phone from Virgil Adams of Newark Central that the Russians have replaced Salvi with another agent, already in the United States. Tiger phones Lavois, who says he checked Salvi's apartment and found a quarter-pound of heroin in a condom balloon anchored inside a commode pipe. Tiger gets photocopies of Hamilton's files from Bentley, mails the originals to Camille, and reads the copies before retiring.

Next day Tiger gets Randolph to produce Salvi's autopsy, which shows no drug addiction. Corbinet provides Tiger with rare photos of Agrounsky and says he had a hobby of miniaturizing electronic components. Tiger taxis to Belt-Aire, barges into Camille's office, and shows her Agrounsky's pictures. She recalls his unsuccessful application for work, then drives Tiger to her Manhattan apartment to consult her notes on failed applicants. No luck. So after drinks they make torrid love. Tiger, distressed at this use of precious time, rushes to Bentley's office and learns this: Agrounsky must have applied for miniaturizing employment somewhere and may thus be traced; Lavois has information on a big drug purchase and is waiting in Tiger's hotel room, a key to which Tiger provided. First, Tiger learns from Hamilton's hotel clerk that Hamilton wrote an informative letter to himself, sent to General Delivery, which Corbinet will retrieve. Returning to his hotel room, Tiger finds Lavois shot dead, phones Adams, and is told to check the fatal bullet. When told it is a high-velocity .22, Adams says it is the trademark of Niger Hoppes, experienced Soviet killer, now in the United States. Adams says Mason Armstrong is piloting Dave Elroy, a street-smart agent, from Detroit to replace Lavois. Both Tiger and Elroy will room over Shigley's place on 56th Street. Corbinet will furnish Tiger reports from Washington, on applicants denied employment at Belt-Aire. Tiger taxis to Rondine, briefs her concerning the entire case, enlists her aid, but warns the brave beauty of danger. She phones for time off, packs, and exits with Tiger and the tough apartment doorman (see Ron, in The Death Dealers) out a back exit. Ron is wounded by a shot, falls, and becomes a decoy, as Tiger phones for a private ambulance to remove his own presumed corpse, with the unseen assailant watching. The evening papers report the death of T. Mann, a Martin Grady employee living over Shigley's. Hoppes will read and gloat.

Next morning Adams phones Tiger. Rondine awakens, smiling evidently after some satisfactory lovemaking. Tiger must see Elroy, who tells him an informant, Earl Mossky, says Salvi bought a kilo of heroin. Tiger visits Bentley, who has news that a letter has turned up, from Agrounsky and on stationery belonging to Vincent Small, of Eau Gallie, Florida. Corbinet reports no leads developed from those rejected applications Washington sent. Tiger taxis to Rondine, tells her to look over the reject files, lectures her verbosely, and leaves. Armstrong flies Tiger in a converted F-51 from Newark to Eau Gallie, where Small teaches philosophy at a nearby college. Tiger rents a car, finds Small, and learns about Agrounsky. He studied miniaturizing too hard, grew ill, and recovered changed and uncertain about the world condition. Small sends Tiger to Boster, another Agrounsky confidante and also involved in "mini-work" but less able than Agrounsky. Neither Small nor Boster knows where Agrounsky is, but Boster suggests Tiger talk with Dr. George Carlson, Agrounsky's physician. Leaving Boster, Tiger spots an assailant, ducks, and two shots from a .38 miss both men. Tiger tells the police it was an attempted robbery gone wrong. Tiger phones Adams and learns this: Elroy is flying down to help him; Hoppes uses a special inhaler for nasal trouble. Tiger rents a second room, leaves it empty, and parks his car near it.

In the morning Tiger disarms a clever car bomb and goes to Dr. Carlson, who tells him Agrounsky's car accident required pain killers, and he became addicted to heroin. Tiger rewires the car bomb, welcomes Elroy, and tells him to locate possible suppliers of heroin for Agrounsky in Eau Gallie. When a Soviet agent sneaks in to check on the car bomb, it blows him to bits. Tiger finds a detached hand, obtains fingerprints, mails them to Bentley, and hides his .45 behind the air conditioner. Captain Hardecker arrives. His assistant recognizes Tiger as involved with Boster. Hardecker takes Tiger to jail, where Elroy visits him and hints about seeking Agrounsky's drug supplier.

At 8:00 the next morning Hardecker, having phoned Tiger's named higher-ups, cooperates and releases him. Tiger returns to his motel and finds the manager happy because Grady wired an enormous sum to pay for damages caused by the car-bomb explosion. Phoning Tiger to meet him at a nearby bar, Elroy tells him a dealer known as Fish is a uniquely big drug supplier and was seen earlier with Agrounsky, who, short of money, sold some of his heroin and therefore was to be supplied by Salvi in New York. Tiger registers at the Sand Dunes Motel as T. Gerrity. Bentley phones this: Henri Frank, a Soviet agent and Florida drug pusher, was the man whose fingerprints Tiger sent him; Bentley is forwarding Tiger rare German-made Bezex inhalers, which he has learned Hoppes uses and which are available in Miami; two of the inhalers are booby-trapped with cyanide gas. Tiger recalls the name Henri Frank as that of a rejected applicant for Belt-Aire work. Tiger phones Camille Hunt; when she remembers few details about Frank, he asks her to fly to Eau Gallie. Tiger visits Hardecker; he says Frank was on his missing-persons list and gives Tiger photos of him. Tiger finds Boster at Small's house, learns from both that Agrounsky acted like an addict and bought fish from a man named Wax, and warns both that Agrounsky could sabotage America's missile program. Tiger returns to Hardecker, who tells him Agrounsky, a subject of a security clearance, was friendly with two prostitutes and also Helen Lewis, from Sarasota. Elroy finds Tiger and tells him a big drug buy was made from Sonny Kipton, who had connections in the Myrtle Beach area and was recently murdered because he sold diluted drugs. Tiger takes Camille from the rainy airport to his motel, tells her Frank is dead, and goes with her to Lisa McCall, a prostitute Hardecker said Agrounsky visited. Lisa, who remembers Camille from a South American adventure, theorizes that contact with a decent woman, perhaps a technician in his laboratory, left Agrounsky so frustrated he visited Lisa for relief. While Camille showers in an adjoining room in his motel, Tiger phones Bentley and learns Agrounsky while in North Carolina sold two patents for quick drug money. Tiger tries to phone Helen Lewis but learns she is in Rome. Camille emerges, and she and Tiger make incendiary love. Elroy phones, directs Tiger to a deserted house, where he— with Camille along—finds a drug addict named Beezo McCauley shot dead, by Hoppes's trademark weapon. Tiger reasons that the fellow was paid to steer Hoppes toward Agrounsky, got high, and was eliminated. Tiger takes Camille, nauseated and chilled, to the motel, drives to Small, and demands that he and Boster remember more about Agrounsky.

Tiger checks with Corbinet, now in Eau Gallie too; he says Randolph is trying to get Tiger off the case, then adds that Hamilton was doing some blackmailing on the side. Back at the motel, Tiger finds Camille having taken sleeping pills for her cold, and Hardecker in Tiger's dark adjoining room. He has learned of Beezo's death and finds Tiger exciting enough to aid. Tiger connects Agrounsky, Frank, and Helen Lewis for him. When Hardecker leaves, Tiger, sensing "the *thing*," that is, Hoppes's nearness, rigs a dummy in his lighted room. When it is fired at, Tiger exits, is shot at, kills an assailant in a rainy palm grove, spots Hoppes on an adjoining roof, fires, misses, and is jumped by a heavy whose neck he fatally breaks. Hoppes escapes. Elroy delivers to Tiger the package of boopy-trapped Bezex inhalers Bentley expressed to Florida. Tiger rouses Camille. They drive to a gas station, where Tiger phones Small, who remembers a stranger asked about Agrounsky's list of real-estate options. Tiger phones Hardecker to protect Small and Boster. Tiger slips past cops at Boster's home but finds him tortured and left for dead in his back workshop. Boster tells him Hoppes forced him to reveal Agrounsky's hideout at Leesville, North Carolina. Tiger phones Corbinet to tend to Boster, drives Camille to the airport, tells her to fly back to New York, and locates Armstrong. Tiger phones Bentley and learns Rondine has special information for his ears only. Learning Hoppes just chartered a Comanche for Leesville, Armstrong and Tiger fly there through rain, belly-land near the beach, see the Comanche and the murdered pilot, learn from a storekeeper where Wax's fish house, frequented by Agrounsky, is, and find it. They seek out Agrounsky's beach house and find him dead of a heroin overdose, his by-pass control humming in his lap. Hoppes must be nearby. Tiger warns Armstrong to help but stay low, while he circles the other way. A shot rings out. Tiger spots Armstrong wounded in a sand dune. Tiger outguesses Hoppes, finds him, and they exchange shots. After a struggle, Tiger, wounded below a rib, breaks his wounded but potent adversary's jaw and drowns him, returns to Armstrong, and bandages his head. Tiger returns to Agrounsky's digs, phones Rondine, learns from her that Hamilton's self-mailed document, just found, revealed that Camille is a Soviet mole, planted at Belt-Aire and the object of Hamilton's blackmailing efforts. Surprise. Camille enters. She helicoptered from Eau Gallie, killed the pilot, has the drop on Tiger, disarms him, has him empty his pockets in fear of his vaunted gimmicks, and gloats. Planning to shoot him soon, she first sneezes, finds a Bezex inhaler he had, sniffs it for relief, and dies shooting the floor vainly.

In *The By-Pass Control,* Tiger reflects Spillane's political philosophy. Tiger describes liberals, often bearded and in sneakers, with red-tinted brains, possessed of college-bred notions, being superstupid droolers of the Moscow line, and needing military-style discipline. When Tiger hears Small discuss philosophy, he ridicules Plato and Aristotle for lacking a realistic vision. The most notable stylistic feature of *The By-Pass Control* is its similes and metaphors, best when thunder storms are personified as laughing at puny humans, worst when the rear stairs used by passengers deplaning are called "anus-like"; twice Tiger compares sex and military combat, best when postorgasm is likened to a parachute collapsing on tired jumpers. In the light of America's September 11, 2001, disaster, Tiger's fearing Manhattan "could all come tumbling down in a single second" is scary. Sherri Molinou, whom Spillane married in 1965, had already posed for the cover of *The By-Pass Control.*

BYRNES, LENNIE. In *The Death Dealers,* he is an eager young agent, about age twenty-five, whom Martin Grady sends to help Tiger Mann. Byrnes guards Edith Caine by posing as a journalist reporting on U.N. translators.

C

CABILLA, PEDRO. In *The Last Cop Out,* he serves the spiciest food in Cuban Miami and marvels at Artie Meeker's ability to eat it in quantities.

CABLE. In "The Flier," the Cable-Hurley Supplies Company provides Felix Ramsey with demotion bombs for Cat Fallon's P-51.

CABLE, S. C. In *The Erection Set,* he is an owner of Cable Howard Productions, a movie company. Sharon Cross and Lee Shay work for him, and Walt Gentry helps bankroll him. Cable entertains lavishly, and his company shoots part of the movie *Fruits of Labor* at the little town of Linton. Is the name Cable Howard a takeoff of Clark Gable, movie actor, and Howard Hughes, movie producer?

CABOT, VIC. In "The Affair with the Dragon Lady," he was the radioman aboard the Dragon Lady.

CAHILL, MRS. In "Stand Up and Die!," she bakes biscuits which her son, Trumble Cahill, sneaks to Mitch Valler.

CAHILL, TRUMBLE. In "Stand Up and Die!," he is a spunky little kid whose telling neighbors he saw Mitch Valler and Caroline Hart passionately kissing puts them both in harm's way. Trumble soon adores Mitch Valler and therefore helps him. Mitch will presumably keep his promise and return to care for the boy.

CAINE, AGNES. In *Day of the Guns,* born in 1896, she is Richard Caine's wife and the mother of their five children.

CAINE, DIANA. In *Day of the Guns,* she is the daughter of Agnes and Richard Caine, was reported killed early during the war, but in reality defected as Rondine Lund to the Nazis, loved and was loved by Tiger Mann during the war, and was later killed. Her sister Edith Caine pretends to be Rondine, who if alive would be age thirty-nine. Mann thinks she had plastic surgery, because Edith would be age twenty-eight. This Rondine is also mentioned in *The By-Pass Control* and *The Death Dealers.*

CAINE, EDITH. In *Day of the Guns,* she is the daughter of Agnes and Richard Caine. When Tiger Mann first sees her, she is a U.N. translator. He thinks she is Rondine Lund, his former lover and an ex–Nazi spy. Through fear that the Caine family will be blackmailed or exposed because of Rondine, Edith does not expose the machinations of Gretchen Lark, her associate and alleged friend. In the end, virginal Edith proves her love for Mann. In *Bloody Sunrise,* Edith, whom Mann calls Rondine, must delay her wedding to Tiger because he is off on another mission. Caught up in it, Edith hints that she may not wait further. When threatened with torture by Sonia Dutko, Edith is amazingly courageous. Tiger rescues her. In *The Death Dealers,* once again she agrees to delay her wedding to Tiger. She is attacked by Malcolm Turos but rescued by Tiger. In *The By-Pass Control,* Rondine helps Tiger and Wally Gibbons fake Tiger's death, then goes with Tiger to a nice apartment over Shigley's place, where they evidently consummate their love. At least, in the morning she "smiled in that pleased way women have after a perfect night." Later, she phones Tiger that Camille Hunt, with whom he also slept, is a Soviet mole.

CAINE, JOHN. In *Day of the Guns,* he was the son of Agnes and Richard Caine. He was killed in the war.

CAINE, PATRICIA. In *Day of the Guns,* she is the daughter of Agnes and Richard Caine. Patricia married an army officer.

CAINE, RICHARD. In *Day of the Guns,* born in 1892 and died in 1951, he was the husband of Agnes Caine and the father of their five children.

CAINE, RUTH. In *Day of the Guns,* she is the daughter of Agnes and Richard Caine. Ruth married an army officer.

CAINE, VERNON. In *Day of the Guns,* he is the bachelor son of Agnes and Richard Caine. Vernon is in the admiralty service.

CALDWELL. In *Day of the Guns,* he owns an old loft into which Ernie Bentley moves.

CALDWELL. In "The Veiled Woman," he is Mrs. Eric Fullerton's butler and answers the phone when Karl Terris calls.

CALLAHAN, MRS. RALPH. In "Killer Mine," she is the retired policeman's wife. Ralph asks Lieutenant Joe Scanlon to speak softly because his wife is a light sleeper.

CALLAHAN, RALPH. In "Killer Mine," he is an honest, retired policeman who gives Lieutenant Joe Scanlon advice.

CAMBELL, RITA. In *The Twisted Thing. See* Grange, Myra.

CAMINO, SEÑOR. In *The Delta Factor,* José tells Morgan that Señor Camino escaped from the United States and came to the island.

CAMISOLE, MARTHA. In *One Lonely Night,* she attends the Communist meeting in Brooklyn. Henry Gladow introduces the bespectacled girl, "just out of her teens," to Mike Hammer as his secretary.

CAMP, EDDIE. In *The Last Cop Out,* he is a criminal working for Francois Verdun.

CAMPBELL, HENRY. In *The Last Cop Out,* he testified that he saw Mark Shelby near the place where Merkowitz and Manute were murdered but was threatened with castration if he didn't retract his statement. He complied.

CANDID, MURRAY. In *My Gun Is Quick,* he is a "fat monkey" deep in city vice and corruption. He manages the Zero Zero Club, bosses call girls, but is not in primary charge. He has Mike Hammer beaten up.

CANERO, PETIE. In *Survival . . . Zero!,* he is a friend of Eddie Dandy, who says Canero saw Mike Hammer at police headquarters after Lipton Sullivan was murdered.

CAPRINI. In *The Last Cop Out,* he and another man with the same name were killed in Chicago ten years or so earlier by a sadistic hit man who then cut out their navels.

CARBITO. In "Killer Mine," he is a criminal, with Gordon, that the mob fears Gus Wilder might testify against.

CARBOY, PHIL. In "Everybody's Watching Me," he is a well-financed drug dealer, outwitted by Vetter.

CAREY. In *The Delta Factor,* Morgan mentions that Carey was an army buddy of his, killed in an explosion.

CAREY. In "The Seven Year Kill," he works at the Phoenix newspaper office and apprised Joe Stack of Phil Rocca's interest in reading about Rhino Massley's supposed death.

CARL. In *Survival . . . Zero!,* he is one of Woodring Ballinger's gunmen, challenged by Mike Hammer and murdered by Stanley, William Dorn's hired killer.

CARLO, FRANKIE. In *The Deep,* he owned a gun Roscoe Tate took long ago and tried unsuccessfully to shoot Deep with.

CARLSON, DR. GEORGE. In *The By-Pass Control,* he was Louis Agrounsky's physician in Eau Gallie, Florida. He tells Tiger Mann that Agrounsky, though treated for substance abuse, has remained a heroin addict.

CARLYSLE. In *The Snake,* he was evidently killed in Los Angeles by Marv Kania. The name "Carlysle" may be a misprint.

CARMEN. In "The Screen Test of Mike Hammer," he is a man Helen killed after she killed Gus and blamed Carmen for doing so.

CARMEN. In "Tomorrow I Die," he and Bernie are members of Auger's gang. Both die when their getaway car crashes down a gully.

CARMEN. In *The Twisted Thing,* he is a liquor supplier for Nelson's casino.

CARMICHAEL, ROY. In *Vengeance Is Mine!,* it is mentioned that he has an office in the building in which Anton Lipsek has his studio.

CARMINE. In "Killer Mine," Lieutenant Joe Scanlon remembers his grocery store in the old neighborhood.

CARMINE. In *Survival . . . Zero!,* he told Caesar Mario Tulley's friend that Beaver is staying at the Stanton Hotel.

CARMODI, BEVO. In *The Last Cop Out,* he stole money collected by Cubans in Miami for a new attack on Fidel Castro.*

CARMODY, FRANK. In *The Killing Man,* he is a loyal FBI agent who participates in the search for Penta.

CARNEY. In "Return of the Hood," he is one of Pete-the-Dog's spies.

CARNEY, ALAN. In "The Veiled Woman." *See* Terris, Karl.

CARPENTER, MISS. In *One Lonely Night,* she is a reporter who wrote about Ethel Brighton's engagement to a starving Communist artist.

CARRIGAN. In *The Girl Hunters,* Barliss Henry reminds Mike of "the fire at Carrigan's" ten or fifteen years ago. This may be a reference to one of Mike's early cases.

CARROLL, JOYCE. In *The Last Cop Out,* he is the subject of an article by Meyer Davis, a journalist. Captain Bill Long complains that it almost ruined a case he was pursuing. Was Spillane aware of the name of Joyce Carol Oates (1938–), who was publishing novels of violence and deprivation at about the time *The Last Cop Out* appeared?

CARSI, PATROLMAN. In *The Killing Man,* he was on duty near where Harry Bern and Gary Fells were shot to death in the supposedly secure safe house in Brooklyn.

CARTER. In *The Delta Factor* he is a U.S. Treasury Department trouble-shooter, involved in questioning Morgan about the missing $40 million.

CARTER, SONNY. In *Bloody Sunrise,* he is named as a British agent who may have shot Spaad Helo in the upper right arm.

CARVER, LILY. In *Kiss Me, Deadly,* she knew Berga Torn and died by drowning. A woman who knows Dr. Martin Soberin took her name and helped him run a drug-smuggling ring. Mike ignorantly befriends this "Lily" until he discovers her identity and actions, after which he burns her to death.

CASALES, DON. In "Kick It or Kill!," Artie phones Kelly Smith that Casales is a Los Angeles hood, works for Carter Lansing, and is the owner of the car Benny Quick is driving.

CASATOR, RICHARD. In "The Seven Year Kill." *See* Massley, Rhino.

CASE, BERNICE. In *The Delta Factor,* she is a lonely, pleasant prostitute who lived at Mrs. Gustav Timely's house, knew Gorman Yard and his vicious friends, offers to help Morgan, and is strangled for trying. Spillane is unusually tender in dramatizing certain prostitutes. (*See* "Sex Is My Vengeance.")

CASE, MRS. RICHARD. In *The Last Cop Out,* she is married to a phony politician, but they have been separated for three years.

CASE, RICHARD ("LITTLE RICHARD"). In *The Last Cop Out,* he is a three-hundred-pound criminal, allegedly in real estate and in politics, but in reality the pipeline to Mark Shelby's mob. Shatzi Heinkle stabs him to death.

CASE, VINCENT HARLEY. In *Day of the Guns,* he is a British U.N. representative. He has a Scottish background.

CASEY. In *Black Alley,* he owns a cheap saloon where Dr. Ralph Morgan was drinking when Mike was shot at the nearby waterfront.

CASEY, AL. In *The Body Lovers,* he is a crime reporter who tries to follow leads provided by Mitch Temple. After Temple's murder, Casey and Mike work together.

CASEY, INEZ. In *The Long Wait,* she is Gracie Harlan's fellow waitress. Eddie Parkman intends to kill Gracie but by mistake stabs Inez to death instead.

CASS, LARRY. In *The Erection Set,* he was Sharon Cass's father and worked for the Barrin family.

CASS, SHARON. In *The Erection Set,* this virginal little blonde, age thirty-two, grew up in Linton, lives on East 55th Street, New York, works for S. C. Cable, seduces Walt Gentry nonintimately, and reluctantly helps Dog Kelly. In the end, it is revealed that she knew Dog when she was age ten and he left. So they finally make love, and all is well.

CASSANDRO, PETEY. In *Vengeance Is Mine!,* Captain Pat Chambers tells Mike that Cassandro and George Hamilton, gunmen from Detroit, have appeared in New York City. Either Cassandro or Hamilton may be the thug Velda shot in Clyde Williams's apartment.

CASSIDY. In "Killer Mine," he is a policeman working with Lieutenant Joe Scanlon.

CASTLE, ARNIE. In "The Affair with the Dragon Lady," he was a crewmember aboard the Dragon Lady.

CASTRO, FIDEL (1927–). Cuban revolutionary leader and Communist prime minister. In *The Death Dealers,* Tiger Mann reminds Virgil Adams that Seaton Coleman and Porter Lockwood let Castro "get away with" something damaging to the United States. Castro is also in the background of "The Flier."

CASWELL. In *The By-Pass Control,* Tiger Mann remembers this agent as having been fatally careless in handling a car bomb.

CAT. In *The Deep,* he was a member of the Knights Owl Club, acted as its doorman, and achieved his name through cat-burglar skills. Cat is now terminally ill with tuberculosis. He is loyal to Deep, helps him at every turn, and is fatally shot by Artie Hull. Cat's philosophy is this: "This world isn't worth living for or dying over. . . . Everybody's money hungry and trying to kill each other off like crazy."

CAVELLO, LIEUTENANT JOE. In *The Snake,* he is one of Captain Pat Chambers's men and provides information on the murder of Thomas Kline, and on Marv Kania and Basil Levitt.

CAVENDISH, MILLARD. In "The Veiled Woman," he is an AEC agent who questions Karl Terris.

CHAMBERS, CAPTAIN PAT (real name: Patrick Chambers). In *I, the Jury,* he is Captain of Homicide in New York City. He and Mike Hammer are close friends. Pat shares more information with Mike than Mike does with Pat. Both try to solve six related, sequential murders, but Mike usually stays ahead in their professional race and always wins.

In *My Gun Is Quick,* he and Mike Hammer cooperate, at considerable risk to Pat's career, in solving the murder of Nancy Sanford. Pat is called "young" at one point.

In *Vengeance Is Mine!,* once again, he and Mike work together to solve several murders. Pat lies to substantiate Mike's alibi at one point, only to be exposed by the ambitious D.A. Pat is unavailable at the climax, because he is seeking Jean Trotter's killer ineffectively.

In *One Lonely Night,* Pat and Mike work together on the murders of Charlie Moffit and Oscar Deamer. Mike does not share information with Pat about subversive Soviet actions. But at the end, Pat will receive considerable credit.

In *The Big Kill,* Pat and Mike work together, are often at odds, but remain basically cooperative when Mike seeks to solve the murder of William Decker and soon proves a threat to Lou Grindle, Toady Link, and Ed Teen, all of whom are involved in racketeering.

In *Kiss Me, Deadly,* Pat once again cooperates with Mike as, single-handedly, Mike breaks up the drug-smuggling masterminded by Dr. Martin Soberin and involving, among others, Al Affia, Carl Evello, William Mist, and a woman posing as Lily Carver.

In *The Girl Hunters,* Pat is disgusted with Mike, who has been an alcoholic for seven years. Pat reluctantly takes Mike to Richie Cole, dying in a hospital. Pat is viciously critical of Mike, partly because Pat also loves Velda.

In *The Snake,* Pat gets over his disgust with Mike, still is fond of Velda, but helps Mike when Sue Devon, the adopted daughter of Simpson Torrence, is threatened, and during Mike's attempts to find Black Conley, one of Sue's mother Sally Devon Torrence's would-be lovers.

In *The Twisted Thing,* Mike drives from Sidon into New York City, where Pat helps him by letting him read Herron Mallory's lengthy rap sheet.

In *The Body Lovers,* Pat cleans up after Mike's bloody activities and brain-storms with Mike to try to make sense out of the murders of Maxine Delaney,

Helen Poston, and Mitch Temple, the suicide of Theodore Gates, and the disappearance of Greta Service.

In *Survival . . . Zero!,* he helps Mike by cleaning up after the deaths of Lipton Sullivan and Larry Beers. Pat, again mentioned as a bachelor, is preoccupied by government efforts to contain the threat of germ warfare.

In *The Killing Man,* Pat cooperates with various authorities while also aiding Mike. It is mentioned that the two served in the U.S. Army together.

In *Black Alley,* when Pat thought Mike was killed, he held a memorial service for him. Pat helps Mike minimally, by cooperating with Homer Watson, the Treasury agent, and by accepting Ugo Ponti, the multiple killer, at the end.

In "The Night I Died," Pat declines to help Mike find Carmen Rich.

CHARLES. In *The Erection Set,* he was the former butler for the Barrin household.

CHARLIE. In *Kiss Me, Deadly,* he is a morgue assistant.

CHARLIE. In *The Snake,* he is a bartender at a place on 49th Street off Broadway. Mike meets Jersey Toby there.

CHARLIE HOP SOONG ("LEECHEE CHUCK"). In *The Death Dealers,* Tiger Mann recalls this man's selling litchee nuts on Columbus Avenue.

CHARMAINE. In *The Erection Set,* she is a prostitute who plays amorously with Leyland Ross Hunter while Dog Kelly is with Marcia, her roommate. Charmaine tells Dog she attended Erasmus High School in Brooklyn. Spillane graduated from Erasmus in 1939.

CHASER, JULIAN. In *The Deep,* he was robbed and killed for thirty cents, according to a person living near Tally Lee.

CHELLO, LOU. In *Survival . . . Zero!,* he is mentioned as a criminal rival of Woodring Ballinger.

CHERYL. In "The Gold Fever Tapes," she is assigned to the news agency where Fallon works. She helps him find the missing gold. In reality, she is an undercover police official. Cheryl, uncommonly sexy, and Fallon make love in their limited spare time.

CHET. In *The Death Dealers,* he is an agent. Martin Grady tells Tiger Mann that, according to Chet, the federal authorities hope to embarrass Tiger.

CHEVESKY. In *Day of the Guns,* he is mentioned as someone Mann knew or knew about during the war.

CHICK. In "Man Alone," he was a cabbie waiting behind Guy Rivera the night Leo Marcus was supposedly killed.

CHOBEAY. In *Bloody Sunrise,* Clement Fletcher names Chobeay and Wells as a pair who told him about uranium strikes near Vera Cruz.

CHOO, MAXINE. In "Return of the Hood," according to Pete-the-Dog, she saw two foreigners at the Big Top after they put Karen Sinclair in a getaway car.

CHOPPER, THE. In *The Erection Set,* Dog Kelly orders The Chopper and Hobis to guard Sharon Cass and Lee Shay, and to help Dog around the movie set at Linton.

CHOPS, PERRY. In *The Last Cop Out,* he was a narcotics dealer caught by the father of two boys he was trying to get hooked on heroin. The father helped him drop from a five-floor rooftop.

CHRISTY, MA. In "The Gold Fever Tapes," she runs a seedy place where Fallon meets Cheryl.

CHURIS, VIDOR. In *Day of the Guns,* he is a vicious Russian killer. He works with Gretchen Lark. Tiger Mann traces him through his love of Russian movies and eventually kills him.

CICA, ANTHONY ("TONY"). In *The Killing Man. See* DiCica, Anthony.

CILON, AKTUR. In *The Ship That Never Was,* he is an assassin from Grandau. He is an explosives expert and works with Embor Linero.

CISSIE. In *The Last Cop Out,* she is the hostess at her place on East 55th Street where Mark Shelby and Francois Verdun face off briefly.

CIVAC, MARTA SINGLETON. In *The Girl Hunters,* she inherited a machine-manufacturing fortune in Chicago, was a widow, married Rudolph Civac (*see* Erlich, Gerald), moved to New York City, hired Velda to guard her, but was kidnapped by Gorlin, stripped of her jewelry, and murdered.

CIVAC, RUDOLPH ("RUDY"). In *The Girl Hunters. See* Erlich, Gerald.

CLAIRE. In "Together We Kill," she was a French partisan, about twenty, who helped Joe blow up a German-held bridge during World War II. Seven years later they meet in New York. Claire is a Broadway star; Joe, an engineer. They will marry.

CLARENCE. In *The Erection Set,* he and Danny are doormen at Lee Shay's apartment building.

CLARK, DR. In *The Twisted Thing,* he put stitches in the cheek of the man whose mouth Mike Hammer tore open.

CLARK, JOHN. In *The By-Pass Control,* he lives in Buffalo, New York. Niger Hoppes stole his driver's license.

CLAUSIST, MOE. In "Killer Mine," he owns a hock shop above which Harry Wope has a small room.

CLEHOE. In "Killer Mine," he runs a deli in Marta Borlig's neighborhood.

CLENDENNING. In *The Body Lovers,* he and Davis when old sold their Long Island property to Gerald Ute some ten years earlier.

CLEO. In *The Body Lovers,* she is a loose Greenwich Village resident who is an artist-illustrator for fashion magazines. After "two sour early marriages," Cleo tries unsuccessfully to get Mike to bed but still gives him information about Dulcie McInnes and Greta Service. Cleo must content herself with a painting she made, while nude, of Mike nude.

CLINTON, DAVID. In *The Killing Man,* he is a hospitality orderly, with three years of service, who prevented a mysterious doctor from giving Velda a shot.

CLINTON, GEORGE. In "The Flier," he is a member of Celeda's so-called quiet sect but still supplied Cat Fallon with vital information.

CLOUGH. In *The Last Cop Out,* he is a client of Francois Verdun and is about to leave New York from La Guardia Airport.

COBRA, THE. In *The Last Cop Out,* he and Lupe are guards outside Leon Bray's door. Both are killed, as are others near Bray.

COGGINS, DETECTIVE. In "The Pickpocket," he is a police officer who used to harass Willie until Willie was instrumental in the apprehension of a shooting suspect.

COHEN, SID. In *Survival . . . Zero!,* he is mentioned as the father of a burglar caught by Jenkins and Wiley, two detectives Mike Hammer knows.

COLBY, VANCE. In "The Bastard Bannerman," he is a criminal who came to Culver City, got engaged to Anita Bannerman but enjoyed night sessions with

Irish Maloney, and associates with Popeye Gage and Carl Matteau in a Syndicate land-grab scheme. Colby killed Chuck Maloney. Cat Cay Bannerman exposes him. When visiting Irish, Colby called himself Arthur Sears.

COLE, ANN. In *The Girl Hunters,* she was Richie Cole's wife. She died of cancer in 1949.

COLE, ARTHUR ("NOCKY"). In *The Big Kill,* he and his fellow thug, Glenn Fisher, accompanied William Decker on his safe-cracking assignment. The two act as private detectives, follow Mel Hooker, are beaten up by Mike, leave New York for Philadelphia, and are shot to death by the police there. Dying, Cole implicates Toady Link.

COLE, BILLIE. In "Return of the Hood," he saw, according to Pete-the-Dog, the one-eared man involved in moving Karen Sinclair.

COLE, RICHIE. In *The Girl Hunters,* he was an Office of Strategic Services captain during the war, working with Lester Bender, Alex Bird, and Velda, among others. He was an undercover FBI agent, working under Art Rickerby as a union seaman, and, at age forty-five, was fatally shot by Gorlin.

COLEMAN, HARRY. In "The Seven Year Kill," Joe Stack tells Phil Rocca that Harry Coleman, Joe's friend, works at the Blue Sky Motel and will "treat you right."

COLEMAN, JEROME. In *The Killing Man,* he is a government official from Albany who appears in New York City and thereafter helps search for Penta.

COLEMAN, SEATON. In *The Death Dealers,* he and Porter Lockwood are dangerously thoughtless liberal politicians whose giveaway attitude is jeopardizing America's relationship with Teish El Abin.

COLFACO. In *The Last Cop Out,* Mark Shelby recalls that Gill Burke threw both Colfaco and Bennie off a rooftop to their death eight years earlier.

COMBOLT, PIERRE. In *The Day the Sea Rolled Back,* it is mentioned that he lost a two-masted ship the previous year.

CONLEY, BLACK ("BLACKIE"). In *The Snake,* he double-crossed Sonny Motley, his fellow robber, during their 1932 armored-car heist, escaped to a Catskills hideout with the loot, but died in the woods there in a stolen taxi. Mike mistakenly thinks Conley is still alive. When Mike and Velda finally find Conley, Motley follows the pair and is about to kill them both when Conley's dead finger, on his rifle, is jiggled, the result of which is Motley's being shot dead. The Motley-Conley heist, as it was called, may be Spillane's subtle way of spoofing the name of Malcolm Cowley (1898–1989), the distinguished American literary critic who regarded Mike Hammer as a sadomasochistic paranoiac and Spillane as a danger to the public for sanctioning his behavior.

Bibliography: Malcolm Cowley, "Sex Murder Incorporated," *New Republic* 126 (February 11, 1952): 17–18.

CONNELY, EDDIE. In *Kiss Me, Deadly,* he is a reporter who works the police beat and gives Velda information about the Mafia.

CONNORS. In *Day of the Guns,* in reminiscing about the war, Mann mentions that he saved Connors in Poland.

CONNORS, EDDIE. In "The Gold Fever Tapes," he is a police official who aids Fallon by helping him with a graphic voice-print pattern.

CONSTANTINO. In *The Deep. See* Alverez.

CONWAY, JOE. In "The Flier," he was a member of Cat Fallon's 252 Fighter Squadron during World War II, and now runs a New Jersey shop rebuilding propellers. By phone, he provides Fallon with vital information. (At one point, he is named, or misnamed, George.)

COOK, MISS. In *The Twisted Thing,* she is a lesbian librarian in Sidon with whom Myra Grange associates to establish Myra's alibi. Dilwick grabs Miss Cook and ties her up with Myra in Herron Mallory's boathouse. Mike Hammer refers to Miss Cook as Legs for obvious reasons.

COOLEY, JACK. In "Everybody's Watching Me," he was a drug dealer, once Helen Troy's lover, and was killed by Mark Renzo. Vetter finds Cooley's heroin stash.

COON, JOE. In "The Seven Year Kill," he is one of Mannie Waller's hoods. Coon follows Phil Rocca to Phoenix and is killed near Rhino Massley's former ranch.

COOPER, BUD. In "Stand Up and Die!," he was a person Caroline Hart praised as being uniquely able to handle a certain mule.

COOPER, DIXIE. In *The Big Kill,* he was a shark who loaned William Decker money to hook him so that Ed Teen could force Decker to become a safe-cracker for him.

COOPER, DONAN. In "Stand Up and Die!," he was the local postmaster until he was killed, presumably by the Harts.

COOPER, ED. In *Vengeance Is Mine!,* he is the *Globe* sports editor. Mike gets information from him concerning Rainey's sports arena. In return, Mike promises him an eventual scoop.

COOPER, OLIVER. In "Stand Up and Die!," he became the local postmaster when his brother Donan Cooper died. Oliver helps Mitch Valler and agrees to care for Trumble Cahill.

COPELY, WILLIAM ("BILL"). In *Bloody Sunrise,* he is an agent, age thirty-six, who works for Raymond Watts in New York. While tracking Sonia Dutko, he is murdered and his death is staged to look like suicide.

COPPOLA. In *The Deep,* he is a corrupt "guiding force" behind City Hall politicians. Evidently Deep cut him in the stomach years ago. The name Coppola undoubtedly derives from that of Michael ("Trigger Mike") Coppola (1904–1966), New York Cosa Nostra political boss. His first wife allegedly heard him discuss plans to kill Joseph R. Scottoriggio, was called to testify, but died before she could do so. Coppola bragged to his second wife about killing her.

Bibliography: Sifakis.

CORBETT, LILLIAN. In *Vengeance Is Mine!,* she is a model who is pinched by Anton Lipsek at the Bowery Inn.

CORBETT, SERGEANT. In *Survival . . . Zero!,* Mike Hammer asks him to get in touch with Captain Pat Chambers for him.

CORBINET, CHARLIE. In *Day of the Guns,* he was a general during the war and was Tiger Mann's commanding officer. He is now a right-wing extralegal agent, well financed by Russell and Perkins, and wielding great power. He aids Tiger, who calls him colonel. In *Bloody Sunrise,* Corbinet again aids Tiger, once to the extent of pulling rank and forcing Hal Randolph to let up on Tiger. In *The Death Dealers,* Corbinet's distinguished military record is summarized. Once again, he aids Tiger, mainly by running interference for him with the federal agents. In *The By-Pass Control,* he aids Tiger again, by phone from New York and also through flying from New York to Eau Gallie, Florida, to aid personally there.

CORNER, SIMON. In *The Erection Set,* Dog Kelly mentions him as a rival in London trying to take advantage of Dog's departure. Dog later learns that Le Fleur has killed Corner.

CORNING. In *The Body Lovers,* he was a sex pervert who served time three years earlier, escaped, and supposedly burned to death. The report, ultimately false, of his being sighted provides Captain Pat Chambers with a troublesome lead.

CORRIGAN, JIMMIE. In *The Last Cop Out,* he is a policeman who walked toward the pawnshop of Turley, saw Ted Proctor with a gun, and shot and killed him.

CORTEZ. In "Return of the Hood," Ernie Snow tells Ryan that Fly used to be supplied heroin by Cortez.

COSTELLO, FRANK (1891–1973). New York City Syndicate gambling boss and political fixer, born Francesco Castiglia in Lauropoli, Calabria, Italy. In 1950 he voluntarily spoke before a U.S. Senate Commerce Committee sub-committee about gambling. In 1951 he testified before the Kefauver Committee of the U.S. Senate, Washington, D.C., which established organized crime's connections between New York and Miami. In *Kiss Me, Deadly,* Mike casually says that he could easily show where Costello's sworn testimony was false.

Bibliography: Estes Kefauver, *Crime in America,* ed. Sidney Shalett (Garden City, N.Y.: Doubleday, 1951); Sifakis.

COULTER, DAN. In *Black Alley,* according to Bud Langston, Coulter in-vented a virtually impenetrable body armor, failed to patent it or interest the government in it, peddled it elsewhere, and died in a factory explosion.

COULTER, PAULINE. In *The Snake,* Joey Adams tells Mike Hammer that Pauline Coulter recently saw Annette Lee, Sally Devon Torrence's old friend. Mike, surprised Annette is still alive, goes to see her.

COULTER, ROXY. In *The Twisted Thing,* Roxy, a "luscious redhead," was a nurse, then a striptease artist, and finally, calling herself Helen Malcom, Rus-ton York's governess. When Ruston sees Mike Hammer kissing Roxy, he shoots at her and wounds her in the shoulder.

COULTER, TREETOP. In "Return of the Hood," he was a rival drug lord for whom Ernie South peddled. South soon took over Coulter's "business."

COURTNEY. In *The By-Pass Control,* he is a new agent under Hal Randolph. Courtney is impressed by Tiger Mann.

COWAN, BILL. In *One Lonely Night,* he is a reporter on the *News* who is friendly with Marty Kooperman of the *Globe.*

COX, CAPTAIN. In "Kick It or Kill!," he is the swaggering but cowardly head of Pinewood's police force. Kelly Smith embarrasses him, perhaps enabling Cox to reform.

COX, EMMA. In "Kick It or Kill!," she is the ex-wife of Captain Cox and the sister of Dr. McKeever, whom she helps hide Dari Dahl, Ruth Gleason, and Kelly Smith.

COYNE, LEWIS. In "Return of the Hood," he was killed in a gunfight outside a cafeteria at the time Karen Sinclair was wounded.

CRAFT, WILBER. In *Survival . . . Zero!,* he is mentioned as a prisoner in Sing Sing, caught in a million-dollar lottery swindle.

CRAMER, STANLEY ("STAN"). In *The Erection Set,* he is an engineer, retired after working in the Barrin family factory. He and his cronies, Jason, Juke, Pat, and Stoney, help Dog Kelly by finding plans for the antigravity device. Cramer is excellently characterized.

CRAMER, WALTER. In "Kick It or Kill!," according to Artie, Cramer is the "nobody" who rented the Cadillac Sergei Rudinoff paid for and drove to Simpson's drug-lord meeting.

CRANE, BIG JAKE. In "The Flier," he is a knowledgeable person in Brooklyn who asked Nick Mahoney to provide George Clinton with information about Andro Marcel.

CRANE, MRS. ROBERT. In *Survival . . . Zero!,* her being the suspicious type makes Eddie Dandy doubt Robert Crane's story that he was in the hospital visiting a girlfriend.

CRANE, ROBERT. In *Survival . . . Zero!,* he is a State Department official involved when a man dies in the subway after being exposed to a bacterial weapon. Crane is Teddy Finlay's boss and dislikes Mike Hammer.

CREIGHTON, OLIVER ("OLLIE"). In *The Day the Sea Rolled Back,* he rents his dune buggy to Petey Betts and Jake Skiddo.

CRISTY. In "The Flier," "Verdo and Cristy" was a code signal Cat Fallon and Tucker Stacy used.

CROCKER. In *The Last Cop Out,* he is a munitions salesman whom Eric Schmidt mentioned in conversation with Francois Verdun.

CROSETTI. In "The Seven Year Kill," he is one of Phil Rocca's neighbors.

CROSS, CHARLIE. In "The Affair with the Dragon Lady," he was the engineer aboard the Dragon Lady.

CUDDER. In *The Erection Set,* Al DeVecchio, according to Dog Kelly, handled the bookkeeping for the Cudder Hotel group.

CUDDY, BILL. In *The Twisted Thing,* he is a harmless clamdigger who found Ruston York's pajamas bottoms, which Ruston threw onto the beach in order to be rescued.

CULLEN. In "Me, Hood!," he is mentioned as a hood from Elizabeth, New Jersey. He was assigned to kill Ryan at his apartment but failed to do so.

CULLEN, BIRDIE. In "Everybody's Watching Me," he was a criminal allegedly killed by Vetter before he could testify before the grand jury.

CURTAIN, JOHN. In *The Death Dealers,* he is a member of the British embassy and attended the party given for Teish El Abin.

CUTLER, KAY. In *The Big Kill,* she is a residually attractive actress, claiming to be in her early thirties. Marsha Lee introduces her to Mike Hammer at a Greenwich Village theater rehearsal.

CUTTER, ALBERT. In *Bloody Sunrise,* he is a CIA agent, cooperating with Thomas Watford and seeming to distrust Tiger Mann.

D

DAHL, DARI. In "Kick It or Kill!," she is the voluptuous proprietress of the Pinewood hotel where Kelly Smith is staying. Her sister Flori Dahl was a drug addict. Once Dari realizes Smith is not a drug addict, she falls in love with him. She takes his gun and goes to kill Simpson, is captured and tortured for a show, and is rescued by Smith.

DAHL, FLORI. In "Kick It or Kill!," she was Dari Dahl's sister, became a drug-addicted prostitute, and committed suicide in New York City.

DAILEY, ED. In *The Girl Hunters,* he owns a bar in Brooklyn. Mike Hammer and Bayliss Henry go there after examining Richie Cole's apartment nearby.

DALE, BOB. In *The Body Lovers,* he is a reporter who read a note by Mitch Temple connecting the murders of Maxine Delaney and Helen Poston.

DALY, INSPECTOR. In *I, the Jury,* he investigates crimes connected with narcotics and appears at the scene of Bobo Hopper's murder. Daly is reluctant to cooperate with Mike Hammer, because Mike embarrassed him in an earlier narcotics case.

DALY, JOHN. In *The Erection Set,* he is a waiter at S. C. Cable's party in Linton. By mistake, Daly is wearing a nameplate reading "Ferris."

DAMAR, LARRY. In *The Day the Sea Rolled Back,* he is Vincent Damar's son, age twelve. When the sea rolls back, Larry and Josh seek the *Blue Tuna,* locate it, find the *Nantucket Belle* and its lost treasure, evade Bud and Joie Jimson, and return safely to Ara Island. Larry brings an uncut diamond back from the *Nantucket Belle* and thus saves Vincent from financial ruin. In *The Ship That Never Was,* he and Josh (named Josh Toomey here) rescue Vali Steptur, proceed to Montique Island aboard the *Sea Eagle* ahead of their fathers, are befriended by Princess Tila there, outwit would-be assassins Aktur Cilon and Embor Linero from Grandau, find the *Tiger,* set it adrift, and watch it explode over the Grandau submarine killing all of Princess Tila's enemies.

DAMAR, VINCENT ("VINCE," "VINNIE"). In *The Day the Sea Rolled Back,* he is a widowered scientist. Vincent, who owns the *Blue Tuna,* a forty-two-foot ex-navy cutter, and his son, Larry Damar, seek treasure in sunken vessels. Bud and Joie Jimson deliberately caused the *Blue Tuna* to lose water and sink. In *The Ship That Never Was,* Damar and his friend Timothy Toomey follow their sons to Montique Island on Damar's *Blue Tuna II* but arrive too late to do anything but congratulate the boys for saving Princess Tila and her island subjects.

DANADO, MARIO. In *The Erection Set,* he owns a New Jersey mortuary where Teddy Guido's remains are on a shelf.

DANDY, EDDIE. In *Survival . . . Zero!,* he is a WOBY-TV reporter whose suspicions concerning the dangers of chemical and biological warfare result in his being taken into protective custody by federal authorities. Dandy and Mike Hammer are friends.

DANDY, MRS. EDDIE. In *Survival . . . Zero!,* she is the reporter's wife and the mother of their children. Because of his family, Dandy worries more than Mike Hammer does.

DANIELS. In *The By-Pass Control,* it is mentioned that Niger Hoppes killed Daniels in Madrid some time ago.

DANNY. In *The Erection Set,* he is an ex-policeman now employed with Clarence as a doorman at Lee Shay's apartment building.

DARPSEY, CHARLIE. In "Killer Mine," he was identified as a criminal from Brooklyn involved in the Canada armored-car heist. He does not figure in subsequent action.

DARTMOUTH. In *Bloody Sunrise,* this is a code word Tiger Mann uses in a conversation with Virgil Adams of Newark Central.

DAVE. In *The Deep,* he is a gunman who phones Lenny Sobel at the time Deep is being held for Holiday.

DAVE. In *Kiss Me, Deadly,* he is a knowledgeable black-market bookie whom Mike Hammer phones for information.

DAVE. In "The Night I Died," he is one of Carmen Rich's bodyguards.

DAVEWELL. In *The Erection Set,* Al DeVecchio, according to Dog Kelly, established Davewell Products.

DAVIS. In *The Body Lovers,* he and Clendenning, ten years earlier, let Gerald Ute buy their Long Island property.

DAVIS. In "Killer Mine," when Lieutenant Joe Scanlon and Larry Scanlon were kids, they rigged a harness to pretend they were hanging Davis, to scare adult neighbors.

DAVIS, MEYER. In *The Last Cop Out,* he is a nosey columnist who wants to find out why Gill Burke has returned to official police work.

DAVITSON, CHARLIE. In *The Long Wait,* he was a construction contractor for whom John McBride and George Wilson worked.

***DAY OF THE GUNS* (1964).** Novel. (Characters: Beaver, Carmen Bellotica, Ernie Bentley, Brian, Agnes Caine, Diana Caine, Edith Caine, John Caine, Patricia Caine, Richard Caine, Ruth Caine, Vernon Caine, Caldwell, Vincent Harley Case, Chevesky, Vidor Churis, Connors, Charlie Corbinet, Dell, Devlin, Barney Dodge, Evans, Gettler, George Gifford, Wally Gibbons, Gorbatcher, Martin Grady, Cal Haggerty, Gregory Hofta, Ted Huston, Peter Johnson, K, Ron Kelly, Krouse, Gretchen Lark, Marty Lehman, Tiger Mann, Stephen Midros, Alexis Minner, P. J. Moriarty, Morvitch, Captain Murray, Pedro, Hal Randolph, Price Richard, Seliga, Burton Selwick, Mrs. Burton Selwick, Smith, Smithwick, Standish, Stovetsky, Joe Swan, Max Sweiber, John Fredericks Talbot, Toomey, Vance, General Von Selter, Thomas Watford, White, Tommy Williams, Wilson.)

Tiger Mann, a wartime American spy in Germany, fell in love with Rondine Lund, Nazi spy there, in 1945. He saved her life and made love with her; then she shot him almost fatally. Now, in 1964, he suddenly finds Rondine near the United Nations headquarters in New York employed as a seemingly young translator from England and calling herself Edith Caine. He tells her he will gutshoot her one fine day. That night he puts pillows in his hotel bed to resemble himself, hides outside the window, and misses being killed by two gunmen whose bullets he removes from the bed. Next morning, Tiger, who is opposed both to Russian Communism and to anti-Americanism in the U.N., drops in on Rondine, who hides her surprise that he survived and whom he joshes for having had a face lift. Next, he warns a politically influential import-exporter named Thomas Watford that his cushy days are numbered unless he provides information about "Edith Caine." A ballistics specialist tells Tiger that last night's bullets measured 7.65 millimeters. Charlie Corbinet, Tiger's former commanding officer and presently a pro-American, antigovernmental businessman who now "rolled in millions," agrees to use secret contacts to learn about Rondine, long thought dead. Wally Gibbons, a former O.S.S. agent and now a Broadway journalist, responds to Tiger's request by giving him excellent photographs of Edith (to circulate among plastic surgeons) and a list of her current friends, namely British businessman and government adviser Burton Selwick, Hungarian translator Gregory Hofta, and U.N. secretary Gretchen Lark. Tiger lets himself into the Gramercy Park apartment of John Fredericks Talbot, British embassy friend of Rondine's. Tiger finds evidence of burned papers and a fancy Colt. Tiger visits the midtown apartment of Hungarian freedom-fighter Stephen Midros, who promises to check on Hofta. Tiger traces a call from Rondine, spots her with Selwick at a bar, sees Selwick with a tall redhead and suddenly appearing ill; and when Rondine goes to Tiger's apartment, he greets her with a .45 and promises to destroy her scheme and then kill her, then orders her out.

Two days pass. Martin Grady, reliable contact, sends Toomey to tell Tiger a U.N. leak is helping Russia learn how America is establishing bases in friendly countries. Midros introduces Tiger to Hofta, who proves reliable and knows about the dangers, but to whom Tiger declines to mention Rodine's involvement. Tiger outwits a tail, and the two exchange nonfatal fire in his hotel-room corridor. Toomey appears and helps chase the gunman, who left his Russian 7.65-millimeter automatic and blood on the floor. Toomey agrees to check on Talbot and Gretchen for Tiger, who visits Gibbons and gets a rundown on Edith's impeccable London family.

Friday turns rainy. Watford, working with Toomey, summons Tiger to a meeting with several serious agents and rebukes Tiger. One sneering agent fails to get information from Tiger but does reveal that one of the Russian gunmen trying to kill Tiger is Vidor Churis, whom Tiger wounded in the hand two years ago. Tiger finds Rondine leaving work at the U.N. with a redhead. Selwick's friend, she is Gretchen Lark. Tiger takes Rondine to dinner. On the way by cab to her expensive apartment, he slyly disarms her small automatic; once there, he promises again to kill her, reminisces, listens to her Caine family tree, forces her to strip to check for body plastic surgery, laughs when she pulls her clipless weapon, and leaves. On the way to his apartment, he is shot at from two cars but is missed, kills both pursuers, and takes a thousand-dollar bill from one assailant. From London, Tiger learns Rondine Lund may be using the name of a dead woman of that name. Tiger phones Gretchen, impresses her by taking her to dinner at Dell's Oriental-style side-street place with fancy food and provocative dancers, notes her arousal, and taxis to her place with her and goes to bed with her. Gretchen knows nothing helpful concerning Edith.

Next day, Tiger first checks with Watford, who warns Tiger he may be attacked again; goes with Corbinet to the British embassy, participates in talk about the U.N. leak, amiably asks that Edith be rechecked; and, finding Wally, reminisces about wartime intrigues, chats about Gretchen, and promises him a scoop soon. At the U.N., Selwick debates well against the Russians but gets sick again. Corbinet tells Tiger he must confiscate the thousand-dollar bill because it came from a Russian diplomatic transfer. Hofta, nearby, wonders if Rodine poisoned Selwick. Tiger encounters Rondine and gloatingly promises, again, to kill her soon. A friendly phone call informs Tiger that Churis may soon be spotted attending a Russian-language movie in Manhattan. Tiger visits Rondine in her apartment, tells the now frightened beauty he knows she blackmailed the superdecent Caine family into letting her take dead Edith Caine's identity. Tiger returns late to his apartment, loaned to Toomey, only to find him shot dead. In Toomey's pocket is a report that a German plastic surgeon may have operated on Rondine. Tiger checks into a nearby hotel, obtains Soviet assassin Alexis Minner's address from Hofta, summarizes events to himself, and sleeps.

Saturday at 10:00 A.M. Tiger tours with some alerted firemen around Minner's place to case it. Tiger calls on sexy Gretchen, busy painting Selwick's portrait, takes her back to Dell's for lunch, boasts about his violent past, has Bentley make a key to let him into Minner's apartment, and reports to Corbinet, who equips him with special tiny spherical grenades. Tiger rants further to Wally about American pinko eggheads, promises him a scoop, lets himself into Minner's expensively furnished but sloppy place, finds sodium pentothal and poisons, lifts three thousand-dollar bills from a bundle, and hears three gunmen enter. He has rigged the foyer light to fizzle, and in the darkness manages the deaths of all three—and by their guns. Before dying, Minner reveals nothing. Tiger checks with Bentley, who warns him about the instability of the minigrenades; taxis to Corbinet, who must keep the three bills, since they are from the Russian legation; escorts Gretchen to Dell's to see an erotic floor show, learns from Dell that Churis may attend that Russian film, then drops Gretchen at her place, outside which another attempt to shoot him fails. Tiger concludes Rondine had him staked out at Gretchen's building.

Dull Sunday Tiger improves by mailing a report to Grady. He calls Watford and evades cops rushing to the street pay phone he used. Tiger sits through several showings of the Russian film, finally spots Churis and a colleague, and follows their cab to a crummy top-floor apartment in Greenwich Village. All he hears when Churis phones is "Selwick" before he bursts in. Churis escapes. Tiger shoots the other; dying, he says "the girl." Tiger concludes Rondine is going to use sodium pentothal, again, on Selwick, who thus leaks British U.N. secrets. At 9:45 P.M. Tiger taxis to Rondine's, forces her into the taxi, and away they go to Churis's apartment. Tiger shows Rondine his tiny grenades and uses one to blow out Churis's steel door. They find Gretchen's address on some paper and head for it. Silencing Rondine, who is sad and critical, Tiger bursts in, is wounded in the side by Churis, shoots him fatally up his nose, but suddenly is confronted by Gretchen, with a gun. Selwick sits nearby, thoroughly drugged with the truth serum. Obviously the mastermind, Gretchen plans multiple murders here, including Tiger versus Churis, plus a love-nest killing of "Rondine" and Selwick. "Rodine," who is really Edith Caine, explains that the real Rondine was her older sister, Diana, who defected as Rondine Lund to the Nazis, and thus so shamed the Caine family that blackmail followed. While Gretchen is busy sneering, Edith gets a grenade from Tiger's pocket, flips it at Gretchen's feet, and the explosion carries her out the window. Edith undresses and removes stern Mann's lingering doubts by proving her non-Rondine identity—that of a virgin.

Day of the Guns is Spillane's answer to the James Bond 007 novels by Ian Fleming (1908–1964), which began with *Casino Royale* (1953), hit a high point with *From Russia with Love* (1957), and were translated to the big screen starting in 1962. Like Bond, Tiger Mann hates enemies of his country, is a mercenary killer, is provided gimmicky weapons, successfully lusts for women, drinks in a sophisticated manner, and cooperates minimally with allies. In *Day of the Guns,* Edith Caine's resemblance to her sister Diana Caine when Diana was younger rings changes on the mistaken-twin plot Spillane used in *One Lonely Night.*

Bibliography: Collins; Jerry Palmer, *Thrillers: Genesis and Structure of a Popular Genre* (London: Edward Arnold, 1978); Julian Symons, *Bloody Murder: From the Detective Story to the Crime Novel,* 3rd rev. ed. (New York: Mysterious Press, 1992).

THE DAY THE SEA ROLLED BACK (1979). Novel for juveniles. (Characters: Bill Andra, Doug Andrews, Mrs. Betts, Petey Betts, Pierre Combolt, Oliver Creighton, Larry Damar, Vincent Damar, Bud Jimson, Joie Jimson, Johnny, Josh, Sergeant Arthur Lander, Captain Henry Logan, McKee, Captain Stephen Morelli, Steve Percy, Reggie, Jake Skiddo, Arnie Snyder, Timothy.)

Vincent Damar, a widowered, financially depleted scientist from Long Island, and Larry, his son, age twelve, live on Peolle Island, in the Caribbean Sea southeast of Miami. Vincent owned the *Blue Tuna,* an ex-navy cutter, and sailed it off Ara Island nearby, in search of the *Nantucket Belle.* Her crew took Spanish coins from the *San Simon,* which sank in 1732, but they mutinied and also sank, in 1852. Bud Jimson and his brother Joie sabotaged the *Blue Tuna* and hope to find the treasure for themselves. One day Larry and his chum, Josh, a native Caribbean lad, while their parents are away, see the sea roll back for some miles, leaving a sea bed of varied and often hideous vegetation. They locate the blown-up *Blue Tuna,* find the *Nantucket Belle,* and escape the murderous intentions of the Jimsons, who are well aware of what the boys have learned. Various natives also rush around the exposed sea bed for what they can salvage. Vincent is beside himself when he learns of the unique oceanic phenomenon and cannot locate Larry. He and Josh return safely, and Larry brings Vincent what proves to be an enormous uncut diamond from the *Nantucket Belle*. This find will keep Vincent from bankruptcy and Larry from having to quit being home-schooled by his bright, loving father. When Spillane was twitted for writing nothing of novels featuring adult violence, he decided to write a book for young readers. In fact, he announced plans to write six such books. Only *The Ship That Never Was* (1982) has followed, thus far. *The Day the Sea Rolled Back* was a Junior Literary Guild Selection for 1979.

DEAMER, LEE. In *One Lonely Night*, he is a rising conservative politician. Captain Pat Chambers gets Mike Hammer to help Lee, who is revealed in the conclusion to be Oscar Deamer, Lee's vicious, hypocritical twin brother. *See* Diana and Edith Caine in *Day of the Guns*, for a similar use of look-alikes.

DEAMER, OSCAR. In *One Lonely Night*, he is Lee Deamer's twin brother and impersonates him. It is Lee, not Oscar, who was crushed under the subway train. Oscar killed Charlie Moffit, sought microfilms of an American secret weapon for his Soviet cronies, but in the end is unmasked and choked to death by Mike Hammer. Oscar's hypocritical reactionary rantings make him resemble those of Senator Joseph McCarthy (1908–1957), whose fear of Communist threats, domestic and elsewhere, began in 1950, a year before Spillane published *One Lonely Night*.

***THE DEATH DEALERS* (1965).** Novel. (Characters: Virgil Adams, Sergeant Anderson, Augie, Henry Balfour, Casey Ballanca, Ernie Bentley, Carmen Beship, Bradley, Jack Brant, Lennie Byrnes, Edith Caine, Fidel Castro, Charlie Hop Soong, Chet, Seaton Coleman, Charlie Corbinet, John Curtain, Patrolman Delaney, Dog, Flood, Lieutenant Dick Gallagher, George, Yamu Gorkey, Martin Grady, Buddy, Dick, Gretch, Harry, James Harvey, Haskell, Frankie Hill, Hollendale, Carl Jenner, Jim, Johnson, Vey Locca, Porter Lockwood, Maxie McCall, MacKinley, Tiger Mann, Walter Milos, Peter Moore, Stephen Pelloni, Phil, Hal Randolph, Parnell Rath, Ron, Rubin, Mrs. Leo Rubin, Leo Rubin, Sarim Shey, Sloan, Talbot, Teddy Tedesco, Teish El Abin, Tillson, Tom, Tom Lee Foy, Lily Tornay, George Tung, Malcolm Turos, Wheeler, Mrs. Wheeler, Louis Wickhoff.)

Walking down Broadway, Tiger Mann senses a tail, becomes evasive, and grabs Lily Tornay, who confesses she is after him on orders from the American State Department and Interpol. When she mentions Teddy Tedesco, he says Teddy, an old friend, is dead. She says no, he has disappeared in Selachin, near Saudi Arabia, and needs help and, further, her mission requires Tiger's cooperation. He moves to the Barnes House, phones his fiancée, Edith Caine, whom he calls Rondine, to delay their wedding day, and meets Lily at the Taft Hotel. She briefs him: Two years ago an engineer for AmPet, an American oil company, discovered a vast, hard-to-recover oil reserve in Selachin; Teish El Abin is a childless old king there; the United States sent two experts to advise him; they were killed; the Soviets are wooing Teish; America could lose disastrously; Teish is coming to New York tomorrow, with his young fiancée, Vey Locca, to negotiate with Americans; if Teish dies, control of Selachin passes to Sarim Shey, anti-American; Pete Moore, an American agent, is in Selachin seeking Tedesco; Tiger is to provide extra protection for Teish; Malcolm Turos, a Communist killer whom Tiger wounded in the neck in Brazil, damaging his voice, seeks revenge on Tiger.

Next morning Tiger sees Jack Brant, an American businessman disillusioned because of mistreatment in Saudi Arabia, whose authorities sought him for killing "a couple of gooks" who attacked him. Brant agrees to dragoon three disgruntled Saudi ex-employees now in the United States who will gain access to Teish's entourage. Eric Bentley, Tiger's special-equipment confrere, will provide gear for them. Tiger visits Lily in her room, lectures her on the need to fight, no holds barred, Communist slimeballs and cruel Arabs indifferent to their people's plight; if she doesn't follow Tiger's directions, she may wind up in a Mideast harem. On to the U.N. Tiger meets Charlie Corbinet, an ex–intelligence officer heading an anti-Communist, dirty-methods organization; alerts him to Teish and Turos; learns Teish is to be blanketed with security; and meets Rondine, who doubles as translator and British secret agent. She says she is ordered to stick close to Tiger to interfere with his work but would prefer helping him. He reports to Bentley; Brant arrives with "Tom, Dick, and Harry," Brant's Saudis for whom Bentley provides Arabic robes and to whom Tiger explains how to get close to Teish tomorrow. Tiger phones Talbot, Rondine's U.N. associate, now missing. Tiger taxis to her hotel, breaks down Rondine's door, and finds her tied so as to choke herself to death. Revived, she says Turos, identifiable by her description, did it to antagonize Tiger. Tiger phones Lennie Byrnes, assigned to aid him, to come and guard Rondine.

In the morning Tiger phones Virgil Adams at Newark Central for photos of Turos, goes to Bentley's loft, is soaked in a dye tub to have an Arab's complexion, dons a suitable robe, meets Tom, Dick, and Harry, and proceeds with that eager trio, robed and spouting Turos's language, to the dock where Teish will disembark. They bribe their way aboard. Tiger pretends to be a mute. They meet canny Teish, oily Sarim, and gorgeous Vey. Hal Randolph leads a welcoming group of federal agents aboard and silently spots Tiger. Tiger taxis to George's bar, meets Brant, and orders Harry, a Selachin army veteran, to prepare for further work. In his hotel room, Tiger showers off the dye, takes delivery of photos of Turos, and is warned by Corbinet's phone call that Randolph is about to question him. When Randolph arrives, Tiger briefs him about Teish and Turos, and obtains Randolph's grudging permission to remain armed. Tiger asks Lieutenant Dick Gallagher, a friendly police officer, to get him and Harry into Teish's reception at the Stacy Hotel. Talbot is also there, having met Teish in Selachin earlier. He says Teish is a philanderer with a hankering for pornographic movies. He introduces Tiger to Teish and Sarim. Tiger calls himself a rich oilman representing AmPet. He and sexy Vey shake hands lingeringly. Sudden action: When a previously televised showing of the gloating Teish turns snowy, a repairman waddles in; Tiger sees he has a poisoned needle, pushes Vey away, seizes the weapon; a bearded man fatally slugs the repairman and disappears; Tiger, sensing sabotage of the rooftop TV antenna, rushes up with Gallagher; they pursue a secret saboteur, who falls off the building to his death; Tiger concludes that the slugger, his beard hiding his wounded neck, was Turos. Over Sarim's and Randolph's protestations, Teish persuades Tiger to escort Vey to her room while he continues with official meetings.

Tiger phones and taxis around. Martin Grady, Tiger's well-positioned superior, will send an expert to brief him on oil terminology. Harry tells Tiger that at the reception Sarim told Teish, in their language, that the Americans plotted the assassination attempt. Harry adds that the guy with the damaged voice mentioned his dislike of litchi nuts here in New York. Corbinet says Turos got the poison for the needle in Brazil. Lily tells Tiger that Tedesco is alive in Selachin, after which Tiger packs her clothes and checks them with a hotel clerk to keep her from leaving. Tiger arranges for Byrnes and Harry to work at Teish's reception tomorrow. When Tiger revisits Lily, he finds her murdered by Turos, who left a gloating note. After reporting this to Corbinet, Tiger returns to Vey for drinks. When she pirouettes sensually, he tears off her dress but remarks that they will make love only when *he* says so. They report to Teish, who reveals that he will deal with AmPet, asks Tiger to show Vey around Manhattan, and hints Tiger is to impregnate Vey for a heir to the Selachin throne. Tiger taxis with Vey to the Turkish Gardens, where they have drinks and see a slinky dance, after which Vey does a voluptuous striptease with a ruby in her navel, after which Tiger spots Turos, who, however, escapes. Tiger tells Vey about Turos but not about himself. She sketches her background: Chinese-Russian mother, Irish-Japanese father; Vey danced in Morocco; Teish saw her there, took her to Selachin, where his wife conveniently died. Back in her Stacy suite, she disrobes, they make love, and he removes the winking ruby.

Awakening to rain at noon, Tiger learns from Corbinet that the Senate is investigating Grady. He obtains a miniature tape recorder from Bentley. He meets Rondine at the U.N. She tells him this: Teish will demand an American loan, to be repaid if his oil can be extracted; two liberal American politicians, Seaton Coleman and Porter Lockwood, are seeking to smother AmPet under government controls. Byrnes and Harry, working at the Stacy, give Tiger a recording of Sarim warning Teish that the Americans want to kill him and grab his country's oil. In the lobby, Tiger phones Vey, who wants him to escort her at 8:00 P.M. to the fifth-floor ballroom reception. Tiger spots a service exit to a side alley, reconnoiters, and sees Sarim smoking a cigar outside, then a taxi leaving, and also learns Sarim has reserved an extra room adjacent to Teish's nine-room suite. Casey Ballanca, an experienced engineer sent by Newark Central, meets Tiger and briefs him on oil lingo. Tiger sees Rondine and Talbot in the ballroom, goes up to Vey's room, inserts her ruby into her navel, and starts in the elevator to the ballroom with her. Another elevator arrow indicates a party has dropped straight to the basement. Tiger dashes there, finds the elevator man shot dead, two guards and an American official badly wounded, and a taxi whisking Teish into captivity. Officials, including Randolph, confer. Tiger shows Randolph how the elevator circuit was "gimmicked" by Turos to stop only at the basement. Reporters are told Teish is "indisposed," and the party continues. Sarim and Vey are ordered to remain silent about Teish. Tiger takes Rondine's recorder to Harry, who translates the foreign conversation. Sarim said this: Americans grabbed Teish; Sarim will govern Selachin; Vey will be exiled; AmPet will be dumped. Harry says Vey then left the room, and Sarim conferred with men from Washington, D.C. Tiger tells Byrnes to give Adams the recording and guard Rondine. Randolph drags Tiger to another set of federal agents, all of whom Tiger insults. He astonishes an oilman there with his knowledge of the oil industry. He seeks Sarim in the ballroom, but he has vanished. The police let Tiger search Sarim's extra room. He finds Vey beaten, stabbed in the stomach, but alive only because the navel ruby deflected the blade. He orders Corbinet to tend to Vey, phones Adams, and gets the address of an East Side tailor who told an informant that he sold a small, old suit to a man with a damaged voice.

Tiger hastens there and learns that the suit was for a man in "a nightgown" held outside in a car belonging to a Communist named Yamu Gorkey who lived over a store nearby. Going there, Tiger finds Gorkey guarding Teish. Gorkey wounds Tiger in the side, but Tiger shoots him dead, rescues Teish, quickly counters his anti-American fears, and makes him use Gorkey's phone to order his Selachin army back home to rescue Tedesco and Moore. Teish implies gratitude that Vey may provide him a son. Tiger clarifies details by phoning Adams and Corbinet, suddenly realizes that Vey's ruby resembles a litchi nut, and taxis to a Chinese laundry and learns from a smiling worker that litchi nuts are processed near Flood's Warehouse. That is where Turos would be rooming and holding Sarim to force him into additional pro-Soviet concessions. Tiger taxis there, scouts around, determines which rooms Turos would have, and evades his trip wires. Inside, he smells Sarim's cigar, sees his corpse, and bursts in on Turos. Gunfire. Though wounded again, Tiger smashes Turos's head with his .45 butt, ties him up to choke to death slowly, says "Kismet, buddy" to him, and leaves. Tiger will see a doctor, then Rondine, then the authorities.

Action in *The Death Dealers* takes place in 1964, during the time of the New York World's Fair of that year. Tiger Mann, the narrator, adopts an occasional intimate tone, as when, for example, he says, "Well" and "You see." He knows his New York, but shows the reader mostly its nocturnal, dreary side. When Tiger is having a bad time, he says, "It always rained on nights like this."

"THE DEATH OF THE TOO-CUTE PROSTITUTE" (1965). *See* "Man Alone."

DECKER. In *The Deep,* Sullivan reminds Deep that Deep and his young ruf-fians used Decker's basement as a meeting place long ago.

DECKER, MRS. WILLIAM. In *The Big Kill,* she was the young wife of William Decker, encouraged him to reform, had a son with him, died of cancer, and left her husband with huge medical bills. John Vileck praises her to Mike.

DECKER, WILLIAM ("BILL"). In *The Big Kill,* he was a reformed safe-cracker who married, had a son, and tried to go straight for four years. When he was lured into gambling and lost, he was forced back into safe-cracking, was accused of holding out on Ed Teen and his criminal associates, and was killed by Arnold Basil. Decker hid the loot—certain microfilms—in his little kid's overalls, took him to a bar for safety, and went out to his death.

DECKER, WILLIAM JR. In *The Big Kill,* he is the Deckers' active little boy, just over a year old. When Mike temporarily shelters him, the kid likes to handle his .45. He accidentally kills Marsha Lee with it.

DEEP ("DEP"). In *The Deep,* he is the two-hundred-pound narrator. Twenty-five years ago he left a successful criminal gang in New York City to his partner Bennett. But when Bennett is murdered, Deep, now just over forty, returns, works with Augie, Wilson Batten, Cat, Helen Tate, Roscoe Tate, and others to combat Holiday, the hidden leader of the criminal syndicate in New York City who controls Lenny Sobel and his underlings. After many killings, Deep solves the case and brings a measure of justice to the city. He and Helen evidently will have a future together. Spillane manages to have Deep commit only one killing, that of Tate. Al and Peddle die in the K.O. melee; Augie is killed by James and Reeves; James and Cat, by Hull, who dies by falling; Tally, by Tate; Reeves, by Sullivan. Who killed Mattick?

THE DEEP **(1961).** Novel. (Characters: Al, Alverez, Dr. Anders, Augie, Wilson Batten, Bello, Bennett, Benny, Bimmy, Charlie Bizz, Brogan, Lew Bucks, Frankie Carlo, Cat, Julian Chaser, Coppola, Dave, Decker, Deep, Delray, Dixie, Ed, George Elcursio, Mrs. Gleason, Grady, Dr. John Halpern, Hardy, Harold, Holiday, Artie Hull, Sergeant Ken Hurd, Hymie, Lew James, Jocko-boy, Benny Krepto, Betty Ann Lee, Tally Lee, Walter Lico, Martin, Benny Mattick, Maury, Moe, Morgan, Mort, Sig Musco, Hugh Peddle, Pedro, Morrie Reeves, Moe Schwartz, Petie Scotch, Lenny Sobel, Spanish John, Stashu, Carlos Stevens, Sullivan, Henny Summers, Helen Tate, Roscoe Tate, Teddy the Lunger, Thelma, Tony, Vernon.)

After evidently being away for twenty-five years, Deep, a former hood, reappears in his old New York neighborhood after hearing his loyal gang member Bennett has just been murdered. He buys drinks at a bar for a girl named Tally Lee, who expresses delight at Bennett's demise, because he got her sister, Betty Ann Tate, so hooked on heroin that she committed suicide. Tally is terrified, though, when Deep identifies himself.

Deep goes to the office of Wilson Batten, a lawyer whom Deep knew in the old days and who says Bennett's will specifies this: Deep is to get $10,000 now, will inherit the vast crime empire of Bennett, who feared he would be murdered, but only if in one week Deep "determines" who killed him to the satisfaction of Roscoe Tate, a newspaper columnist; otherwise, Batten is the heir. Deep scares Batten, formerly a gang member himself, and persuades opportunistic Augie, Batten's aide, to come work for him. Deep goes to Tate, who comes from and still lives in the same neighborhood, dislikes Deep for bothering Tate's half-sister Helen Tate, and would like Deep to find and kill Bennett's killer and then be destroyed by the police.

Deep goes to a meeting of criminals at the Knights Owl Club (the K.O.), Bennett's old haunt. Benny Mattick, a successful drug dealer, is nominating himself to replace Bennett as gang leader—until, that is, Deep announces he will do so, slaps Mattick viciously, slugs Dixie worse, promises Charlie Bizz he will rule "for keeps," and departs, taking Cat, a clever, loyal robber, along with him.

Deep visits Tally's apartment. She is sick. Helen, a former lover of his, says she is Lenny Sobel's girl now, criticizes Deep's dead crony Bennett's leading Tally's sister astray, and hopes Deep dies soon. She tries to hit him, but he slaps her and takes her in a taxi with him to the Signature restaurant, where Sobel hangs out. After the two have a leisurely lunch, Sobel appears, with Al and Harold, his bodyguards. Deep insults all three, slaps Al when he objects, announces he is taking over Sobel's big criminal organization, and leaves for Martin's bar with Helen, who alternately despises and half-admires Deep. He phones Pedro, a derelict, and Augie. Pedro arrives. According to Batten, Pedro found Bennett's body in Bennett's apartment. Pedro admits he took not only Bennett's watch—a gift from Deep—and sold it, but also Bennett's wallet, which Deep tells him to hold for him. A cop, also phoned, accepts $100 from Deep and gives him the police report on Bennett's death. Helen taxis home. When Al tries to sap Deep, he kicks Al unconscious and moves into Bennett's apartment, shabby outside but lush within. Augie arrives and calmly says he'll help Deep, whose initial success but eventual demise will enable him to take over the money-making gang. Checking the apartment, Deep concludes Bennett was killed elsewhere, then placed here. Deep rejects Augie's theory of a syndicate hit on Bennett, who, Deep says, was killed close up by a friend. Augie says Bennett did not collect jewelry or cash. Augie leaves. Cat phones Deep that two gunmen imported from Philadelphia are approaching to get him. Deep is ready when they arrive, with Hugh Peddle, a crooked councilman, in charge. Deep insults "Hughie," declines his offer to buy Deep out, intimidates the gunnies—Lew James and Morrie Reeves—and with Cat's sudden arrival ejects them. Deep and Cat stay put overnight.

A big day follows. Cat arouses Deep. They reminisce. Augie brings details of Bennett's organizational plans. Deep informs Tate, in his old tenement, that Helen said she saw Bennett's corpse, which must have been on the street and was therefore planted in his apartment later. Tate will aid Deep but warns him not to hurt Helen. Dell takes Augie to Bimmy's tavern, where Mattick has a back-room office. Deep bursts in on Mattick, drugged-out Dixie, Peddle, Sobel, and his goons Harold and Al. Sobel refuses to let Deep take over all operations and orders Harold and Al to dispose of Deep. Deep, however, shoots Harold in the pelvis, Al in the arm, and Sobel in the buttocks, and orders Mattick to cooperate—or else. Deep goes to see Tally but at her entrance is knocked unconscious by a wrapped bottle. Reviving, he goes upstairs, only to find Tally murdered, by what proves to be the same bottle, and Helen knocked out. He tends to Helen, assures her he didn't attack them, hides his .38 under garbage in the dumbwaiter, and phones Batten and the police. Sergeant Ken Hurd, a vicious cop who grew up in the neighborhood, arrives. Augie and Cat are brought in from a nearby bar, have alibis, but are held. The medical examiner judges Deep's head injury exculpates him. Hurd takes Augie, Cat, Helen, and Deep to "the Green House," a secret police building. He grills Deep, who turns sarcastic, gets knocked down twice, but smashes Hurd in the mouth before being sapped by another cop. Deep revives and tells Hurd to make a certain phone call. Batten arrives and gets Deep and his friends out. Cat and Augie return to Bennett's old pad. Deep and Helen kiss wildly in the taxi back to Tally's. Deep retrieves his .38 and phones Cat and Augie. Cat is to locate Dixie; Augie is to ferret out "a power package" Bennett must have collected against someone high up. Deep takes Helen along and barges in on an off-Broadway late dinner Peddle is hosting. Deep says that during his twenty-five years away he became something "Big," with fearsome allies, and hints that Bennett had evidence, still hidden, on Peddle. Cat informs Deep, by phoning Augie, that Dixie is at the Merced Hotel. Arriving there, Deep threatens Dixie to cold-turkey him; so he confesses that Bennett, hours before he was murdered, sent him out for liquor for a party. Deep concludes that someone knew Dixie would waste time by first getting fresh drugs for his habit. Deep forces Dixie to name Dr. John Halpern as likely to minister to wounded gunmen. Helen taxis to her home, while Deep and Cat return to their pad. They get shot at on entering. Deep, missed, wounds one, chases another outside and into the sights of Sullivan, the beat cop on duty, who kills the second thug—Reeves. Authorities in squad cars arrive with Hurd in charge, trace blood tracks showing that the man Deep wounded escaped, but also find Augie, riddled by both gunmen and dead. They thought their target was Deep. To prove Deep's alibi, Hurd phones Peddle and Helen, whose cabbie he also questions. Hurd tells Deep he made that call. Cat notes Hurd's sudden, surprising respect for Deep and also wonders what he was doing while away those twenty-five years. Deep and Cat bed down in Cat's nearby squalid room, which has a dusty couch from the K.O.

The morning paper features Tate's latest condemnation of Deep. Cat seeks the whereabouts of Lew James, the gunman Deep wounded. At Hurd's office, Deep makes a detailed statement, sees Tate and Helen there, and is valuably informed by Hurd that Bennett was shot by a punk's homemade zip gun. Over coffee, Tate rebukes Helen for associating with both Tally and her sister, Betty Ann Tate, and tells Deep he is preparing Deep's obituary. Deep returns to his apartment, now guarded by Sullivan. The two look around but find nothing helpful. Deep goes to the K.O., reminisces with Henny Summers, the old janitor, still there. Deep reminds Henny of a coin flip long ago: Deep lost, turned the criminal setup over to Bennett, left the scene for twenty-five years. Henny recalls that Bennett, just before his murder, planned for a big-liquor K.O. party. On to Batten's office. Deep is startled when Batten says Bennett, though a clever criminal, was "a retarded adult." Batten still awaits Deep's death, to be followed by his own cushy bribe-taking future.

Deep goes to Helen, who plans dinner for two. To excite him, she flashes briefly, but he wants to talk instead. She says she consorted with Sobel to get him to be charitable toward the have-not neighbors and in the hope he would nail Bennett, who caused Betty Ann's suicide. Deep and Helen go to Mattick's apartment. They are shot at and find Mattick murdered. Deep phones Tate: Tate should pretend that he legitimately called on Mattick and found him dead, and will thus have a scoop. Helen begs Deep to stop all action. He can't. Cat has learned that James is resting in the Westhampton Hotel and will meet Deep there. When Deep arrives, he finds James shot again and dead, and Cat mortally wounded. Deep chases the killer to the roof; they fight, and the killer falls to his death three stories down. Deep recognizes him as Artie Hull. Cat tells Deep to query the Westhampton clerk, then dies. Deep finds the clerk, bribes and threatens him, and learns that James phoned Peddle.

Peddle lives in the tenement district which he controls politically but in which he enjoys a luxurious penthouse. Deep breaks into it but is suckered. Peddle is not there, but Sobel is, with several thugs, including Ed and Tony. They take him to a hideout near Yankee Stadium. Tony knocks him out. They tie him in a chair and present him to Holiday, a suave gentleman in charge of everything criminal in town. Holiday wants to know where Bennett's "stuff" is. Deep doesn't know, gets slapped viciously by big Maxie, and understands almost everything once Holiday summarizes his various murderous orders. Deep is horrified when Sobel suddenly says Helen knows and ought to be brought in. Holiday makes some phone calls and learns that Helen was spotted leaving her place with Peddle. Holiday leaves, to establish his alibi. Ed lies down for a nap. Tony departs to eat. Sobel batters Deep, gets sick in the process, orders Ed to guard him in the bedroom, gets drunk, answers orders over the phone, and is about to leave in a panel truck to find and kill Peddle and grab Helen. But Deep, now out of his ropes, grabs Sobel, dislocates his shoulder, and ties him up, ties up sleepy Ed, conks Tony when he returns, and ties him up. Deep drives the truck to the K.O., sneaks in through the coal chute to the furnace room, and finds Bennett's stuff under a concrete block inside slide-out shelves, and phones not only Tate to come for the latest scoop but also Hurd for help. Deep spies on Helen, being tortured by Al, with Peddle uneasy nearby. Holiday's gangsters attack, killing Al, Peddle, and another. The police arrive, firing. In the melee, Deep drags Helen to safety. Back near the furnace, Helen admits that she talked to Tate about Bennett's unrequited love for her but adds that Tate is her deceased father's stepson, hence not his half-sister. Deep responds: Tate never shook the squalor of his upbringing, stayed through lust for Helen. Tate appears, with the zip gun he used on Bennett leveled at Deep, who taunts him into a reckless attack, draws, and kills him. Helen is aghast, then says Deep couldn't avoid the old K.O.'s murderous ways—until, that is, Hurd storms in and congratulates Lieutenant Deep for a job well done.

Spillane's love-hate affair with New York City is evident in *The Deep*. He knows the vibrant city well, likens action in it to "an unending living drama" on "a macadam stage," says that guns, cars, and voices make "music perfectly suited to the city," and reels off street names precisely. The novel is hard to follow, with too many telephones and taxis, pronouns with obscure antecedents, and speakers in puzzling dialogue sequences. Characters are not skillfully named. There are two Bennys, plus Bello, Bennett, Bimmy, and Bunny; Carlo and Carlos; two Charleses; two Georges; two Johns; two Lews; and two Moes, plus Morrie. The action is surreal; when Deep needs someone, that someone is almost immediately where he looks.

DEKKER, MANOS. In "Return of the Hood," he is the international spy expert, working for the Soviets. He captures Karen Sinclair, with the assistance of Alex and others, and holds Karen in a hotel room above Ryan's room. Ryan finds both, kills Manos, and rescues Karen.

DEKKER, SAL. In *The Delta Factor,* he was an army buddy of Morgan's, was tortured by the Germans, escaped, was mangled in a land mine, was rescued and hospitalized, and went to Australia. According to official accounts, he farmed and died there. In reality, Dekker stole the $40 million Morgan was accused of stealing, stashed the money, went to Australia, killed a farmer named Marty Steele, went as Marty Steele to the island controlled by Carlos Ortega, and tries to use Morgan to cover his escape. He kills Rosa Lee and Whitey Tass, and is about to kill Kimberly Stacy, Joey Jolley, and Morgan when Morgan kills him.

DEL. In *The Girl Hunters,* he processes a wire photo for Hy Gardner. The picture turns out to be one of Velda taken in eastern Europe.

DELACORT, LUCY. In *The Body Lovers,* Mike chides Mitch Temple, a reporter, about his falling for Lucy Delacourt and therefore not writing a story about the "house she ran."

DELANEY. In *The By-Pass Control,* he is an intelligence agent up from Washington, D.C., to New York.

DELANEY. In *Kiss Me, Deadly,* he is a factory representative of the company that made the safes in Carl Evello's home. Delaney opens them for the police.

DELANEY, DR. In *Survival . . . Zero!,* he is the physician who, Mike Hammer recalls, stitched Lipton Sullivan's eyebrow wound after a neighborhood fight long ago.

DELANEY, MAXINE. In *The Body Lovers,* she was a pretty, redheaded West Coast stripper and call girl, then a Chicago model, and finally a victim of Belar Ris and other sadists. An Oregon relative declines to accept her body for burial.

DELANEY, PATROLMAN. In *The Death Dealers,* he is a policeman whom Tiger Mann phones to ask how he can get Malcolm Turos's photographs to Lieutenant Dick Gallagher.

DELL. In *Day of the Guns,* he runs a sleazy joint called the Hall of the Two Sisters. Mann takes Gretchen Lark there. Dell provides Mann with leads as to Vidor Churis's whereabouts.

DELRAY. In *The Deep,* this is the name of a rival gang when Deep, Augie, and Bennett were young.

***THE DELTA FACTOR* (1967).** Novel. (Characters: André, Angelo, Herm Bailey, Señor Camino, Carey, Carter, Bernice Case, Sal Dekker, Inspector Jack Doherty, Juan Fucilla, Lisa Gordot, Melvin Gross, Malcolm Hannah, Professor Francisco Hernández, Baldy Hines, Joey Jolley, José, Art Keefer, María López, Little Joe Malone, Max, Morgan the Raider, Carlos Ortega, Raymond, Rice, Mr. Roberts, Captain Romero, Luis Rondo, Señora Rondo, Rosa Lee, Russo Sabin, Victor Sable, Saxton, Kimberly Stacy, Marty Steele, Lou Steubal, Whitey Tass, Lily Temple, Mrs. Gustav Timely, Toppett, Ma Toppett, Mario Tullius, Major Turez, Valente, Lieutenant Valente, Vince, Gavin Woolart, Gorman Yard.)

For three years after a $40 million New York heist, Federal authorities suspected Morgan the Raider, the narrator. Convicted and imprisoned, Morgan soon escaped. They catch him only when a car driven by a punk hit Morgan and he was hospitalized. The physician who treated him had him fingerprinted and thus the police were alerted. When Morgan is released, Gavin Woolart of the State Department, Rice of the CIA, Carter of the Treasury Department, and Inspector Jack Doherty of N.Y.P.D. spirit him to a secret location for questioning. The federal men care little for the still-missing money, which Morgan half-denies knowledge of, and will make it worthwhile if he agrees to go on a dangerous mission. Liking adventure anyway, he agrees to appear as a criminal on a certain foreign island, be imprisoned in its Rose Castle (built by the Spaniards in 1620) where Victor Sable is jailed, and spring Sable, an aging scientist with secrets valuable to the United States. Kimberly ("Kim") Stacy, an able, beautiful federal agent, will go along as his wife.

During three free days, Morgan seeks evidence as to the location of the $40 million. Information he gets from Joey Jolley, a jewelry fence, and Mrs. Gustav ("Gussie") Timely, a knowledgeable landlady, link Bernice Case, a prostitute, and Gorman Yard, a well-heeled criminal imprisoned in Elmira, New York, for a hit-and-run offense committed in Syracuse. Morgan gets Kim to check on Yard in detail and determine whether money he flashed came from the $40 million, serial numbers of which are recorded. After making some phone calls, he locates Bernice and persuades her to take him to her room for conversation. She reveals that Yard, a vicious man she would never sell sex to, had sleazy friends. She knows Morgan was accused of stealing millions, and he lets her theorize he stashed it in Gussie's old house, where Bernice says she used to live. She mentions a high-up criminal named Whitey Tass, also involved, and agrees to nose around for more information, if he will comfort her for one nonsexual night. He does.

Morgan calls an old army friend, Al Keefer in Miami, and gets him to make travel arrangements for him. Little Joe Malone, another buddy, supplies him with weaponry and burglary tools. Kim tells Morgan her sources report that Yard was killed in a prison workshop accident and that no heist money has surfaced. Morgan and Kim go to Georgia, are quickly, officially married, and drive to Florida for a nonintimate honeymoon at a motel. By phone, Kim learns from her superiors that certain people already know of their movements. Morgan calls Joey and is told that Yard's death was no accident, that Tass is a politically powerful criminal, and also that Bernice has just been strangled.

In the morning Morgan and Kim drive to Miami, where he picks up $20,000 from a bank account, under the name of M. A. Winters, arranged by Woolart. The bank also has a safe-deposit box in his new name. The pair proceed to the Keys, get a motel room, and enjoy some poolside beer. Keefer appears on cue, explains his flight plan and communication signals for Morgan and Kim, whom he eyes appreciatively in her bikini. Keefer says that Carlos Ortega, the island dictator, is protected by Russo Sabin, a hatchet man, is wooing regional Communists for a political takeover, and can be tempted by the millions he believes Morgan has.

Keefer flies Morgan and Kim to a boat near their target island. José, its skipper, takes the pair to a car. They register as the Winterses, in the lush

Regis Hotel in Nuevo Cádiz, the capital of the small, unstable Central American country that Ortega rules by controlling the military. But he needs money to strengthen his hold on the Communists and Victor Sable's intellectual secrets to woo them. Nuevo Cádiz combines dazzling gambling casinos, a depleted economy, concealed poverty, and a democratic figure-head president both liked and powerless. Rose Castle is on a peninsula four miles distant. While Kim shops, Morgan begins to gamble. Kim returns. Marty Steele, an American gambler with a twisted face, warns Morgan about crooked croupiers. An old Chevy is in the parking lot. Morgan wins at craps, attracts a crowd, cashes in $12,000, and is approached by a flashy woman named Lisa Gordot, whom Kim later identifies as a dangerous jet-set foreign national. Morgan and Kim go to an off-beat restaurant for a late steak and are shot at when leaving. Morgan identifies the spent shell casing as an American .38, hides his .45, and, accompanied by Kim, is taken to Russo Sabin, director of police, who, after smoothly warning him, lets the couple return to their honeymoon. Awaiting them in their room is Ortega, with his bodyguard, Major Turez. Ortega's slick manner does not conceal his ruthless power, as he calmly offers to launder the millions of dollars "Mr. Morgan" has.

Morgan does some bar-hopping until an American bartender, hearing him name Lisa Gordot, reveals that Lisa is dangerous, that Sabin lusts for her, and that Angelo, the Regis bell captain, can aid him. Morgan returns to the Regis, helps Lisa win $12,000 by backing his fourteen lucky rolls of the dice, gets her room number from her, and is warned by Angelo about Sabin. Morgan enters Lisa's room, phones Kim his whereabouts, and talks to Lisa. She is virtually a captive here and needs $50,000 to escape and clear herself of blackmailers back home. For his help, she agrees to gain what information she can. Moreover, after some drinks she disrobes and poses invitingly—until Kim, having picked her lock, bursts in and takes Morgan away. Back in their room he manages to explain Lisa's usefulness through her knowing Sabin.

The next morning Morgan mollifies Kim by kidding her in the shower; the two, trailed by Ortega's goons, go from bar to bar until they arrive at the Orino Bar, where Keefer told Morgan to make contact with someone singing "Green Eyes." The buxom soloist is Rosa Lee, who explains that she has a secret radio and knows a Rose Castle guard named Juan Fucilla, who can be bribed to help. She says cadres of local rebels stand ready to throw off Ortega's dictatorship. That evening, Morgan leaves Kim in their room and sneaks out of the hotel by a route Angelo described. At Rosa Lee's, he radios Keefer for news: Joey has told Keefer that Tass appears connected to Yard's and Bernice's murders. Fucilla enters, and Morgan agrees to supply heroin for him to sell to Rose Castle prisoners with rich families. Fucilla warns that Sabin gets payoffs from all drug deals. Morgan expects Fucilla's aid regarding Sable. Rosa Lee startles Morgan with a quick, hot kiss.

Morgan returns to Kim, who voices jealousy upon smelling Rosa Lee's perfume on him. The two go to the gaming tables, and find a hurricane warning posted and several tourists planning to leave. Marty chats with Morgan about the weather and also about women, saying Morgan has all the luck. Morgan spots Lisa, teary eyed until he tells her he'll help her escape, as a diversion to distract Sabin. Turez escorts Morgan to Ortega, and they tell him that he was spotted talking at the Orino with Rosa Lee, further, that an anonymous tip reported his taxi ride to Rosa's house, where she has been found strangled. Morgan lies his way out, after which Ortega tells him he has only a short time to decide to let him launder the $40 million. Morgan returns to the Regis, asks Angelo to check into Fucilla, peels off $5,000 from a hidden bundle, and pays Angelo with it to convert Kim's passport into one for Lisa. She, grateful, promises to make it up to Morgan one fine day. Suddenly Kim notes that some money with Morgan's bundle has serial numbers from the missing $40 million. All along, Kim has been suspicious.

The new day is bright, but the hurricane is approaching. Lisa will disguise herself as a maid and get to the airport; her avoidance of Sabin will outrage and hence divert him. Angelo drugs a guard with wine and drives Morgan to Rosa's house. Morgan checks the evidence and discerns that she was attacked while eating. He radios Keefer, who reports the imminent arrival of supplies by boat for Morgan, says his airplane blew a cylinder and can't fly just now, and adds that Joey, terrified for some reason, is also on the boat. Kim says her contact reported that one of Ortega's men tried to hit Morgan's Miami safe-deposit box, was chased off, and is holed up somewhere.

The weather report next morning is alarming. Hotel windows are being boarded, and all but die-hard gambling tourists are flying off the island. Kim goes shopping as a diversion, while Morgan treats drinkers and pretends to become hopelessly drunk. José lands his boat, bringing Joey, who says Tass has connected him somehow with the deaths of Yard, who tried to double-cross Tass, and of Bernice, who was queried by Morgan. Suddenly Morgan tells Kim he never stole the $40 million but did scoop up some of it in the room he had at Gussie's and after the presumed thief left part of the loot there. Kim wonders who shot at Morgan here on the island.

Morgan meets Fucilla in the men's room, for his approval of the heroin sample José brought. In his Volvo, Fucilla drives Morgan to Rose Castle and introduces him to Captain Romero and Lieutenant Valente, the inside drug dealers. Romero wants Morgan to deliver two kilos of heroin fast. Morgan demands $20,000—a bargain, Romero thinks. Morgan is aware of an impending doublecross. Morgan is proudly shown the fiendish torture chambers and the obedient, drug-addicted inmates. These include Victor Sable, recognized by his photos and sitting at a desk busily writing. Morgan is loaned the Volvo to get the heroin, which he says is stashed in town. A group of medics arrives at the Regis, to help if the hurricane hits and causes injuries. Morgan notes Tass among them. In his room, Morgan tells Joey to keep calm. He orders Kim, answering Sabin's phone call pretending to be Lisa, back to their room. He calls Rondo, Kim's contact, and (as Winters) orders a six-passenger Queenaire plane. He has Angelo wrap and tape two kilos of confectioners' sugar, and bring the package along as heroin, with some sandwiches. He hears an airplane heading northwest, bearing Lisa to safety. Plans are well developed. Sabin will be distracted. The getaway plane will be waiting. Kim will hide Joey from Tass's view. But once outside, Morgan finds Kim slugged unconscious, Tass shot dead, and Joey groggy. Morgan drives Kim and Joey in Fucilla's Volvo to the airport to wait, uses a field wagon to block the car of pursuers as he gets to Rose Castle, and hides the packages of sugar in some bushes.

What follows is three-climax derring-do. First, Morgan enters the castle; reports to Romero, Valente, and Fucilla, receives $20,000, shoots Romero and Fucilla dead, persuades Valente to cooperate. Morgan decks a guard, frees Sable, learns from him of his importance to the Free World, stops the electric generator, causes darkness throughout. Valente produces a flashlight, kills a guard. Beside Romero's and Fucilla's corpses, Valente rips his uniform and is willingly slugged by Morgan to appear a scarred, surviving hero. Morgan finds grenades in Romero's office, phones Angelo, learns Ortega and Sabin are heading for the castle. Once outside, Morgan shoots the parapet guards, drives Sable toward the airport, kills Ortega, Sabin, and their henchmen with four grenades, and finds a Chevy wrecked at the road-blocking wagon.

Second, at the airport Morgan grabs a parachute from an old B-25; finds Marty Steele, his face lift spoiled by his Chevy accident and now revealed as Sal Dekker, an army buddy long thought dead in Australia but now boasting he stole the $40 million, lived with Gussie, and left some loot there so Morgan would be blamed. Dekker explains his temporarily bought freedom here on the island, and prepares to shoot Kim, Joey, then Morgan. But Morgan kills him.

Third, Morgan surrenders to Kim's contact, Rondo, the Queenaire pilot. Rondo, Morgan, Sable, Kim, and Joey take off for Miami. Morgan anticipates prison time, until Kim says Dekker's boast about hiding the money where Captain Henry Morgan (1635?-1688) hid his may lead to the recovery of Dekker's missing stash. Morgan and Kim agree they are truly married. Morgan spots a boat below, right where he ordered Angelo to tell Keefer to have it. Sable keeps Rondo from viewing Morgan. Kim, nodding her eternal love, salutes him with the two-fingered Victory sign and other index across as Delta, the female symbol. Morgan puts on the parachute and leaps.

Morgan, the hero of *The Delta Factor,* like Mike Hammer and Tiger Mann in their novels, demeans women by calling them "baby," "doll," "girl," "kid," "kitten," "kitty cat," and "sugar," and voices dislike of America's generous foreign aid programs and big insurance companies. Unlike Mike and Tiger, however, he is sensible enough to call himself a stupid sucker. As elsewhere, Spillane's figures of speech in *The Delta Factor* run the gamut from the clever—when Morgan and Kim kiss at their forced wedding ceremony, "it was more like a couple of fighters touching gloves before the first round began"—to the foolish—when, much later, Kim's "full breasts [were] pouting against the restraint of her clothes."

DEMAREST. In "The Veiled Woman," he works for the Attorney General.

DEMENT. In "The Flier," Cat Fallon tells Del Reed that he flew films to and from laboratories for Dement Pictures during location shoots.

DERTELLI. In "The Flier," George Clinton tells Cat Fallon that Andro Marcel is said to have killed Dertelli and Smitty Bones.

DeVECCHIO, AL. In *The Erection Set,* he was a captain in the air force with Dog Kelly. He is now a New York businessman, up from Hell's Kitchen. Dog gets him to cooperate by reminding him of deals he made concerning Cudder, Davewell, and Warton.

DEVIN, SAM. In "The Flier," he was Tucker Stacy's attorney, about sixty but still quick. He helps Cat Fallon in his investigation of Stacy's murder.

DEVLIN. In *Day of the Guns,* Mann recalls that Devlin used torpedoes to blow a safe to get the Morvitch papers in Yugoslavia during the war.

DEVLIN, MYRNA. In *I, the Jury,* she was a drug addict whom Jack Williams aided in going cold turkey. The two were to marry, but Jack was murdered. Mike Hammer tries to comfort her. Charlotte plants heroin on her and murders her after the dinner party held by Esther and Mary Bellemy.

DEVOE. In *The Big Kill,* this is the name of a stupid family Joan works for and impresses with a phony French accent.

DEVON. In *The Snake,* he was Sally Devon Torrence's first husband, was presumably Sue Devon's father, and is now deceased.

DEVON, SUE. In *The Snake,* she is Sally Devon Torrence's daughter and was adopted by Simpson Torrence, Sally's second husband, after Sally's death. Sue, age twenty-one, lovely, petite, but unbalanced, is rightly afraid that Torrence wants her dead, and runs away. Velda protects her. Mike Hammer persuades her to return home. In Sue's cuddly teddy bear Mike discovers a long-missing letter from Sally incriminating Torrence.

DEWEY. In *The Girl Hunters,* he owned a newstand on Lexington Avenue. In his eighties, he held a message about Velda for Mike, was murdered by Gorlin, and wills the stand to Duck-Duck Jones.

DeWITT. In "The Flier," he is a reporter in Celada, wrote about Tucker Stacy, and helps Cat Fallon when he is investigating Stacy's murder.

DIAMOND, MARTY. In *Black Alley,* it is mentioned that Marcos Dooley owed Diamond $5,500. This is presumed evidence that Dooley did not rob from Lorenzo Ponti.

DIAZ, GENERAL ORTEGO. In *The By-Pass Control,* Lisa McCall recalls seeing Camille Hunt in a Rio bar and says Camille killed two men to protect General Ortego. This hint as to Camille's violence ought to have made Tiger Mann suspicious of Camille but did not.

DiCICA, ANTHONY ("TONY"). In *The Killing Man,* he was a World War II veteran, then a criminal with knowledge as to the whereabouts of a huge cocaine cache. He was injured by a head blow causing him to lose his memory. When he recovered, he went to Mike Hammer's office for help but was murdered and mutilated there by Penta. Like Spillane, DiCica attended Erasmus High School in Brooklyn.

DiCICA, MARIA LOUISA. In *The Killing Man,* she was Victorio DiCica's wife and then widow, and Anthony DiCica's mother. Anthony provided his mother with $300,000 and two houses. She kept her husband's toolbox, which her son took when he was mentally disturbed.

DiCICA, VICTORIO. In *The Killing Man,* he was Maria Louisa DiCica's husband and Anthony DiCica's father. Victorio, a cabinet maker, was killed in a holdup in 1960. Anthony then murdered the killer. Anthony kept his father's toolbox, initialed "V. D."

DICK. In *The Death Dealers,* he is an ex-Selachin native now in Brooklyn. Jack Brant gets him to help Tiger Mann. Dick's friends are Tom and Harry.

DICKERSON. In *The Snake,* he is repeatedly mentioned as a super boss of the Syndicate. He never appears.

DIDSON. In *I, the Jury,* he is the supervisor of Bobo Hopper, who delivers packages as directed by Didson.

DIGS, LUCY. In *The Body Lovers,* she is a prostitute too self-respecting to touch Orslo Bucher.

DIKER, RAY. In *Kiss Me, Deadly,* he is a *Globe* reporter—skinny, stingy, and able. He gives Mike Hammer information about Nicholas Raymond.

DILLON. In *The Twisted Thing,* when Mike Hammer seeks a physician who treated a man he wounded, one physician's housekeeper says her employer treated only Dillon, who accidentally shot himself in the foot.

DILWICK. In *The Twisted Thing,* he is a crooked policeman in Sidon, in cahoots with Herron Mallory. Mike Hammer stops him from beating up Billy Parks, outwits Dilwick often, learns he has snatched Myra Grange and Miss Cook and hidden them in Herron Mallory's boathouse, and shoots him dead there.

DINERO, LOUIE. In *The Long Wait,* he owns a fine steakhouse, employs Wendy Miller (*see* West, Vera) as a popular singer, and warns John McBride to treat her respectfully.

DINES, JERRY. In *The Last Cop Out,* he apprised Mark Shelby of the vote in Chicago to kill Papa Menes.

DiNUCCIO, JOE. In "Me, Hood!," he owns a bar on 49th Street and Sixth Avenue. Ryan uses it as a meeting place.

DIXIE. In *The Deep,* he was part of Deep's and Bennett's Knights Owl Club group years ago. Now a useless drug addict, he works ineffectively for Lenny Sobel.

DODGE, BARNEY. In *Day of the Guns,* he is Mann's informative friend.

DOE, JANE. In "Man Alone," this is the name Madaline Stumper assigns to a prostitute who told her Mildred Swiss was preparing to travel. Both Mildred and "Jane" were of European extraction.

DOG. In *The Death Dealers,* he is an agent who, alerted by Virgil Adams, told Leo Rubin to be on the lookout for a man whose voice was damaged. Ruben then helps Tiger Mann.

DOHERTY, INSPECTOR JACK. In *The Delta Factor,* he is a friendly New York policeman who witnesses the attempts by federal authorities to question Morgan about the missing $40 million.

DOLLY. In *The Body Lovers,* she is a prostitute who cannot stand Orslo Bucher.

DONAHUE. In *The Long Wait,* he is the state auditor whom Vera West threatened and whom John McBridge visited for information.

DONAVAN. In "Killer Mine," he owns Donavan's Dive, where Lieutenant Joe Scanlon goes for information.

DONNINGER. In "Man Alone," this is the name of a bar which Patrick Regan frequents. It is located at Sixth Avenue and 49th Street.

DONOVAN. In *Bloody Sunrise,* the written message in code asking him to call "Mr. Donovan" alerts Tiger Mann that he must phone London.

DOOLEY. In "Man Alone," he was a cabbie waiting behind Guy Rivera and Chick the night Leo Marcus was supposedly killed.

DOOLEY, MARCOS. In *Black Alley,* Mike Hammer and Captain Pat Chambers knew Dooley in the army. Dooley, formerly in the navy, was daring in combat in Germany. He steers both Mike and Pat into police work. He was a menial laborer for Angelo Ponti, a deceased Mafia don. Dying after being wounded by Ugo Ponti, Dooley asks to speak only with Mike and gives him enigmatic information about the Mafia's missing $89 billion. Mike uses Dooley's service serial numbers to trace their location.

DOOLEY, MARVIN. In *Black Alley,* he is an ex–navy man.

DOOLEY, MRS. MARCOS. In *Black Alley,* she is Marcos Dooley's deceased wife and Marvin Dooley's mother. He lives in New Brunswick, New Jersey, and is a ne'er-do-well, visited by Mike Hammer for information and bribed by Ugo Ponti.

DORN, WILLIAM. In *Survival . . . Zero!,* he heads Anco Electronics and the March Chemical Company, with Park Avenue offices. Renée Talmage poses as his accountant. Beaver's stealing Dorn's wallet, with a map of sites of canisters containing biological-warfare weapons, results in all the trouble. Dorn's crooked Soviet colleague is Joseph Kudak. Mike Hammer kills Stanley, Dorn's hired killer, after which, confronted with prison, Dorn and Renée commit suicide by swallowing cyanide capsules.

DOUGLAS, LESLIE ("LES"). In "The Bastard Bannerman," he owns the Cherokee Club.

DRAGO, HOWIE. In *Black Alley,* he is one of Ugo Ponti's gunmen, turned part-time businessman. Mike relishes insulting him. Drago's partner is Leonard Patterson.

"THE DREAD CHINATOWN MAN" (1975). Short story. (Characters: None named.) When four of his fraternity brothers from their college at Fort Hays, Kansas, visited Spillane in New York City, he impressed them by telling off the man offering to sell them Chinatown tour tickets. Thirty years later, however, Spillane still fears and avoids the fellow—even though by now "books, movies and TV have made" Spillane famous.

DREW, CHARLIE. In *The Twisted Thing,* Mike Hammer recalls seeing Roxy Coulter at a New Year's party Drew once held in Atlantic City.

DRUTMAN, NAT. In *The Girl Hunters,* he owns the building where Mike's office is located. In *The Snake,* Mike borrows a .32 from Drutman. In *The Killing Man,* he is still the building manager. Spillane had an air force buddy named Nat ("Sporty") Drutman, to whom he dedicated *Bloody Sunrise.*

Bibliography: Johnston.

DUBRO, ERTICIA. In *The Erection Set,* she was a nanny for the Barrin family. She skinny-dipped with Leyland Ross Hunter. Dog Kelly humorously black-mailed Hunter by photographing the scene. Erticia later married a gardener.

DUGAN, TOM. In *I, the Jury,* he is a *Chronicle* reporter Mike Hammer knows.

DUKE. In *I, the Jury,* he is a college student who appears at Harold Hines's dormitory immediately after Mike Hammer shoots George Kalecki.

DUKE. In *Kiss Me, Deadly,* he is a Mafia man Mike Hammer ruptures with a kick.

DUKES. In "Stand Up and Die!," Caroline Hart tells Mitch Valler that "Mr. Dukes" could read, "fore his eyes went." Literacy is rare in her community.

DUMONT, PIERRE. In *The Erection Set,* he was an agent in Marseilles for Dog Kelly, who says Dumont was superficially wounded.

DUNCAN, CHESTER ("DUNC"). In "The Girl Behind the Hedge," he is a successful businessman who gets revenge on Walter Harrison, after he steals Adrianne, Duncan's fiancée, and indirectly causes her death.

DUTKO, SONIA. In *Bloody Sunrise,* she is a beautiful Russian skier who allegedly defected during the 1956 Olympics, came to the United States, became a ski instructor and a film adviser, and comes to New York allegedly to rendezvous with Gabin Martrel, who is in love with her. Her mission is to kill him. She fools Tiger Mann until the last minute, when he escapes her clutches, rescues Edith Caine and Wally Gibbons, and kills Sonia. She called herself Helen Wells when she taught skiing and registers in the Shrevesport Hotel as L. Grace before she kills Ann Lighter.

DUVAL, ALI. In *The Body Lovers,* he is an Algerian-French criminal. As a steward on the *Pinella,* he smuggles for Belar Ris and pays Lorenzo Jones to provide loose girls for him to deliver to Ris. If Ali is in Ris's mansion when Mike blows it up, he will figure as part of Mike's kill count.

DUVAL, THELMA B. In *I, the Jury,* Captain Pat Chambers names her as a drug addict in rehab.

DuVALLE, FRANCISCO. In *The Killing Man,* he was Bennett Bradley's twin brother. Mike's testimony four years earlier caused DuValle, who murdered fourteen people, to be executed. This fact caused Bradley (as Penta) to try to kill Mike.

E

EARL. In *The Girl Hunters,* he was one of Mike's remembered war buddies.

EARLE. In *The Erection Set,* Dog Kelly remembers that Earle said showers are slick.

EARLY, INSPECTOR. In "The Girl Behind the Hedge," he questions Chester Duncan about the death of Duncan's rival, Walter Harrison. Duncan's explanation is satisfactory.

ED. In *The Body Lovers,* he is a waiter at the Blue Ribbon.

ED. In *The Deep,* he is one of Holiday's goons. When he naps, Deep could kill him but merely gags and ties him up.

EDDIE. In *The Killing Man,* he is a guard assigned with Tunney to Lewis Ferguson's cabin. Penta kills both men. (If Mike Hammer had not wasted valuable time verbosely summarizing evidence to Velda, he might have saved both Eddie and Tunney.)

EDSON. In "Man Alone," he is the assignment cop who tells Patrick Regan about certain papers Sergeant Jerry Nolan was working on for Regan.

EDWARDS, BUCKY. In "Everybody's Watching Me," he is an alcoholic city reporter.

ELCURSIO, GEORGE. In *The Deep,* he was impressed when Deep and others, long ago, dropped bricks on rival gang members' heads. Deep recalls that Elcursio had earlier been a member of the Vernon gang in Chicago.

ELKINS, WILLIE. In "Kick It or Kill!," he rents a pick-up truck to Kelly Smith.

ELLIOT, DR. In *The Erection Set,* he prescribed pain pills for Sheila McMillan to ease the painful memories of repeated rapes.

ELLISON. In *My Gun Is Quick,* he is a private investigator. Velda tells Mike Hammer that she has recommended Ellison to handle work Hammer would find too routine.

ELROY, DAVE. In *The By-Pass Control,* he is an agent whom Mason Armstrong flies from New York to aid Tiger Mann after Dan Lavois is murdered. Elroy, tall, lean, age thirty-two, proceeds to Eau Gallie, Florida, and locates drug pushers who may be involved with Louis Agrounsky, the object of Tiger's search.

EMBLER, ELLIOT. In *The Erection Set,* he has the compromising photographs of Dennison Barrin abusing Rose Porter. This character's name may be Spillane's harmless play on that of Eric Ambler (1909–1998), the distinguished mystery writer.

THE ERECTION SET **(1972).** Novel. (Characters: Louis Albo, Joe Allen, Barney, Barrin, Alfred Barrin, Cameron Barrin, Dennison Barrin, Mrs. Barrin, Veda Barrin, Beansey, Arnold Bell, Bertram, Beth, Betterton, Big Benny, Bridey-the-Greek, Brown, S. C. Cable, Larry Cass, Sharon Cass, Charles, Charmaine, The Chopper, Clarence, Simon Corner, Stanley Cramer, John Daly, Mario Danado, Danny, Davewell, Al DeVecchio, Erticia Dubro, Pierre Dumont, Earle, Dr. Elliot, Elliot Embler, Farnsworth, Forbes, Raul Fucia, Garfield, Marvin Gates, Pam Barrin Gates, Walt Gentry, Greco, Guido, Teddy Guido, Hal, Hamilton, Harvey, Mrs. Havelock, Bud Healey, Helgurt, Hobis, Roland Holland, Hunter, Leyland Ross Hunter, Jansen, Jason, Jason, Jerry, Joe, Juke, Kelly, Dog Kelly, Ernie Kirrel, O'Keefe, Dick Lagen, Le Fleur, Chet Linden, Linton, Lisa, El Lobo, Lucy Longstreet, Louise, McMillan, Cross McMillan, Sheila McMillan, Marcia, Marco, Markham, Meehan, Mona Merriman, Shekky Monroe, Montgomery, Jimmie Moore, Old Snarly, Pat, Peggy, Rose Porter, Bibby Potter, Sylvia Potter, Purcell, Mel Puttiche, Mrs. Bennie Sachs, Sergeant Bennie Sachs, Blackie Saunders, Kurt Schmidt, Morrie Shapiro, Lee Shay, Fred Simon, Lucella Barrin Simon, Mrs. Simon, Stash, Count Stazow, Stoney, Strauss, Tag, Mel Tarbok, Darcy Taylor, Thorpe, Cubby Tillman, Tobano, Sergeant Vince Tobano, Hiram Tod, The Turk, Voorhies, Ferris Weal, Willis, Woodring.)

After twenty-some years in Europe following service during World War II as a combat pilot and his discharge in 1946, Dogeron ("Dog") Kelly, the narrator of much of the story, returns in June to New York City, bunks with Lee Shay, an old buddy, and meets and impresses Rose Porter. She is Lee's bright prostitute friend. [Parenthetical material in the summary indicates scenes that Dog does not narrate and is unaware of.]

(Rose summarizes her sexual history and expresses interest in Dog.)

Lee is startled when Dog shows him $2 million, brought from Europe.

Dog reports to Leyland Ross Hunter, his family's aging lawyer. They renew acquaintance after a thirty-year hiatus. Dog was the bastard son of the wife of a now-deceased man named Barrin, head of Barrin Industries, who owned an estate called Mondo Beach on Grand Sita, a waterfront area an hour from New York, and a factory at Linton, a nearby town. Dog's happily accepting $10,000 in company stock—legally possible if no immorality can be discovered in his past—from that man's estate would frustrate Dog's cousins, Alfred Barrin and Dennison Barrin, who grew up hating and being hated by Dog, and hope to inherit Barrin's leavings. Dog also has three disreputable female cousins—Pam Barrin Gates, Lucella Barrin Simon, and Veda. To validate his continued immorality, Dog takes Hunter to two prostitutes, and the four have a tousled night.

(Hunter remembers evidence he obtained through Interpol that Dog, for whom he searched, may have hijacked some Nazi gold.)

(Lee, counting Dog's money, is terrified and is about to put the $2.5 million down the incinerator.)

Dog has a solution: Dog goes to a bank across the street and deposits the sum, legally counted. He visits Rose in her apartment, and they simultaneously chat and have intercourse. He says he has plans for her.

Dog goes to the Weller-Fabray haberdashery, writes a check, and orders a wardrobe to be ready in a day. The manager is an agent Dog knows. Dog goes to Al DeVecchio, an old army buddy, now a success and in a plush office. They reminisce cryptically about combat and DeVecchio's present ability to scare even Mafia members. DeVecchio summarizes the perilous financial condition of Barrin Industries and the stupidities of Dog's cousins—now in jeopardy. Dog says he knows, because he secretly bought Barrin's devalued stock and is prepared to fight Cross McMillan, a rival from their childhood days who wants Barrin's company, which is developing an antigravity machine.

(DeVecchio, an army captain during the war, remembers the daredevilry of Dog, a major. DeVecchio wonders if Dog was really El Lobo, who supposedly ruined the European black market with American mob money.)

Dog calls on his friend Chet Linden, who came to New York a week ago from London. They discuss obscure European actions, and Linden says he bought some depleted Barrin Industries stock before McMillan could get it. Linden adds that his organization barely voted to spare Dog's life. Dog says he is going to Walt Gentry's party this evening but not through Linden's influence.

(Sharon Cass is aware that S. C. Cable, her boss and co-owner of Cable Howard Productions, Hollywood film makers, wants her to seduce Gentry, their host tonight, to get him to invest $5 million in a new venture. Raul

Fucia, an ultraconceited ladies' man, comes on to her slickly. She tells him she is a virgin and would castrate him if he couldn't restrain his visible erection. Dog eavesdrops, introduces himself, queries her about virginity, and walks off. Sharon, though fingering a green engagement ring, appears inexplicably excited by Dog. Gentry approaches, propositions her unsuccessfully, but amiably says he will invest the desired $5 million anyway.)

Dog meets Mona Merriman, a gossip columnist, age sixty-one but sexy. They kiss, talk dirty, and feel each other. Up comes Dick Lagen, a political columnist. He says he has heard of a Dogeron in Istanbul and Paris. Both men admit liking belly dancers. Walt defines Sharon to Dog as a challenging sex pot and introduces the two. She tells Dog she grew up in Mondo Beach, where her father, deceased, worked for Barrin Industries. He tells her he may not get the $10,000 the estate owes him. The two leave, have dinner and some drinks, and go to her East Side apartment. They kiss, and he returns to Lee's place. When Lee, scared, says some men are watching his movements, Dog calls Chet and demands that surveillance cease.

Hunter, who recalls that he knew Sharon's father, has Willis, his limousine chauffeur, drive Dog, Sharon, and himself to the Barrin family mansion at Grand Sita. Though unexpected, the three find Dog's cousins—Alfred, Dennison, Lucella, Pam, and Veda—and Pam's chortling husband there. The upshot of the explanation by Hunter of Dog's stepfather's will: Dog will lose all if Alfred, who domineers the others, can prove immorality in Dog's past; if Alfred insists on trying (which he does), Dog can seek evidence of immorality in his cousins' past, with a three-month time limit; if both sides find such evidence, Dog inherits all. Hunter has engaged rooms at a local inn; he and Willis retire, and Dog drives Sharon in the limousine to Mondo Beach, nearby, where they skinny-dip, then lie partially nude until morning. McMillan, with an option to buy Barrin family land at Mondo Beach, brings Sergeant Bennie Sachs to press trespassing charges, until Dog explains the beach is Barrin family property.

Dog and Sharon see Hunter at the inn. Dog gives a check for $250,000 for the beach land to Hunter, who is handling the sale, but tells him to inform the cousins, who must then return McMillan's $50,000 option. Willis drives to New York, drops Hunter at his office, garages the car, and leaves. Dog sees they are followed by Markham, a gunman, and Bridey-the-Greek, an icepick killer—Old World killers he knows were hired by The Turk to kill him. Leaving Sharon in the limo, he separately lures Markham and Bridey to the garage men's room, and mutilates Markham's head and Bridey's face and genitals. Back at Lee's apartment, Dog finds his wardrobe delivered (with a coded message), learns by phone from DeVecchio that Farnsworth Aviation wants to subcontract a gadget to Barrin Industries and that McMillan is a corporate raider. Dog calls Hunter, asks him to tell the cousins that the beach land was sold to Ave Higgins, Inc., backed by a long-lost Barrin relative, but not that Dog owns the dummy corporation. Dog adds that Hunter, now his attorney, will receive a package soon, then illegally purchases a .45, with accoutrements.

Dog joins Lee and Rose at a West 47th Street restaurant, and they discuss the near-identity of sex and murder thrills. (Francois Verdun, in *The Last Cop Out*, will agree that murder is orgasmic.) Lagen enters and tells Dog he is digging into his past but has discovered nothing untoward. Dog seems menacing, and Lee squirms. When the Weller-Fabray manager relays a warning to Dog from their European agents, Dog says he is retired and wants to stay retired. At Lee's place, Dog greets two police officers, who show him nauseating photos of Markham and Bridey; Dog says he has witnesses to account for his time. Alone with Lee, Dog says he mangled the two in those photos.

At 3:00 A.M. Linden orders Dog to a meeting at the Automat. When he finds Linden there with two gunmen, Dog listens to Linden's warnings, threatens all three with his .45, and leaves to drive Sharon to Linton, her home town, where the Barrin factory is located near Mondo Beach. They stop at a rundown club owned by old Hiram Tod, who remembers Dog and his feisty parents. Tod tells Dog that authorities, including Bennie Sachs, hushed up a sex scandal involving Alfred. While Sharon checks for gossip about Alfred from Tod's niece, Louise, a waitress at the local country club, Dog visits Sachs, who dislikes McMillan and all the Barrins and therefore tells Dog that Alfred bribed his way out of the scandal. Sharon says Louise recalled a Barrin factory explosion just before in which an engineer named Stanley Cramer was slugged. Dog and Sharon visit Cramer, who remembers her parents fondly. He recalls that the explosion destroyed a safe containing old papers. Dog and Sharon drive to her vacant old homestead, undress revealingly, and inactively sleep in her old bed.

Late next morning Dog enters Lee's apartment, finds him slugged, tied, and weighted down in the bath tub with a trickle from the faucet about to drown him. Dog revives him, has him dress, and welcomes the police he knows the would-be killers would have alerted. After getting rid of them, he asks Lee to describe his assailants. That evening, Dog attends a bash Cable Howard Productions throws to celebrate merging with Gentry and starting plans to produce a film based on *Fruits of Labor,* a nineteenth-century sex novel. Many guests are there. Lagen tries to needle Dog about Barrin family scandals. McMillan, annoyed at losing the land deal, is there with Sheila, his tall, sinuous wife, who introduces herself to Dog and tells him McMillan should retire with their sufficient fortune. Mona the columnist asks Dog for some usable gossip and tells him that Sheila's uncompromising frigidity has made her husband commercially ruthless.

The Weller-Fabray agent phones Dog: Heroin is heading from Marseilles to the United States; The Turk knows about Markham and Bridey and is sending another killer after Dog; from Lee's description, one of his assailants is Arnold Bell of Belgium. Hunter tells Dog that Markham and Bridey, both hospitalized, paid the bill and checked out, and that Tobano had them followed. Dog visits Tobano, has him make a phone call to an evidently potent office for clearance, and learns where Markham and Bridey are separately staying. During lunch,

Dog gives Hunter a check and tells him to buy him a certain house and have it restored as it used to be. Hunter tells Dog this: Alfred and Dennison think a relative has bought the Mondo Beach property; they sought wealthy marriages but failed; they need money to complete contracts their factory has accepted for special products; McMillan would like to grab the factory. Dog visits DeVecchio, reveals part of his mission, and induces the terrified fellow to identify some mob figures to help him intercept the Marseilles heroin shipment. Dog dines with Sharon, Cable, and Gentry at a restaurant and watches Sharon blackmail Cable into shooting much of *Fruits of Labor* in Linton; otherwise Gentry wouldn't finance the film.

Dog goes to the hotel where Markham roomed and finds him shot dead. He alerts Tobano, who soon finds Bridey murdered. The Turk's hit men failed and paid the price. Dog meets Lee for breakfast but answers few questions. Dog and DeVecchio, in the latter's office, watch a television report connecting the murders with The Turk. DeVecchio says he has been checking, wonders if Dog is El Lobo, is told no, tells Dog the Guido brothers would provide leads to mob members expecting the heroin from Marseilles, asks if Dog were implicated in the black market in Europe, and is told yes.

Dog orders agents Hobis and The Chopper to guard Lee and Rose.

The next dawn finds Dog driving a rented car to Linton for breakfast. He ponders a puzzling note Lee said the doorman gave him for Dog. It concerns "Ferris" and "655." Dog learns Barrin Industries is hiring; calls on Pam and Veda (Lucella is away drunk); terrifies them by revealing his knowledge of their sexual escapades and by saying he owns Barrin Industries and they must vote as he demands; and forces them to undress in front of Harvey, the amused butler, as revenge for his being flogged as a child because they lied about him. Dog calls Sheila from Tod's; when she sashays in, he indulges in frivolous sex talk, then drives off with her to the beach, where they perform muscular love. She warns him that McMillan will want revenge. Alone again, Dog calls Hobis and The Chopper, learns that word has it Dog has been fingered as the recipient of the Marseilles heroin, gets a message Cramer wants to see him soon, goes to the five cousins' mansion and pleases all with news that Linton is to be the scene of a movie shoot, and evades a would-be assassin when Harvey alerts him and he drives away by a rear road. As dawn breaks, Dog meets Tobano, who says he hates drug traffickers. He goes to Lee's apartment, packs, and heads for a hotel and some sleep.

Lagen's latest column details news about the filming of *Fruits of Labor* at Linton, northeast of New York. DeVecchio informs Dog that McMillan may have enough proxies to take over Barrin Industries. A frightened agent tells Dog the syndicate thinks Dog has the missing heroin, demands it, or will kill him. At a party for movie people in Cable's penthouse, Dog meets Mona; they discuss McMillan's commercial ambitions and, of course, sex. Suddenly, after Dog remembers aerial combat, he and Sharon are together. She tells him her long-time fiancé, whose ring she fingers, was reported missing in action during the war. She undresses; Dog scrutinizes her body parts, then leaves. On deserted, rainy streets, Dog senses an enemy gunman (identified as one who tried to drown Lee), wounds him, cannot make him talk, admits he killed El Lobo and is the Dog, and blasts the gunman's stomach. Dog stays in the old Mondo Beach house where he was conceived. At sunrise, on the beach, Marvin Gates, Pam's henpecked husband, appears, wants to help Dog, tells him Alfred and Dennison are homosexuals, and leaves. Dog visits Cramer, who is playing cards with Juke and Stoney, two retired factory workers. They recall that the factory explosion was followed by someone trying to jimmy a new safe containing papers about experimental alloys. Leaving them to discuss former erections, Dog visits Sachs, who tells him four prostitutes were beaten up a few years ago in Linton but didn't press charges. By phone Hunter says the man Dog killed was a French criminal in the United States illegally. Hunter agrees to represent Dog at the family stockholders' meeting.

Cable moves his company to Linton and gives a party at a hotel. Dog hires Rose to seduce Alfred and others and film the action. A hired waiter's wrong nameplate reads "Ferris." The real Ferris is elsewhere. Dog suddenly recalls 655 as the number of a post office box used for communications. Dog visits Lucy Longstreet, a retired brothel madam, and Beth, her black assistant. Lucy mentions the immorality of Dennison and Alfred, the latter more dangerous, and adds she knows Sharon's fiancé but won't name him. Returning to the hotel party, Dog observes the drinking and dancing, and also Hunter and McMillan with legal papers. Sheila McMillan gets Dog to drive her to her nearby inn. Attacked by gunmen, Dog kills all three—by head shot, car wheels, and neck chop. He takes Sheila, smiling in total shock, to his family beach house, undresses and fingers her tenderly, and lets her sleep in his bed.

The morning paper theorizes incorrectly about the killings. Dog, who has already replaced his .45 barrel, calls Chet and orders him to have agents sanitize his rented car instantly. Over lunch, Rose tells Dog nothing much happened last night with Dennison but she'll see him again. Sachs fires Dog's .45 into a toilet tank but naturally will find an innocent round. Dog buys secret information from Beth.

(Sheila McMillan, quiet in Dog's bed, concludes that Dog knows her having been repeatedly raped has left her unable to meet her sex-eager husband's needs.)

Dog returns, and at Sheila's request they shower, inspect each other, and make multipostured love, therapeutic for her.

Rain delays the film shoot. Dog suddenly remembers Ferris, a canny agent from 1948 named "Ferris" Weal. McMillan wins the stockholders' vote and plans to deplete Barrin Industries by antilabor tactics. Dog gives Hunter a scrawled will. Hobis and The Chopper, disguised as movie-crew workers, warn Dog of danger. Lagen gets Dog and Sharon into his Cadillac and gloats that his research confirms the following: Dog in England in 1946 loaned money to a fellow pilot named Roland Holland, who got rich and bankrolled Dog, who moved from black-marketeering to drugs to murder, and who will soon be murdered. Dog's nods scare Sharon, who, nonetheless, when they are alone says she profoundly loves only Dog.

Rose, in anguish, tells Dog about photos Elliot Embler took proving nearly impotent Dennison's sexual masochism with her. Dog tells her Lee still needs and will marry her. Dog tells Sharon to check recent employees over age seventy. He obtains the photos, drives to Lucy's, is warned in time by her to capture three thugs who followed him from Cramer's place. They tie them up, and Lucy will tell the cops she and her girls caught them trying to rob them. One girl gives Dog a letter from Stoney of possible blackmailing value. At the Barrin factory, Dog finds Sharon. The address of one aging employee leads Dog, with Sharon, to long-lost Ferris, who says he is interested in anti-pollution programs, warns Dog he is now the enemy's target, calls Bell uniquely dangerous, and gives Dog the missing heroin in a casket in Ferris's truck. Sharon registers her disgust. Dog drives Ferris's loaded truck, forces Chet's address on Long Island from the Weller-Fabray manager, drives there, shows Chet (who has been ordering Dog's execution) and a big cop named Vince the heroin casket, leaves it with Vince, takes Vince's car, and drives off with Sharon. Dog's car, left at Ferris's, explodes when a kid tries to steal it. Hobis tells Dog that European agents report Le Fleur shot The Turk and was killed by a Le Fleur enemy. Dog tells Hobis about the casket.

Dog attends the Barrin family meeting. Hunter pays Dog $10,000 in presumably worthless stock. Alfred owns Grand Sita. Dennis has Mondo Beach. McMillan owns the factory. Dennison reveals pornographic photos of Dog and Sheila. When Dennison insults Dog's mother, Dog smashes Dennison's teeth and tears off one of his ears. Pam wants to call a doctor. Marvin confesses he took the photos. Dog is indifferent. Veda vomits and faints. Driving off, Dog and Hunter are followed by two Volkswagens.

Barrin Industries cannot handle Farnsworth's work, which will be done at McMillan's other factories. Sachs identifies the exploded car as Dog's. McMillan actually thanks Dog for helping Sheila get over her sexual hang-ups, says he has called off killers he hired to get Dog, presents him with a deed to the presumably useless Barrin factory, and leaves. Cramer and other old fogies, accompanied by Sharon, enter and show Dog plans, just located, for the antigravity device, which will prove invaluable. Bell fires a .22 bullet near Dog's head, as one professional's challenge to another. Dog drives Sharon in her car to her abandoned childhood house, which Hunter caused to be restored on Dog's orders. Upstairs, she disrobes, gets him to do so also, feels him, tells him she is aware that the "Vince" in possession of the heroin is a policeman (he is Sergeant Vince Tobano), and listens to Dog: Holland enriched Dog, who became an undercover agent in the black market, then the international drug scene; Chet will be criticized for doubting all this. Sharon says her little green engagement ring was one Dog himself gave her when she was ten and he left Linton. They are making love when Bell enters, stupidly taunts Dog instead of firing quickly, and is defaced by Dog's under-the-pillow .45.

"The Bastard Bannerman" has plot elements redacted in *The Erection Set*. *The Erection Set*, Spillane's longest novel, interestingly experiments with multiple first-person narrators, the most voluble being Dog Kelly. The novel has three intertwined plots: Dog wants to clean up the drug traffic; Dog wants revenge on the Barrin clan; Sharon wants Dog. Sex, money, and killing are thus also linked. Action proceeds at breakneck speed, and time is handled here as excitingly—and as unrealistically—as Shakespeare handles it in *Othello*. The key word in Spillane's title is functional. Nonsexual action can usually be counted upon to give way to sexual action when a good erection develops. The f-word is used thirty-six times, to accompany patches of milder, previously used vulgarities. (*The Last Cop Out* will outdo *The Erection Set* in this matter, until the word becomes a kind of mantra.) Spillane's overuse of breast limning is predictable by 1972, but his sudden fixation on feminine pubic hair is new and cheap (and briefly touched on again in *The Last Cop Out*). Rumor has it that Spillane here sought to emulate such other sex-conscious best-selling authors as Harold Robbins and Irving Wallace. The movie title *Fruits of Labor* may hint at Spillane's abiding aversion to homosexuality. Images in *The Erection Set* are of varied effectiveness: Sheila McMillan's smile is charmingly depicted as slow like the sun rising; Tod's loss of sexual urge is startlingly like a pilot light gone out; a mixed, one-sentence image, to be rejected, is the night compared to a blanket cutting one's vision like a "cheesy knife" and simultaneously muting the city's lion roar punctuated by taxi horns. Once again, rain in Spillane treats the city ambivalently. Rain is New York's mouthwash, to be gargled and spat down the gutter; yet rain can never cleanse the skin of the city's buildings. Spillane makes good use of his experiences with movie-wise people. Spillane's second wife, Sherri Molinou, posed for the cover of *The Erection Set*. Its first paperbound edition (New American Library, 1972) is rendered unattractive by a few dozen typos as well as many punctuation and grammatical gaffs.

ERLICH, GERALD. In *The Girl Hunters*, he was a wartime double-agent, who spied with and against Richie Cole and Velda, among others, changed his name to Rudolph Civac, married Marta Singleton (*see* Civac, Marta Singleton), and was killed by Gorlin.

ERNIE. In *The Killing Man*, Mike Hammer and Captain Pat Chambers meet at Ernie's Little Place for a beer and a chat.

ESCALANTE, MARIA. In *The Killing Man*, she is the Mexican cleaning lady at the building in which Mike has his office. She describes Anthony DiCica's killer.

ESCALANTE, TOMAS ("SPANISH TOM"). In "Me, Hood!," he and Alfredo Lias are sailors involved in stealing and selling heroin. Escalante is stabbed to death in the Battery. Why would Spillane nickname Escalante "Spanish Tom" when he was from Lisbon?

ETCHING, STAN. In "Me, Hood,!" he and his brother, Stash Etching, gained a reputation for killing Fletcher. Ryan outwits the two when they try to kill him. Ryan gutshoots Stan.

ETCHING, STASH. In "Me, Hood,!" he drives Ryan, held by his brother Stan Etching in the back seat, for what they plan to be Ryan's last ride. Ryan disarms Stan, shoots him, and orders both brothers out of the car.

EVANS. In *Day of the Guns,* he operates a phone in Newark for Toomey and thus provides Mann with information.

EVANS, GLORIA. In "Kick It or Kill!," she was lured into drugs, dirty dancing, and prostitution by Simpson, is permanently ruined, and remains defiant when Dari Dahl tries to help her. Sonny Holmes remains her loyal boyfriend.

EVELLO, CARL. In *Kiss Me, Deadly,* he is an important Mafia figure. His boss is Dr. Martin Soberin. Evello's associates include Al Affia and William Mist. Carl's half-sister is Michael Friday. When he leads some thugs to squeeze Mike Hammer for information, Mike chokes him unconscious, lets the thugs think Evello is Mike, and one of them kills Evello.

"EVERYBODY'S WATCHING ME" (1953). Short story. (Characters: Balco, Boyle, Phil Carboy, Tony Briggs, Jack Cooley, Birdie Cullen, Bucky Edwards, Finney, Captain Gerot, Detective Sergeant Gonzales, Gordon, Gulley, Sling Herman, Johnny, Lou, Morgan, Nick, Patty, Mark Renzo, Rocco, Mrs. Stacey, Tommy, Helen Troy, Vetter, Webber.) The narrator, calling himself Joe Boyle, strengthens himself for eighteen months working in a corrupt, drug-riddled town by pushing carts filled with scrap metal. He pits Gulley, Mark Renzo, and Phil Carboy, rival drug dealers, against one another. He meets and makes love with Helen Troy, who has been working for Renzo ever since her former lover Jack Cooley, another drug dealer, was killed. A shadowy figure named Vetter both frightens criminals and puzzles police, through his reputation as a killer. After fights at Renzo's place, in town, and at a pier, many thugs are dead, Helen escapes, and Joe reveals that he is Vetter. The first installment of "Everybody's Watching Me" appeared in the initial number of *Manhunt,* the popular pulp that succeeded *Black Mask;* the story was republished as "I Came to Kill You" (1964).

F

FALLON. In "The Gold Fever Tapes," he is allegedly a disgraced policeman sent to prison but only to get information on the theft of 800 pounds of gold. Once out, Fallon becomes a reporter, kills would-be killer Arthur Littleworth, gets help (and love) from Cheryl, leads to Reading's exposure, and solves the case. Rare among Spillane heroes, Fallon does not smoke.

FALLON, CAT. In "The Flier," he flew a Mustang P-51 in Europe during World War II, later was a failed crop-duster with his wartime buddy Tucker Stacy, and inherited Stacy's estate in Celada, Florida, after Stacy was murdered because of anti-Castro activities. While investigating, Cat calls upon friends old and new to help him; resists the sexiness of Lois Hays and Sharon Ortez; bombs the *Leona,* loaded with Russian nuclear warheads and headed for the Panama Canal to embarrass the United States; returns to Celada; and escapes Lois's murderous treachery. Macho Cat says that Sharon, a girl, shouldn't have been sent to do a man's job, and tells Lois that fornication is "a functional necessity that comes at my own time and choosing."

FALLON, CHARLIE. In *The Big Kill,* he was an important racketeer who liked pretty actresses, had Toady Link get him photographs of them, womanized and developed heart trouble, and died in 1940, ten years ago. Mike Hammer tardily discovers that when Fallon was threatened by his associates, Lou Grindle and Ed Teen, he had Toady make microfilms incriminating the pair but by mistake mailed them not to Robert, the D.A. then, but to Marsha Lee, an actress he liked. Fallon's mistress, Georgia Lucas, was pressured into causing his death by stealing his nitroglycerin tablets.

FARMER, ARLEEN. In "The Veiled Woman." *See* Fullerton, Ann.

FARNSWORTH. In *The Erection Set,* he heads Farnsworth Aviation, which has contracts with the Barrin family factory.

FAT JOHN. In *Bloody Sunrise,* he runs a sleazy place. Tiger Mann bribes him to use it as a hideout. Fat John is killed by two Soviet agents when Tiger hides Sonia Dutko there.

FAT MARY. In "Killer Mine," she works at Tony's Pizza, gives Lieutenant Joe Scanlon information about René Mills, and is probably Tony's wife.

FATER, WILL. In "Killer Mine," he is a gunman, associates with Benny Loefert, shoots at Lieutenant Joe Scanlon, and falls from a roof to his death.

FEATHERS, HANK. In "The Bastard Bannerman," he was a wild friend of Cat Cay Bannerman's father, Max Bannerman. Now a reporter in Culver City, he helps Cat.

FELLS, GARY. In *The Killing Man,* he and Harry Bern, ex–CIA agents turned rogues and working for Libya, are ordered to kill Penta. Either Fells or Bern kills Richard Smiley while tracking Penta, who kills both of them.

FERGUSON, LEWIS. In *The Killing Man,* he is a cooperative CIA agent assigned to work under Bennett Bradley. Ferguson heads the raid after the trailer containing cocaine has been located. He knows the region, near Kingston and Phoenica, New York, since he has access to a cabin nearby. Spillane once lived in Newburgh, New York, forty or so miles south.

FERRO, MACK. In *The Last Cop Out,* he and his cousin Marty Stackler are ordered by Richard Case to capture Shatzi Heinkle. Shatzi kills Marty and Case, and mortally wounds Mack, who kills him.

FIELDS. In *I, the Jury,* Charlotte Manning names him as the person she was with at the moment Myrna Devlin was murdered. Not so.

FINERO. In *Survival . . . Zero!,* his is the Steak House where Mike Hammer finds Woodring Ballinger and, later, Heidi Anders.

FINGERS, WILLIE. In *The Snake,* Sonny Motley names him to Mike Hammer as a member of his old mob. Fingers is still in prison in Atlanta.

FINLAY, TEDDY. In *Survival . . . Zero!,* he is a State Department official working under Robert Crane.

FINNEY. In "Everybody's Watching Me," he works at Mark Renzo's Hideaway Club.

FINNEY, MRS. In "Kick It or Kill!," she runs a Pinewood rooming house that doubles as a summertime brothel. She associates with Gloria Evans.

FISH. In *The By-Pass Control. See* Frank, Henri.

FISHER, GLENN. In *The Big Kill*, he and Arthur Cole were lookouts when William Decker went on his safe-cracking assignment. The two act as private detectives, follow Mel Hooker, are beaten up by Mike Hammer, leave New York for Philadelphia, and are shot to death by the police there.

FISHER, MISS. In *The Last Cop Out*, she was Artie Meeker's teacher long ago. When he draws a map for Papa Menes, Meeker feels that his old teacher would have been proud of him.

FLEMING, MORRIS. In *The Girl Hunters*, he is the old night watchman at Mike's office building. Gorlin kills him.

FLETCHER. In "Me, Hood!," he is named as murdered in Canarsie by Stan Etching and his brother, Stash Etching.

FLETCHER, CLEMENT ("FLETCH"). In *Bloody Sunrise*, he is an old friend of Tiger Mann, who rescued him during a military operation in Panama. Fletcher, in his mid-fifties, is now a sailor off the *Maitland*. His suspicions that Soviet agents were hiding an uranium bomb aboard cause him to be murdered by drowning.

"THE FLIER" (1964). Short story. (Characters: Manuel Alvada, Barrett, Smitty Bones, Cable, George Clinton, Joe Conway, Big Jack Crane, Cristy, Dement, Dertelli, Sam Devin, DeWitt, Cat Fallon, Gonzeles, Lois Hays, Jones, Juan, Duncan Knight, Lerner, Dominick Lolla, Nick Mahoney, Andro Marcel, Captain Rob Olsen, Sharon Ortez, Felix Ramsey, Del Reed, Peter Claude Satworthy, Smith, Tucker Stacy, Whitey Thompson, Charlie Traub, Lieutenant Trusky, Slim Upgate, Verdo.)

Cat Fallon, the narrator, is an aviator, first as a combat pilot in World War II and later as a failed crop-duster with an old buddy, Tucker ("Tuck") Stacy. Later, Stacy owned and developed the Capital K airport, in Celeda, near Miami, died mysteriously in an over-water flight, and willed everything to Cat. Cat flies his P-51 Mustang to Celeda to check into matters. Lieutenant Trusky, a Celada police officer, and Del Reed, a state government attorney, find Cat at a bar, say they are investigating Stacy's contacts, but learn little from them.

Lois Hays, whom Cat remembers as a reporter, finds him in his hotel room, calls herself Karen Morgan now, and says she is a reporter investigating Cat. She says Tuck crashed at sea in mild weather. She undresses in a ploy to gain information from Cat, but he spurns her with rude comments about his sexual prowess.

At the airport, Cat checks with Charlie Traub, Tuck's chief mechanic, and Sam Devin, Tuck's attorney. Sam produces a cryptic note from Tuck, telling him to recall "Verdo and Cristy" and not to choke on a banana. When Cat asks whether Tuck was involved with anti-Castro elements in Miami, Traub and Devin merely say Tuck was honest. Concluding that Tuck wanted to involve him in some mission, Cat checks into Tuck's motel room at his airport complex, where he is confronted by Sharon Ortez with a .38. She orders him to let her associates examine Tuck's papers. Cat disarms, undresses, and ejects her.

Next morning Cat gives Trusky and Reed permission to scrutinize Tuck's papers at the airport. They suspect Tuck of having Cuban connections—very dangerous in these politically sensitive times. Lois enters. Reed, who says he knew her earlier, leaves with Trusky. Lois mentions bananas puzzlingly. Cat returns to his room, is knocked unconscious, comes to bound and gagged, and is queried by their leader—called Marcel by one of his two thugs. They found Tuck's note. Who are Verdo and Cristy? Cat doesn't know. They sap him again and depart.

Sharon Ortez awakens Cat, turns apprehensive when he mentions the assailants' concern about bananas, warns him, and vanishes. Back at the airport, Traub confesses to Cat that Tuck was involved with anti-Castro personnel. Cat calls George Clinton, a knowledgeable contact in Celeda recommended by an influential friend, learns that Andro Marcel distributes drugs from Red China into the United States, and asks him to check on Tuck's Cuban connection. Cat finds Lois at their hotel, mentions bananas to her, gets an army buddy named Jack Conway in New Jersey on the phone, and asks him to try to identify Verdo and Cristy. Cat again calls Clinton, who has just learned that Tuck flew over Cuba and dropped weapons and ammo to anti-Castro forces, and, more significantly, was involved politically.

Despite the approach of a Caribbean hurricane designated Ingrid, Cat flies his P-51, with Lois along, to Miami, where he gets information on Tuck from a reporter named DeWitt, a search pilot named Captain Rob Olsen, and a fisherman named Peter Claude Satworthy. Reed got Cat's flight plan, followed Cat, and brings along two federal agents, Jones and Smith. It seems that Tuck and an anti-Castro engineer named Gonzales learned that Castro and the Russians offloaded nuclear warheads from Russian vessels (after the 1962 Cuban Crisis) and placed them on a boat with the code name *Banana,* poised to do damage somewhere. On his way back to Florida, Tuck's sabotaged plane was blown up. Gonzales was found strangled. To gain information, Smith sticks with Cat in a hotel room adjoining Lois's. Marcel enters, shoots Smith dead, and drugs Cat.

Cat comes to in a room near water, naked and tortured by Marcel and his two bullies. After electric-shock treatments to his testicles, Cat suddenly recalls that "Verdo and Cristy" was a code signal Tuck and Cat used, and meaning "record this message." In agony, Cat would reveal this secret, but Sharon, having followed Marcel, enters and shoots his three torturers dead, admires his nude body, then unbinds him. He phones Traub to check Tuck's "Verdo and Cristy" tapes, saved at the airport. Tuck's message is this: *Banana,* really a Liberty ship named *Leona,* is heading for the Panama Canal, to be exploded there; the Communists will exploit this tragedy as an American plot to force Central American countries to need increased American military presence against indigenous anticapitalist revolutions. Cat gets a munitions friend of Clinton's to load two demolition bombs under his P-51 wings, calls Jones to apprise him of everything, including Smith's death and his dead killers' location, and learns *Leona's* coordinates from Jones. Sharon kisses Cat volcanically for a quick take-off.

Cat finds the *Leona* and drops both bombs. One loosens her bottom plates, and she sinks and explodes underwater. Cat returns to the Capital K airport, almost deserted because of Ingrid. He lands but leaves his coughing engines on, in case. Sharon rushes up for an embrace and calls him "big one." Lois appears, weapon leveled. She was in league with Marcel and the other Castro agents, gloats about tomorrow's news report of Cat's insane bombing of an innocent Cuban vessel, but before she can shoot both Cat and Sharon—in heroic self-defense, she says—backs into the P-51 propeller and becomes a crimson cloud in Ingrid's wind.

"The Flier," initially titled "Hot Cat," was reprinted in *The Flier,* which included "The Seven Year Kill" and which was an immensely popular Corgi (London) paperback.

FLO. In *Bloody Sunrise,* her name is signed as the author of a letter addressed to William Copely breaking off their engagement. This letter is put in his hand by Soviet agents, who then stage his "suicide."

FLO. In *My Gun Is Quick,* she is mentioned as the wife of Nat, a jeweler friend of Mike Hammer's.

FLOOD. In *The Death Dealers,* he owns Flood's Warehouse, next to which litchi nuts are sold. Tiger Mann uses this lead to find Malcolm Turos.

FLORES, DIEGO ("DAGO"). In "Me, Hood!," he is a runner for Sid Solomon. Ryan did Flores a favor once; so he warns Ryan that Stan and Stash Etching are gunning for him.

FLORIO, MANUEL. In *The Killing Man,* he owns the Pompeii Bar on 6th Avenue and can vouch for the accuracy of Mike's alibi when he is suspected of killing Anthony DiCica.

FLY. In "Return of the Hood," he is a miserable drug addict working for Primo Stipetto. Fly befriended Lisa Williams, whom Primo abuses. When Fly captures but cannot hold Ryan, Primo kills him.

FLYNN. In *Vengeance Is Mine!,* he is a bartender working at a bar around the corner from Mike Hammer's apartment building. Mike and Captain Pat Chambers meet there.

FORBES. In "The Bastard Bannerman," he is a man who Sidney LaMont tells Cat Cay Bannerman can vouch for LaMont's integrity.

FORBES. In *The Erection Set,* Dog Kelly embarrasses Veda Barrin by reminding her of her long-ago lesbian relationship with a governess working at the Forbes estate.

FORBES, CHARLIE. In *The Body Lovers,* he was the photographer that took the secret picture of Belar Ris and Naku Em Abor.

FORCE, CHARLES ("CHARLIE"). In *The Snake,* he is the talented young New York D.A. He dislikes Mike, who warns him a few times. Ultimately Force proves cooperative.

FOREMAN. In *Kiss Me, Deadly,* he is a Mafia thug. When he and others charge Mike Hammer, Mike blinds Foreman. Foreman's cohorts then evidently kill Foreman when he is no longer useful.

FOREMAN, BALDIE. In *The Last Cop Out,* he and Vito Bartoldi work for Leon Bray, check on Bray, find him dead with others, and are soon blown up themselves.

FOUNTAIN. In *Bloody Sunrise,* he runs a lingerie-catalog business in the Tomlinson Building. Spaad Helo uses the office as a communication center. Sonia's ordering lingerie there alerts Tiger Mann.

FRANCIE. In "I'll Die Tomorrow," she was one of Rudolph Lees's victims, whom he bought to torture by biting.

FRANCIS ("FRAN"). In "Together We Kill," she was Joe's temporary girlfriend but never a match for unforgettable Claire.

FRANK, HENRI. In *The By-Pass Control,* he is a Soviet agent, born in Austria, age fifty-two. He was rejected for employment by Belt-Aire Electrics as unstable. He tries to kill Claude Boster, kills Beezo McCauley, rigs a car bomb to kill Tiger Mann, but when Tiger rewires it is killed by it. At one point Frank is called Fish.

FRED. In "The Bastard Bannerman," he is a police sergeant whom Lieutenant Travers orders to seize Cat Cay Bannerman's .45.

FRIDAY, MICHAEL. In *Kiss Me, Deadly,* she is Carl Evello's half-sister, living in luxury on his ill-gotten gains. Mike Hammer asks her to help him crack the drug-smuggling ring by bravely providing Carl's phone records. She does so and then disappears from the action. Mike is fixated on her warm, wet, sensual mouth.

FUCHIE. In "Killer Mine," Lieutenant Joe Scanlon tore off Fuchie's goatee and warns Al Reese to leave Paula Lees alone or he will injure Reese too— by tearing off his ears.

FUCIA, RAUL. In *The Erection Set,* Sharon Cass threatens to castrate this oily adventurer when he offers sexual dalliance.

FUCILLA, JUAN. In *The Delta Factor,* he is Rosa Lee's cousin, in his late forties. Fucilla is the dishonest head guard at the Rose Castle. Morgan tempts him with a supposed shipment of heroin and kills him, along with his superior, Captain Romero.

FULLERTON, ANN. In "The Veiled Woman," this beautiful blonde, about twenty-five or -six years old, works for the Communists, tries to obtain Karl Terris's cosmic-energy secrets, but through love for Terris kills her associate, Sergi Porkov, and makes love with Terris. He then kills her (à la Mike Hammer: gunshot in belly). She uses the alias Arleen Farmer. Karl calls her Sadie for no known reason.

FULLERTON, ERIC. In "The Veiled Woman," he is Ann Fullerton's father.

FULLERTON, MRS. ERIC. In "The Veiled Woman," she is Ann Fullerton's mother. She believes Ann was killed in a warehouse fire and says so when Karl Terris phones her.

G

GABIN. In *Survival . . . Zero!,* Mike Hammer has duplicates of Beaver's photograph made at Gabin's Film Service.

GABLE, HERMAN. In *My Gun Is Quick,* he is a man who paid Mike Hammer $2,500 for finding his valuable lost manuscript. The task took Mike forty-eight tiring hours.

GAETANO. In *Black Alley,* members of this Mafia family were waiting, according to Mike Hammer, to gun for rival Pontis in the crime-family feud on the waterfront.

GAGE, POPEYE. In "The Bastard Bannerman," he is a Syndicate enforcer who accompanies Carl Matteau and batters Cat Cay Bannerman. Cat and Hank Feathers render Popeye harmless by preventing him from getting his necessary heroin fix.

GALLAGHER, LIEUTENANT DICK. In *The Death Dealers,* he is an honest policeman who helps Tiger Mann gain access to Teish El Abin. In return, Tiger gives Gallagher photographs of Malcolm Turos to circulate.

GALLO. In *The Last Cop Out,* this is the name of a crime family engaged in toppling former syndicate leaders from power.

GARCIA. In "The Seven Year Kill," he is a policeman under Johnny's command in Phoenix and works with Aldridge.

GARDINER, HAVIS. In *The Long Wait,* he is Lyncastle's bank president. He embezzled, cast blame on John McBride, bankrolled Lenny Servo, was a murderer, and is shot dead by McBride.

GARDNER, HY (1908–1989). Author and radio and television host. Gardner was born in New York City, attended Columbia University, served in the U.S. Army during World War II (1942-1945), and rose to the rank of major. He wrote gossip columns for the *New York Herald Tribune* (1951-1966), thereafter syndicated them into the 1980s, and contributed to periodicals. He hosted radio and television programs, was a filmmaker and actor, and appeared in *The Girl Hunters* (1963), based on Spillane's 1962 novel of that name. Gardner's books include *Champagne Before Breakfast* (1954), *So What Else Is New!* (1959), *Tales Out of Night School* (1959), *Hy Gardner's Off-Beat Guide to New York* (1964), and with his wife, Marilyn Gardner, *Glad You Asked That* (1976). Gardner retired to Miami, Florida, where he died. Spillane knew and liked Gardner and his wife, Marilyn Gardner. He put Hy in several novels. In *The Girl Hunters,* Hy appears as a captain in special forces during the war. He is now a *Trib* reporter in New York, appears on television, and helps Mike Hammer with information. In *The Snake,* Hy helps Mike by providing information about Black Conley and Sonny Motley. In *The Body Lovers,* Hy gives Mike what information he can. His greatest service is telling Mike the phone number of Belar Ris, whose mansion Mike can therefore blow up. In *Survival . . . Zero!,* Mike mentions that Hy has sensibly left New York.

Bibliography: Obituary in *New York Times,* June 19, 1989; Sam Riley, *Biographical Dictionary of American Newspaper Columnists* (Westport, Conn.: Greenwood Press, 1995).

GARDNER, MARILYN. Author. She was the wife of Hy Gardner (1908-1989), writer and entertainer, and wrote *Glad You Asked That* (1976) with him. Spillane knew both Hy and Marilyn Gardner, and put Marilyn in one novel. In *The Girl Hunters,* she is Hy Gardner's pretty wife. In Hy's office, she hugs Mike pleasantly.

GARFIELD. In *The Erection Set,* Dog Kelly gets word from Betterton and Strauss in London that Dog successfully trapped Garfield and Greco, both presumably in Europe. Hence the two are out of action.

GATES. In "The Seven Year Kill," Phil Rocca remembers him as a spineless editor who refused, through fear, to publish Rocca's exposé of criminal activities in New York City.

GATES, MARVIN. In *The Erection Set,* he is Pam Barrin Gates's alcoholic, henpecked husband. He tries to help and also hurt Dog Kelly, who nonchalantly ignores him.

GATES, PAM BARRIN. In *The Erection Set,* she is Dog Kelly's cousin, whom he despises.

GATES, THEODORE ("TEDDY"). In *The Body Lovers,* he is a photographer for fashion magazines. Dulcie McInnes tells Mike that Teddy photographed Greta Service. Dulcie's betrayal of Teddy leads to his disappearance and indirectly to his suicide.

GELLIE, BOB. In *Kiss Me, Deadly,* he is an expert auto mechanic who finds two explosive devices in the new car that Mafia representatives offered Mike Hammer. Later, some thugs beat Gellie up, but he doesn't talk and will recover.

GENTRY, HELEN. In "Killer Mine," she was pursued by René Mills once he had money.

GENTRY, WALT. In *The Erection Set,* this man, whose full name is Walt Gentry III, met Dog Kelly in the army, is a rich bachelor, and gently lusts for Sharon Cass. Dog meets her at a party hosted by Gentry. Gentry agrees to bankroll S. C. Cable's movie production of *Fruits of Labor.*

GEORG. In *The Ship That Never Was,* he is an inhabitant of Montique Island.

GEORGE. In *The Girl Hunters,* he was one of Mike's war buddies.

GEORGE. In *One Lonely Night,* he is a policeman who mans the radio. He tells Mike Hammer that Paula Riis phoned for police protection, which arrived too late.

GEORGE. In *The Snake,* he works at the Blue Ribbon on 44th Street and loans Mike fifty dollars so he can rent a car and drive to Black Conley's supposed hideout. In *Bloody Sunrise,* George handles messages from Charlie Corbinet to Tiger Mann. In *The Death Dealers,* Tiger, Jack Brant, and Harry meets at George's to discuss strategy. In *The Body Lovers,* George lends Mike his car, which Mike drives to Bradbury, on Long Island. In *Survival . . . Zero!,* Mike meets Velda and others at the Blue Ribbon. It is mentioned that George is married.

GEORGE. In "Tomorrow I Die," he is Sheriff LaFont's deputy. He is too badly injured to help Richard Thurber foil Auger's gang of bank robbers.

GEORGE. In *The Twisted Thing,* Mike Hammer uses the phone of George and his wife, Mary, to tell Sergeant Price about Myra Grange's disappearance.

GEORGE. In *Vengeance Is Mine!,* he is a clerk at the hotel in which Chester Wheeler was murdered.

GEORGIE. In *My Gun Is Quick,* he is a friend of a homosexual to whom Mike Hammer talks briefly at Monica's.

GEROT, CAPTAIN. In "Everybody's Watching Me," he is a ranking city police officer who seeks evidence against Mark Renzo and Phil Carboy.

GERRITY. In *Black Alley,* he owns or owned a trucking company from which Marcos Dooley rented vehicles used to transport $89 billion in cartons.

GERRITY, T. In *The By-Pass Control. See* Mann, Tiger.

GETTLER. In *Day of the Guns,* Tiger Mann recalls killing him, along with Krouse, in 1945 during the war.

GEYFEY, CONGRESSMAN. In *Kiss Me, Deadly,* he is a crooked Washington politician with connections to Carl Evello, whose lawyer he was in the West. Did Spillane choose this name because it slightly echoes the last name of honest, crime-fighting Estes Kefauver (1903–1963)?

GHENT, MARTHA. In *The Twisted Thing,* she is Rudolph York's sister, Richard Ghent's wife, and the mother of Richard Ghent Jr. and Rhoda Ghent. She is domineering and selfish.

GHENT, RHODA. In *The Twisted Thing,* she is the daughter of Richard and Martha Ghent, and Richard Ghent Jr.'s sister.

GHENT, RICHARD. In *The Twisted Thing,* he is Martha Ghent's henpecked husband, and the father of Rhoda Ghent and Richard Ghent Jr.

GHENT, RICHARD JR. In *The Twisted Thing,* he is the son, in his early twenties, of Richard and Martha Ghent. Mike Hammer, who calls him a half-"pansy," catches him rifling the files of his uncle, Rudolph York, in search for the man's will.

GIBBONS, ADRIAN. In "The Gold Fever Tapes," he would probably tell Fallon the route an illegal gold shipment would take but for the fact that he is in a Mexican jail for rape.

GIBBONS, WALLY. In *Day of the Guns,* he was an O.S.S. agent during the war and knew Tiger Mann. He has been a successful Broadway columnist for the *News* for almost twenty years and provides Tiger with information in return for a scoop when the action ends. In *Bloody Sunrise,* Gibbons reluctantly provides Tiger information, hides Sonia Dutko for him, is captured by Sonia, and would have been killed by her but for Tiger's intervention. In *The By-Pass Control,* Gibbons helps Tiger fake his death near Edith Caine's apartment by calling an ambulance to take away the alleged corpse.

GIESLER, COLONEL. In *The Girl Hunters,* Hy Gardner names him as an SS colonel, in the German army, who killed prisoners during the Battle of the Bulge and was killed when, while he was a prisoner himself, the truck he was in hit a land mine. Spillane may have been thinking of Hermann Giesler, one of Adolph Hitler's favorite architects, when he named this fictional Nazi.

GIFFORD. In "The Seven Year Kill," he provided a photograph for the newspapers of Rhino Massley in his coffin. Massley quietly pretended to be dead for a moment.

GIFFORD, GEORGE. In *Day of the Guns,* Mann recalls that Gifford during the war liked a woman Chevesky also liked.

GILFERN, MORT. In "Return of the Hood," is a Communist sympathizer in whose Print Shop three Soviet spies hold Karen Sinclair. Ryan invades the place, kills two Soviets, badly injures the third, and rescues Karen—temporarily.

GILL, JOE. In *Vengeance Is Mine!,* he is a mild private investigator. Since he owes Mike Hammer a favor, Mike pressures him into getting information about Chester Wheeler.

GINGER. In *The Long Wait,* she is a redheaded bar-girl at the Last Resort.

"THE GIRL BEHIND THE HEDGE" (1853). Short story. (Characters: Duncan, Chester Duncan, Inspector Early, Harrison, Walter Harrison, Martha, Evelyn Vaughn.) Inspector Early questions Chester Duncan about the supposed suicide of Walter Harrison, his business rival. Did he cause Harrison's death? No, says Duncan, and explains. He and Harrison were old friends. But when Harrison, a handsome, conceited womanizer, stole Adrianne, Duncan's fiancée, married her, proved faithless, and let her die, Duncan planned revenge. He invited Harrison to his Long Island home and let him see Evelyn Vaughn, a gloriously beautiful blonde, across the bay, sitting near a hedge. She ecstatically waved at Duncan. Harrison preened, waved, attracted her pleased attention. Totally, hopelessly in love, he got Duncan to give him the Vaughn family's New York City address. Duncan named a small hotel off Fifth Avenue. Harrison went there, saw her, committed suicide. Why? The ever-smiling girl "was a hopeless imbecile," Duncan explains. "The Girl Behind the Hedge" is unusual for being the first significant fictional work by Spillane to use, in part, the technique of third-person narration. "The Girl Behind the Hedge" was republished as "The Lady Says Die" (1966).

***THE GIRL HUNTERS* (1962).** Novel. (Characters: Aliet, Lester Bender, Pat Bender, Bernie, Alex Bird, Carrigan, Captain Pat Chambers, Marta Singleton Civac, Ann Cole, Richie Cole, Ed Dailey, Del, Dewey, Nat Drutman, Earl, Gerald Erlich, Morris Fleming, Hy Gardner, Marilyn Gardner, George, Colonel Giesler, Gorlin, Benny Joe Grissi, Mike Hammer, Bucky Harris, Bayliss Henry, Injun Pete, John, Cortez Johnson, Duck-Duck Jones, Greta King, Laura Knapp, Senator Leo Knapp, Red Markham, Mason, P. J. Moriarty, Gary Moss, Ray, Art Rickerby, Dr. Larry Snyder, Annie Stein, General Stoeffler, Augie Strickland, Sugar Boy, Ted, Dennis Wallace.)

Mike Hammer sent Velda to guard rich Marta Singleton Civac. While giving a party in New York City Marta, her husband, Rudolph Civac, and Velda disappeared. Marta was found dead in the river, her jewelry stripped from her. Blaming himself, Mike became an alcoholic bum.

Seven years passed, and it is now 1962. Captain Pat Chambers, disgusted, drags Mike to a hospital where Richie Cole, dying, will speak only with Mike. Pat says a bullet dug from Cole matches another that killed Senator Leo Knapp three years earlier. Cole tells Mike that he gave a message for him to newspaper vender Dewey, that Mike must seek The Dragon, and that Velda is alive. Mike suspects Pat was in love with Velda too. Mike, hospitalized, clams up to Pat and Dr. Larry Snyder, who needles him about his alcoholism but praises him for his instant recovery. FBI agent Art Rickerby visits Mike, tells him Cole was an agent and like a son to him, wants to cooperate with Mike, and proceeds to spring him from the hospital.

Mike goes to Dewey's one-room apartment but finds the man murdered. Mike visits his old office, kept intact by the grateful owner of the building. Musing in old surroundings, Mike wonders if Dewey's death relates to Cole's and Knapp's. Rickerby tells Mike that Cole worked as an undercover seaman. Mike gets the lowdown on Knapp, an anti-Red, anti-union conservative, from Hy Gardner, a newspaper pal, then drives to Phoenicia, upstate, to interview Laura Knapp, Leo's gorgeous blonde widow. She is hospitable, tells Mike a robber killed Leo and took paste jewelry from their opened wall safe. Given the combination, Mike deliberately triggers the safe's secret alarm. Two cops appear, but Laura gently waves them away. Mike meets Rickerby at a downtown Automat, reports about Laura, her safe, and the paste jewelry, says nothing about Velda, and is told Cole "disobeyed orders." Mike goes to his office building, passes Morris Fleming, a watchman, enters his office, is slugged, recovers, and finds the place searched. He retrieves his old .45, makes his way to a dock saloon, decks two would-be bouncers, and spots Bayliss Henry, a retired, canny newsman. He remembers Mike's exploits, says, yes, he knew Cole, suspected him of being undercover, and leads him to

Cole's Brooklyn apartment. They sneak in, and Mike finds letters dated 1944 and old army pictures of Cole, some with Velda. As they leave, they are shot at but missed. Mike visits Rickerby at his office and learns this: Cole was married; he was a wartime Office of Strategic Information (O.S.I.) captain in England; his buddies included Lester Bender, killed in 1945, and Alex Bird, now owner of a Marlboro, New York, chicken farm; Cole's wife died of cancer in 1949; Cole's girlfriends included manicurist Pat Bender, who was Lester's sister, stewardess Greta King, and a nameless third.

Next day Mike returns to Cole's neighborhood, and finds and pockets the bullet shot at him. He encounters the police at his office building, there because Morris has been murdered. In his office is Pat, who brought Laura Knapp with him. Contrite, Mike mollifies Pat, gets him to go check Velda's possible military background, and gives him the bullet for ballistics testing. Laura stays, says she misses Leo, guesses Mike misses Velda, connects to two, says she wants to kill their victimizer, and hires Mike for $5,000 cash. They lurch into lovemaking on his office couch. Mike meets Rickerby at a bar and is told this: Cole, to whom Velda was close in Paris, was involved in an operation called Butterfly Two, worked to track Gerald Erlich, a Nazi spy, whose network the Communists took over to rule the world; Cole sought illegal gold shipments; The Dragon is a team of pro-Red excutioners, called Tooth and Nail. When Mike promises to get Cole's killer, Rickerby agrees to federalize and arm Mike. He visits Hy's office, gets him to check into The Dragon, takes him to meet Pat—Dr. Snyder is there too—and learns from Pat that Velda was an O.S.I. agent during the war. Pat whispers, yes, he was in love with her too. At a bar, Hy tells Mike that he was a captain in special services, knew about Butterfly Two, Erlich was a prisoner presumed killed by a land mine. Hy gives Mike a photo of Erlich. Mike rents a car, drives to see Laura, is pursued then passed by a fellow, angular-faced like an Indian, in a Buick. She says her husband Leo was a major general in procurement during the war and did no spy work. She doesn't recognize Erlich's photo. A poolside radio is suddenly smashed by a pistol shot. Mike dashes about but sees only that departing Buick. Laura lets him inspect stuff in Leo's war trunk. Disappointed at finding nothing relevant, the two make love again.

Back in Manhattan that night, Mike walks in the rain, thinks of Velda, goes to his office, and finds Rickerby there. He gives Mike written permission to go armed, says Erlich could have exposed Soviet and other schemes for world domination, was killed five years ago in East Germany by Gorlich, known as The Dragon, asks Mike to capture Gorlich for Rickerby to kill. Phoning, Laura says she and Pat will meet him at Moriarty's bar. First, Mike goes to Hy's office. Hy shows him a wire photo, just arrived, of Velda in East European garb, says Communists sought to kill her, says she is not in Europe now, and hands him more information on promissile Leo's opposition to "the knot-headed liberals and 'better-Red-than-dead' slobs." Pat relays an eye-witness description of the man who shot at Mike and Henry; it matches Mike's memory of the thug driving the Buick. Mike concludes he is Gorlich, The Dragon. Pat tries to relate Laura's stolen paste gems, just recovered from a pawnshop, Cole's "gem smuggling," and Velda's assignment to guard bejeweled Mrs. Civac. Pat hands Mike a photo of Rudolph Civac. Civac is Erlich.

Laura drives Mike to her upstate mansion. He sleeps until afternoon. She expresses profound love for him, wants him to find Velda and decide between the two women, and listens attentively as he summarizes: Erlich dreamed of world domination; "the Commies" soon wanted Erlich dead; he survived, got to the United States, married rich Marta Singleton; by coincidence Velda guarded the two; "Red agents" killed Marta, spirited Erlich and Velda to Europe; Velda pretended to cooperate with Erlich "in the goddamn Russian country" all these years while Mike sank into alcoholism; Erlich and Velda escaped; Erlich was shot; Velda and Cole got home; Velda recommended Mike, but Cole, dying, spoke insufficiently to Mike, "a drunk." Mike and Laura swim. He sees her shotgun barrel down in the beachhouse mud, lectures her on such possibly fatal carelessness, makes sudden fierce love with her, and drives her car back to Manhattan.

Mike meets with Hy, tells him everything, and says Cole must have smuggled Velda home on a tramp steamer and ashore with someone's help. Mike and Hy at Grissi's find Bayliss, who says Cole disembarked off the *Vanessa,* and had a friend named Red Markham, now at a nearby flophouse. Red says Cole's friend Dennis Wallace offloaded Velda in a crate. They find Wallace in a rooming house, tortured and murdered. The landlady says his visitor looked like an Indian. Mike alerts Pat, leaves Hy to brief him, and departs. Mike guesses Wallace revealed to Gorlin that Alex Bird had a truck and used it to transport the crate with Velda in it to his Marlboro farm. Mike rushes there, and finds Alex slugged but silenced by an immediate heart attack. Mike and Gorlin see each other, and fire and tussle. Mike, triumphant, decides not to put an ax through the unconscious loser's skull but instead secures his hand to a barn floor with a twenty-penny nail. He phones Rickerby to come see and proceeds to Laura's. While she showers, she lets him rest and swim. Then he summarizes: Pat rightly connected Laura's and Marta Civac's gem thefts; Leo surprised Gorlin seeking safe-held documents, shot him; Laura provided the enemy state secrets mentioned by Leo and overheard in Washington conversations among Leo and his friends in high places; Dewey indubitably hid Velda's address in a note in *Cavalier,* Mike's favorite magazine (and one of Spillane's); Mike will therefore be the surviving girl hunter and rescue Velda soon (and regain Pat's friendship). Mike plugs Laura's shotgun with bathhouse mud and starts walking away just as she reappears, naked and armed. He looks down the shotgun's "yawning chasms," turns his back, and immediately hears an "unearthly roar." She aimed to shoot him.

The Girl Hunters is a fast-paced, incredibly plotted comeback Mike Hammer novel, published ten years after *Kiss Me, Deadly.* Velda, while never appearing in *The Girl Hunters,* unifies its action. This novel is notable for the best imagery Spillane managed to its date, the most graphic accounts of sexual intimacy yet, Mike's descent into alcoholism and instant recovery (cum several beers), his giving up smoking, his killing no one, and his first quoted utterance of "shit." Amusing is Spillane's satirizing of that dreadful newcomer into modern English, the pervasive misuse of "like." Spillane is addicted to the word "grin" (and variants): *The Girl Hunters* features a tiresome fifty-two, with menacingly toothy Mike leading with thirty-three, and Laura next with eight.

Bibliography: Gay Talese, "It's a New Killer for Mike Hammer," *New York Times,* June 19, 1962.

GLADOW, HENRY. In *One Lonely Night,* he is a pro-Communist American who leads meetings of fellow travelers and Soviet agents in Brooklyn. He introduces Mike Hammer to Martin Romberg as his "traveling companion" and Martha Camisole as his secretary.

GLEASON. In *The Deep,* she was Tally Lee's next-door neighbor. When Tally overdosed on sleeping pills, Mrs. Gleason cared for her.

GLEASON. In *The Snake,* Sonny Motley names him to Mike Hammer as a member of his old mob. Gleason is dead.

GLEASON, RUTH. In "Kick It or Kill!," she is one of the girls lured by Simpson into heroin addiction. She went to New York City with Flori Dahl, returned to Pinewood, helps Kelly Smith, and goes with Dari Dahl to Simpson's mansion. When Lennie Weaver, her supplier, will not provide her a fix, she kills him with a pointed stick.

GLEN. In *The Last Cop Out,* he drove Louise Belhander from Decatur, Illinois, but they never got to California, their hoped-for destination.

GLORIA. In "Together We Kill," she was Joe's girlfriend, temporary because he could never forget Claire.

GLOVER. In *The Deep. See* Mort.

GODFREY, IRENE. In *The Long Wait. See* Harlan, Gracie.

GOLDEN, MANNY. In "Me, Hood!," he is an ex-policeman, dismissed in 1949 on a charge of graft. He is in cahoots with Big Man and is "shilled" and murdered in front of Ryan's apartment.

"THE GOLD FEVER TAPES" (1973). Short story. (Characters: Paddy Ables, Walter Head Ardmore, Henry Borden, Cheryl, Ma Christy, Eddie Connors,

Fallon, Adrian Gibbons, Al Grossino, Arthur Littleworth, Loco Bene, Lucas, MacIntosh, O'Malley, Patsy, Marlene Peters, Reading, Sophia, Stiles, Charlie Watts, Squeaky Williams.) Fallon, an ex-cop, discharged for being on the take, was befriended by Squeaky Williams in prison. Both are now out. Fallon works for a news agency. Squeaky repairs radios and other sound equipment. When Squeaky is killed to silence him, Fallon wants to see justice done. He gets hold of a tape Squeaky left. By playing it, Fallon learns that a mysterious gang has stolen eight hundred pounds of gold and is planning to ship it to Europe. With the help of Cheryl, the news agency's sexy secretary, Fallon outwits not only the police, some of whom are after him for alleged involvement, but also Reading, supposedly a rare-book dealer with materials in a safe to be sent abroad, but in reality the murderous head of the gang. When the authorities arrive at Reading's office, Fallon has the crook in hand and demonstrates that the gold has been remade into the safe, deceptively painted black.

GOLDWITZ, IZZY. In "Return of the Hood," he owns the Cafeteria. Ryan observes him counting Wally Pee's numbers take for him at the Cafeteria. Pedro is Izzy's busboy.

GOMP, JOEY. In "Return of the Hood," he is a drug dealer, operating on 96th Street, and named by Ernie South as one of Fly's suppliers.

GONZALES. In "The Flier," he was an anti-Castro engineer murdered by Castro forces.

GONZALES, DETECTIVE SERGEANT. In "Everybody's Watching Me," he works under Captain Gerot, is in cahoots with Culley, and is killed in a drug raid.

GONZALES, JUAN. In "Me, Hood!," he was a minor criminal involved with Henry Billings, Tomas Escalantes, and Alfredo Lias, and was thrown in front of a truck and killed. Knowing he was in danger, Juan left thousands of dollars for his wife, Lucinda.

GONZALES, LUCINDA. In "Me, Hood!," she is Juan Gonzales's frightened widow, living at 54th Street and Tenth Avenue. Juan left her a substantial sum of money. She reluctantly confides in Ryan.

GOODWIN, ARNOLD ("STUD"). In *The Snake,* he was imprisoned by Simpson Torrence on a rape charge and vowed to shoot him on sight when released. Mike Hammer learns, however, that Goodwin was killed in a car accident a few months ago and hence is not a suspect in the attempt on Sue Devon's life.

GORBATCHER. In *Day of the Guns,* he and Smith are named in connection with Tiger Mann's fake fire-inspection ploy. Tiger wants to case Alexis Minner's apartment.

GORDON. In "Everybody's Watching Me," he works with "Joe Boyle" collecting scrap metal.

GORDON. In "Killer Mine," he is a criminal, with Carbito, that the mob fears Gus Wilder might testify against.

GORDOT, LISA. In *The Delta Factor,* she is an attractive jet-set gambler at the Regis Hotel. Morgan uses her to distract Russo Sabin, who lusts for her, and helps her escape Sabin. Morgan resists her well-displayed physical attractions.

GORGE. In *Day of the Guns,* this is the name by which Alexis Minner identified his associate, whom Tiger Mann has just killed.

GORKEY, YAMU. In *The Death Dealers,* he owns the 1963 Chevy Malcolm Turos used to transport Teish El Abin in. Gorkey is known in his East Side neighborhood as an unpopular Communist. When Tiger Mann finds Gorkey guarding Teish, they exchange gunfire; Tiger is wounded, and Gorkey is killed. Spillane obviously patterned Gorkey's name after that of the Russian writer Maxim Gorky (1868–1936).

GORLIN. In *The Girl Hunters,* he is the Tooth half of The Dragon, an assassination team (*see also* Knapp, Laura). Gorlin, a KGB agent, has an angular face, with high cheek bones, making him resemble an Indian. In his search for Velda, he killed Marta Singleton Civac, Gerald Erlich, Dewey, Morris Fleming, and Dennis Wallace, and causes Alex Bird's fatal heart attack. Gorlin is immobilized when Mike nails his hand to Bird's barn floor.

GORMAN, FRANCIS. In *The Snake,* he was a bootlegger who encroached on the territory of Howie Green. When Gorman was murdered (perhaps by Black Conley), Green was suspected of being involved.

GOSTOVICH. In *Survival . . . Zero!,* she is a gossipy old lady in Lipton Sullivan's neighborhood. To Mike Hammer, she usefully describes a suspect who turns out to be Larry Beers.

GRACE, L. In *Bloody Sunrise. See* Dutko, Sonia.

GRACIE. In *The Last Cop Out,* this is the name of a diner Jimmie Corrigan says he frequented.

GRADY. In *The Deep,* he is a waiter at the Pelican bar.

GRADY. In "Stand Up and Die!," Caroline Hart tells Mitch Valler that Grady shot her father in the back, crippling him, and therefore was killed along with all other Gradys.

GRADY, BILL. In "Return of the Hood," he is an army buddy of Ryan's, a bachelor, a nationally syndicated columnist, and a reliable source of information for Ryan. A conservative living in the West 72nd Street hotel, Grady tells Ryan he laments America's "playing big brother to all the slobs in the world, [while] the Soviets are laying the groundwork for our own destruction if the surface negotiations don't go their way."

GRADY, MARTIN. In *Day of the Guns,* he is an influential right-wing agent with access to a great deal of money. He exercises enormous bribe power and is therefore helpful to his friend Tiger Mann. In *Bloody Sunrise,* Grady owns two magazines and is the well-to-do, well-connected boss of an extra-legal intelligence network. He orders Tiger to protect Gabin Martrel, the Russian defector, and helps him in the venture. In *The Death Dealers,* Tiger calls on Grady to help him in his association with Teish El Abin and in his pursuit of Malcolm Turos. In *The By-Pass Control,* Grady's hiring Doug Hamilton provides the beginning of Tiger's search for Louis Agrounsky. Remaining behind the successive scenes, Grady provides Tiger with information and money.

GRAFTON. In "Killer Mine," he owns a store near which Harry Wope tells Lieutenant Joe Scanlon he saw Al Reese.

GRAHAM, ARTHUR. In *The Twisted Thing,* he and his brother, William Graham, are Rudolph York's materialistic, parasitic nephews. They scramble to find their uncle's will and thus cause Mike Hammer trouble.

GRAHAM, WILLIAM. In *The Twisted Thing,* he and his brother, Arthur Graham, are Rudolph York's selfish nephews and hope to inherit from him. Their conduct disgusts Mike Hammer.

GRANGE, MYRA. In *The Twisted Thing,* she is a lesbian and is Rudolph York's laboratory assistant, with an apartment in Sidon. Formerly a nurse, whose real name was Rita Cambell, she was in on York's taking Herron Mallory's infant son, calling him Ruston York, and calling him his son. Myra blackmails Rudolph with this knowledge. Rudolph hires Alice Nichols, his niece, to pose with Myra as a pair of lesbians, be secretly photographed, and thus neutralize Myra. Mike Hammer saves Myra, now between thirty and forty years of age, from Dilwick and Mallory.

GRANGER. In "The Veiled Woman," he is an FBI agent. Karl Terris slugs him and ties him up.

GRANT, LEO. In "The Seven Year Kill," he was the Phoenix mortician involved in the fake photograph of nondead Rhino Massley. Grant and Dr. Thomas Hoyt, also involved, were then killed in a staged jeep accident on October 2, 1965.

GRAVES, RUSSELL. In *The Killing Man,* he is a sports reporter for the *Manchester Guardian.* Petey Benson tells Mike about Graves, who provides Mike with information about the grisly murder of an American in the Manchester area.

GREBB, INSPECTOR SPENCER. In *The Snake,* he is the police officer under whom Captain Pat Chambers serves. When he was a rookie back in 1932, Grebb was involved in arresting Sonny Motley. Mike Hammer is sarcastic toward Grebb at first. But when aware that Grebb came up through the ranks honestly, Mike observes this at one point: "He [Grebb] came in with the patient attitude of the professional cop, always ready to wait, always ready to act when the time came."

GRECO. In *The Erection Set,* Greco, a Spaniard, and Garfield were evidently rivals in Europe of Dog Kelly, who set a trap removing them from action.

GREEN, HOWIE. In *The Snake,* he was a friend, now deceased, of Black Conley. Green was a bootlegger, then a real-estate agent. Because Conley killed a man (perhaps Francis Gorman) for Green, he was able to pressure Green into getting him a Catskills hideaway. According to Sonny Motley, Conley killed Green before Conley and Motley pulled off their 1932 heist.

GREEN, LEW. In *The Snake,* Velda is forced by Del Penner to tell Mike Hammer to meet her at Lew Green's bar. Mike does so, walks into a trap, and is taken to Penner to be warned.

GREEN, MOE. In "Return of the Hood," he was killed during the shootout outside the Cafeteria, during which Karen Sinclair was wounded.

GREEN, SY. In "Return of the Hood," to terrify Ernie South, Ryan reminds him that Ryan so frightened Sy that his "mind is going on him now."

GREENBLATT. In "Man Alone," Patrick Regan mentions to Sergeant Jerry Nolan the Small-Greenblatt spy case, involving secret police work Regan handled.

GREENIE. In *The Body Lovers,* he saw Orlso Bucher get into a car with a diplomatic license plate. Mike Hammer cannot interview Greenie, a drunk according to Max Hughes, because he was killed by a truck two months earlier.

GREGORY. In *The Body Lovers,* he is named as a political reporter for a national magazine.

GREGORY. In "The Veiled Woman," he is a Communist thug. Karl Terris kills him.

GRETCH. In *The Death Dealers,* when an East Side bar-girl wonders if Tiger Mann is a cop checking into Buddy's pulling a gun on Gretch, Tiger says he isn't.

GRIF, JOEY. In *The Last Cop Out,* he blows up the Big Board meeting in Chicago with a bazooka, on Papa Menes's orders. Thirty-two men die.

GRIFFIN, DR. In *The Twisted Thing,* he is a Sidon physician. When Mike Hammer asks him if he recently treated any wounded man, he says he didn't.

GRINDLE, LOU. In *The Big Kill,* he is a racketeer, in his forties, working under Ed Teen. Grindle is flashy, at home on Broadway and in Harlem. Grindle and Teen caused the death of Charlie Fallon, their superior in the rackets, but in the fallout are blackmailed. When Teen has Mike Hammer in his clutches, Grindle approaches, Mike breaks his front teeth, but is mercilessly battered by Grindle. After Mike escapes, he returns and shoots Grindle dead.

GRISSI, BENNY JOE. In *The Girl Hunters,* he owns a lowdown bar near the docks. Mike meets Bayliss Henry there. Grissi's name may reflect Spillane's interest in the Mafia, a colorful member of which was Jake ("Greasy Thumb") Guzik (1887–1956).

Bibliography: Sifakis.

GROOTZ. In "Killer Mine," he is Sergeant Mack Brissom's fat partner in police headquarters.

GROSS, MELVIN. In *The Delta Factor,* he is mentioned as having lived at Mrs. Gustave Timely's house.

GROSSINO, AL. In "The Gold Fever Tapes," he is a police lieutenant with whom Fallon confers.

GROVE, IRVING. In *Survival . . . Zero!,* he owns the Grove Men's Shop on Broadway. Mike Hammer interviews him about his stolen wallet without developing any useful leads.

GROVE, MRS. IRVING. In *Survival . . . Zero!,* Grove tells Mike that his wife drags him to the theater.

GUIDO. In *The Erection Set,* he and his brother Teddy Guido are bungling, cheating mobsters. He is in South America when Teddy Guido is murdered.

GUIDO. In *The Last Cop Out,* he is Mark Shelby's cousin. He owns a grocery store in which Shelby changes clothes to preserve his anonymity after he visits Helga Piers.

GUIDO, TEDDY. In *The Erection Set,* he and his brother bungled rackets at the waterfront and the airport, and cheated the syndicate. Teddy is killed by a hand grenade.

GULLEY. In "Everybody's Watching Me," he operates boats for the purpose of picking up drug shipments. In cahoots with Phil Carboy and Mark Renzo, Gulley dies in a car accident probably engineered by Vetter.

GUS. In "The Screen Test of Mike Hammer," he was a man Helen killed and blamed Carmen for killing.

H

HAGGERTY, CAL. In *Day of the Guns,* he was an agent whom, Mann recalls, Rodine Lund killed in Hamburg during the war.

HAL. In *The Erection Set,* Rose Porter, a prostitute, remembers Hal as rather tender.

HAL. In "The Seven Year Kill," he and Jolly are two of Mannie Waller's hoods. They pursue Terry Massley, slug Phil Rocca, and get viciously kicked by him in revenge.

HALL, CHARLES. In *The Last Cop Out,* he rented a car, drove along beside Stanley Holland, and killed him. Hall was from Elizabeth, New Jersey.

HALLOWAY, FRED. In "The Affair with the Dragon Lady," he was a crew-member aboard the Dragon Lady.

HALPER. In *I, the Jury,* he lives in Poughkeepsie, New York, and knows Eileen Vickers's father, R. H. Vickers. When Mike Hammer phones him, Halper says only that Vickers now dislikes his daughter and will have nothing to do with her.

HALPERN, DR. JOHN. In *The Deep,* he is a disgraced physician. Dixie tells Deep that Dr. Halpern has "a drug store on Amsterdam" Avenue in New York City and patches up wounded criminals.

HAMILTON. In *The Erection Set,* he was a member of a theater chain who bailed out Veda Barrin once, when she was in trouble over gambling losses.

HAMILTON, DOUG. In *The By-Pass Control,* he was an electronics expert. He founded Belt-Aire Electronics in 1946 and was hired by Martin Grady. Hamilton got greedy, tried to blackmail Camille Hunt, and was tortured and murdered by Vito Salvi. Hamilton left a document behind which implicated Camille and which Edith Caine finds and tells Tiger Mann about.

HAMILTON, GEORGE. In *Vengeance Is Mine!,* he and Petey Cassandro, according to Captain Pat Chambers, are Detroit gunmen reportedly in New York. Either one of the two may be the thug Velda shoots in Clyde Williams's apartment.

HAMMER. In *The Twisted Thing,* Mike Hammer mentions his father as one who comforted him when he hurt himself as a child.

HAMMER, MIKE (real name: Michael Hammer). He is the rough, womanizing, sadistic former New York City cop, now a private detective. Velda is his admiring, critical, beautiful, big secretary. Hammer is the narrator of all of his stories.

In *I, the Jury,* Hammer says he spent two years in jungle combat against the Japanese in World War II. He is now 190 pounds. Jack Williams saved his life; so when Jack is murdered, Hammer vows to find and gutshoot the killer. On the way to learning Charlotte Manning is the guilty one, Hammer helps Captain Pat Chambers solve the murders of Harold Kines, Eileen Vickers, George Kalecki, Bobo Hopper, and Myrna Devlin. Also, along the way, Mike drinks and smokes excessively, makes wild love with Mary Bellemy, and prematurely proposes marriage to Charlotte. When he first speaks with Miss June, at her brothel, he calls himself Pete Sterling.

In *My Gun Is Quick,* Mike says he was born in New York City and his apartment is 9-D. His meets Nancy Sanford by chance in a hash joint. When she is murdered, he determines to solve the crime, which leads him to Arthur Berin-Grotin, her rich grandfather, to his bodyguard Feeney Last, to Murray Candid, involved in call-girl crimes, and to reformed call girl Lola Bergan, and—with Captain Pat Chambers's cooperation—to uncovering citywide vice and corruption. Mike's double standard is manifest when he wants Lola all for himself even while intimate with other women. When Mike meets Candid, he calls himself Howard Martin, a cop from Des Moines, and seeking call girls for a party. When he seeks photographs left at the Quick Pix office, he signs in as J. Johnson.

In *Vengeance Is Mine!,* Mike's chance meeting Chester Wheeler in New York City leads to their drinking together and winding up in Wheeler's hotel room. When Wheeler is found dead, Mike must prove Wheeler did not commit suicide. In doing so, he exposes the murderer not only of Wheeler but also of Rainey, three models, and sleazy photographer Anton Lipsek. In the process, he encounters bewitchingly beautiful Juno Reeves, Anton's associate. At one point, Mike dreams of being in a foxhole.

In *One Lonely Night,* when Captain Pat Chambers introduces Mike to Lee Deamer, after Mike has shot a Soviet agent on the George Washington Bridge and seen Paula Riis commit suicide there, Mike connects Deamer and the bridge incident and determines that Lee is being impersonated by his evil twin brother Oscar Deamer. In the process, Mike, though troubled by bad memories, sleeps with Ethel Brighton and Linda Holbright, becomes tentatively engaged to Velda, and kills several people. Mike recalls being wounded in the war. Drinking and smoking excessively, he is least attractive in *One Lonely Night.* He calls himself "a ruthless bastard," says he is "evil for the good," and relishes his memory of macheteing a Japanese soldier to death.

In *The Big Kill,* Mike witnesses William Decker's murder, which orphans the man's son. Mike's investigation leads him to identify Decker's killer; to solve the murders of Arnold Basil, Mel Hooker, and Toady Link; indirectly to cause the deaths of Arthur Cole, Glenn Fisher, and Martin; and to kill Johnny and Lou Grindle. Mike exposes Ed Teen, mastermind of New York City's racketeering empire, which he grabbed after Charlie Fallon was murdered. Mike saves the life of Georgia Lucas, sleeps with Ellen Scobie, but resists Marsha Lee's wiles.

In *Kiss Me, Deadly,* Mike tries to aid Berga Torn; after she dies, he tracks down the killers. This leads him, often with Captain Pat Chambers's help, to Al Affia; Carl Evello and his beautiful half-sister, Michael Friday; William Mist; and others. After escaping murder plots by the Mafia against him, Mike is captured and mauled, but escapes, sees to the killing of Evello, guesses that a key to the crimes is in Berga's stomach, proceeds to the office of Berga's physician, Dr. Martin Soberin, kills him and kills Berga's other betrayer, a woman posing as Lily Carver, Berga's friend.

In "The Screen Test of Mike Hammer," Mike identifies Helen as a killer and chokes her to death.

In *The Girl Hunters,* Mike has spent seven years as an alcoholic bum after Velda's disappearance. This binge cost him Captain Pat Chambers's friendship. Mike recovers, follows leads provided by dying Richie Cole, and meets FBI agent Art Rickerby and Laura Knapp, the widow of Senator Leo Knapp. With help from Hy Gardner and Bayliss Henry, Mike connects Knapp's murder and Cole's to The Dragon, an assassination team composed of Laura and KGB multiple-killer Gorlin, both of whom get their comeuppance. At novel's end, Mike is about to rescue Velda.

In *The Snake,* Mike finds Velda ensconced in an apartment and guarding Sue Devon, who has been adopted by Simpson Torrence. Thugs try to grab Sue, and gunfire follows. Mike investigates Torrence, a rising politician. Doing so leads Mike to crack the fall-out of a 1932 heist by Sonny Motley, jailed for thirty years, and by Black Conley, Motley's disloyal partner, who disappeared with the loot. Mike's pursuit of Marv Kania, hired to kill him, and other activities delay the consummation of his love for Velda.

In *The Twisted Thing,* Mike is hired in Sidon, outside New York City, by Rudolph York, a rich, widowed scientist, to find his brilliant son, Ruston York, allegedly kidnapped. Mike is confused by parasitic members of Rudolph's family, is impeded by Dilwick, a crooked cop, and aided by Sergeant Price, an honest state trooper. Mike follows evidence to Myra Grange, Rudolph's blackmailing laboratory assistant, and her criminal associate, Herron Mallory—really Ruston's father. Ruston defines himself to Mike as "a thing," fatally twisted by his supposed father's educational experiments on him. While pushing his investigation, Mike often deprives himself of sleep and food, and smokes more than forty-five cigarettes.

In *The Body Lovers,* Mike connects Maxine Delaney's and Helen Poston's murders to the disappearance of Greta Service—all beautiful women. Doing so leads him to kill Orslo Bucher, investigate Lorenzo Jones, a pimp, Ali Duval, a smuggler and kidnapper, and Belar Ris, a hypocritical U.N. representative. Mike is aided by Cleo, a fading Greenwich Village artist, and Dulcie McInnes, a fashion editor and Ris's attractive but dangerous hostess.

In *Survival . . . Zero!,* his friend Lipton Sullivan's murder leads Mike to investigate persons whose wallets were stolen by Beaver, who roomed with Sullivan and was a pickpocket. Mike uncovers a plot by William Dorn, from whose wallet Beaver kept a map incriminating Dorn and Soviet agent Joseph Kudak in a plot to destroy the United States. In foiling their scheme, Mike causes the deaths of Dorn, Dorn's accountant Renée Talmage, Kudak, and Stanley, who was Dorn's killer, among others. Spud Henry names Mike "Mikey." Mike reminisces about growing up near Columbus Avenue and 110th Street and says he is getting tired after twenty years of investigative work.

In *The Killing Man,* Mike's investigation into Anthony DiCica's torture and mutilation murder in Mike's office involves him in the murders of Richard Smiley, Harry Bern, and Gary Fells, and the attempted kidnapping of Velda— all the work of the mysterious Penta, who turns out to be Bennett Bradley, a State Department hypocrite. Mike also helps locate a trailer containing cocaine. Mike is aided by Captain Pat Chambers and General Rudolph Skubal, and helps Candace Amory of the D.A.'s office, with whom he incidentally has a brief but fiery amour. Mike reveals that he was born in Brooklyn, had some FBI and Police Academy training, and has quit smoking. He still drinks excessively.

In *Black Alley,* Mike takes eight months in Florida to recover from bad abdominal gunshot wounds, sustained in a waterfront fracas during which he killed Azi Ponti, who wounded him. Mike can no longer drink alcohol or even pack a gun comfortably. He returns to New York and receives enigmatic comments from Marcos Dooley, his dying army buddy, concerning $89 billion in missing Mafia money. Mike's search for it involves him with Lorenzo Ponti, his disloyal son Ugo Ponti, and his henchmen, Howie Drago and Leonard Patterson. Mike's progress both toward solving the mystery, and toward marrying Velda at last, is hampered by his occasional relapses into dangerous poor health. Ultimately, he outguns Ugo and survives—as does Velda, to whom he is insufferably bossy.

In "The Night I Died," Mike falls in love with the beautiful but corrupt Helen Venn, locates the Syndicate boss Carmen Rich for her, is betrayed and stabbed by her, feels spiritually destroyed, finds her two years later, and kills her.

Bibliography: David Geherin, *The American Private Eye: The Image in Fiction* (New York: Frederick Ungar, 1985); Christopher La Farge, "Mickey Spillane and His Bloody Hammer," pp. 176–85 in *Mass Culture: The Popular Arts in America,* ed. Bernard Rosenberg and David Manning White (Glencoe, Ill.: Free Press, 1957).

HAMPTON, ASHFORD. In *The Ship That Never Was,* he was the master British shipbuilder who in 1791 built the beautiful but jinxed *Tiger* in the Cremington Boatyards, England.

HAND, KID. In *The Snake,* he is a criminal who watched Velda. When he seeks to kill Sue Devon, he is shot dead by Basil Levitt.

HANLEY, WALT. In *The Body Lovers,* he works for Krauss-Tillman and hired Mike for unspecified jobs, one of which takes him out of town for a week.

HANNAN, MALCOLM. In *The Delta Factor,* he is mentioned as an army buddy of Morgan's who blew up a German troop train but was also killed as a consequence of the explosion.

HANSON. In *The Last Cop Out,* he was a policeman who investigated the hit-and-run murder of Joe Scanlon.

HANSON, JOHN. In *I, the Jury. See* Kines, Harold.

HARDECKER, CAPTAIN. In *The By-Pass Control,* he is the chief of police at Eau Gallie, Florida. He helps Tiger Mann in his search for Louis Agrounsky.

HARDY. In *The Deep,* it is at his bar that Deep discusses Bennett's murder with Tally Lee.

HARDY, RICHARD. In *The Body Lovers,* he works for the R. J. Marion Realty Company, which owns the Greenwich Village building in which Greta Service lived. He cannot help Mike locate Greta.

HARKIN, COOKIE. In *The Big Kill,* he is the columnist Harry Bailen's leg-man, notable for his ugliness and his success with women. Cookie bribes people for stories to sell to Bailen. Because of his many connections, Cookie helps Mike identify Arthur Cole, gunman, and locate Georgia Lucas, the late Charlie Fallon's ex-mistress.

HARLAN, GEORGE. In *The Long Wait,* Gracie Harlan, not George Harlan, is the Harlan sought by Alan Logan and John McBride.

HARLAN, GRACIE. In *The Long Wait,* she was an actress who incorporated her last name. She met Lenny Servo, pleased but then displeased him, wrote Robert Minnow a letter to be opened in case of her death, passed information to Troy Avalard, and committed suicide through fear. When Gracie was a waitress with Inez Casey, she called herself Irene Godfrey.

HARLAN, WILLIAM. In *The Long Wait,* this Harlan, like George Harlan, is not the Harlan being sought by John McBride.

HARMODY, LEO. In *Kiss Me, Deadly,* he is a friend of Carl Evello. He is a guest at one of Evello's parties.

HARNEY, DONALD. In *The Body Lovers,* he is an attorney who defended Harry Service and tried hard to get him a light sentence.

HAROLD. In *The Deep,* he is one of Lenny Sobel's goons. Deep shoots him in the pelvis.

HAROLD. In "Tomorrow I Die," he is the mayor of the small town the bank of which Auger and his gang rob. Harold, who is politically ambitious and evidently practices law, favors charging into the holed-up robbers, even if it means killing Sheriff LaFont, whose daughter Carol he is engaged to. Richard Thurber slugs him to prevent this from happening.

HARRIS. In *Black Alley,* she is mentioned as Slipped Disk Harris's daughter.

HARRIS, AL ("BIG AL"). In *The Last Cop Out,* he was Mark Shelby's contact man, formerly in Atlanta, Georgia. Harris suffers from tuberculosis and lives in Baja California.

HARRIS, BUCK. In "Return of the Hood," Ryan scares Ernie South into talk-ing by recalling the time Ryan put Harris in a wheelchair permanently.

HARRIS, BUCKY. In *The Girl Hunters,* this bar owner has a letter written by Dewey in which Dewey wills his newstand to Duck-Duck Jones.

HARRIS, ELENA. In "The Seven Year Kill," she is a beautiful actress and nurse. She accompanied Rhino Massley from New York to Phoenix, went with him to Rio de Janeiro after his "death" was staged, and evidently tired of him when his money ran out.

HARRIS, SLIPPED DISK. In *Black Alley,* he was a friend of Marcos Dooley's. Harris was a former bootlegger, then a supplier of fine Canadian whiskey. He injured his spine lifting liquor crates. His supplies were cached in a cave near Newburgh, New York. Marvin Dooley, Dooley's son, tells Mike about Harris.

HARRISON, NORMAN. In *The Body Lovers,* he is a political correspondent in New York, covered a senate conference in Washington, D.C., returns home, and aids Mike and others trying to trace Mitch Temple's movements. Spillane undoubtedly chose the last names of Norman Harrison and Richard Salisbury, who are fellow journalists, because of his familiarity with the famous *New York Times* correspondent Harrison Salisbury (1908–1993).

HARRISON, WALTER. In "The Girl Behind the Hedge," he was formerly a friend of Chester Duncan until he stole Duncan's fiancée from him, married her, was unfaithful, and let her die. Duncan points out gorgeous Evelyn Vaughn to Harrison, a dreadful womanizer. He falls totally in love and commits suicide, in utter despair, when he discovers that Evelyn is an imbecile.

HARRY. In *The Death Dealers,* he is an ex-Selachin native and army veteran now in Brooklyn. Jack Brant gets him to help Tiger Mann. Harry's friends are Tom and Dick. Tiger selects Harry for special work, notably preparing special food for Teish El Abin and translating recorded conversations of Teish and his aides. Tiger tells Harry to call himself Harry Smith.

HARRY THE FOX. In *The Snake,* Sonny Motley names him to Mike Hammer as a deceased member of his old mob.

HART. In "Stand Up and Die!," he is the evil patriarch of a family bent on securing land for its uranium. The crippled old man has four sons, including Clemson Hart and George Hart, and one daughter, Caroline Hart. Mitch Veller outwits him, breaks his wheelchair, and avoids his effort to have him hanged. Ultimately, all the Harts but Caroline die in an explosion meant for Mitch.

HART, CAROLINE. In "Stand Up and Die!," she is old Hart's gorgeous, sexy daughter. She was engaged to Billy Bussy until Mitch Valler parachuted into her arms, outwitted her father's evil plans, and persuaded her to leave her hillbilly environs with him.

HART, CLEMSON. In "Stand Up and Die!," he is one of four sons of the old man.

HART, GEORGE ("BIG GEORGE"). In "Stand Up and Die!," he is the first son of the old man. Mitch Valler tangles with George and breaks his jaw.

HARVEY. In *The Big Kill*, he owns the Greenwich Village nightclub where Georgia Lucas is a substitute singer.

HARVEY. In *The Erection Set*, he is the Barrin family's taciturn, secretly smiling butler. Harvey enjoys seeing Dog Kelly embarrass his dissolute, hypocritical employers.

HARVEY. In *The Twisted Thing*, he is Rudolph York's loyal butler. He is courteous to Mike Hammer, who wonders at first if perhaps this time the butler did do it.

HARVEY, JAMES. In *The Death Dealers*, he sells litchi nuts, according to George Tung, who tells Tiger Mann that he and Harvey, whose mother was Chinese, are cousins.

HASKELL. In *The Death Dealers*, he is an important State Department official who confers with Teish El Abin.

HAVELOCK, MRS. In *The Erection Set*, she is a rich widow whom Dennison Barrin pursued unsuccessfully.

HAVER, EARNIE. In "The Night I Died," he was one of Helen Venn's lovers.

HAWKINS, ED. In *The Killing Man*, he leaves the office building where both he and Mike Hammer work and is almost killed when Penta drives by shooting at Mike.

HAYNES, PETER F., III. In "Me, Hood!," he owns a business in which Carmen Smith is a vice president. The position is a front for her criminal activity.

HAYS, LOIS. In "The Flier," she is an attractive journalist who Cat Fallon remembers interviewed him in Germany about a clandestine operation he was part of in Hungary. Now calling herself Karen Morgan and saying she works for Duncan Knight, she gains Fallon's confidence but is in reality a pro-Castro agent, aids Andro Marcel against Fallon, finally threatens to kill Fallon and Sharon Ortez, but steps back into his P-51 propeller, and dies.

HAYS, MISS. In *The By-Pass Control,* she is Henry Stanton's old-fashioned secretary, in her mid-fifties. They work at Belt-Aire Electronics.

HAYS, WILLIAM R. In *The Last Cop Out,* he is a fabric salesman from East Orange, New Jersey. Though innocent, he resembles a man sought by Francois Verdun, who has Hays tortured and killed.

HAZELTON, TOMMY. In *The Last Cop Out,* he is a person who, Papa Menes recalls, was arrested for violation of the Mann Act. Therefore, Menes has Louise Belhander fly from Florida to New York while he is driven by Artie Meeker. This is a plot weakness, because Louise, an adult, is Menes's willing associate.

HEALEY, BUD. In *The Erection Set,* Dog Kelly recalls that Bridey-the-Greek wounded Healey with an ice pick and made him a paralytic.

HEALEY, JIMMY. In *Survival . . . Zero!,* he and his friend, Vance Solito, are members of the so-called Marbletop bunch. Mike sees both of them in the elevator of the hotel where Beaver lived and was murdered.

HEINKLE, SHATZI. In *The Last Cop Out,* he is a resourceful, perverted, cross-eyed killer, age forty-five, working with Bingo Miles for Francois Verdun in pursuit of Gill Burke. Shatzi enjoys torturing victims with hot irons and has a habit of cutting out and saving their navels. Shatzi turns against Verdun, kills him, and also Richard Case, Marty Stackler, and Mack Ferro, who kills Shatzi before dying.

HELEN. In "The Screen Test of Mike Hammer," she kills Gus and Carmen, and tells Mike Hammer that Carmen killed Gus. When Mike says she did the killing, Helen pulls a gun but Mike chokes her to death.

HELEN. In "Together We Kill," she was Joe's temporary girlfriend but no match for Claire.

HELENA. In *The Ship That Never Was,* she is an inhabitant of Montique Island and serves Princess Tila.

HELEN THE MELONS. In "Man Alone," she worked as a hat-check girl at the Climax, was Al Argenio's well-endowed but abused girlfriend, escaped to Brooklyn, and helps Patrick Regan by revealing Argenio's addiction to playing the stock market.

HELGURT. In *The Erection Set,* in reminiscing about the war, Dog Kelly recalls that Helgurt shot down Bertram and Dog shot down Helgurt.

HELM, SIMON. In "The Bastard Bannerman," he is a Culver City real-estate agent. Cat Cay Bannerman fakes an interest in some land purchases in order to gain information from Helm about Vance Colby's criminal ambitions.

HELO, SPAAD. In *Bloody Sunrise,* he is a cunning Soviet killer, who traveled from California to Mexico to New York assigned to work with Sonia Dutko to kill the Russian defector Gabin Martrel. He tries on several occasions to kill Tiger Mann, who kills him.

HENAGHAN ("HENNY"). In *Survival . . . Zero!,* he is a public-works official who tells Mike Hammer where certain construction sites are located.

HENDERSON, BUNNY. In *Survival . . . Zero!,* he is a rich, playboy jet-setter who gave Heidi Anders a diamond-studded compact.

HENDERSON, NICHOLAS ("NICK"). In *The Long Wait,* he works in the bus station and is John McBride's loyal but timid friend. Nick leads McBride to Vera West and helps him in other ways.

HENLEY, MUMPY. In *Survival . . . Zero!,* he dislikes Mike Hammer, who once caused his arrest. Henley informs Jenkins and Wiley, two detectives, about Mike's being in Lipton Sullivan's apartment.

HENRI. In "Together We Kill," he is a waiter at the off-Broadway bistro where Joe meets Claire.

HENRY. In *I, the Jury,* he is an expert garage man who souped up Hammer's harmless-looking "heap," so that it can out-race police in pursuit.

HENRY. In *The Twisted Thing,* he is the gatekeeper at Rudolph York's estate. Henry is rendered unreliable when Ruston York substitutes sleeping pills for his aspirin.

HENRY, BAYLISS ("PEPPER"). In *The Girl Hunters,* he is a retired old newsman. Mike Hammer encounters him at Benny Joe Grissi's bar and asks him to help him locate Richie Cole's Brooklyn apartment and Red Markham's flophouse pad.

HENRY, MILES. In "Man Alone," Spud tells Patrick Regan that Henry delivered two pictures, both painted by Popeye Lewis, to the boss of the Climax, who had bought them.

HENRY, MRS. SPUD. In *Survival . . . Zero!,* she evidently henpecks her husband.

HENRY, SPUD. In *Survival . . . Zero!,* he is the ex-heavyweight doorman at William Dorn's apartment building. Mike Hammer knows him and kids him about his twelve children.

HERMAN. In *The By-Pass Control,* he and Bert live near Edith Caine.

HERMAN ("HERM"). In *The Ship That Never Was,* he has a marine service shop in the Florida Keys. Vincent Damar communicates with him by radio.

HERMAN, BERNIE. In *The Big Kill,* he owns a bar. Dixie Cooper proves to Mike Hammer that William Decker repaid him a loan by saying Herman saw him do so.

HERMAN, SLING. In "Everybody's Watching Me," he is remembered by Vetter as a pursued man standing as though "ready to go for something in his pocket."

HERNÁNDEZ, PROFESSOR FRANCISCO. In *The Delta Factor,* José tells Morgan that this man was abducted from the United States by Carlos Ortega.

HILBAR, RUSSELL. In *I, the Jury,* he is dean of men at the college attended by Harold Kines. When Hammer threatens to slap him around, Hilbar gives him Kines's dormitory room number.

HILL, DENNY. In *Survival . . . Zero!,* he reports to Mike Hammer, his friend, that he saw Velda.

HILL, FRANKIE. In *The Death Dealers,* he is an agent whom Lennie Byrnes summons to guard Edith Caine.

HILO. In "Killer Mine," he is a person Harry Wope says he works for.

HILQUIST, RAY. In "Man Alone," he was a bookie whose association with Mildred Swiss was terminated by an arranged car accident killing him. Her "suicide" was arranged because she knew too much about Leo Marcus.

HINES. In "The Seven Year Kill," Gates, Phil Rocca's spineless boss, worked for Hines and Best, who are evidently newspapermen.

HINES, BALDY. In *The Delta Factor,* he tells Morgan that Gorman Yard used to flash fifty-dollar bills in Hines's delicatessen.

HINNAM, I. In *The Long Wait,* he is a real-estate agent, eager to sell the flophouse where Inez Casey was murdered.

HOBIS. In *The Erection Set*, Dog Kelly orders Hobis and The Chopper to guard Sharon Cass and Lee Shay, and to help Dog in other ways.

HODGES, CHIPPER. In *Survival . . . Zero!*, he is an informant who reports to Mike Hammer that Woodring Ballinger has left his apartment without packing.

HOFTA, GREGORY. In *Day of the Guns*, he is a Hungarian translator in the U.N. Rondine Lund knows him. He helps Mann.

HOLBRIGHT, LINDA. In *One Lonely Night*, she is an unattractive fellow-traveling doorkeeper at the Brooklyn Communist meetings. Mike Hammer flirts a little with her, whereupon she visits his apartment, looking prettier. When they make wild love, it is the first time for her.

HOLIDAY. In *The Deep*, he is the seemingly decent power behind the criminal syndicate in New York City. His main underlings are Hugh Peddle and Lenny Sobel. After the killings are all cleared up, Deep will inevitably expose Holiday.

HOLLAND, ROLAND ("ROLLIE"). In *The Erection Set*, he was one of Dog Kelly's army buddies. After the war, Dog loaned Holland money. Very bright, Holland became wealthy, remained in Europe, and helped Dog.

HOLLAND, STANLEY. In *The Last Cop Out*, he was Papa Menes's drug lord and killer, posing as a businessman in Cleveland. One day he is shot dead in a parking lot. His real name was Enrico Scala.

HOLLENDALE. In *The Death Dealers*, he is an agent whom Lennie Byrnes recalls aiding "in Formosa."

HOLLINGS, MATT. In *Survival . . . Zero!*, he is mentioned by Eddie Dandy as an official in charge of disposing of nerve gas some time ago. Dandy's suspicions were aroused when he saw Hollings with Robert Crane of the State Department.

HOLMES, MARVIN. In *The Big Kill*, he is a well-heeled resident in an apartment one floor above Marsha Lee's. For a time, it was erroneously thought that Decker was ordered to crack his safe in the belief that it was loaded with money.

HOLMES, SONNY. In "Kick It or Kill!," he is Grace Evans's loyal boyfriend. He attacks Lennie Weaver and is slugged. He leads Kelly Smith to Simpson's private dock.

HOLMES, WILLIS. In "Me, Hood!," he is an ex-policeman, dismissed on a 1949 graft charge. He is wounded in front of Ryan's apartment and is not expected to survive.

HOMER. In *Vengeance Is Mine!,* he is a rich man who, with his hotly clinging mistress, visits the Bowery Inn for thrills. Homer wins at the gambling table there, briefly.

HOOD, ELAINE. In "The Affair with the Dragon Lady," she is a Broadway actress, Vern Tice's girlfriend, and then his wife.

HOOKER. In *Bloody Sunrise,* he and James are assigned by Newark Central to aid Tiger Mann.

HOOKER, MEL. In *The Big Kill,* he was William Decker's friend at the docks. He was involved in betting at the race track with Decker. When Hooker is murdered, Mike Hammer concludes that Toady Link ordered the killing.

HOOVER, CARL. In "Return of the Hood," during gunplay outside the Cafeteria, at the time Karen Sinclair was wounded, Hoover was killed.

HOPKINS. In *Bloody Sunrise,* this is the name of a woman registered in the Shrevesport Hotel. Tiger Mann briefly wonders if she is really Sonia Dutko, but she is not.

HOPPER, BOBO. In *I, the Jury,* he is a simple-minded but lovable friend of Mike Hammer's. Bobo used to run numbers for George Kalecki, is ambitious to be a beekeeper, now innocently delivers heroin for Charlotte Manning, and is shot to death by her.

HOPPES, NIGER. In *The By-Pass Control,* he is a Soviet agent, who escaped from Canada, returned to Russia, and is now in the United States, seeking Louis Agrounsky for his by-pass control. He kills Don Lavois in New York and goes to Florida after Agrounsky. He tries but fails to shoot Tiger Mann, tortures Claude Boster for information about Agrounsky, and follows that lead to Leesville, North Carolina, where Tiger follows him and kills him there.

"HOT CAT" (1964). *See* "The Flier."

HOWARD. In *The Erection Set,* he is S. C. Cable's partner in Cable Howard Productions, a movie-making company.

HOWELL, VIRGINIA. In *The Body Lovers,* she is a downtrodden prostitute whose pimp, Lorenzo Jones, beats her up. Mike Hammer intervenes and slugs Jones.

HOWIE. In *The Long Wait,* he is a casual friend of Carol Shay.

HOYT, THOMAS ("TOM"). In "The Seven Year Kill," he was an alcoholic physician in New York. The mob "straightened him out and put him back in business," in Phoenix. Hoyt helped fake Rhino Massley's "death." Hoyt and Leo Grant, a mortician also involved, were then killed in a staged jeep accident on October 2, 1965.

HUGGINS, MAMIE. In "Me, Hood!," she works in Ryan's neighborhood.

HUGHES, MAX. In *The Body Lovers,* he is a friendly bartender in a Bronx "slop chute." Max tells Mike Hammer what he can about Orslo Bucher's activities.

HULL, ARTIE. In *The Deep,* he is a syndicate hit man. After Hull kills Lew James and mortally wounds Cat, Deep chases him to the roof, off which he falls to his death.

HUMPY. In *I, the Jury,* he is a hunchback in his forties. He shines shoes on Park Avenue.

HUNT, CAMILLE. In *The By-Pass Control,* she is a Soviet mole, planted in Doug Hamilton's Belt-Aire Electronics company in New York, where Tiger Mann, seeking leads to Hamilton's murder, encounters her. She supplies Tiger with leads to Henri Frank, and she and Tiger make love in her Manhattan apartment. She flies to Eau Gallie, Florida, at Tiger's request, to aid in finding Louis Agrounsky, whom Camille and Niger Hoppes, her Soviet associate, are seeking. Camille follows Tiger to Agrounsky's beach house in Leesville, North Carolina, and is about to kill Tiger but, having a cold, sniffs a cyanide inhaler meant for Hoppes and dies. Camille, calling herself Helen Lewis, has a safety address in Savannah, where she consorted with Agrounsky.

HUNTER. In *The Erection Set,* he was Leyland Ross Hunter's father, and liked Dog Kelly's great-grandfather.

HUNTER, LEYLAND ROSS. In *The Erection Set,* he is an old lawyer friend of the Barrin family and Dog Kelly. Dog helped him become sexually active again by introducing him to Charmaine. Dog obtains Hunter's essential help with legal matters.

HURD, SERGEANT KEN. In *The Deep,* he is a tough policeman. He grew up in the same neighborhood as Deep, Bennett, and the other ruffians, but remained honest. Once he hears of Deep's true identity, Hurd treats him with grudging respect.

HURLEY. In "The Flier," Felix Ramsey gets demotion bombs from the Cable-Hurley Supplies Company for Cat Fallon's P-51.

HUSTON, TED. In *Day of the Guns,* he is a political editor for the *News,* for which Wally Gibbons writes columns.

HYMIE. In *The Deep,* he owns the deli patronized by Roscoe Tate, among others.

HYMIE. In "Me, Hood!," he had a drug store near Ryan's apartment.

HYMIE THE GOOSE. In "Me, Hood!," he is named by Stan Etching as a gunman.

I

"I CAME TO KILL YOU." *See* "Everybody's Watching Me."

"I'LL DIE TOMORROW" (1960). Short story. (Characters: Brisson, Francie, Joan, Rudolph Lees, Marco Leppert, Lulu, Buddy Riley, Tim Sheely, Lew Smith, Theresa, Cindy Valentine.) Rudolph Lees is a professional hit man, whose appearance is deceptively genteel. He has deftly killed almost fifty people. He uses his fees to buy women to torture sexually. When he is hired to kill a man named Riley, everything backfires. The man wears a bullet-proof vest, which sustains his bullets, and shoots Lees in the head. As he dies, Lees recognizes Riley as "Buddy," his first victim, whom he shot into the water, didn't finish off, and identifies by an ear shot during the war. Riley recovered and waited to set him up.

INJUN JOE. In *The Girl Hunters,* he is or was a sailor aboard the *Darby Standard.* Red Markham says Gorlin resembles Injun Joe. His nickname obviously derives from the name of the villain in *The Adventures of Tom Sawyer* by Mark Twain.

***I, THE JURY* (1947).** Novel. (Characters: Bellemy, Esther Bellemy, Mary Bellemy, Betty, Captain Pat Chambers, Inspector Daly, Myrna Devlin, Didson, Tom Dugan, Duke, Thelma Duval, Fields, Halper, Mike Hammer, Henry, Russell Hilbar, Bobo Hopper, Humpy, John, Miss June, George Kalecki, Kathy, Harold Kines, Charlotte Manning, Ronald Murphy, Pete, Virginia R. Reims, Big Sam, Charles Sherman, Silby, Conrad Stevens, Henry Strebhouse, Velda, Eileen Vicker, R. H. Vickers, Harmon Wilder, Jack Williams.)

Mike Hammer, private detective, is called to the scene of the torture-murder of Jack Williams, gutshot by a .45 dum dum in his apartment. Williams saved Mike's life in combat against the Japanese two years earlier, at the cost of an arm. Williams, formerly a New York City policeman and after the war an insurance investigator, was engaged to Myrna Devlin, a drug addict whose rehabilitation he financed. Vowing to find and kill the murderer, Mike comforts Myrna and learns from Captain Pat Chambers that Jack threw a party last night, attended by Myrna; Harold ("Hal") Kines, who drove her to her home in Westchester; George Kalecki, a rich ex-bootlegger with a Westchester mansion, with whom Kines lives; the pretty Bellemy twins; and Park Avenue psychiatrist Charlotte Manning, a gorgeous blonde with a "ritzy clientele."

Next day in Mike's office, Velda, his assistant, a beautiful, tough brunette, provides details concerning people on Jack's guest list. Mike loses a tail Pat put on him, barges in on Kalecki, and when Kines tries to conk him with a vase flattens him, threatens and insults both men, and hears their alibi for last night. Back at Pat's office, Mike learns that Myrna may have been involved with drug pushers using post-office box drops.

Mike calls on Charlotte Manning in her attractive office, hears her alibi—she left with the Bellemy twins—and learns she treated Jack's depression at Myrna's request. Mike goes to Charlotte's apartment, is admitted by her black maid, Kathy, and looks around briefly. Over beers, Pat tells Mike that Kalecki was shot at last night by the same gun that killed Jack, and that Kalecki and Hal quickly got an apartment in the city, at the Midworth Arms, where the Bellemys live. Mike lets himself into Kalecki's place, finds a .45 and a photograph of Hal looking older than he should. When the two men enter, Mike queries them and swaggers out. Calling at the Bellemys' apartment, Mike is seductively admitted by Mary, who says Esther is out shopping. Mary's alibi seems credible.

In the office, Velda spots Mary's lipstick on Mike's ear. He goes to the Hi-Ho Club, a former speakeasy, whose black owner, Sam, and a mentally challenged friend of Mike's named Bobo Hopper, tell him about Kalecki's numbers runners operating out of the club. Bobo, who delivers messages, says he no longer works for Kalecki. When two blacks at the bar jump Mike, he breaks the hand of one and the teeth of the other. He returns to Charlotte's place. She dismisses her maid and serves Mike chicken and fries. Hoping he will catch Jack's killer but warning him to take care, she compares his manliness to the wimps she counsels; they kiss and do some body pressing; he leaves, unnerved and promising to return.

In the morning Mike illegally enters Jack's apartment via a neighbor's air shaft and finds Jack's diary. Its contents indicate that an Eileen Vickers is in trouble in a call house, which Mike phones and enters, admitted by "Miss June." He is introduced to Eileen, now calling herself Mary Wright. She cries when Mike tells her Jack has been murdered. She tells him that she was seduced in college in the Midwest a dozen years ago by a John Hanson and that Jack knew about it and was trying to help her. Mike calls Pat, and the two locate pertinent college yearbooks—the police seized some from Jack's apartment—find Hanson's picture, and identify him as "Hal Kines." Mike hastens to the call house, only to find both Eileen and Hal shot dead. Pat arrives, scours the premises with Mike and has an aide photograph patrons and girls, but no killer is found. Nor is Miss June. Bullets from the same .45 killed Jack, Hal, and Eileen.

Next morning Mike phones and learns Charlotte is caring for a friend's baby in Central Park at 68th Street. He goes there and briefs her on the latest murders. Kalecki drives by, shoots at Mike, but misses. His bullet, retrieved, is not a dum dum. Mike takes Charlotte to her apartment, where though aroused by her sudden nudity he declines her offer. After Mike reports Kalecki's near miss, he and Charlotte theorize that Hal went to kill Eileen but a killer killed them both. Charlotte says Hal, supposedly a pre-med student, met her when she lectured at his college. They agree he ruined girls and forced them to work in Miss June's call house. When the police pick up June, Pat lets Mike question her. She says she escaped her house by a hidden passageway. Thinking the killer followed her that way, Pat and Mike inspect the area but find nothing. Mike visits Mary Bellemy, who pretends she is her absent staid twin Esther, but Mary's nymphomania rises and the two drink and make love. She invites Mike to a tennis party in the Bellemy estate on Saturday. Myrna and Charlotte will attend. Mike goes home. Suddenly thinking dead Hal might keep records of his pimping in his college room, he drives three hours north to Packsdale, rouses and scares the dean there, is given Hal's room number, and goes there. Grazed by a bullet, he shoots back and kills Kalecki. Mike discovers that Hal deposited blackmailing evidence against Kalecki in a New York City bank. Kalecki burned most of the papers before Mike broke in. The "hick cops" clear Mike once he has them phone Pat. Mike returns to Charlotte's place, summarizes events, and sleeps on her sofa until afternoon.

Near Lexington Avenue, Mike spots a murder scene. Bobo has been shot. A scared druggist nearby explains to Pat, and Inspector Daly of narcotics as well, that Bobo spilled some heroin, begged for some boric acid to replace it, rushed out, and got shot. Pat informs Mike that five persons he named are currently in drug-rehab programs. Is there a connection to Bobo? Missing his wallet, Mike rushes back to Charlotte, finds it in her sofa, and watches in her darkroom while she develops pictures of a patient under hypnosis.

Mike leaves his suit to have the bullet hole repaired, goes home, and gets a phone call from Pat. The same .45 killed Bobo. Mike takes Charlotte to a double-feature and on for sandwiches and beer. He proposes marriage to "kitten" and is accepted. Next day he picks up Myrna, who remains sad, and they drive to the Bellemys' estate to dine and then watch a tennis match. Mike drinks at the bar, naps in his assigned room, greets Charlotte, who has arrived by train. They sit near sexy Mary Bellemy at dinner. During the tennis match, Myrna pleads a headache and leaves. Mary lures Mike away from

Charlotte, and the two make love in the shadows. A maid suddenly screams. Mike leads others into the mansion, where Myrna has been shot dead. Mike posts guards to prevent the crowd of 250—guests and crashers—from leaving, and calls Pat. He locates some white powder found near Myrna's corpse and pockets it. Squads of cops arrive, question everyone, find no clues, and let everyone depart. Mike drives Charlotte back to town.

Sunday and part of Monday pass, largely wasted on cigarettes, beer, and the comics. Suddenly Mike has the solution. For "a fin," a druggist tells him Myrna's powder is heroin. Mike sneaks into Charlotte's apartment. When she enters, he covers her with his .45 and recites proof of her guilt: Jack trusted her; Jack suspected Hal; Hal, Kalecki's accomplice, had the goods on Charlotte and was blackmailing her; Charlotte followed Hal to Miss June's brothel, killed him, killed Eileen, and followed June out; Charlotte fired at Kalecki from outside his house; on the street Kalecki shot at her, not at Mike; Bobo innocently delivered heroin to Charlotte's addicted patients; when he spilled heroin, Charlotte shot him; Charlotte killed Myrna when the latter found heroin to be delivered to two of the Bellemys' guests. Charlotte had money but wanted more, to be independent of all men. Although Charlotte undresses, totally, before Mike and approaches provocatively—to grab her concealed .45, hidden behind him—he keeps his vow to Jack Williams and fatally gutshoots her. When she asks, "How c-could you?" he famously replies, "It was easy."

Spillane originally planned to use the plot of what became *I, the Jury* in a comic book to be titled *Mike Danger* but could not peddle it. He said he wrote the novel in nine (or maybe nineteen) days, to earn $1,000 for a down payment on acreage at Newburgh, New York, on which to build a house. The novel was a smash hit, ultimately selling 8 million copies in paperbound. Its blockbuster ending has been quoted scores of times, in praise and derogation of Spillane.

Bibliography: Collins and Traylor; Juddith Fetterley, "Beauty and the Beast: Fantasy and Fear in *I, the Jury,*" *Journal of Popular Culture* 8 (1975): 775-82.

J

JACK. In *The Long Wait*, he is a bellhop-pimp at the Hathaway House. McBride tips him well and learns from him where to encounter the brothel madam McBride calls Venus.

JACKIE. In *Black Alley*, he is a trucker loader who helps Mike Hammer get out of his apartment building undetected.

JACKIE. In *Survival . . . Zero!*, she is a prostitute working near Columbus Avenue and 110th Street. She knows Beaver.

JACKSON. In "Man Alone," he was a policeman at the switchboard who was too busy to monitor adequately the tip phoned in about the $5,000 bribe Patrick Regan supposedly received.

JAKE. In "The Night I Died," he is a Bowery bum who tells Mike Hammer that Carmen Rich killed Marty Wellman. The story is false.

JAMES. In *Bloody Sunrise*, he and Hooker are assigned by Newark Central to aid Tiger Mann.

JAMES, LEW. In *The Deep*, he is an expensive killer from Philadelphia, imported with Morrie Reeves to eliminate Deep. James, a junkie, is shot by Deep, bandaged by Dr. Anders, but then murdered by Artie Hull. When James arrives in New York City, he registers in a hotel as Charles Wagner, George Wagner's brother. George is really Reeves.

JAN. In *The Last Cop Out,* he and Lucien, both homosexuals, are assigned by Francois Verdun to guard Leon Bray. Both have their throats fatally cut by a masked man.

JANIE. In *The Twisted Thing,* she is a drunk girl at the Bayview honky-tonk.

JANSEN. In *The Erection Set,* he is a kid just out of reform school. He tries to steal Dog Kelly's rented car; but Coss McMillan's men have wired it, and it explodes and kills Jansen.

JASON. In *The Erection Set,* he is an agent in Paris whom Dog Kelly's agents are in touch with.

JASON. In *The Erection Set,* he is one of Stanley Cramer's old cronies. Jason and Pat help Cramer by finding material concerning the antigravity device for Dog Kelly.

JASON. In "Tomorrow I Die." *See* Trigger.

JEAN. In "Together We Kill," she was Joe's girlfriend—briefly, because Claire was matchless.

JEFF. In *The Killing Man,* he is the doorman of the apartment building where Mike lives. Two thugs slug Jeff to get at Mike.

JENKINS. In *Survival . . . Zero!,* he and Wiley are detectives investigating Lipton Sullivan's murder.

JENKINS, HARVEY ROBINSON. In *One Lonely Night,* he is a former matinee idol, down on his luck. Oscar Deamer hires him to impersonate Oscar, then gives him money for liquor, and kills him.

JENKINS, JEW. In "Killer Mine," Lieutenant Joe Scanlon recalls that long ago this old man was mugged by Mischelle Stegman, whom Joe then identified.

JENNER, CARL. In *The Death Dealers,* he is a *Journal* reporter seen by Tiger Mann talking with Seaton Coleman.

JENNER, JACK. In "The Bastard Bannerman," he is the person whose car was bumped by Vance Colby, who was visiting Irish Maloney's apartment for amorous purposes. A neighbor recorded his license number. This helped Cat Cay Bannerman expose Colby's criminal activities.

JENSON, HAPPY. In "Return of the Hood," he is a waiter at Chuck Vinson's saloon. He is worried about the trouble Ryan is in.

JERRY. In *The Erection Set,* he was an air force buddy of Dog Kelly having something to do with British Spitfires.

JERSEY TOBY. In *The Snake,* he is a reformed criminal, is now a pimp, and reluctantly provides Mike Hammer with information.

JIM. In *The Death Dealers* and in *Survival . . . Zero!,* he is the big bartender at the Blue Ribbon.

JIMMIE. In "Kick It or Kill!," he owns a bar where Kelly Smith and others meet to plan strategy.

JIMMY. In *My Gun Is Quick,* he runs a snack bar where Mike Hammer grabs a quick steak.

JIMSON, BUD. In *The Day the Sea Rolled Back,* he is the vicious older brother of Joie Jimson. The two sabotaged the *Blue Tuna,* owned by Vincent Damar, and seek the treasure in the *Nantucket Belle.* When the sea rolls back, the Jimsons go to the sea bed, see Larry Damar and Josh, try unsuccessfully to kill them, and may be lost when the sea rises again.

JIMSON, JOIE. In *The Day the Sea Rolled Back,* he is the stupid brother of Bud Jimson, who bullies him. The two may perish when the sea rises again.

JOAN. In *The Big Kill,* she is one of Cookie Harkin's informants. She works for the Devoe family, whom she impresses with a fake French accent.

JOAN. In "I'll Die Tomorrow," she was a huge victim whom Rudolph Lees paid to torture sexually. He planned to play with Joan and Theresa together later.

JOCKO-BOY. In *The Deep,* he is a bartender who tries unsuccessfully to keep Tally Lee from talking to Deep about Bennett.

JOE. In *The Erection Set,* he is a man hired by Dog Kelly to help guard the Cable Howard Productions party.

JOE. In "The Night I Died," he supposedly has taken over Marty Wellman's bar up the Hudson River. Actually, Carmen Rich owns it.

JOE. In "The Seven Year Kill," he is one of Mannie Waller's henchmen. He slugs Phil Rocca with his gun muzzle.

JOE. In "Together We Kill," he is an engineer in New York. Seven years earlier, during World War II, Claire, a French partisan, helped him blow up a bridge. They made love and promised to meet. They do and will marry.

JOHN. In *The Girl Hunters,* he is an Irish bartender working in P. J. Moriarty's saloon.

JOHN. In *I, the Jury,* he lives adjacent to Jack Williams. Mike Hammer uses John's apartment to gain illegal access to Jack's after Jack is murdered.

JOHN. In *Kiss Me, Deadly,* he is the helpful superintendent in Mike Hammer's apartment building. His wife cares for Lily Carver when Mike hides her in his apartment.

JOHNNY. In *The Big Kill,* he is one of Ed Teen's gunmen. When he is taking Mike Hammer for a one-way ride, Mike finds his .32 in his car and kills Johnny.

JOHNNY. In *The Day the Sea Rolled Back,* he is a helicopter pilot who flies Vincent Damar from Miami to Ara Island to look for Vincent's son Larry.

JOHNNY. In "Everybody's Watching Me," he is Mark Renzo's right-hand man.

JOHNNY. In "The Seven Year Kill," he is an important Phoenix police officer who is summoned by Joe Stack to aid Phil Rocca at Rhino Massley's former ranch.

JOHNSON. In *Bloody Sunrise,* he is the London intelligence agent who phones Tiger Mann about Spaad Helo. In *The Death Dealers,* Johnson phones Newark Central from London that Interpol was "all het up" because Lily Tornay was murdered. In *The By-Pass Control,* Johnson briefs Tiger about Niger Hoppes.

JOHNSON, CORTEZ. In *The Girl Hunters,* Mike Hammer is reminded by Bayliss Henry of Mike's gunfight with this man and his Red Hook gang.

JOHNSON, J. In *My Gun Is Quick. See* Hammer, Mike.

JOHNSON, JOSEPH. In *My Gun Is Quick,* this is the name of a man seeking to hire Mike Hammer, according to Mike's secretary, Velda.

JOHNSON, MARK. In *My Gun Is Quick,* along with Joseph Johnson, this man wanted to hire Mike Hammer, according to Velda.

JOHNSON, PETER. In *Day of the Guns,* he is a London agent who attempts to gain information for Tiger Mann about the Caine family.

JOHNSTON. In *Kiss Me, Deadly,* he is a policeman assigned to watch Mike's apartment. Mike asks him to guard Lily Carver. She evades him.

JOLLEY, JOEY ("JOE"). In *The Delta Factor,* he runs a Greenwich Village gin-mill and fences jewelry. He recommended that Mrs. Gustav Timely rent a room to Gorman Yard. Morgan asks him to check on Whitey Tass, a criminal. Joey does so, gets scared, comes to the island, and is pursued by Tass, who, however, is murdered. Morgan helps Joey escape.

JOLLY. In "The Seven Year Kill," he and Hal work for Mannie Waller, seek Terry Massley, beat up Phil Rocca, and are viciously kicked by Rocca.

JON. In *The Ship That Never Was,* he is a Montique Island inhabitant.

JONES. In *Bloody Sunrise,* he and Smith are two able, taciturn men under the command of Hal Randolph, who obviously gives them fictitious names. Tiger Mann badmouths both.

JONES. In "The Flier," he is a government internal bureau man, superior to Del Reed and working with Smith.

JONES, DUCK-DUCK. In *The Girl Hunters,* he is a longtime friend of Mike's. Duck-Duck replaced Dewey at his newstand, which Duck-Duck inherits.

JONES, LORENZO. In *The Body Lovers,* he is pimp with a string of girls, including Virginia Howell, Greta Service, and Roberta Slade. He delivers women to Ali Duval for Belar Ris's sadistic amusement. When Mike Hammer catches Jones beating up Virginia, he batters Jones. When Roberta leads Mike to Jones, Mike pumps him for information, batters him horribly, takes $3,000 from him, and gives it to Roberta for her escape and that of other prostitutes to a better life. At the Sandelor Hotel, Jones registers as J. Lorenzo.

JONES, SIGMUND ("PAPA"). In "Killer Mine," he owns a candy store. Upstairs, René Mills and Noisy Stuccio roomed and conducted their pimping work.

JONESY. In "The Affair with the Dragon Lady," he helps rescue the downed F-100 pilot.

JORDAN, HENRY. In *The By-Pass Control,* he is mentioned as owning a pick-up truck in Leesville, North Carolina. Presumably, Louis Agrounsky bought it last year.

JOSÉ. In *The Delta Factor,* he works for Art Keefer, has a boat, gets Morgan to the island, and delivers Joey Holley and a sample of heroin to Morgan.

JOSEPH. In *Vengeance Is Mine!,* he is a wealthy young man who visits the Bowery Inn with his date for thrills.

JOSH. In *The Day the Sea Rolled Back,* he is Timothy's son. Both are native Caribbeans. Josh and Larry Damar to explore the sea bed when the sea rolls back. They both escape the murderous intentions of Bud and Joie Jimson. In *The Ship That Never Was,* Josh's full name, Josh Toomey, is given.

JOSIE. In *Survival . . . Zero!,* she is mentioned by Heidi Anders as a friend.

JUAN. In "The Flier," he is a thug working under Andro Marcel. The two, plus an unnamed colleague, torture Cat Fallon.

JUKE. In *The Erection Set,* he and Stoney are two of Stanley Cramer's cronies. The three, all retired after working for Cameron Barrin, play cards and help Dog Kelly.

JUNE, MISS. In *I, the Jury,* she is a madam whose brothel politicians and businessmen frequent. Harold Kines and Eileen Vickers are murdered there. Miss June, "a frowsy blonde about fifty," escapes through a secret passageway, which Charlotte Manning also uses.

K

K. In *Day of the Guns,* he is named as the Russian who assigned Stovetsky a post in the U.N. K may well be Nikita Khrushchev (1894-1971), head of the Soviet government from 1958 to 1964.

KALECKI, GEORGE. In *I, the Jury,* he is a numbers racketeer, rich through bootlegging in Prohibition days and now living in a mansion. Working with Harold Kines, to shake down Charlotte Manning, cost him his life. To gain seeming respectability, Kalecki called himself George K. Masters when he bought a .45.

KANIA, MARV. In *The Snake,* he is a hardened killer, about twenty-eight, who evidently killed Angelo, Carlysle, Vince Pago, and Schulburger in various cities. He was imported from St. Louis to kill Mike Hammer. During Kania's attempt on Sue Devon's life, Mike gutshoots Kania, who dies ghoulishly laughing at the end.

KATE. In *Vengeance Is Mine!,* she is a friend whom Connie Wales, when with Mike Hammer, meets at Neil's Bowery bar. Connie says Kate is "from upstate."

KATHY. In *I, the Jury,* she is Charlotte Manning's peppy black maid. Spillane's handling of her lingo is demeaning and ludicrously inaccurate. For example, Kathy addresses Hammer as "y'all." Another example of demeaningly recording black talk comes when the black bartender employed by Esther and Mary Bellemy answers Hammer thus: "Don' nobody come in 'cept de girl [Myrna Devlin]. She's daid."

KATZ, SIGMUND. In *Survival . . . Zero!,* he is a tailor near Columbus Avenue and 110th Street. He tells Mike that he saw Carl and Sammy a short time earlier.

KAWOLSKI, MATT. In "Return of the Hood," he owns an eatery by the docks. Karen Sinclair is hidden nearby.

KAWOLSKY, LEOPOLD ("LEE"). In *Kiss Me, Deadly,* he was an ex-boxer, a bartender for Ed Rooney, and Berga Torn's bodyguard and lover. Right after her murder, Kawolsky was murdered by being pushed in front of a truck. Eddie Connely, Mike's journalist friend, gives Mike information about Kawolsky.

KEEFER, ART. In *The Delta Factor,* he was an army buddy of Morgan's. Described as big and tough, and as having "looked on the world and thrown it away," Keefer helps get Morgan to the island, information by radio once he is there, and out again to safety.

KELLY. In *The Erection Set,* he was a wild Irish employee in the old Barrin factory. Dog Kelly was his illegitimate son. The mother, though pregnant, married a Barrin, who then ostracized the elder Kelly and probably had him murdered.

KELLY, DOG ("DOGGIE"; real name: Dogeron Kelly). In *The Erection Set,* Dog Kelly, the narrator of most of the novel, was the black-sheep cousin of the Barrin family, since he was the illegitimate stepson of a Barrin who married the mother and caused Dog's father's death. Dog's cousins are Alfred Barrin, Dennison Barrin, Veda Barrin, Pam Barrin Gates, and Lucella Simon. Dog was an All-American in college football, became a major in the army air force and a combat ace, and flew with Walt Gentry, Roland Holland, Al DeVecchio, and Lee Shay. Dog took his discharge in Europe in 1946, bankrolled Roland Holland to wealth, became rich himself, and learned Arabic, French, Spanish, and Turkish. Experienced in black-market and drug activities, Dog becomes an undercover agent, is suspected of being the drug boss El Lobo, returns to New York twenty-some years later, sleeps and kills around, causes a heroin shipment to be intercepted, financially embarrasses his cousins, and woos and wins Sharon Cass. By having Dog dislike martinis, Spillane hoped to evoke readers' memories of 007, the martini-loving hero of the James Bond novels of Ian Fleming (1908–1964).

KELLY, RON. In *Day of the Guns,* he is a young fireman. Mann uses him and his boss Captain Murray as decoys so Mann can approach Alexis Minner's apartment.

KEVIN, ARTHUR ("SLICK"). In *The Last Cop Out,* he is one of Mark Shelby's investigators. At one point, Francois Verdun tries to reach Kevin but cannot, since Kevin has been shot dead.

"KICK IT OR KILL!" (1963). Short story. (Characters: Jake Adler, Harry Adrano, Helen Allen, Artie, Calvin Bock, Don Casales, Captain Cox, Emma Cox, Walter Cramer, Dari Dahl, Flori Dahl, Willie Elkins, Gloria Evans, Mrs. Finney, Ruth Gleason, Sonny Holmes, Jimmie, Carter Lansing, Dr. McKeever, Mrs. McKeever, Moe, Rita Moffet, Nat Paley, Margie Provetsky, Benny Quick, Rayburn, Bob Rayburn, Red Dog Wally, Sergei Rudinoff, Bonnie Ann Shaefer, Grace Shaefer, Simpson, Kelly Smith, Mort Steiger, Sergeant Hal Vance, Lennie Weaver, White, Woody.)

Kelly Smith is trying to recover from a gunshot wound by vacationing at Pinewood, outside New York City, but finds the town dominated by a man called Simpson. This villain gets local girls hooked on heroin, and with a squad of criminals forces them to dance, be whipped in his hilltop mansion, and be sex slaves to visiting drug lords, soon to include Sergei Rudinoff, a Soviet diplomat. Kelly is aware of a Cuba-China-Russia drug-smuggling network. Pinewood police, led by Captain Cox, and the locals are both fearful of Simpson and pleased by tax revenue and other money he provides. Kelly falls in love with the hotel proprietress, Dari Dahl, whose drug-addicted sister committed suicide. Dari sees Kelly take painkillers, assumes he too is a drug addict, and spurns him until she learns better. Then they fall in love. Some of Simpson's thugs dump Gloria Evans, exploited, sado-whipped, and now useless, back in town. Kelly evades a pair of thugs but is wounded by another, whom he kills. Dr. McKeever treats Kelly, whose delayed recovery prevents his stopping Dari from taking his gun and offering herself as a fresh, attractive dancer for Simpson, in hopes of killing him. Kelly tells McKeever to summon reinforcements from New York City and gets Gloria's boyfriend to show him Simpson's private dock. Kelly invades the mansion, kills several bullies, sets fire to the place, and hears mop-up gunfire from the authorities outside. Before escaping the flames with Dari, Kelly kills Rudinoff and Simpson—in reality an influential senator. Kelly has ample time to tell Dari he is Al Braddock, a federal agent.

Ruth Gleason could not kick heroin, hence killed Weaver; hence the title "Kick It or Kill!" Given Spillane's plotting techniques, Smith's lecture to McKeever is fascinating: "Lack of coincidence can eliminate chance. Coincidence can provide it. I was the coincidence [i.e., by appearing in Pinehood]." Dari's persuading Smith to surrender his gun foolishly to her has interesting parallels in myths, legends, and cowboy literature.

KIERNAN. In *The Last Cop Out,* he was Helen Scanlon's lover when she was eighteen. He proved callous.

KILEY. In *The Snake,* he is one of Captain Pat Chambers's men. He and Lew Nelson are assigned to check on Basil Levitt.

"KILLER MINE" (1965). Short story. (Characters: Commissioner Arbatur, Beamish, Bloody Mary, Phil Borley, Marta Borlig, Sed Borlig, Sergeant Mack Brissom, Inspector Bryan, Bunny, Ralph Callahan, Carbito, Carmine, Cassidy, Moe Clausist, Clehoe, Charlie Darpsey, Davis, Donavan, Fat Mary, Will Fater, Fuchie, Helen Gentry, Gordon, Grafton, Grootz, Hilo, Jew Jenkins, Sigmund Jones, Doug Kitchen, Paula Lees, Bummy Lentz, Benny Loefert, Steve Lutz, Hal McNeil, Billy Menter, René Mills, Kitty Muntz, Murphy, Mrs. Murphy, Norman, Captain Oliver, Polack Izzie, Pops, Ray, Al Reese, Ronnie, Sergeant Nick Rossi, Scanlon, Lieutenant Joe Scanlon, Larry Scanlon, Hymie Shapiro, Rose Shaw, Smith, Sam Staples, Mischelle Stegman, Strauss, Noisy Stuccio, Tony, Trent, Gus Wilder, Henry Wilder, Harry Wope.)

When four murders are committed in Lieutenant Joe Scanlon's rundown former neighborhood, Joe is ordered to return to it, pretend Marta ("Marty") Borlig, a childhood friend now an undercover policewoman, is his girlfriend, and investigate. The latest victim was Doug Kitchen, Joe's friend and a decent shipyard worker. Joe and Marty are single; she is a little younger, big, and beautiful. They resume their acquaintance and reminisce about their families. Joe's favorite sibling among ten was Larry "Chief Crazy Horse" Scanlon, long gone, missing in action in World War II. As boys playing with chums, Joe was a cop in Cops and Robbers; Larry was an Indian in Cowboys and Indians. Marty mentions a brother, now studying dentistry. Joe and Marty consult three earlier victims' rap sheets, provided by Sergeant Mack Brissom. The dead are Hymie Shapiro, Noisy Stuccio, a pimp, and René Mills, who roomed with Noisy until Mills hit the lottery. Joe suspects the killings, all by an expert with one .38, are connected to political corruption and gang warfare.

On Saturday Joe and Marty start gossip about their renewed friendship by sauntering into their old neighborhood. Joe is remembered as a cop, but Marty is thought to have an office job elsewhere. They enter Donavan's musty bar for beer. Playing it tough, Joe punches a wise guy slow to make room for Marty. When the district political boss, Al Reese, threatens to have Joe's badge lifted and pokes Joe with his finger, Joe breaks it and shouts a general warning. Loefert, an uptown ex-con mobster, watches, amused. Marty changes to casual dress, kisses Joe briefly, and they go to Tony's pizza place. His wife, Fat Mary, when Joe questions her about Mills, produces well-worn Cadillac ads she says Mills left just before he was shot. Joe takes Marty home, calls several car dealers, and learns Mills had money enough to shop for a Cadillac. Joe kisses Marty passionately and leaves. On the street he braces Loefert, with a prostitute named Paula Lees, as a neighborhood wake-up call.

Joe goes to his office on Sunday and hears this from Brissom: Charlie Darpsey, suspected of an armored-car robbery and a killing in Canada, may be heading for New York; Loefert has been seen with Beamish, Will Fater, and

Steve Lutz, high-paid gunmen. Joe hints at a bar that Reese is a stool pigeon. After lunch and a movie, Joe and Marty have supper at a grill and meet Hal McNeil, the loyal beat cop who knew the murder victims.

Leaving Marty at her place, Joe has two beers and talks with Harry Wope. He knew Joe's father and says Reese has hired someone to get Joe. Joe locates Paula, persuades her to admit she saw Doug get killed, but learns only that the assailant yelled strangely. Joe calls on Ralph Callahan, a retired policeman living nearby. He tells Joe the mob may be watching for a witness against them named Gus Wilder, who reportedly jumped bail in Toledo recently and may be back in the city.

The next morning Brissom tells Joe the gun used in the Canadian heist was found in the Bronx; so that killer may be in the city. At a diner Marty tells Joe that Fat Mary recalled Mills's flashing rolls of money and buying expensive whiskey. Joe, aware that neither money nor whiskey was found in Mills's apartment, concludes (somehow) that he was hiding Gus Wilder. Joe visits Henry Wilder, Gus's stepbrother, at his dry-cleaning establishment, is told that Rose Shaw, one of Mills's prostitutes, is coming in for some clothes, waits for her, and follows her to her room. By treating Rose gently, he learns that Mills dumped her and another girl, had plenty of money in small bills, and was hiding someone. Joe tells Rose he'll ask a photographer he knows to try her for modeling. In late afternoon Joe goes to Donavan, is told Reese is at Bunny's "fag joint," and goes there. He humiliates Reese, and with him Fater and Lutz, by patting them down, then threatens to tear off Reese's ears if he doesn't let Paula alone permanently. Joe dines with Marty at her place. She tells him that police reports indicate that the mob ordered Loefert, Fater, and Lutz into the neighborhood and that the mob has fingered Gus.

Tony tells Joe and Marty that Mills was both stupid and scary, and suddenly knew or had something Reese demanded to share. Joe and Marty check Mills's apartment and find evidence that someone else had lived there. They conclude this: Noisy investigated; the stranger killed him; Noisy had told Hymie; the stranger killed him; Doug chanced to see Paula witness this killing; the stranger, whooping, killed him. Joe, told by McNeil on patrol to call Brissom, learns this: Chicago police arrested a man who revealed that a big heist, undoubtedly the Canadian one, was hijacked by a masked man who dropped a paper with Sigmund Jones's phone number. Joe concludes this: Gus was the hijacker, phoned his stepbrother through Jones, came to New York, roomed with Mills, and is the killer. McNeil tells Joe that Reese talked tonight with Loefert and Fater at Bunny's place. After checking with Henry Wilder to verify the timing of Gus's call, Joe and Marty start home but are shot at. Marty sustains a shoulder wound. Joe rushes to the building roof opposite them and chases a gunman, who falls from a rusty fire escape to his death. He was Fater.

Authorities handle Fater's body. Bryan and Oliver tell Joe about increased political pressure to solve these killings and give him two more days to try.

Joe goes home with Marty. They make splendid love. He returns to the streets, alone, his cover blown. Wope informs him that Reese offered to pay Fater for killing Joe and that Reese was seen with Paula. Wondering whether Reese and Gus are in cahoots, Joe approaches Paula's apartment, hears shots, is fired on, gets to the roof, sees his assailant on the street, returns, and finds Lutz, Beamish, and Reese shot dead, with evidence that Reese had been torturing Paula. Dying, she tells Joe only this: Reese offered her a job if she would meet someone; Reeve was to arrive first; but the other appeared first. Bryan and Oliver supervise the medical team and give Joe until morning to solve everything. Joe calls Brissom, who reports that Gus is no longer a suspect, since he committed suicide in Ohio days ago and his body was just found. Joe, certain of events now, returns to the deserted building where the Scanlon brood grew up. Well-trodden stairs. A musty room. He finds his twin brother, Larry "Chief Crazy Horse" Scanlon, long missing. It seems that Larry got into postwar black-marketeering, then more crimes, heard of that Canadian heist, stole from its getaway truck, and made his way back to the old Scanlon stamping grounds. Larry boasts of killing everyone trying to shake him down. He shouted a Crazy Horse warwhoop when he had to nail Doug. Joe guesses the loot is safe under the family's stairway. Yes. Having heard all, Joe, whom Larry shot at earlier, offers to arrest Larry. No way. In gunplay following, Joe kills his twin.

"Killer Mine" has a clever plot, deliberately tangled by two red herrings: The reader suspects that Joe Scanlon's superiors may be motivated by criminal political connections; and Gus Wilder, considered a suspect, killed himself before the action starts. Joe drinks Pabst beer in 1965; after Spillane began advertising Miller in 1973, his heroes change brands.

***THE KILLING MAN* (1989).** Novel. (Characters: Nolo Abberniche, Candace Amory, Petey Benson, Harry Bern, Bing, Bennett Bradley, Byers, Frank Carmody, Patrolman Carsi, Captain Pat Chambers, David Clinton, Jerome Coleman, Anthony DiCica, Maria Louisa DiCica, Victorio DiCica, Nat Drutman, Francisco DuValle, Eddie, Ernie, Maria Escalante, Gary Fells, Lewis Ferguson, Manuel Florio, Russell Graves, Mike Hammer, Ed Hawkins, Jeff, Kimball, Sergeant Klaus, Jason McIntyre, Madge, Julius Marco, Meg, Dr. Burke Reedey, Marty Santino, Bill Sheen, General Rudolph Skubal, Richard Smiley, Phillip Smith, Victor Starson, Tony, Juan Torres, Tunney, Velda, Richard Welkes, Edwina West, Ray Wilson.)

Mike Hammer enters his office one Saturday noon to meet a client he has never met, but finds Velda slugged unconscious and a corpse at Mike's desk— mouth taped, face and chest sliced, fingers chopped off and displayed, killed by a spike in his forehead. A note signed "Penta" says, "You die for killing me." Did someone mistake the victim for Mike? Mike calls Dr. Burke Reedey and the police. Reedey and Meg, his nurse, get Velda to the hospital. Officials handle the murder scene and the victim. Captain Pat Chambers takes Mike's statement. In the victim's pocket they find his name, Anthony Cica, and address, break into his tenement apartment, and find 7.65 cartridges and precision hand-tools in an ornate box, initialed "V. D."

On Sunday morning, Mike calls Reedey and learns that Velda is better. Pat orders Mike to headquarters, where he learns that Cica—really DiCica—delivered stationery Velda ordered for the office. Mike meets Candace Amory, a beautiful assistant D.A., and Jerome Coleman, who is from Albany. Mike is ordered to keep confidential the name Penta, whom Mike denies knowing anything about. A cleaning woman tells Mike she saw a big man in a raincoat near his office yesterday. Over a beer at the Olde English Tavern on Third Avenue, Petey Benson, a knowledgeable reporter, tells Mike that Candace worked for the FBI in Washington, D.C., and is a bright, single, dangerous lawyer.

At 8:00 P.M. Mike briefly visits Velda in the hospital. He tells her to pretend she is too sick to talk to anyone. On the street, three men jump Mike. He breaks one man's nose, another's teeth, but is drugged, taken to a garage, given sodium pentothal, and queried. When he denies knowing any Penta, the men leave. Dazed, Mike walks out and notices the garage is labeled Smiley's. Pat, when informed next day, says witnesses saw Mike dragged into a black Mercedes with a broken taillight. Pat says DiCica had been slugged, was hospitalized, developed amnesia, but was recently released and worked at the stationery shop. Pat takes Mike to a meeting called by Coleman and Candace, with Bennett Bradley (State Department), Frank Carmody and Phillip Smith (FBI), and Lewis Ferguson (CIA) present. When asked, Mike says, yes, some people can lie when given sodium pentothal. One official tells him Penta killed a CIA agent who before dying may have revealed vital information concerning nuclear capabilities of a Third World country. Pat takes Mike to meet Ray Wilson, a former intelligence expert, now a policeman near retirement, whom Pat has briefed. They agree Mike's assailants were probably government agents and wonder whether the killer sought DiCica, not Mike. Mike answers a message to meet a stranger at Charlie the Greek's. When the stranger asks about DiCica and seems responsive, Mike theorizes: DiCica was left alone until he recovered his memory, then was hunted. The stranger says certain people figure DiCica sought Mike for protection and told Mike some secrets. Mike hands him a bullet as a challenge to his boss.

Benson tells Mike that Candace, in a teenage essay, expressed the determination to be president and gives Mike her private number. Mike calls for a supper date. They meet and exchange confidences: Mike says the authorities want him to kill Penta; Candace doesn't know the name of the American agent Penta killed, but the murder occurred near Manchester, England. Candace and Mike go to her apartment. He wins a bet by stating her ambition to be president; shocked and losing, she is supposed to undress. He says she needn't; she does anyway—as he leaves. Mike checks on Velda, calls Benson, gets the name of a Manchester journalist—Russell Graves—calls him, and is promised details about the murder of an American near Manchester, if available.

Mike checks the neighborhood of Smiley's garage. A codger named Jason McIntyre is cleaning it and gives Mike something he found, a broken-off partial plate. At a coffee shop Mike has a sandwich and learns that Smiley is a show-off with money he says he regularly wins at the tracks. Mike gives the partial to Pat, who will have it checked against dental records of FBI and CIA agents. When Mike sees Velda, she tells him she recorded the phoned request, presumably by Penta, for an appointment and put it in a certain file. Mike plays it in his office, then pockets it. That night Graves calls from England with information that an American was murdered, with five fingers chopped off. Next morning Mike returns to Smiley's, only to find him clubbed to death. Mike calls the authorities. Pat, and then Coleman and Candace, appear. After routine questioning, Mike gives Pat the tape of Penta's voice.

Mike visits Wilson, who has computer links to international law-enforcement agencies and tells him about three victims of killings and finger mutilations. These unsolved murders—of a drug dealer, a kidnapper, and an art thief—were criminal cases, twelve years old. The killer has now, however, become a political terrorist, who also thinks Mike killed Penta. Mike fends off reporters, talks with Pat and Candace, and learns Smiley's killer wore boating shoes now being traced. Back in his apartment, Mike returns Graves's call and learns British intelligence agents warned Graves not to investigate murders involving cut-off fingers. Mike invades a meeting of Bradley, Coleman, and Candace; brushing aside their annoyance, he says he knows recent murders are political and terroristic. Bradley admits that federal authorities for eleven years have sought Penta, suspected of nine political assassinations; but he wonders why Penta is after Mike. Mike takes Candace to a tavern, introduces her to Benson, asks him to check on DiCica, and drops Candace by taxi at her apartment.

Mike works out, has a steam bath, muses about who ordered DiCica killed, takes flowers to Velda, and accompanies Pat to confer with Ferguson and Bradley. Ferguson has the dental plate Mike gave Pat and grudgingly tells Mike it came from the mouth of a ex–CIA agent named Harry Bern, who with his partner, Gary Fells, were trained by General Rudolph Skubal but are now renegades. Bradley orders Mike to drop the Penta investigation but says Mike can pursue DiCica leads because Penta gunned for Mike, not DiCica. Alone with Mike, Pat reveals this: DiCica killed two mobsters and took an envelope from them; his enemies cracked his head too hard, waited because he lost his memory, searched his place but found nothing. Mike visits Benson, whose computer links reveal this: Victorio DiCica, Anthony's father, was a cabinet maker (the toolbox marked "V. D." was his), was killed in a holdup in 1960; Anthony, by then a street crook, killed the murderer, got off for lack of evidence, and associated with Juan Torres, a notorious drug dealer; Maria Louisa DiCica, Anthony's mother, is well off through his generosity; someone is watching her two houses; mobsters think DiCica recovered his memory, confided in Mike; they want Mike. Mike goes to Candace's apartment; while she gradually dresses, he says he can help her nail DiCica's killer and thus advance her career.

At the entrance to his apartment building, Mike is jumped by two thugs, breaks one man's nose and groin-kicks the other, forces one to talk, and learns the pair were hired by the boss resenting the bullet challenge. After the police arrest the pair, Pat arrives and says the tape Mike gave him is to be aired on TV. Not wanting Velda to see the broadcast, Mike rushes to the hospital and learns that a strange doctor was prevented by an alert orderly from giving her a shot, and quickly left. Velda tells Mike the stranger's voice was that of the man who phoned their office Saturday for the appointment. In the foyer are Pat, Reedey, and Bradley. Mike tells Bradley he doubts Penta, merely named in that note on his desk, is involved.

Mike goes to his office, locates Rudy Skubal's address, leaves, and is shot at but missed by a drive-by passenger with an Uzi, phones Candace, and accepts a lift from her to her apartment. She says the envelope DiCica took from his murder victims specified the location of a tractor-trailer full of cocaine worth $905 million. She lectures Mike about the escalating production and consumption of cocaine, and wonders with Mike about Penta's relationship to DiCica. Mike wants only DiCica's killer, because he slugged Velda. To the tune of the *Dante Symphony* by Franz Liszt, Mike and Candace make exhaustive love. Next morning, Mike drives to Long Island and Skubal's solar-powered, electronically guarded minifortress, employing eighty people. Mike is ushered past his gorgeous CIA "secretary" Edwina West into Skubal's presence, is awed by his gigantic sophisticated computers, and briefs him about DiCica, Penta, Bern, and Fells. Skubal reveals this: The CIA assigned the name Penta to an unknown multiple killer and finger chopper connected to the Red Brigade; Bradley was reported shot by Penta and is soon to be reassigned; Penta is in America for high-level work, perhaps involving someone Mike doesn't know; Penta killed three politicians on orders from Arabs in Libya, where Bern and Fells recently worked; those two, wanted by the CIA and the FBI, have one safe house left, in Brooklyn. Skubal retreats for his nap. Mike and Edwina enjoy muscular embracing, prematurely ended when the Brooklyn address is given to him. Mike returns home.

Mike calls Pat, gives him the safe-house address, and meets with Pat, Bradley, Ferguson, and Carmody. SWAT members break into the house, find Bern and Fells shot dead, and locate the Mercedes that trailed Mike in their garage. A thorough search of the house produces $42,000 in cash and a letter revealing this: Penta was assigned to kill the vice president of the United States, didn't follow orders immediately because of his desire, first, to get DiCica to tell where the cocaine was hidden; Bern and Fells, assigned to kill Penta, were killed by Penta. When Mike calls Candace from Pat's office, she reports that Wilson discovered that the cocaine—worth a billion dollars—was transferred from one trailer to another. Its drivers were then killed, and it is missing. Mike reports by phone to Skubal, who says Penta has access to the Brooklyn safe house. Mike is still Penta's target because he thinks DiCica told Mike where the cocaine trailer is. Mike and Pat are mulling over things when suddenly Mike spots DiCica's father's toolbox, kept with Pat as evidence. Mike calls Candace to come to Pat's at once and explains: DiCica, though with memory loss, took the toolbox because it seemed precious to him. Breaking its bottom, Mike finds a coded message. Mike orders Candace to send a copy to Washington, D.C., but to let Ray try at once to decode the message, and says it may lead to the trailer.

Mike rushes to the hospital, spots a phony guard at Velda's door, calls Pat for reinforcements and watches as Velda, sedated, is gurneyed to the parking lot by a phony orderly. Pat and other personnel arrive. Both criminals are killed, and the survivors rush to Candace's apartment. Present are Bradley, Ferguson, Coleman, Carmody, and Reedey. Wilson reports that the code, now broken, suggests that the trailer is at a barn by Lake Hopatcong, northwest of Kingston, New York. Ferguson, a skier, has access to a cabin there. Bradley coordinates efforts of a convoy of men. Candace loans some clothes to Velda, to whom Mike explains the case and who accompanies him to Ferguson's cabin. It will serve as a well-provisioned safe house. Dawn follows the first night. Mike prepares breakfast for Velda, their two guards outside, and himself. Pat radios a delay because of an interagency argument Bradley says he will settle. A cold front sweeps in. Mike prepares logs for the fireplace, and by chance while twisting piled-up newspapers under the kindling sees an illustrated report of Francisco DuValle's execution. Mike's testimony four years earlier of this multiple murderer convicted him. When Mike covers DuValle's beard and unruly hair with Velda's white facial cream, DuValle is the spitting image of Bradley. All is clear: Bradley, obviously DuValle's brother, is Penta, ordered in Europe to kill the vice president but sidetracked by news of the execution and determined, first, to kill Mike and find the cocaine. Mike shoves Velda through an attic hatch, creeps outside, finds the guards dead, returns, sees Bradley up the hatch and pulling on Velda, shoots both of his legs, gloats as the hypocritical fellow drops to the floor, and tells Velda to radio the authorities. Twisting in pain, Bradley snarls about DuValle, his twin, quotes the message he left in Mike's office, scrambles for a hidden .38, but gets a .45 round from Mike through his head.

Spillane brings action in *The Killing Man* au courant by referring to AIDS, the Black Panthers, CNN, computer networking, Libya, Mafia "made men," Middle Eastern terrorists, Qaddafi, the Red Brigade, and Uzis. He skillfully describes body language and translates its possible import. Dirty talk is kept to a minimum, but the final word is an obscenity. The narrative moves at lightning speed, but the reader must pause at monstrous coincidences, for example, the "V. D." toolbox in Pat's office for Mike to rest his feet on, Ferguson having a cabin near where the cocaine is stashed, and Mike's seeing

DuValle's picture on a weeks-old paper he is about to burn. His publishers paid Spillane $1.5 million for *The Killing Man.* In addition, an excerpt of it was published in *Playboy,* in December 1989, illustrated by Daniel Torres.

KIMBALL. In *The Killing Man,* this is the name of the estate where General Rudolph Skubal lives.

KIMBALL, GUY. In "Together We Kill," he offers Joe an engineering job in Bolivia.

KINES, HAROLD ("HAL"). In *I, the Jury,* he is racketeer George Kalecki's criminal associate. Kines claims to be a medical-school student, looks about twenty-three, but in reality has gone from college to college—at least twenty-seven of them, according to Captain Pat Chambers—registering briefly and corrupting naive young female students, whom he forces into prostitution. One such victim is Eileen Vickers. When he follows Eileen into Miss June's brothel, Charlotte Manning, whom Kines is blackmailing, follows him and kills both Kines and Eileen.

KING, GERALDINE. In *The Snake,* she is Simpson Torrence's gorgeous political-party secretary. She comes on to Mike Hammer, with little success. At his request, she gets Sue Devon, Torrence's adopted daughter, to safety. She expresses a sense of freedom on learning that Torrence has been murdered.

KING, GRETA. In *The Girl Hunters,* Art Rickerby tells Mike that she is an American Airlines stewardess and was one of Richie Cole's girlfriends.

KIPTON, SONNY. In *The By-Pass Control,* he was a drug dealer murdered for diluting heroin.

KIRKLAND, DR. In *The By-Pass Control,* he attends to Tiger Mann when he is wounded by Vito Salvi in New York.

KIRREL, ERNIE. In *The Erection Set,* he was one of Dog Kelly's army buddies. He may have seen Dog in Marseilles.

KISS ME, DEADLY **(1952).** Novel. (Characters: Al Affia, Andy, Carlo Barnes, Mousie Basso, Bernstein, Lily Carver, Captain Pat Chambers, Charlie, Eddie Connely, Costello, Dave, Delaney, Ray Diker, Duke, Carl Evello, Foreman, Michael Friday, Bob Gellie, Congressman Geyfey, Mike Hammer, Leo Harmody, John, Johnston, Leopold Kawolsky, Walter McGrath, Charlie Max, William Mist, Moffat, Clancy O'Brien, Pascale, Harvey Pullen, Nicholas Raymond, Ed Rooney, Sammy, Sugar Smallhouse, Dr. Martin Soberin, Toscio, Carmen Trivago, Berga Torn, Harvey Wallace, Mrs. Harvey Wallace, Velda.)

While driving to New York City one Monday night, Mike picks up an attractive female hitchhiker, nude under her trench coat. A car passes them. They get to a police barricade. When a cocky county cop asks if he saw a hitchhiker, Mike says he and his wife saw nothing. The cop says a sanitarium patient just escaped. Mike and the girl drive on, stop for gas, and she gets out briefly (and mails Mike a message). They are soon blocked by a car. A gunman emerges, Mike slugs him, is sapped unconscious, and comes to as five or six thugs are torturing the girl. When she provides no information, they kill her, load groggy Mike, who hears but cannot see them, and the girl's corpse into Mike's car, and shove it down an embankment. On Thursday, Mike, his head damaged, is recovering in the hospital. FBI agents and Captain Pat Chambers separately reveal this: Mike was thrown free; his car burned; the girl was Berga Torn, high-level criminal Carl Evello's ex-mistress, who was to testify before a federal committee, suffered a breakdown, was hospitalized under wraps awaiting her recovery, but escaped. Mike tells what he knows but vows to dispense his swifter brand of justice.

Velda visits Mike at his apartment, cautions him about the dimensions of the Berga Torn case, and says Mike's P.I. license and gun privileges are revoked. She will check the sanitarium records, research Mafia members, and infiltrate. Mike taxis to Pat's home. Pat says his files lack information on Evello but offers Berga's Brooklyn address. Mike goes there, checks her rooms, finds evidence that she inquired about passage on the *Cedric* passenger liner, and obtains her former roommate's last name—Carver—and current address. He goes there. Lily Carver, tiny, beautiful, with dazzling white hair, and smelling of rubbing alcohol, has been terrified, she says, by visits from inquisitive police and thugs. Mike gains her confidence—and amorous interest—and checks Berga's luggage, left there. The two girls worked together, Lily says. Mike takes her by subway and cab to his apartment for her safety—and nothing else.

Next morning Velda phones, has some information, and will meet him at the Texan Bar while Lily remains behind, in hiding. Velda gives Mike a rundown on Berga: Swedish-Italian, born in Pittsburgh, 1920; visited Italy in 1940 loaded with money; lovers included Nicholas Raymond (prewar, dead), Walter McGrath, (wartime, out of state), Carl Evello; friends included Leopold Kawolsky, ex-fighter, killed by truck, and Congressman Geyfey, single, seemingly harmless. Mike taxis to an unnamed journalist, retired when wounded by the Mafia for an article he wrote; receives "a folio" of pertinent data; and takes it to a nearby bar. In walks Mousie Basso, a piddling crook who tells Mike the Mafia has hired Charlie Max and Sugar Smallhouse, Miami gunmen, to kill him.

Mike goes to Ray Diker of the *Globe* and gets leads on Raymond, McGrath, and Kawolsky, proceeds to the office of Dr. Martin Soberin, who authorized Berga's sanitarium stay, and learns from Soberin's sexy nurse that William Wieton sent Berga to him. Mike boldly walks around, challenging Max and

Smallhouse to show, and returns to comfort Lily. A growling voice on the phone tells him to accept the replacement car out front, papers all in order, or else. Mike snarls back, and asks a mechanic named Bob Gellie to disarm the car. He removes two explosive devices—one to blow as the engine started; the other after some miles on the road—just in case. Mike drives to Evello's Yonkers mansion; meets Evello's gorgeous half-sister, Michael Friday; crashes a party with her; meets Al Affia and Leo Harmody, two of Evello's associates; and demands to talk with Evello. Mike asks Evello about Berga, is told he merely got tired of her, and sees Congress Geyfey arriving with Velda, already obviously infiltrating, just as he and Friday chat briefly. She says Geyfey, a lawyer, formerly handled Evello's accounts. Mike horrifies her by explaining Evello's Mafia connections. She says Evello and "peculiar" Berga argued one night.

Going home, Mike is snatched by two gunnies. One drives Mike's car; the other sits in back. They drive toward the airport past the Queens Tunnel. Mike kids them about the one bomb his mechanic found. Knowing about the second, the driver slams on the brakes. In the melee, the driver shoots the other heavy when Mike pulls him forward and then shoots himself as Mike grabs his gun. Dumping both men, Mike returns to his apartment. Lily is gone. He phones Pat, who puts out a bulletin for her. Friday phones to invite him to a party Evello is throwing at a Riverside Drive place. Mike has time to seek Max and Smallhouse, finds them at a bar, chokes Smallhouse severely and kicks Max in the face. The Feds, having tailed them, show up and stop Mike. He leaves, meets Friday at the Astor, and they taxi to Evello's party. She begs Mike to spare Evello, corrupt though she now knows he is. Velda, having cozied up to Al Affia and William Mist, Evello's cronies, is a guest. She slips Mike a duplicate of Mist's apartment key and says she has a date with Affia and plans to drug him with chloral and search his apartment. The party breaks up. Mike searches Mist's place and finds a photograph of Mist, Evello, and Berga. Mike phones Pat, who says Max and Smallhouse were arrested but got machine-gunned to death while in a police car. Mike taxis to Affia's messy pad, finds evidence that Velda drugged him insufficiently and has disappeared. Mike phones Pat from Affia's to raid Mist's place and save Velda, waits at Affia's, and finds a blueprint of the *Cedric,* on which Berga unsuccessfully sought passage.

After sleeping into the next afternoon, Mike phones Diker and learns that Kawolsky was Berga's bodyguard and lover and that Raymond made several prewar trips to Italy, gambled badly in Miami, and was "a ladies' man." Mike's building superintendent found Lily hiding in the basement. She is exhausted and scared, but is safe with Mike again. Mike finds the trucker who ran over Kawolsky. He recalls seeing someone fleeing from the accident. Mike says Kawolsky was pushed into the truck's path. Mike goes to a hotel lobby, phones out of town and orders a black marketeer to spread this word: Mike has what the big crooks want. He proceeds to a hotel resident named Carmen

Trivago, who knew Raymond, and batters him into confessing that the Mafia shadowed and finally killed Raymond. Mike goes to Pat's office, tells him Raymond, an international drug smuggler, was murdered, adds he'll barter for Velda, and learns this: Berga's escape from the sanitarium was planned; she walked out with a woman.

Mike taxis to Affia's pad, finds him chopped to death, alerts the FBI, and meets Friday at the Texan Bar, where he phoned her to be. He convinces her to side with decency and against her half-brother, Evello, who used Berga to seek information. Friday remembers Evello made prewar international phone calls and agrees to provide a list to Pat for federal action. They kiss. Mike realizes Mist and others want the drugs Raymond concealed. In his office Mike finds a letter Berga wrote him using his old address on his steering column. Forwarded late, it says "The way to a man's heart—B. T." Thugs crash in, Mike blinds one, groin-kicks another, is conked, revives tied to a mattress on a bed in a dark room, and is beaten and left. He works free by upsetting the flimsy bed, rights it and himself again, and in comes Evello, alone. Mike reasons he helped Berga to escape in hopes of finding drugs Raymond left with her. Evello sneers. Mike chokes him unconscious, puts him on the bed, tells thugs outside that Mike talked, so "put him away." A knifer kills Evello. Mike kills him with a Herculean chop, disables the remaining thug, and tangles him under the two corpses. Mike staggers to a bar, on Second Avenue; phones Pat about the bodies; Pat says one of the dying gunnies mentioned Berga, says Friday's list is helping break numerous federal cases; both men clarify the maze involving Berga, Kawolsky, Evello, Affia, Velda, and the drugs likely on the *Cedric*. Pat promises to locate Mist and check the *Cedric*. Mike senses an elusive clue, will check on Friday, subways home, finds Lily safe, and reads a note Friday sent. Although she wants to see him about something uniquely vital, he falls asleep—and dreams.

Mike by phone next morning learns that Friday has vanished, a search of the *Cedric* proved useless, and Mist has an alibi. Lily, again smelling of rubbing alcohol, says someone called Berga twice in the sanitarium. Mike gets Lily around the police guard, borrows a car from a garageman, and drives with Lily to Friday's wing in Evello's mansion. They locate concealed wall safes. Mike theorizes that Mist is in the clear, lacks the money from the drugs, but has Velda. Suddenly insightful, Mike drives to the morgue, forces the coroner to cut Berga's stomach open, and gets a locker key from it—529, City Athletic Club. He orders the coroner to phone Pat, tells Lily what he found, drives to the club, wraps chilly Lily in his car blanket, and goes inside. He slaps the night clerk into revealing 529 is Raymond's locker on a ten-year basis. Inside, Mike finds two containers of heroin, together with sundry *Cedric* documents. He returns to Lily in the car, gets a duplicate club key made, gives it to her, and gets her back to his apartment, where she is to give the key to Pat. He finds a note from Friday saying "William Mist."

Mike drives to Mist's pad, bursts in, avoids his drawn gun, and slugs him to make him talk. Instead, Mist dies. Thugs start to enter, but Mike hides in the bathroom, sees a bottle of medicine with a certain name on it, and escapes—just as the Feds machinegun the thugs.

Mike goes to a certain dark office, sneaks upstairs, finds and unties Velda, and tells her to grab a cab and rush the club key to Pat. Mike opens another door and says, "Doctor Soberin, I presume." When this fellow, who assigned Berga to the sanitarium, grabs a gun, Mike breaks his fingers, elbows his mouth, and concludes that Soberin misleadingly typed "Wieton" over "Mist," the name in Berga's record. Admitting his action may cause trouble, Mike then shoots Soberin dead. Mike phones police headquarters for the identification of a drowned blonde recently discussed. Her name was Lily Carver. The fake Lily enters, with drawn .45, and hisses that she loved Soberin. Catching on, Mike tells her this: Soberin, whom she loved, used her only for "power and money"; she killed and replaced Berga's friend, the real Lily; set up Berga, identified Velda, told Affia; Affia razzed Mist about it; insulted, Mist killed Affia; she stayed with Mike for information, warned Mist to escape; it's all over. But "Lily," calling Mike "a deadly man," shoots him in the side. He is given a final cigarette. She says Soberin "would take me like I was"; disrobes, revealing hideous, deforming burns from "knees to . . . neck"; leans close, gun at his belly and says, "Deadly[,] . . . kiss me." With a handy lighter, Mike sets the residual alcohol in her puckered wrinkles afire, and she tumbles and burns to death.

Kiss Me, Deadly, 1952, is neatly structured, with vivid opening and ending chapters, but betrays Spillane's likely fatigue. Mike and Velda have pledged their love for one another. What should follow is delayed a decade. The next Mike Hammer novel is *The Girl Hunters,* published in 1962. Interesting side facts are that in *Kiss Me, Deadly* Mike makes use of taxis nineteen times along Manhattan's often rainy streets; in addition, Velda hops into five, Friday and Gellie one each. Spillane often bothers purists with his slapdash style, not least here when he has Mike describe the false Lily's eyes as "dark wells that could knead your flesh" and when he compares the Mafia to Medusa with its innumerable Hydra heads.

Bibliography: Collins and Traylor.

KITCHEN, DOUG. In "Killer Mine," he was a friend of Lieutenant Joe Scanlon's from childhood. Doug became a night worker at a shipyard and was murdered by Larry Scanlon. By using the name "Kitchen," is Spillane hinting that the boys' tough old neighborhood was Hell's Kitchen?

KLAUS, SERGEANT. In *The Killing Man,* he is a friendly police officer on duty when Mike visits Captain Pat Chambers on Sunday morning, a day after Anthony DiCica's murder.

KLINE, THOMAS. In *The Snake,* he owned a sleazy bar in Brooklyn. After being seen looking at a photograph of Basil Levitt by the police, he is found shot to death.

KNAPP, LAURA. In *The Girl Hunters,* she is the Nail part of The Dragon, composed of Tooth (*see* Gorlin) and Nail. When Mike meets her, Laura, in her early forties, is Senator Leo Knapp's beautiful blond widow. They become intimate, until he concludes that her purpose is to aid Gorlin in his search for Velda. He rigs her shotgun so that, aiming at him, she destroys herself.

KNAPP, SENATOR LEO. In *The Girl Hunters,* he was a major general of procurement during the war. He is called Mr. Missile Man, because of his hard line against pro-Red and pro-union liberals. Gorlin kills Knapp while searching his home safe for documents.

KNIGHT, DUNCAN. In "The Flier," he is a journalist whose column, titled *Washington Inside,* contains criticism of America's military policy. Lois tells Cat Fallon she works for Knight.

KOCH. In *The Last Cop Out,* he was Turley's neighbor and advised him to buy a gun for protection.

KOOPERMAN, MARTY. In *One Lonely Night,* he is a political reporter for the *Globe.* He praises Lee Deamer's conservative stance to Mike Hammer. Nothing comes of Mike's promise of an eventual scoop to Kooperman.

KOPEK. In "Me, Hood!," this is the name of the wreckers hired to demolish Valley Park building in preparation for a housing-development project.

KRAUS. In *The Body Lovers,* he and Tillman hired Mike Hammer to check an accident report concerning the Capeheart Building.

KREPTO, BUNNY. In *The Deep,* Deep recalls that Bunny was killed by Petie Scotch, long ago, at the Knights Owl Club.

KROUSE. In *Day of the Guns,* Tiger Mann says he killed him in 1945, along with Gettler, during the war.

KUKAK, JOSEPH. In *Survival . . . Zero!,* he is a Soviet politician with scientific and commercial interests. When Mike Hammer confirms his suspicions that Kukak is conspiring with William Dorn, he shoots Kukak, unarmed, to death.

L

LACY, JOHN. In "The Seven Year Kill," he was an old-time boxer who inspired Rhino Massley to change his name, which is Jean Stuart Massley, to John Lacy Massley.

LADERO, PETE. In *The Snake,* he is a legman for a political columnist and provides Mike Hammer with information about Simpson Torrence.

"THE LADY SAYS DIE." *See* "The Girl Behind the Hedge."

LAFARGE, BUSTER. In "The Seven Year Kill," he is a retired killer, in his seventies and left by Rhino Massley as caretaker of his former ranch. Phil Rocca forces him to dig up Rhino's empty coffin. Mannie Waller's gunnies raid the place, and Lafarge is killed.

LaFONT, CAROL. In "Tomorrow I Die," she is Sheriff LaFont's daughter, engaged to Harold, the town mayor, until Richard Thurber comes along and helps her see Harold's callousness.

LaFONT, SHERIFF. In "Tomorrow I Die," he is the local sheriff, taken hostage by Auger and his fellow bank robbers. He is tied up and therefore cannot help Richard Thurber foil the outlaws.

LAGEN, DICK. In *The Erection Set,* he is a heavy-set New York political columnist, with Washington, D.C., connections. He tries hard to unearth damaging information about Dog Kelly, who tolerates him humorously.

LAKE. In *The Big Kill,* he is mentioned as a gambler Lou Grindle knows.

LAKE, MISS FLORENCE. In *Black Alley,* she is the obstreperous D.A. who appears before television cameras in Mike Hammer's office. He enjoys razzing her. She soon disappears from any official action.

LAKLAND. In *The Body Lovers,* Velda put evidence she obtained for Mike Hammer in a safe at Lakland's.

LaMONT, SIDNEY ("SID"). In "The Bastard Bannerman," he is evidently a petty Culver City crook. Cat Cay Bannerman squeezes him for information about the Bannerman family.

LANDE, SERGEANT ARTHUR. In *The Day the Sea Rolled Back,* he is a Miami police officer ready to plan crowd control if the coastal populace grows terrified.

LANE, DR. In *Day of the Guns. See* Mann, Tiger.

LANGSTON, BUD. In *Black Alley,* he is a friend of Mike Hammer's, paid by a bureau in Washington, D.C. He tells Mike about Dan Coulter's invention of body armor and loans Mike a sample.

LANSING, CARTER. In "Kick It or Kill!," he is an ex-mobster who owns a Miami airline. One of his criminal employees is Don Casales, whose Cadillac Benny Quick is driving in Pinewood. Kelly Smith suspects Lansing of furnishing transportation for the big-wigs attending Simpson's dirty-dancing party. One guest is Sergei Rudinoff, who has Cuban connections.

LARK, GRETCHEN. In *Day of the Guns,* she is Rondine Lund's sexy, red-headed friend at the U.N., where she is a secretary. Once a nurse, she has a Greenwich Village apartment, and knows Burton Selwick. Tiger Mann sleeps with her, takes her around, and is almost killed before discovering that she has been getting information from Selwick by using sodium pentothal. Rondine kills her.

LARRY. In *The Long Wait,* he is a thug killed by one of his associates when their attempt to take John McBride on a one-way ride misfires.

LARUE, JAKE. In *My Gun Is Quick,* he is a policeman whom Mike Hammer knows and to whom he delivered Feeney Last for possible arrest on a gun-possession charge. Last had a license to carry it, which caused Larue embarrassment.

LARUE, MRS. JAKE. In *My Gun Is Quick,* she is a policeman's wife. When Mike Hammer phones their home, she has to wake up Jake.

***THE LAST COP OUT* (1973).** Novel. (Characters: Aaron, Carl Ames, Pasi Arando, Steve Arando, Vitale Arando, Charlie Argropolis, Andy, Cammie Armstrong, Willie Armstrong, Baggert, Barney, Harvey Bartel, Vito Bartoldo, Louise Belhander, Bennie, Bennie, Berkowitz, Cynthia Berkowitz, Myron Berkowitz, Bert, Bingo, Leon Bray, Anthony Broderick, Gillian Burke, Pedro Cabilla, Eddie Camp, Henry Campbell, Caprini, Bevo Carmody, Joyce Carroll, Mrs. Richard Case, Richard Case, Perry Chops, Cissie, Clough, the Cobra, Colfaco, Jimmie Corrigan, Crocker, Meyer Davis, Jerry Dines, Mark Ferro, Miss Fischer, Baldie Foreman, Gallo, Glen, Gracie, Joey Grif, Charles Hall, Hanson, Al Harris, William R. Hays, Tommy Hazelton, Shatzi Heinkle, Stanley Holland, Jan, Arthur Kevin, Kiernan, Koch, Robert Lederer, Captain William Long, Lucian, Lulu, Lupe, Malone, Manute, Irma Manute, Maria, Artie Meeker, Papa Menes, Sylvia Menes, Bingo Miles, Killer Miller, Looney Mooney, Morrie, Joe Morse, Nicole, Nils, Ollie, Papa Fats, Peppy, Herm Perigino, Sal Perigino, Peterson, Pete the Meat, Victor Petrocinni, Moe Piel, Helga Piers, Moss Pitkin, Florio Prince, Ted Proctor, Dennis Ravenal, Remy, Rierdon, Sal Roma, Rose, Manny Roth, Mrs. Manny Roth, Sadie, Helen Scanlon, Joe Scanlon, Mrs. Joe Scanlon, Erik Schmidt, Sergeant Al Schneider, Lennie Scobie, Herman Shanke, Mark Shelby, Mrs. Mark Shelby, Teddy Shu, George Spacer, Marty Stackler, Statto, Matt Stevenson, Taggart, Trent, Turley, Francois Verdun, Vigaro, Woodie.)

(The paragraphs that follow are often short, because each paragraph summarizes the action of a separate scene.)

Mark Shelby, educated at mob expense, has been named the leader of a syndicate crime family in Manhattan. In a single month five of his subheads have been killed. He asks why of his lieutenants, including Leon Bray (computer expert), Arthur ("Slick") Kevin (supervisor of other city bosses), Remy (in charge of investigations), and Richard Case (weapons expert and friend of the police). The attacks, Shelby concludes, represent a take-over effort.

Captain William ("Bill") Long, of Homicide, after telling the upset commissioner that the puzzling murders are personal or for business, meets Gillian ("Gill") Burke at the Automat and sympathizes. Gill, discharged from the police force two years earlier for being violent and uncooperative, is happy as a well-paid private security guard. Gill says the mobsters are welcome to kill off each other, but Long fears innocent lives may be lost.

Shelby brings in Francois Verdun, a polished, well-rewarded hit man with a string of successes.

Teddy Shu in Chicago calls old Papa Menes, his crime boss in a Miami hotel, to tell him Verdun is in New York and Menes can expect action. A delivery boy brings Shu's coffee order and shoots Shu dead.

George Spacer and Carl Ames, two thugs, wait to report Shu's death to Menes until 10:00 A.M., because Menes wants never to be disturbed until such hour. Menes has already heard about Shu's death and has his theory confirmed, by calls to Chicago, that Shu's killer worked at a deli and is long gone. Menes orders his sedan and decamps secretly.

Bill Long meets Robert Lederer, assistant D.A., who says the officials want Gill rehired to solve these killings. Long tells Lederer that Gill was close to solving various crimes by his unorthodox methods until political higher-ups were bribed to oust him, that he is furious, but that he will broach the offer.

Gill surprises Long over lunch by saying that he'll think about the offer and that his sources have already told him Verdun, his old enemy, is in town.

Verdun meets with Shelby, theorizes that the recent killings are designed to hit the top echelons of Shelby's organization preparatory to taking over. He tells Shelby to order his men to stay visible even though it is risky.

Gill meets Lederer and his staff, accepts the assignment, but demands— and is promised—freedom and cooperation, and a dollar-a-year pay.

Gill beats up Verdun's two bodyguards, enters Verdun's office, throws down a challenge, and shows his badge, to prove his official status. Gill recognizes Verdun's receptionist. She is Helen Scanlon, whose honest testimony got a hit man acquitted, but who lost her job as an actress and could find work only with Verdun. Gill forces Helen to a grill for iced tea for her, beer for him. She is bitter that her father, Joe Scanlon, was a policeman killed in the line of duty, and criticizes Gill's reputation and methods.

Behold Menes, with a henchman named Artie Meeker, in Homestead, Florida. Menes gets a letter from Verdun about Gill but replies by coded telegram to do nothing about Gill yet. Menes smells fear near him.

Shelby, whose wife is frigid in their Trenton, New Jersey, home, keeps Helga Piers, a busty Swede, as a mistress in an East Side apartment. He visits Helga, and her "oralistic activity" makes him briefly forget Gill, Menes's power, and the killings.

Gill studies a photograph of Shelby given him by Long. Gill wants to recheck the murder of Berkowitz and Manute, photographers, supposedly by a robber named Ted Proctor, who was killed by the police. The photographers created pornographic movies. Gill thinks the closed case has syndicate connections.

Helen rings Gill's bell, enters, apologizes for rebuking him, and agrees her father was killed to keep him from producing evidence against the syndicate. The two kiss, and she leaves. He thinks he ought to tidy up his slovenly rooms.

Stanley Holland, transferred from Los Angeles to Cleveland on Menes's order, rebuilt his boss's drug organization, bribed and killed two crooked cops just last week, and now feels secure. He is shot dead in the parking lot of his office building.

Gill meets with Long, and they theorize that Menes is lying low, waiting, and plans to emerge at the top.

Shelby and Verdun face off during a nice little dinner, mistrusting but needing each other. Verdun thinks the CIA or the FBI may be behind these killings. He also warns Shelby about Gill, always Shelby's enemy and now back with the police.

Menes has Meeker draw lines on a big map to Phoenix, Cleveland, Seattle, San Diego, and Dallas, then orders Meeker to fetch Louise Belhander, that little Miami prostitute he likes.

Menes bribes a bartender to use pass keys to two cottages on the Keys coast. Menes and Meeker engage in varieties of conduct with two prostitutes. Menes feels better and thinks death, blindfolded, can't find him.

Consulting his map, Menes is reminded of the Pennsylvania town where he married Sylvia, whose father was a rabbi, who was soon inferior in bed, and who now plays canasta in Miami. Menes hates Jews, kills them when he can, and remembers uneasily that Shelby is one-quarter Jewish.

Meeker calls New York and learns the Cleveland police are tracing Holland's killer through photos of him taken by the security camera where he rented a car, giving the name Charles Hall of Elizabeth, New Jersey. Meeker tells Menes he'll have a copy of the photo tomorrow.

Long also has a copy of the killer's photo, shows it to Gill, who doesn't put much faith in it, because one can go in disguise to a kill.

Gill visits Harlem and asks Willie Armstrong, a black buddy from army days, to check into the whereabouts of Henry Campbell, whose last address was on Bleecker Street.

For a $5 bribe, Ted Proctor's pudgy, snoopy landlady tells Gill this: Ted's effects included some old papers; he never had a gun; he drank up spare money at Barney's nearby.

Turley, a pawnbroker, tells Gill that Ted was drunk, waved a gun at him, and robbed him two years ago.

Plump Cynthia Berkowitz tells Gill she saved her husband's papers for tax purposes and lets him study them. The photo shop of Berkowitz and his also dead partner, Manute, sold at auction for about $2,000. Gill leaves for a supper date with memorably kissable Helen.

Verdun and Kevin enter a Brooklyn garage loft and check on a man that Verdun's thugs, Bingo Miles and Shatzi Heinkle, have brought in, tied, and are guarding. He is William R. Hays, a New Jersey fabric salesmen, according to his papers. He closely resembles the photo of the man who may have shot Holland. Verdun inks Hays's fingers to take prints and leaves. Hays wets his pants.

At a restaurant during dinner, Helen gives Gill a photo she filched from a batch Verdun received, checked, and distributed to cohorts. Recognizing it as a copy of the photo of the man thought to have killed Holland, Gill concludes Verdun has an informer among the police. Helen volunteers to accompany him home to set his place in order.

A man watches the two leave, makes a phone call, and tries but fails to follow them.

While Gill mixes drinks and relaxes, Helen brings on a sweat cleaning up his place, then has a shower. Gill is disappointed when she emerges all dressed, kisses him lightly, and leaves. Looking about, he wonders if she snooped through his papers.

After making some phone calls, Kevin tells Verdun that Hays did time for auto theft and assault, has been clean eight years, and is liked by his current boss. Leaving with Kevin, Verdun orders Shatzi and Bingo to torture Hays anyway, in case he knows something.

Gill realizes that Verdun employed Helen when no one else would. Maybe she is in cahoots with Verdun.

Shatzi awakens Verdun from a comfortable sleep in his hotel, says Hays died, and is told to "dump it."

Gill shows Long and Lederer the photo and accuses their departments of having a leak. Long says a tortured corpse was found in Prospect Park this morning. One hand was smeared with ink. Gill gets Jimmie Corrigan, an honest cop, to describe how he was forced to shoot Proctor, who killed Berkowitz and Manute.

Gill gets Sergeant Schneider to show him Proctor's fingerprints, found on the murder weapon. Another policeman enters with a photo of Hays's body. His navel has been cut out. Gill recalls that the Caprini gang used that gruesome technique in Chicago, Denver, and Minneapolis ten years ago and orders a file check.

Following Armstrong's directions, Gill enters a black ghetto, locates Campbell, and gets him to admit he saw Shelby near where Berkowitz and Manute were murdered. He was threatened with castration, retracted his statement, and thus enabled Shelby to fake an alibi. Gill gives Campbell $100.

Meeker frequents a Cuban Miami restaurant featuring incredibly peppery food. When he leaves it one night, he does not notice he is spied on by a man who then makes a phone call.

Bray, Shelby's accountant, is like an automaton in a castle, well guarded, it would seem. But one night someone in a gas mask slits the throats of two "faggot" sentries and gasses three others to death. Bray calls the garage, nearby, for his car, starts to leave but is shot dead.

When Bray delays, the two men in the garage go to his office, see numerous bodies, and then are blown to bits by slow-fused dynamite carefully placed.

Helen, still working in Verdun's office, hears someone hint someone saw her dining with Gill. Fearing Verdun will be suspicious, she boldly tells him she accepted Gill's invitation to pump him for information but failed. Pleased, Verdun offers Helen a bonus to cultivate Gill and learn all she can.

The newspapers are full of items about the gang-war killings and explosion. Lederer and Long tell the police commissioner their only lead, coming through Gill, is to a murderer named Bingo Miles, known for cutting off his victims' navels—and his own navel. (Actually, Shatzi Heinkle is this pervert.) As the cops leave, they see Richard Case. Long doesn't like him, but his superior says Case has political clout helping the police.

Shelby regularly visits Helga by circuitous routes. He fails, once, to see a raggedy old man behind him, taking down part of his taximan's license plate number.

Verdun checks with Eric Schmidt, an accomplished weapons expert, whose friend sold a certain type of bullet to a man with a still-scabbing tattoo.

Menes is ordered to participate in a conference call, listens, grows irate, and feels tempted to have a soldier of his blow up the place where the so-called Big Board meets.

Gill praises Helen for her fast thinking with Verdun, drives her to her home, but on the way questions Turley, who sold Proctor the gun he used in the Benkowitz-Manute robbery during which Corrigan killed Proctor.

Shelby stays for hours at Helga's, gets a disturbing phone call, hits Helga to relieve his pressure, then gives her $200 for her trouble. Helga entertains visions of torturing Shelby some day.

Helen, experienced in sex after a rape and an abandonment, is nicely relaxed after gentle lovemaking with Gill, who, however, feels both too independent and too endangered to commit himself.

Verdun drinks alone, gets furious at developments, and would kill Shelby but for Menes's protection of Shelby. Why did Shelby kill those Jewish photographers simply for photographing Shelby with a prostitute? Verdun calls Kevin's number to plan a trap for Helen to set for Gill. No answer, because Kevin has been shot dead.

When the Big Board drafted gunmen from Miami, Herman Shanke (Herman the German) saw a chance to fill the vacuum with the Arando family and to outwit Menes, who once had him beaten up. Shanke sends Moe Piel to Manhattan for weaponry.

Lederer tells his associates, and Gill, that they should check rumors in Miami, but Gill says trouble will center in New York, where the big money is. Long says an informant reported that a man named Shatzi has a navel scar. Alone with Long, Gill suggests seeking Shatzi and adds that the department has a leak.

Verdun dictates letters to Helen, who tries to pump him by saying Gill visited a pawnshop. Verdun gives Helen theater tickets that a client says he can't use.

Shelby is assembling from memory information lost in Bray's office, plans to eliminate Italians from the organization, and fears Gill. The man tailing Shelby files his final report and dreams of sunbathing in Florida.

Shelby suspects Helga, searches her apartment in her absence, and happily fondles a candle he gave her to place near a religious statue.

Piel drives to Manhattan to buy weaponry, reports to the old garage he was given directions to, but is seized by Bingo and Shatzi, who heat some irons to torture him with and who call Verdun.

Verdun is annoyed that Piel died of shock, tells his clumsy thugs to dump his corpse and that of the gun dealer (whom they murdered), booby-trap some ammunition to explode in Herman the German's face, and ship everything down to Herman. First, Shatzi cuts the navels from both corpses.

Helen treats Gill to the theater and afterwards tells him Verdun provided the tickets. Fearing a trap, Gill drops Helen home by taxi, then continues, followed by Bingo and another (Shatzi). Shots ring out. Gill kills Bingo. Shatzi escapes. The police laboratory reports that Bingo's clothes have garage residue similar to that found on Piel's corpse, discovered in a New Jersey meadow.

When told of events, Verdun uniquely feels fear and orders a hit on Shatzi, who was in the car when Bingo was killed. Shatzi, thinking Verdun ordered Bingo killed, disappears ahead of Verdun's soldiers.

Long questions Gill and Helen but gets nowhere.

In a cab, Helen expresses fear. Gill says she must quit working for Verdun. She suggests a weekend in New Jersey. He agrees, half-proposes marriage, and leaves her at her place to pack.

Menes is unconcerned. The Board orders him to kill Herman. OK. Gill is bothering Verdun. Fine. Meeker will soon fetch that prostitute. Lovely.

Verdun feels he is being stalked, gets to his apartment, has a shower, emerges, and is mutilated and fatally stabbed.

Shatzi stands there, thinking Verdun needn't have sent soldiers after him. He was always loyal. He cuts out the dying man's navel and promises to keep it.

Long calls Gill: Shatzi is on the run, sought by two Brooklyn gunmen. Gill says he and Helen are going to spend the weekend at the Clipper Inn in Jersey.

While Menes is sodomizing Louise Belhander, she nonchalantly reads a telegram to him signed "Verdun." She remembers hitchhiking to Florida, being picked up by a man named Verdun, and being raped and tortured by him. She remembers his name because her grandfather was killed in Verdun, France.

While driving Helen to New Jersey, Gill talks to her about a cop's life, which she says her mother understood, and also, hesitantly, about love. Gill used to think love was for children.

Shelby gets word from Chicago that he can assume charge of New York activities while Menes is in hiding. Shelby, pleased, plans to upset Herman soon. Among Verdun's papers Shelby finds a note saying Eddie Camp is tracing bullets and a tattoo. Shelby leaves word for Camp to phone him. Case, that politician with an in with the police, visits Shelby and tells him that Shatzi, Verdun's man, killed Verdun and cut out his navel, and that Gill is missing.

Long calls Gill with details of Verdun's mutilation-murder by Shatzi, seen leaving Verdun's place and missing.

In a cheap hotel room, Shatzi ecstatically studies Verdun's navel, pickled in rubbing alcohol, and is ambitious to collect Shelby's and his crony Remy's navels too.

Eavesdropping on Menes and Meeker, Louise learns of Verdun's death and Shelby's desire to replace Menes as syndicate leader in New York. She takes beer cans the men discarded and has a policeman friend identify Menes and Meeker from their fingerprints. She consults newspaper files on them in the local library.

Gill tells Long he will take steps to protect Helen if Lederer doesn't stop pressuring her. Long says information is coming from the Los Angeles plastic surgeon who remade Holland's face. They discuss Herman and wonder about Menes's possible whereabouts.

Shelby gloats about laundering vast sums of money soon. He learns that the tattoo, still scabbing, read "DS" and "WV." Remy says the letters mean "Deputy Sheriff, West Virginia."

Gill grills Myron Berkowitz, the lawyer-nephew of the murdered photographer Berkowitz, and learns this: Berkowitz probably filmed intimate scenes for blackmailing purposes, ordered a device for microfilming, and hinted about soon becoming rich. Gill, in summing up the evidence, recalls that the police found a pickpocket's cache of wallets hidden in Proctor's room. He checks police records and takes down the names of persons whose wallets were returned to them.

Herman plans a bloody feud between his soldiers and Menes's. Menes worries about his murderous past but knows his Miami and feels pretty secure. The Board voices continued faith in him. Meeker drives him back to the Keys.

Shelby and Case meet at a shoddy bar. Case says that the police have located Shatzi uptown but that two of Case's men, Marty Stackler and Mack Ferro, are eager to spirit Shatzi to a Brooklyn location. Shelby orders the pawnbroker shot. Gill is the only block to his rise to full power and must also be hit. Meanwhile, a driver parks a booby-trapped truck in Miami but then learns, to his horror, that Verdun, who gave the order, is dead.

Long talks with Gill and Helen. The tattooed deputy has been murdered and had Gill's card on him and a small arsenal in his room. A police report informs Long that Shatzi killed Stackler and Ferro kidnapped Shatzi. Gill says Shatzi probably is in Statto's warehouse in Brooklyn. Gill takes Helen to his place for safety, gets a coded phone message, but can't act on it because Long tells him a prowl car will pick Gill up at once.

While being driven toward the garage, Shatzi takes his knife from his sock and kills both Case and Ferro, who, dying, shoots Shatzi dead. The authorities arrive. Gill is amused when Lederer plans a cover-up for Case, now identified as Shelby's informant.

Herman and his men move the truck loaded with armament to their Miami garage, where it explodes, thus eliminating that threat to Menes and his organization. The Board in Chicago, alarmed at adverse Miami publicity, vote anyway to kill Menes, who, however, orders a trigger man in Chicago to fire a bazooka, which eliminates the Board, kills thirty-two men, and injures others. The news so delights Menes that he is especially virile with Louise. He invites her to travel to New York with her. She agrees, planning his death.

The country is outraged by news reports. Shelby is worried, concludes that Menes—an example of "shitless senility"—was responsible, and determines to kill him.

Meeker drives Menes and Louise to Jacksonville. She flies alone to New York. Meeker takes Menes on to New York.

The authorities, with Gill and Long, convene. Questioned, Menes had a sufficient alibi, they say. Gill scoffs at Lederer and the others; predicts that Menes and Shelby will fight with horrible bloodshed; predicts one will emerge in total control; when asked, says the solution is to kill both.

Alone, Long asks if Gill is serious. Yes.

Shelby is aware that West Coast criminals favor him while Midwesterners support Menes. Menes taunts Shelby on the phone by hinting at a secret Menes knows. Shelby needs Helga; so he rushes there, maneuvers to satiety, and falls asleep. She was expecting her real lover, Nils, evidently delayed at the airport. She just bought a tabloid with photographs of syndicate leaders. Shelby was one, and she thought all along he was a grocer from Trenton. She figures she and Nils ought to kill Shelby to avoid trouble.

Helen is distressed that Gill and Long are arguing about Gill's dismissal from the police.

Helga reexhausts Shelby, who turns suspicious when there is a phone call for her (it was Nils), phones Menes, and is told Gill was checking Turley's pawnshop. Shelby beats Helga horribly and leaves.

Gill, parked near Turley's with Long and Helen, says this: Shelby was the brains behind everything, killed Berkowitz and Manute, gave Proctor the gun to pawn; Proctor was waving it toward Turley when Corrigan entered and shot Proctor in self-defense. Shelby rushes toward Turley, sees Gill approach, fires; Gill ducks; Turley is hit, dies; Long shoots Shelby but suspects Gill of aiming at Turley.

After Lederer's men clean up the scene, Gill takes Long and Helen to Helga's apartment, aware of Shelby's assignations there. They find Helga horribly bloody and chopping at Shelby's candle. Helen cleans her up. Helga identifies Shelby from her magazine photograph and says he suspected Nils, who arrived late, saw her condition, and decamped. In the candle, Gill finds microfilms Shelby had Berkowitz make detailing syndicate activities for his protection. Long still suspects Gill.

A certain European immigrant shoe-shine lad overheard stock tips from Wall Street customers, amassed a fortune, built a castle on Long Island, lost everything in 1929, and committed suicide. Now Menes owns that hideaway. Louise, with Menes there, has accepted $5,000 from him but plots revenge.

While Long vainly seeks Menes and suspects Gill will murder him, government experts use evidence from the microfilms to arrest dozens of criminals.

Menes, guarded by Meeker and Remy outside, is cavorting with Louise, who begins to domineer the aroused pervert.

Helen gets Gill to deny he planned Shelby's death, questions no more, and the two make tumbling, explosive love. "What's Shinola?" she asks. Gill says it's shoe polish. When she says Verdun hinted Menes might be hiding at Shinola, Gill calls Long about the former shoe-shine man kidded for Shinola-like pretentiousness. Gill, Long, and Helen rush to Long Island.

Louise gets Menes into the proper position and replicates an act of sodomy for him with a .38 barrel, then fires. His guards observe the kneeling remains and leave. Likewise Louise.

Gill, Long, and Helen find Menes. Long calls in. Gill only half-denies all guilt to Helen. They go home.

The Last Cop Out has an unusual form. Narrated from an omniscient point of view, it is in sixteen numbered chapters, each with between two and eleven abrupt scenes—totaling ninety such shifts. It is Spillane's most sexually explicit novel, with diction to match. Gill Burke's strategy of taking the law into his own hands, his praise of good cops' brutality, and his dislike of the Miranda law all seem to reflect Spillane's own mind set. The popularity of *The Godfather* (1969) by Mario Puzo (1920–1999) probably inspired Spillane to concentrate on crime-family action in *The Last Cop Out*.

LAST, FEENEY. In *My Gun Is Quick,* he is a criminal from the West Coast, involved in procuring call girls to ship to New York City, where he associates with Arthur Berin-Grotin, allegedly as his bodyguard. Last is involved in killing Nancy Sanford, Ann Minor, and Lola Bergan, and is killed at a pier shack by Mike Hammer, who regularly calls him a greaseball.

LAVOIS, DON. In *The By-Pass Control,* he is a big, tough agent who worked with Tiger Mann in France in 1943 and later in Panama. Lavois finds evidence of cocaine in Vito Salvi's apartment. While waiting in Tiger's apartment for Tiger, Lavois is killed by Niger Hoppes.

LEAVY. In "The Seven Year Kill," he owns a store near where Phil Rocca lives.

LEDERER, ROBERT ("BOB"). In *The Last Cop Out,* he is the assistant D.A. He comes from a wealthy family, dislikes Gill Burke, and is mostly bluster. When Richard Case is murdered, Lederer covers up the circumstances.

LEE. In *The Long Wait,* he worked at Philbert's store five years earlier.

LEE, ANNETTE. In *The Snake,* she knew Sally Devon Torrence and cared for her until Sally died. Now pushing ninety and somewhat feeble-minded, Annette tells Mike Hammer about Sally, Black Conley, and Simpson Torrence. The dialogue between Mike and Annette is one of Spillane's most charming sequences.

LEE, BETTY ANN. In *The Deep,* she was Tally Lee's younger sister. Bennett got Betty Ann, a prostitute, hooked on heroin, and she committed suicide, at age sixteen, by jumping off a building. Roscoe Tate is callously critical of Betty Ann.

LEE, MARSHA. In *The Big Kill,* she is a fading but still sexy actress. When Mike Hammer incorrectly theorizes that her apartment was broken into by William Decker by mistake, Marsha leads Mike on. In reality, she has been blackmailing Ed Teen and Lou Grindle for a decade. When Decker takes the incriminating microfilms from her safe, Marsha hopes Mike can find them. He catches her wrecking his furniture searching for them. She is accidentally shot by Decker's little boy, who is playing with Mike's .45. In *The Girl Hunters,* Captain Pat Chambers, while disgusted with Mike, reminds him in front of Laura Knapp that he caused Marsha's death.

LEE, TALLY. In *The Deep,* she is the late Betty Ann Lee's sister. Tally knows something about Bennett, talks loosely to Deep, and is therefore murdered at her 103rd Street apartment.

LEE, TED. In *Vengeance Is Mine!,* he is evidently a business associate of Chester Wheeler. According to Joe Gill, Lee wired Wheeler $5,000 to New York City, which Wheeler needed to pay off a blackmailer.

LEEDS, JOHNNY. In *Black Alley,* he and McClain are surveyors in Albany. Mike Hammer pretends to be interested in buying certain property so as to gain information about Slipped Disk Harris's land holdings.

LEES, PAULA. In "Killer Mine," she is a prostitute victimized by Benny Loefert and Al Reese. Lieutenant Joe Scanlon tries to help her but is too late to prevent Reese from luring her to meet Larry Scanlon, who tortured her fatally.

LEES, RUDOLPH. In "I'll Die Tomorrow," he is a hit man whose victims number perhaps forty-six or forty-eight. He uses money earned to buy women to torture sexually. His first target was Buddy Riley, whom he did not finish off and who bided his time, hired him to kill and rob Riley himself, and kills Lees.

LE FLEUR. In *The Erection Set,* he is a French narcotics boss whose shipment of heroin has been stolen. Suspecting Dog Kelly, Le Fleur wants his drugs back or Kelly dead. Le Fleur kills Simon Corner and The Turk, and is killed by the relative of another man Le Fleur killed.

LEHMAN, MARTY. In *Day of the Guns,* he is a junkie who helps Dell in his efforts to locate Vidor Churis for Tiger Mann.

LENTZ, BUMMY. In "Killer Mine," Lieutenant Joe Scanlon tells Paula Lees that Lentz, who once bothered her, won't do so any more, because he recently died after drinking "bad booze."

LEO. In *Survival . . . Zero!,* Little Joe tells Mike that Beaver may be at Leo's. The lead proves false.

LEO. In "Tomorrow I Die," he is a member of Auger's gang of bank robbers. He goes with Auger to pick up the loot hidden by Richard Thurber and is presumably killed by the police.

LEPPERT, MARCO. In "I'll Die Tomorrow," he was a Mafia courier whom Rudolph Lees killed for hire.

LERNER. In "The Flier," this is the last name of the couple who saw Sharon Ortez after Art Fallon ejected her from his motel room naked.

LESTER, MARION. In *Vengeance Is Mine!,* she works for Anton Lipsek and Juno Reeves as a model. Connie Wales knows and dislikes her. She lied to Mike Hammer, that Chester Wheeler dated her discreetly. When the truth is about to come out, Lester is murdered.

LEVITT, BASIL. In *The Snake,* he is a former private detective. Simpson Torrence and Charles Force got him off on separate criminal charges. Torrence hires him to kill Sue Devon, but he is killed during gunfire at Velda's apartment involving Kid Hand, also killed.

LEWIS, CANDY. In *Kiss Me, Deadly. See* Velda.

LEWIS, CONNIE. In *The Snake,* she provides brief shelter when Velda takes Sue Devon to Connie's place for safety.

LEWIS, EDITH. In *The By-Pass Control. See* Hunt, Camille.

LEWIS, POPEYE. In "Man Alone," he is a painter whose inherited wealth enables him to live comfortably with Edna Rells and throw lavish parties. He and Edna were at the Climax when Patrick Regan was drugged.

LEWISON, BRUCE. In *The Killing Man. See* Bradley, Bennett.

LIAS, ALFREDO ("FREDO"). In "Me, Hood!," he and Tomas Escalantes are sailors involved in a drug shipment aboard the *Gastry.* Involved with Juan Gonzales and Henry Billings, Lias is shot and dies before Ryan can get him to identify Lodo.

LICO, WALTER. In *The Deep,* he owns the Blue Pheasant Inn, where Hugh Peddle is dining when Deep barges in on him threateningly.

LIGHTER, ANN. In *Bloody Sunrise,* she is an intelligence operative assigned by Newark Central to Tiger Mann. She reports information well and offers unavailingly to check what she calls Tiger's "stripes" in bed. Tiger sends her to guard Sonia Dutko, and she is murdered. To cover up, her superiors name her as Mrs. Romero of Paterson, New Jersey, to reporters.

LINDA. In *The By-Pass Control,* she is one of Camille Hunt's secretaries at Belt-Aire Electronics.

LINDEN, CHET ("LUCKY LINDY"). In *The Erection Set,* he is an agent back from London to New York. He, along with his associates, is suspicious of their associate Dog Kelly, votes not to kill him, changes his mind, and unsuccessfully tries to do so.

LINDSEY, CAPTAIN. In *The Long Wait,* he is an honest police officer in Lyncastle. He suspects John McBride of murder and embezzlement but reluctantly cooperates with him.

LINDY. In *Survival . . . Zero!,* Little Joe says he used to work near Lindy's, until it closed.

LINERO, EMBOR. In *The Ship That Never Was,* he is a Grandau assassin, working with Aktur Cilon. Linero kills Herbert Mackley.

LINK, TOADY. In *The Big Kill,* he moved up from Hollywood photographer for the late Charlie Fallon to blackmailer of Ed Teen and Lou Grindle. Toady unavailingly hires Arthur Cole and Glenn Fisher to kill Mike Hammer, who is getting close to exposing him. Marsha Lee thinks he has evidence against the two and shoots him.

LINTON. In *The Erection Set,* he was a mill owner and the founder of Linton, the town named after him.

LIPSEK, ANTON. In *Vengeance Is Mine!,* he runs a model agency in New York City, with Juno Reeves. He is a photographer; she, a talent recruiter. They also furnish girls for fashion shows. These girls lure men in his bedroom, where he secretly photographs activities for blackmail. His undoing comes when one such victim was Chester Wheeler, whom Mike Hammer knew and who was murdered.

LISA. In *The Erection Set,* she was Dog Kelly's girlfriend in London when Marco decided not to kill Dog.

LITER, BEN. In "The Night I Died," he is a minor criminal who ineffectively attacks Mike Hammer and Helen Venn, then runs away.

LITTLE JOE. In *Survival . . . Zero!,* he is a beggar whose legs were shot off fifteen years earlier, by a criminal whom Captain Pat Chambers then shot. Little Joe provides Mike Hammer with tips helping him find Beaver.

LITTLEWORTH, ARTHUR. In "The Gold Fever Tapes," he is a hit man from Des Moines. Reading sent Littleworth to kill Fallon, who, however, outwits and kills him. Littleworth's aliases include Little Shim, the Mechanic, Shim Little, and Soho Little.

LITVAK, DAN. In "The Seven Year Kill," he is a knowledgeable New York newsman who helps Phil Rocca, cooperates with the D.A. Cal Porter, and is instrumental in saving Rocca's life.

LOBIN. In *The Long Wait,* he is a crooked Lyncastle cop. He drags Troy Avalard back to Lenny Servo, only to be killed himself by John McBride.

LOBO, EL. In *The Erection Set,* he was a European drug dealer. Dog Kelly, accused of being El Lobo, in reality killed him ten years earlier.

LOCCA, VEY. In *The Death Dealers,* she is the aging Teish El Abin's gorgeous young fiancée, whom he first saw dancing in Morocco. Teish asks Tiger Mann to guard her and implies his gratitude when Tiger sleeps with her because doing so may provide Teish an heir. Malcolm Turos's stab at Vey proved nonfatal because the blade was deflected by the big ruby in her navel. Vey is of Chinese, Irish, Japanese, and Russian ancestry.

LOCKWOOD, PORTER. In *The Death Dealers,* he and Seaton Coleman are foolishly liberal politicians who are jeopardizing America's relationship with Teish El Abin.

LOCO BENE. In "The Gold Fever Tapes," he is a minor criminal whom Fallon persuades to identify Arthur Littleworth for him.

LODO. In "Me, Hood!," he is described as an elusive East Coast enforcer for the Mafia. Pat Shane tells Ryan that Lodo is "a trouble name." *See* Smith, Carmen.

LOEFERT, BENNY. In "Killer Mine," he is an ex-con, uptown mobster who enters Lieutenant Joe Scanlon's neighborhood to make trouble. He associates with Beamish, Will Fater, Paula Lees, Steve Lutz, and Al Reese.

LOGAN, ALAN. In *The Long Wait,* he is a boxer turned journalist. He helps John McBride, drinks too much, is lured by Havis Gardiner to drive off with Looth, is forced off the road, and is badly injured in a crash in which Looth dies.

LOGAN, CAPTAIN HENRY. In *The Day the Sea Rolled Back,* he is named as the captain of the sunken *Nantucket Belle.* Larry Damar and Josh see his skeleton.

LOLLA, DOMINICK. In "The Flier," Cat Fallon recalls that Lolla smuggled him from Germany back to the United States.

LONG, JUDGE. In *Bloody Sunrise,* according to Clement Fletcher's landlady, Judge Long was distressed when the judge's son shipped aboard the *Maitland.*

LONG, WILLIAM ("BILL"). In *The Last Cop Out,* he is Gill Burke's big friend in the police department. Long reluctantly cooperates with Gill but is suspicious of him.

LONGSTREET, LUCY. In *The Erection Set,* she is a semiretired brothel madam on 3rd Street in Linton. She and her maid, Beth, give Dog Kelly information and help him apprehend some thugs.

THE LONG WAIT (1951). Novel. (Characters: Troy Avalard, Barney, Inez Casey, Charlie Davitson, Donahue, Havis Gardiner, Ginger, George Harlan, Gracie Harlan, William Harlan, Nicholas Henderson, I. Hinnam, Howie, Jack, Larry, Lee, Captain Lindsey, Lobin, Alan Logan, Looth, Mac, John McBride, Mrs. Robert Minnow, Robert Minnow, Eddie Packman, Philbert, Pimples, Lenny Servo, Carol Shay, Tucker, Venus, Sergeant Walker, Vera West, Whitman, George Wilson, Jerry Wyndot.)

After five years, John (Johnny) McBride, the narrator, returns to Lyncastle. At the bus station, a fellow he calls Pop is friendly but says Johnny should leave. A stranger also warns him, but Johnny taxis to the Hathaway House, rests overnight, gets a new wardrobe, and visits gossipy Looth Tooth's barbershop. Two cops rush him to Captain Lindsey, who says he is wanted for murder and his fingerprints can prove his guilt. But his fingertips are burned off clean. Lindsey hits Johnny, who slugs him and Tucker, his mean assistant, but wakes up in the hospital with a concussion. Johnny is freed on his own recognizance. The newspapers report him as a longtime suspect in the murder of Robert Minnow, Lyncastle's D.A., who had probed city gambling. Pop tells Johnny that Lenny Servo runs local saloons and gaming rooms, and drives Johnny to Louie Dinero's steakhouse for dinner. Pop, identified as Nicholas ("Nick") Henderson, introduces him to Wendy, a gorgeous blonde singer there who, Nick says, can hide him from danger. Johnny prefers his hotel room.

Next morning Johnny goes to the public library and reads this in old *Lyncastle News* files: Minnow's anticorruption drive ended when John McBride, who attended college two years, was a war hero, became "a dirty bank absconder," killed Minnow, disappeared; only Alan Logan seemed neutral among reporters then. Going outside, Johnny is shot at from a rooftop across the street by a short man. Johnny phones Logan; they agree to meet at a riverside bar. Logan, a tough ex-boxer, recalls angrily that Johnny stole Vera West, Logan's girlfriend, from him, and is incredulous when Johnny says he is really George Wilson. He explains: Wilson and Johnny, looking almost like identical twins, worked together on construction jobs; Wilson seared his hands, including fingertips, saving Johnny from a burning bus; Wilson got amnesia when the bus exploded, remembers nothing about his past, saw his name on his shirt; Johnny died trying to save Wilson in a bridge accident later; Johnny left a letter providing no names but saying he had been run out of Lyncastle five years earlier by "a sadistic bastard" while his ex-girlfriend stood by laughing.

Logan believes Johnny, says he will search Wilson's background, returns to his office to examine photographs of Minnow's murder scene, gives Wilson a picture of Vera, and says someone unknown is Lyncastle's real boss. At a saloon, Wilson is told that Vera, discarded by Servo, might be in the red-light district now. Wilson barges into the bank where Vera worked when McBride allegedly stole money. The manager, Havis Gardiner, calls Wilson "McBride," but expresses doubts that he killed Minnow and lets him look around. Carol Shay, a platinum blonde, is a receptionist for Servo, who has an office with a bodyguard named Eddie Parkman. Wilson enters, insults Servo, who calls him McBride, asks about Vera, throws Eddie around, slugs Servo, and returns to Carol. At a bar, Wilson feeds her nine Manhattans, taxis with her to her apartment, learns nothing about Vera, drops Carol in her bed, and declines her invitation for further action. He goes to the apartment building where Servo keeps an oversexed redhead (named Troy Avalard). From her he learns only that she hates Vera. The building superintendent remembers Vera fondly and says Servo argued last night with someone.

Wilson phones Nick at the bus station, asks him to call Wendy in, and the three chat. She suggests seeing Minnow's widow, still in Lyncastle. Wilson and Wendy find her at home. Recognizing "McBride," she says she told Lindsey five years ago she doubted McBride killed her husband, and says he held in their home safe a letter from a woman who said he should open it only if she died. The night Minnow was killed, he had a call from New York, took the letter to the office, was killed; the letter is missing. Wendy drops Wilson off downtown, where he is knocked unconscious. Three heavies drive him to a quarry to kill him, but he outwits them after begging a cigarette. In the ensuing gunplay, one thug kills another and Wilson takes that one's gun and kills another. The third escapes, and Wilson drives their car back to town and abandons it. He phones Logan and learns Troy was an expensive singer whose contract Servo bought up. Wilson taxis to Wendy's place, sneaks in, and they bed down in faint moonlight.

Over breakfast, Wilson tells Wendy who he is, requests her help in locating Vera, and borrows her car. From Jack, his hotel's friendly bellhop-pimp, he learns Vera could be at a certain Elm House brothel. Records at City Hall reveal Wilson's date of birth, his being orphaned, and his seeing combat army service. He meets Logan, who produces a police circular: George Wilson is wanted for robbery and murder. Logan will keep the information secret, for now. Going to Elm Street, Wilson meets the gorgeous madam Jack recommended. Calling her Venus, Wilson learns she knows Servo and knew Vera. At a joint for some drinks, Wilson is spotted by Tucker and escorted to Lindsey. Experts summoned from Washington, D.C., try unsuccessfully to raise Wilson's fingerprints. Wilson sees a crowd at too-talkative Looth Tooth's barbershop. At a specified roadhouse, Wilson finds Logan, who rushes him to a new murder scene. Inez Casey, a waitress, has been stabbed at a flophouse. After Logan evades the incoming police, he tells Wilson a personals ad asks "J. Mc" to phone a certain number. When he does, a voice says, "See Harlan, Johnny." When Wilson chances to see the one thug who got away last night, he borrows Logan's car, chases him, gets to the car he borrowed from Wendy, continues his pursuit, but sees the thug miss a curve, crash, and die. From the body, Wilson takes $1,000 and a gun, drives to Dinero's, has a steak, and chats with Wendy in her dressing room. She says she just heard that someone saw Vera years ago at the state capital dating someone. When Wendy, suddenly self-critical, refuses to seek Eddie with him, Wilson calls Venus and they go to a recommended gambling joint. Wilson spreads part of his $1,000 around. Two thugs suddenly march him into Servo's presence. Wilson overpowers the thugs, threatens Servo, asks where Vera is, but learns nothing. He and Venus depart. Near the parking lot, they are shot at but missed.

Wilson and Venus drive to an all-night joint for coffee and spot Eddie with a redhead there. Wilson follows him to the parking lot, decks him, but is conked by a cop. He wakes up in a police hospital with a rebandaged head. Lindsey arrives but cannot query him because Gardiner, the banker, has bailed him out and wants to see him. First, Wilson accompanies Logan to a diner to seek a waitress who worked with murdered Inez; she is missing. They proceed to Gardiner's mansion. He explains that the insurance company and the FBI are seeking Vera to see if she embezzled the money. After being allowed to see some investigative reports, Wilson agrees to back away. Getting his car again, Wilson grabs a bite to eat, phones Venus, is warned of trouble by clever answers, and speeds to her aid. He finds Servo watching Eddie torture her for information. Wilson smashes Servo, disarms knife-wielding Eddie, and breaks his arm. Even so, Eddie conks him with an ashtray; both heavies leave, thinking Wilson dead. Venus revives him, tells him someone financed Servo when he first came to town, and wonders whether McBride or Vera did so. All the while, Venus is sensuously dancing and disrobing. Wilson, though weak-voiced, responds amorously.

Logan, found at his favorite bar, tells Wilson that old files mention several Harlans, including an actress using that name. At another bar he sees a cop with a George Wilson wanted poster. Someone alerted the police. Logan?

Wendy? Wilson phones Lindsey for a meet, agrees he is Wilson or McBride, but asks whether Lindsey wouldn't mainly want to collar Minnow's killer. If so, give Wilson a week to locate Harlan, which was the name on an envelope in the Minnow murder-scene photo; meanwhile, Lindsey should find the letter missing from it. When Lindsey agrees, Wilson revisits Servo's apartment building and learns from one of Servo's utility girls that Troy, scared by something, has disappeared. Wilson evades Tucker at the bus station, scares Nick by sneaking into his little office, and is scared when Nick says he is obliged by law to post a Wilson wanted poster. Wilson gets to Wendy's apartment, and the two make love in welcome darkness.

In the morning Wilson drives to the state capital and confers with Donahue, the state auditor, who hints Vera stopped the bank audit by having something on him. In Lyncastle again, he learns from Logan's secretary that a New York newsman just informed him that the Harlan in question was actress Gracie Harlan. Venus shows Wilson a photograph revealing that Irene Godfrey, the suicide victim, was really Harlan. Wilson phones Lindsey urging him to locate and protect Troy. For a disguise, Wilson buys a work shirt and jeans; in a concealed leg slot, he hides his gun. He finds Wendy, who says Tucker's house and car are above his means. Wilson theorizes that Minnow had evidence which Servo stole. Wilson sneaks into Mrs. Minnow's house, with her permission goes to a secret room with a safe, and in it finds a letter from Harlan to Minnow and a ticket for photostat work held at Philbert's store. Wilson phones Lindsey and learns Logan, drunk, was forced off the road and is badly injured; with him was Looth, dead. Wilson drives to the house where Inez was stabbed, starts to look around, but is surprised by Eddie, his arm in a cast, and an adolescent punk Wilson dubs Pimples. They drive Wilson, knocked unconscious, to an abandoned house by the river, tie him to a chair, and go get Servo. Groggy, Wilson wonders whether Servo lusted after Harlan, dumped her for Vera, Vera stole from the bank, Johnny disappeared to protect her. The thugs return with Servo, who batters Wilson; Eddie knifes his ears. Lobin, a crooked cop in Servo's pay, caught Troy trying to leave town and brings her in. Servo beats her sadistically. Servo plans a double murder here and now, but Wilson stalls by saying Troy's hefty bank account will go to relatives. Servo sends Lobin and Pimples to her place for a bank withdrawal slip. Wilson alerts Troy to his hidden gun. Servo knocks her down and kicks her toward Wilson. She seizes his gun, and shoots him dead as he mortally shoots her. She shoots Wilson's ropes loose, begs him to undress her, and dies. He finds a photostat of Harlan's letter taped to her stomach. When Lobin, Pimples, and Eddie return, Wilson shoots the first two dead, breaks Eddie's other arm, and leaves him agonizing. Taking Lobin's gun, Wilson drives Eddie's car to town, phones Lindsey about these killings, and busts into Gardiner's mansion. Wilson starts lecturing Gardiner, who guzzles whiskey the while: Gardiner financed Servo; Harlan shook both down, got greedy then scared, wrote Minnow details; Gardiner juggled the bank accounts, fastened the theft on McBride; Vera aided Servo; Gardiner shot at Wilson from the roof, later from the car aiming not at Wilson but Venus, mistaking her for Vera; Logan phoned Gardiner for a story; Looth talked too much; both had to go; Gardiner, thinking Servo and Harlan would connive against him, sent Eddie to kill her, but he knifed Inez instead; Gardiner occasionally disguised his voice, phoned Lindsey. Gardiner suddenly glances at his window. Wilson ducks and avoids Tucker's shot from outside, turns, shoots Tucker dead, and continues lecturing: Harlan gave the photo to Troy and through fear killed herself. When Gardiner pulls a gun and fires erratically twice, Wilson shoots him in stomach, groin, and head, and tells the screaming housekeeper to phone Lindsey.

Dawn breaks. Wilson drives to Wendy's place, identifies the startled girl as Vera, makes her undress, and would flog her. But she reveals this: Nick had wanted posters of George Wilson two years before she ever met McBride; she has letters attesting to McBride's military heroism; Wilson, knowing he was wanted, would surely have become the fortuitously look-alike McBride upon learning McBride developed amnesia; Servo saved McBride, accused of theft, to control Vera. These last few days, Wendy, confused, acted as she did to make sure of everything. She even filed the personals ad. She checks a stomach scar on Wilson. Proof enough. "Wilson" is really McBride. The real Wilson, dead, was the only criminal. Wendy is Vera. She unfurls their marriage license, issued a month before the bank scandal. They bed down again, this time with lights on.

The Long Wait is Spillane's first non–Mike Hammer novel. Its hero resembles Hammer only superficially. Like Hammer, McBride survives multiple attacks by villains, between which, applying the double standard, he enjoys love-making sessions even as he expects his beloved (Vera's name is close to Velda's) to await his return to her celibately. But unlike Hammer, McBride, with amnesia, often doubts the rightness of his behavior. New American Library editors were so confident of Spillane's drawing power that they authorized an initial paperback printing of *The Long Wait* of 2.5 million copies; it sold out in three weeks.

Bibliography: Collins and Traylor; Johnston.

LOOTH ("LOOTH TOOTH"). In *The Long Wait,* he is the Lyncastle barber whose propensity to purvey gossip costs him his life.

LOPEX, C. C. In *One Lonely Night,* he is the superintendent of the place where Charlie Moffit lived before he was murdered.

LÓPEZ, MARÍA. In *The Delta Factor,* Angelo tells Morgan that Lisa Gordot will be driven in disguise to the airport by María López's brother.

LORING, RITA. In *Vengeance Is Mine!,* she is a model working for Anton

Lipsek and Juno Reeves. Connie Wales tells Mike Hammer that Rita is well over thirty-five.

LOU. In "Everybody's Watching Me," he works for Phil Carboy.

LOUIE. In *The Big Kill,* he owns a bar near the D.A.'s office. Mike and Captain Pat Chambers have some beer there.

LOUIE. In *One Lonely Night,* he owns a restaurant where Mike Hammer and Captain Pat Chambers meet at one point.

LOUISE. In *The Erection Set,* she is Hiram Tod's niece, is a waitress in a Linton country club, and relays gossip about Alfred Barrin to Dog Kelly.

LOUISE. In *Survival . . . Zero!,* she is William Dorn's maid. To silence her, Mike Hammer knocks her out. When Stanley comes looking for her, Mike kills him.

LOWRY, ANN. In "The Seven Year Kill." *See* Massley, Terry (the female).

LUCAS. In "The Gold Fever Tapes," he is a *News* reporter Fallon sees when Charlies Watts is illegally interrogating Marlene Peters.

LUCAS, GEORGE. In "Man Alone," he is an old friend of Patrick Regan's. Lucas came up the hard way in Brooklyn, is a criminal-law attorney, dislikes district attorneys, and advises Regan helpfully.

LUCAS, GEORGIA. In *The Big Kill,* she was Charlie Fallon's last mistress. In fear of Lou Grindle, she withheld Fallon's medicine and thus caused his death ten years ago. Mike finds Georgia, age forty-eight and a fading substitute entertainer, calling herself Dolly Smith, at Harvey's Greenwich Village night club. Mike saves her from Ed Teen's goons and turns her over to Captain Pat Chambers.

LUCERNE, HENRY. In "The Affair with the Dragon Lady," he was the navigator aboard the Dragon Lady.

LUCIAN. In *The Last Cop Out,* he and Jan are homosexuals, are ordered by Francois Verdun to guard Leon Bray, but are killed by a masked man.

LUDEN, MRS. In *Survival . . . Zero!,* she is Sigmund Katz's neighbor, who, Katz says, also saw Carl and Stanley.

LULU. In "I'll Die Tomorrow," she was a savage woman who liked to have Rudolph Lees beat her.

LULU. In *The Last Cop Out,* she warns Francois Verdun that "Freaks speak." Shatzi Heinkle is a genuine freak.

LUM FROG. In "The Seven Year Kill," Phil Rocca has Terry Massley meet him at Lum Frog's for supper.

LUND, RONDINE. In *The By-Pass Control, Day of the Guns,* and *The Death Dealers. See* Caine, Diana.

LUPE. In *The Last Cop Out,* he and the Cobra stand guard outside Leon Bray's door. Both are killed, as are others near Bray.

LUSONG, JAMES. In *The Body Lovers,* he is a U.N. diplomat whom Gerald Ute introduces to Mike at Ute's party.

LUTZ, STEVE. In "Killer Mine," he is a gunman who associates with Beamish, Will Fater, and Benny Loefert. Lutz is killed by Larry Scanlon near Paula Lees's room.

M

MAC. In *The Long Wait,* he phoned Alan Logan to report Inez Casey's murder.

McBRIDE, JOHN ("JOHNNY"). In *The Long Wait,* he went to college two years, served heroically in the army overseas, was wrongly accused of embezzling from the Lyncastle bank, and ran away. He and George Wilson, look-alikes, worked on construction. After an accident resulting in McBride suffering amnesia, Wilson, a murderer, switched identities with him but later died. McBride returns to Lyncastle to clear McBride's name, mistakenly thinking he is Wilson. After much confusion and shooting, McBride is reunited with Vera West, whom he initially suspected of the embezzlement but who in reality is his wife.

MACBRUDER. In "Stand Up and Die!," Macbruder saw the C-47 crash and told everyone. He helps Trumble Cahill aid Mitch.

McCALL, LISA. In *The By-Pass Control,* she is the madam of a brothel in Eau Gallie, Florida, which Louis Agrounsky visited some six times. In Tiger Mann's presence, Lisa tells Camille Hunt she recalls Camille's saving General Ortega Diaz in Rio by killing two men. This hint about Camille's past should have alerted Tiger but did not.

McCALL, MAXIE. In *The Death Dealers,* he is a boxer whom Ron, the doorman at Edith Caine's apartment building, used to know.

MacCAULEY. In "The Bastard Bannerman," Cat Cay Bannerman remembers him as Miles Bannerman's kind servant, who would have helped Cat more but for Miles's viciousness.

McCAULEY, BEEZO. In *The By-Pass Control,* he was a drug addict who gave Niger Hoppes information about Louis Agrounsky, after which Hoppes killed him.

McCLAIN. In *Black Alley,* he and Johnny Leeds are surveyors in Albany. Mike Hammer talks with Leeds but not with McClain.

McDELL, STEVE. In "Man Alone," he is a network radio announcer who helps Patrick Regan locate the cab driver who drove Al Argenio and Madaline Stumper to Long Island.

McDONALD, JEANNIE. In "The Seven Year Kill," she is an upstairs neighbor of Phil Rocca, who borrows clothes from her for Terry Massley.

McDOWELL, OSCAR. In *Bloody Sunrise,* he is a hotel bell captain who gets Tiger Mann the key to a room near where Gabin Martrel is first stashed.

McGAFFNEY, JAKE. "Me, Hood!," he runs a horse parlor, provides Ryan with information, and is at the Spanish shindig with a girl named Bets when Ryan and Carmen Smith go there.

McGILL, SENATOR. In "The Veiled Woman," he is Karl Terris's friend and helps him when the federal authorities are troublesome.

McGRATH, WALTER. In *Kiss Me, Deadly,* he was a flame of Berga Torn's during the war. Mike learns that McGrath was a shady lumber dealer then, has a police record, owns a gun, lives in a Madison Avenue hotel, and likes pretty girls.

McINNES, DULCIE. In *The Body Lovers,* she is a maturely attractive fashion editor for the Proctor Group. Cleo sends Mike Hammer to Dulcie, and she pretends to help him track down Greta Service, during which time they relish some wild sex. From a good Midwestern family—so she says—Dulcie causes Theodore Gates's suicide, plays hostess for Gerald Ute, introduces Mike to Belar Ris, and enjoys watching him torture Greta. She gets her comeuppance when Mike blows up Ris's mansion.

MacINTOSH. In "The Gold Fever Tapes," he and Stiles run a casting factory in Brooklyn where Henry Borden fashioned Reading's safe out of gold.

McINTYRE, JASON. In *The Killing Man,* he is a garageman employed by Smiley. He tells Mike that Smiley has money, supposedly from betting on the ponies, and gives Harry Bern's broken partial plate to Mike.

MACK, EDDIE. In "Me, Hood!," he and Fats Sebull are seen at Pat Shane's restaurant.

McKEE. In *The Day the Sea Rolled Back,* Larry Damar remembers seeing gold coins in McKee's Museum.

McKEEVER, DR. In "Kick It or Kill!," he is a Pinewood physician. He was reluctant to report evidence of local girls' drug addiction and physical abuse. He aids Kelly Smith.

McKEEVER, MRS. In "Kick It or Kill!," she is a Pinewood physician's wife and the sister of Captain Cox's ex-wife Emma Cox. She aids Kelly Smith.

MacKINLEY. In *The Death Dealers,* he is an oilman working for Dursto-Allied, an AmPet rival. He quizzes Tiger Mann and is impressed by his knowledge of the oil industry.

MACKLEY, HERBERT. In *The Ship That Never Was,* he is the Miami linguist who determines that Vali Steptur speaks the Grandau language. Embor Linero, with Aktur Cilon's help, murders Mackley.

McMILLAN. In *The Erection Set,* he was Cross McMillan's father and a commercial rival of Cameron Barrin, Dog Kelly's grandfather.

McMILLAN, CROSS. *The Erection Set,* he is Dog Kelly's lifelong rival and is ambitious to grab Barrin family property and wreck the family. He guns for Dog until Dog sleeps with Sheila McMillan, Cross's wife, and thus warms her sexually after frigidity caused by Sheila's having suffered repeated rapes.

McMILLAN, SERGEANT. In *The Big Kill,* he is a plain-clothes policeman whom Mike Hammer asks to check on Arthur Cole and Glenn Fisher.

McMILLAN, SHEILA. In *The Erection Set,* she is Cross McMillan's frigid tease of a wife. Dog McMillan heats her by some violent sex, for which Cross is grateful.

McNEIL, HAL. In "Killer Mine," he is a long-time beat cop in Lieutenant Joe Scanlon's old neighborhood. His leads help Joe solve the multiple murders.

MADGE. In *The Killing Man,* she is a night nurse at the hospital where Velda is a patient.

MAHONEY, NICK. In "The Flier," he spotted Andro Marcel, told Big Jake Crane, and was asked to learn more. He reported Marcel's drug activities to George Clinton, who passes it on to Cat Fallon.

MALCOM, HELEN. In *The Twisted Thing. See* Coulter, Roxy.

MALEK, MRS. QUINCY. In *The Snake,* she is Quincy Malek's widow. For $500, she gives Mike Hammer information leading to his locating Black Conley's Catskills hideout.

MALEK, QUINCY. In *The Snake,* he was Howie Green's real-estate partner and died of tuberculosis.

MALLORY, HERRON. In *The Twisted Thing,* born in New York City in 1907 of Irish-Russian parents, he is Ruston York's real father. An accomplished criminal, he let Rudolph York take his infant son and raise him as his own, planning to blackmail Rudolph later. Mallory changed his name to Nelson, controlled a casino near Sidon, and worked with Dilwick and Myra Grange. Mike Hammer learns Mallory's identity and works him over shortly before Dilwick kills Mallory.

MALLORY, MRS. HERRON. In *The Twisted Thing,* she gave birth to a baby boy who became Ruston York. She died two days later.

MALONE. In *The Last Cop Out,* he is mentioned as Mark Shelby's Irish predecessor.

MALONEY, CHUCK. In "The Bastard Bannerman," he was sexy Irish Maloney's husband. Irish didn't especially mind when Vance Colby murdered Chuck in the Cherokee Club parking lot, where Chuck worked. But Rudy Bannerman's thinking he killed Chuck enables Colby, Popeye Gage, and Carl Matteau to try to blackmail the Bannerman family.

MALONEY, IRISH. In "The Bastard Bannerman," she is Chuck Maloney's voluptuous wife, then widow, and does strip teases at the Cherokee Club. One of her lovers was Vance Colby, who stabbed Chuck to death. Cat Cay Bannerman interrogates her, regards her as a "nympho," and the two sleep together one night.

MALONEY, LITTLE JOE. In *The Delta Factor,* he leaves burglary tools for Morgan at a New York bus station, at Morgan's request.

"MAN ALONE" (1965). Short story. (Characters: Angie, Al Argenio, Chick, Jane Doe, Donninger, Dooley, Edson, Greenblatt, Helen the Melons, Miles Henry, Ray Hilquist, Jackson, Popeye Lewis, George Lucas, Steve McDell, Leo Marcus, Ted Marker, Walter Milcross, Mutt, Mrs. Jerry Nolan, Sergeant Jerry Nolan, Parker, Ralph, Hymie Reeves, Van Reeves, Patrick Regan, Edna Rells, Guy Rivera, Annie Schwartz, Scipio, Selkirk, Monty Selkirk, Dr. Leonard

Shipp, Small, Spud, Stan The Pencil, Stucker, Madaline Stumper, Sturvesent, Mildred Swiss, Vinnie, Welch.)

Patrick Regan, the narrator, is a dismissed policeman, acquitted by a jury of killing a Syndicate crime boss named Leo Marcus, but rebuked by the judge. Regan remembers being drunk the night of Marcus's death, being taxied by Guy Rivera from the Climax bar to Marcus's home, but not taking $5,000 from him and shooting him six times in the head, as charged. At Donninger's restaurant, Regan meets Sergeant Jerry Nolan, a friend who believes he is guilty. Regan snarls at Jerry's partner, Al Argenio, who found the $5,000 on Regan. Regan locates Rivera, who admits his testimony against Regan in court, though unfavorable, was spotty. He remembers that a red-headed woman helped Regan into his cab that night and thinks Regan was too drunk to shoot anyone. Regan visits the Climax and talks with Ralph, the mean bartender who gave him too many drinks that dreadful night, and also with Spud, a sympathetic old waiter. Present also that night were Stan The Pencil, a bookie; Popeye Lewis and Edna Rells, artists; and Miles Henry, who sold the boss two Popeye paintings. Spud will try to find the redhead.

Regan calls on George Lucas, an old friend now a criminal-law attorney, who agrees to start action to have Regan claim the seized $5,000 and also get his police badge back. Regan meets Nolan at lunchtime, convinces him of his innocence, and tells him about a mickey Ralph must have slipped him and about the redhead. Nolan says Regan might have been dosed with Sentol, a new, conscience-removing mickey. Regan explains this: Marcus owned a string of motels used as Syndicate money drops; Regan was on a secret assignment, gathered evidence against Marcus he gave to six top police officials; evidence included Marcus's murders of a kid and of a witness in Georgia. Marcus was repeatedly shot in the head, fell into his fireplace, and was badly charred. Nolan praises Argenio as tough but unlikable, and says Argenio got a tip about the $5,000 in Regan's apartment and found it remarkably fast. Regan goes around town, asking about Marcus's underworld replacement, goes home, and answers a phone call from Spud, who says the evening newspapers are reporting that the redhead Regan sought was just found drowned.

Regan checks the papers. From her photographs, the victim, Mildred Swiss, looks like a model or a high-class hooker. Regan checks with a childhood pal, Madaline Stumper, nicknamed Miss Mad, now head of a call-girl and modeling agency. She says Mildred was a call girl who associated with Ray Hilquist until he died, and then with other men. Regan silently recalls Hilquist was murdered. Nolan provides Regan with official photographs of Marcus's remains: face obliterated, torso burned in fireplace, one finger and dental plate found. Is Marcus the dead one? Nolan will assemble data on Mildred.

Regan finds Stan the bookie, gains his trust, wonders who gave him the mickey, and alerts him to ask around. Regan walks fifteen blocks to his apartment, lies down, thinks of wartime Nazis, is suddenly suspicious, and finds a can of gas under his mattress released by his weight. He takes the can to Sergeant Ted Marker, who identifies the material as deadly surplus German nerve gas called FS-7. Regan has lunch with Mad, who tells him her girls told her that Mildred two-timed Hilquist by falling in love with Marcus, and he with her, and that the Syndicate warned Marcus to avoid her. When Regan visits Popeye and Edna, Popeye reveals this: Marcus received payoffs for the Syndicate from the Climax, really a lesbian hangout; Helen the Melons was a hat-check girl there, was Argenio's girlfriend, turned against him, and left; Mildred served Regan the mickey that night. Will Regan be accused now of killing her? Marker tells him this: Millie drowned at 5:15 P.M., according to her broken watch, and FS-7 was probably used on two recent Syndicate defectors.

Regan is having supper at his apartment when Mad appears. She tells him rumor has it Mildred boasted of a planned trip, explains that she became a madam to support her ailing parents, cleans up Regan's sloppy pad, showers, and enjoys sudden, nice sex with him. Lucas calls and asks Regan to come see him. On their way out, Regan and Mad are shot at by a silenced gun but missed. Regan finds and pockets three spent bullets. Lucas says bribed informants reveal this: Marcus stole Regan's mob secrets, pleased the mob, but skimmed, thus became a target for killers hired from Chicago. Regan calls Nolan and tells him to check on any missing person whose physique might resemble Marcus's.

Morning rain shrouds New York. Pledging his love to Mad, Regan sends her by cab to her office and locates Helen the Melons in Brooklyn. She says Argenio was too brutally possessive but did give her some bonds. Regan notes their names. He asks Marker to analyzes the three bullets. Lucas tells Regan he has learned that Helen's bonds are junk bonds; Regan infers Argenio is a stock-market addict. Regan visits the dentist who made Marcus's dentures and learns he made a spare set in case one was ever damaged. Nolan reports that a certain missing man's characteristics match Marcus's. Regan gets Walter Milcross, a crooked jeweler who owes him a favor, to search the home of Argenio, who is on a case in Long Island. Marker reports that Argenio had access to a confiscated silencer and also had access to warehoused FS-7 and Sentol. Milcross says he didn't find Regan's papers in Argenio's place but found a severed finger in an ink bottle. Regan summarizes: Marcus stole Syndicate money, got Argenio to steal Regan's evidence against Marcus and plant $5,000 against Regan, even so feared Syndicate vengeance, had Regan drugged, killed and burned a substitute for himself, smashed his spare dentures, when a finger was shot off had a doctor amputate one of Marcus's on the spot, Argenio having found the real one, keeping it to blackmail the living Marcus. Regan calls Mad's office and learns Argenio has seized her.

Regan checks with Mad's doorman, who saw Mad and a man leave by taxi; alerts a radio station to appeal to all cabbies; gets a police escort to a factory region near Long Island City where Argenio and his captive were spotted; and makes his way to a defunct bottling company Regan remembers Marcus used as a racket drop-point. He bursts in on Argenio, sees him torturing the tied-up and half-stripped Mad for information, is missed by Argenio's shot, and shoots Argenio dead. Regan puts his .45 in Mad's lap, loosens her bonds, but turns as he hears Marcus behind him, one hand bandaged after his finger amputation. He gloats he has a secret exit and sights a gun at Regan, who moves on Mad's command as she kill Marcus with Regan's .45. The lovers embrace as police sirens wail.

"Death of the Too-Cute Prostitute," the original title of this story, derives from the fate of Mildred Swiss. The title "Man Alone" is not an improvement. Regan, hardly alone, is helped by at least ten people. The plot is complicated. Regan must prove he didn't kill a criminal who is really alive. Action is slowed when Spillane offers Regan's thoughts on ungrateful public-housing tenants, unclean Harlem, "backwards-collar gooks" opposing gambling, critics of prostitutes, and that rained-on circus called Manhattan. The story is weakened in two respects. Can readers believe that Regan drank too much, was drugged by Pentol, which blurs one's conscience, but happened to take six aspirin, which nullified the conscience-killing effect of Pentol? Also, could Regan, drugged, enter Marcus's house and not shoot his substitute, all the while giving Marcus time to kill that poor slob, burn his face and torso, find the shot-off pinky, summon a physician to amputate his own, place it where it could be found, and locate, break, and scatter his spare dentures—in a couple of hours?

MANGO, STEVE. In *Bloody Sunrise,* he was a sailor aboard the *Maitland.* The authorities had him identify Clement Fletcher's body.

MANN, TIGER. In *Day of the Guns,* he was a World War II counter-intelligence agent. Often wounded, hardened by Communist Cold War villainy, and adept in maneuvers, weaponry, and languages, he boasts of having killed many people who deserved to die. He is now a conservative, freelancing mercenary. He believes in principle but not in law. In 1945 he fell in love with Rondine Lund, a Nazi spy, slept with her, and was gutshot by her. Tiger Mann drinks a little, smokes less, talks dirty, boasts like an overgrown adolescent, and is sometimes incorrect in his conclusions. His seeing Edith Caine at the U.N. and believing she is Rondine contribute to his problems in solving leaks at the U.N. He kills several Soviet agents before determining the culpability of Gretchen Lark, Edith's associate. At one point, he calls himself Frank Wilson; at another, Dr. Lane.

In *Bloody Sunrise,* Tiger puts off his marriage to Edith Caine (whom he calls Rondine out of nostalgia) to follow Martin Grady's order to find Soviet defector Gabin Martrel. In the course of this assignment, Tiger moves from one hotel to three others, is aided by Charlie Corbinet, Clement Fletcher,

Wally Gibbons, and Ann Lighter, among others; meets and soon sleeps with Sonia Dutko, the object of Martrel's affections; stashes Sonia in the empty house of Burton Selwick, a British friend; is stalked by Spaak Helo, a Soviet killer. In the end, he kills Helo, saves Gibbons and Edith, and deliberately causes Sonia's death. In one hotel, Tiger registers as H. Talbot.

In *The Death Dealers,* Tiger is assigned to investigate Teish El Abin and to avoid being killed by Malcolm Turos. Aided by Virgil Adams, Corbinet, and Martrel, among others, Tiger saves both Edith Caine, who is Tiger's fiancée, and also Teish from Turos; is partly responsible for Lily Tornay's murder; sleeps with Vey Locca, Teish's fiancée; and kills Yamu Gorkey and Turos. Tiger admits to feeling older, now being without vinegar, and retaining only piss. He drinks a little, does not smoke, and is monstrously conceited and macho. Tiger is opposed to political "eggheads," the U.N., the Peace Corps, and the IRS. He calls Arabs "gooks with blunderbusses and archaic ideas."

In *The By-Pass Control,* Tiger seeks Louis Agrounsky, a brilliant, drug-addicted inventor of a control which can immobilize America's ICBM system, which he vacillates about using, and which the Soviets want. Tiger kills Vito Salvi, who killed Doug Hamilton, a New York electronics man who knew Agrounsky; consorts with Camille Hunt, Hamilton's personnel manager, who is a Soviet mole and is Niger Hoppes's associate; is aided in Florida by agents Dave Elroy and Mason Armstrong, and Claude Boster and Vincent Small, Agrounsky's friends. At one point Tiger says, "I'm scared, kid," to Camille— for good reason, since, unknown then to him, she is a Soviet mole. Tiger finds Agrounsky, who is dead of an overdose but whose control is active; kills Hoppes; and watches Camille die of a booby-trapped inhaler meant for Hoppes. Tiger registers in various hotels as T. Gerrity, T. Martin, and T. Marvin. In this narrative, Tiger is skillful, ruthless, lucky, and insufferably conceited, and smokes excessively.

In all four Tiger Mann novels, Spillane is clearly capitalizing on the popularity of the James Bond 007 novels written by Ian Fleming (1908–1964); both derring-do heroes are challenged and behave similarly.

Bibliography: Jerry Palmer, *Thrillers: Genesis and Structure of a Popular Genre* (London: Edward Arnold, 1978).

MANNING, CHARLOTTE. In *I, the Jury,* a gorgeous blonde, she is a Park Avenue psychiatrist with ritzy patients. She prescribes them into addiction for profit. She so fools Mike Hammer that he proposes marriage. But when he discovers that she has murdered Jack Williams, Harold Kines, Eileen Vickers, George Kalecki, Bobo Hopper, and Myrna Devlin, all of whom could have implicated her, he shoots her dead. In *Vengeance Is Mine!,* Juno Reeves reminds Mike of Charlotte, and he tells Juno he killed Charlotte. In *The Girl Hunters,* Mike names Charlotte to himself and remembers he shot her. In *The Twisted Thing,* Mike recalls killing the unnamed Charlotte and says doing so, and thus keeping a promise, "killed my soul."

MANNY, PAPA. In "Me, Hood!," he owned a three-floor brownstone off Second Avenue, according to Art Shay, who tells Ryan he now owns it.

MANUTE. In *The Last Cop Out,* he and Berkowitz were photographers. Mark Shelby killed them both when he suspected them of planning to blackmail him.

MANUTE, IRMA. In *The Last Cop Out,* she is the widow of Berkowitz's partner. Both men were photographers.

MARCEL, ANDRO. In "The Flier," he is a dapper, ruthless criminal. He was involved in smuggling drugs from China into the United States and now works for Fidel Castro against anti-Castro Cubans in Florida. Marcel kills Smith, tortures Cat Fallon for information, and is shot dead by Sharon Ortez.

MARCIA. In *The Erection Set,* she is a prostitute who rooms with Charmaine, also a prostitute. Dog Kelly has casual sex with Marcia and then has a friend hire her as a secretary.

MARCO. In *The Erection Set,* he was a gunman who could have shot Dog Kelly outside a London pub but decided not to do so because Dog would have killed him too.

MARCO, JULIUS. In *The Killing Man,* he was a child molester Mike Hammer recalls killing four years earlier.

MARCUS, LEO. In "Man Alone," he is a big-time Syndicate criminal. When he was suspected of skimming, he faked his own murder by using a substitute, implicated Patrick Regan, had one of his own fingers amputated, and absconded. In cahoots with Al Argenio, a crooked policeman, Marcus is found by Regan with Argenio. Regan kills them both.

MARGE. In *The By-Pass Control,* she is a girl in Lisa McCall's brothel.

MARGE. In *The Snake,* she is one of pimp Jersey Toby's girls. Toby tells Mike Hammer that Marge associates with criminals being imported from Chicago to join the Syndicate.

MARGO. In *The Ship That Never Was,* she lives on Montique Island and serves Princess Tila there.

MARIA. In *The Last Cop Out,* she is a fat girl Artie Meeker likes. Pedro Cabilla wonders if Meeker, who loves jalapeño chilies, would burn her if he kissed her in certain specified parts of her anatomy.

MARIA. In "Me, Hood!," she is named as Alfred Lias's date at the Spanish shindig.

MARIA. In *Survival . . . Zero!,* she is Renée Talmage's maid. Renée gave Maria a copy of Beaver's photograph, for William Dorn's use.

MARKER, SERGEANT TED. In "Man Alone," he is a knowledgeable police officer who helps Patrick Regan by telling him about PS-7 and Sentol and analyzing a silencer used by Al Argenio.

MARKHAM. In *The Erection Set,* he is a gunman sent by The Turk with Bridey-the-Greek to kill Dog Kelly. Dog puts both men in the hospital. Markham is later killed for failing in his mission.

MARKHAM, RED. In *The Girl Hunters,* he was Richie Cole's buddy aboard the *Vanessa.* An alcoholic, he tells Mike and Bayliss that Dennis Wallace packed Velda in a crate to get her ashore.

MARLOW, PEPPY. In *Black Alley,* he is a retired cop. Mike has breakfast with him near the precinct house in order to gain information about Slipped Disk Harris, whom Marlow knew during Prohibition.

MARSHA. In *The Body Lovers,* she is one of Dulcie McInnes's employees.

MARSHALL. In *Vengeance Is Mine!,* he is a policeman who interrogates Mike Hammer roughly, when Mike is found in dead Chester Wheeler's hotel room. Mike calls him "Fat Face."

MARTHA. In "The Girl Behind the Hedge," she is Chester Duncan's housekeeper. Going along with Duncan's revenge plan, she announces in Walter Harrison's presence that the Vaughn family has returned to New York City.

MARTIN. In *The Big Kill,* he is Ed Teen's driver and gunman. When he returns to the Islip cottage where Mike Hammer is supposedly being held, Mike has escaped. In ensuing gunfire, Lou Grindle kills Martin by mistake before Mike kills Grindle.

MARTIN. In *The Deep,* it is at his Sixth Avenue bar that Deep takes Helen Tate for coffee.

MARTIN. In *Vengeance Is Mine!,* he is a wealthy fellow who goes to the Bowery Inn. He tips with foolish extravagance.

MARTIN, HOWARD. In *My Gun Is Quick. See* Hammer, Mike.

MARTIN, T. In *The By-Pass Control. See* Mann, Tiger.

MARTINO. In "Return of the Hood," he is a hood who would kill Fly but is expertly stabbed to death by Primo Stipetto and Ernie South.

MARTREL, GABIN. In *Bloody Sunrise,* he is a tired Soviet intelligence officer. A Communist Party member since 1929, Martrel, age fifty-two and never married, defects, largely in order to find Sonia Dutko, thinking the two are in love. Martrel now feels that Communism has contributed to making the world "a vile mess." Assassin Spaad Helo's repeated efforts to kill Martrel fail. In the end, Tiger Mann, assigned to protect Martrel, saves him.

MARTY. In "The Pickpocket," he shot somebody and sent Buster to intimidate Willie, the sole witness.

MARVIN, T. In *The By-Pass Control. See* Mann, Tiger.

MARY. In *The Twisted Thing,* when Mike Hammer learns details about Myra Grange's disappearance, he uses the phone of Mary and her husband, George, to report to Sergeant Price.

MASON. In *The Girl Hunters,* he was one of Mike's remembered war buddies.

MASON, CURLY. In "The Affair with the Dragon Lady," he helped rescue the downed F-100 pilot.

MASSLEY, JEAN STUART. In "The Seven Year Kill." *See* Massley, Rhino.

MASSLEY, JOHN LACY. In "The Seven Year Kill." *See* Massley, Rhino.

MASSLEY, MRS. RHINO. In "The Seven Year Kill," she was Rhino's ex-wife and the mother of Ann Lowry (*see* Massley, Terry). Mrs. Massley put incriminating documents in storage and died.

MASSLEY, RHINO. In "The Seven Year Kill," he is a criminal who framed Phil Rocca, fled with Syndicate funds, faked having polio and needing iron-lung treatment, fell in love with his nurse, Elena Harris, faked his death with the help of Dr. Thomas Hoyt and Leo Grant, went with Elena as Richard Castor to Rio de Janeiro, evidently ran out of money, returned to New York, lured Terry Massley there from Los Angeles in an effort to get documents to blackmail the Syndicate with, tortured Terry, and was killed by Rocca. Rhino's real name was Jean Stuart Massley, changed to John Lacy Massley.

MASSLEY, TERRY. In "The Seven Year Kill," he may be Rhino Massley's missing son. Or did he ever exist? Rhino so despised most females that he may have imagined his daughter was male.

MASSLEY, TERRY. In "The Seven Year Kill," she is Mrs. Rhino Massley's daughter. Rhino thinks "Terry" is the name of his son. When her mother died, Terry, calling herself Ann Lowry, answers a letter from her father and comes to New York. Phil Rocca saves her from Mannie Waller's thugs and, when Rhino catches her and tortures her, kills him. By this time, Phil and Terry are in love. Terry registers as Ann Spencer at a New York hotel.

MAST, JOE. In *My Gun Is Quick,* Mike Hammer goes to his "joint" for some quick, numbing drinks after Mike has killed Feeney Last.

MASTERS, GEORGE K. In *I, the Jury. See* Kalecki, George.

MATHER, CLARENCE. In "The Veiled Woman," he and his wife occupied the steamer cabin contaminated by Lodi Terris's radiation. Both Mathers died.

MATHER, MRS. CLARENCE. In "The Veiled Woman," she and her husband died of radiation exposure.

MATTICK, BENNY ("BENNY-FROM-BROOKLYN"). In *The Deep,* he is an armed heroin dealer with an office in Bimmy's tavern. Deep wrongly thinks Mattick might have killed Bennett. When Mattick tries to seize Bennett's criminal organization, he is murdered in his own Third Avenue brownstone. His nickname was assigned to distinguish him from other Bennys.

MAURY. In *The Deep,* he owns a "hole-in-the-wall diner" on Columbus Avenue near 103rd Street.

MAX. In *The Delta Factor,* he is a bartender who knows Angelo and has him warn Morgan about Russo Sabin.

MAX. In "The Veiled Woman," he guards kidnapped Lodi Terris, whose husband, Karl Terris, kills him.

MAX, CHARLIE. In *Kiss Me, Deadly,* he is a hit man, formerly a policeman, from Miami, hired with Sugar Smallhouse to kill Mike Hammer. When Mike encounters the two at Long John's, he kicks Max violently in the face. Max is later machine-gunned to death by Mafia gunmen.

MAX, RUDY. In "Return of the Hood," he is Ryan's friend. When Fred Stipetto beats him up, Ryan beats up Fred and is therefore wrongly suspected when Fred is killed.

MEEHAN. In *The Erection Set,* he is a businessman who attends a conference held by Alfred Barrin and Dennison Barrin.

MEEKER, ARTIE. In *The Last Cop Out,* he is Papa Menes's loyal worker, running errands, brings him prostitutes, driving him everywhere. Meeker is mainly interested in "broads" and monotonous driving. He escapes the blood-baths at the end. Meeker uses the name John Brill for a letter care of general delivery in Homestead, Florida.

MEG. In *The Killing Man,* she is Dr. Burke Reedey's nurse. The two tend to Velda after she is slugged.

"ME, HOOD!" (**1963**). (Characters: Babcock, Benny, Bets, Big Man, Henry Billings, Cullen, Joe DiNuccio, Tomas Escalantes, Etching, Stan Etching, Fletcher, Diego Flores, 'Fredo, Manny Golding, Juan Gonzales, Lucinda Gonzales, Peter F. Haynes III, Willis Holmes, Mamie Huggins, Hymie, Hymie the Goose, Kopek, Alfred Lias, Jake McGaffney, Eddie Mack, Papa Manny, Maria, Nelson, Lardbucket Pearson, Harry Peeler, Pete-the-Dog, Razztazz, Ryan, Sandy, Turner Scado, Fats Sebull, Mario Sen, Pat Shane, Art Shay, Carmen Smith, Sid Solomon, Stanovich, Lou Steckler, Steve, Jamie Tohey, Mrs. Winkler.)

Some policemen escort Ryan, the narrator and a self-confessed hood, to a taciturn policeman—later called Big Man—who hires him, for unspecified pay, to get Lodo by nefarious means. Ryan suspects the job has international connections. Lodo just killed Henry Billings, who had been assigned the job. Before dying, Billings recommended Ryan as replacement. Ryan has sought Billings ever since he stole $10,000 in gold Ryan liberated in Germany in 1945. Ideas and leads take Ryan to Art Shay, alcoholic but knowledgeable reporter; to Jake McGaffrey's horse parlor; to Juan Gonzales, one of Jake's runners recently thrown in front of a truck and killed; to Juan's widow, Lucinda Gonzales, who says Juan gave her thousands of dollars, from Billings, and also mentioned Lodo; to two thugs following Ryan who say Billings had international criminal connections; to suggestions that the crooked cops hope Ryan will lead to Billings's stash of $12,000, now missing; to a florist shop; and to Carmen Smith, who sent flowers to Billings's funeral.

Carmen, a business executive, professional gambler, and statuesque, over-sexed beauty, sizes up Ryan fast, tells him over lunch at Pat Shane's that she knew Billings and warns Ryan to be careful. So does Pat, who says Lodo recently went gunning for some union representatives. Alone and approaching his apartment, Ryan spots two tails and wounds both. A blast from a nearby thug, later identified as Lardbucket Pearson, kills one before he can talk. Avoiding his apartment, Ryan is approached by a friend named Diego Flores, who says Stan Etching and his brother (later called Stash Etching), among other gunmen, are after Ryan. By stratagems he spots three; slugs one, a Mafia "tap man," and takes $1,400 from him; and taxis to Carmen's apartment. All he wants now, he insists—to her disappointment—is a spare bed.

Alone in the morning, Ryan phones Art, who reports about the two thugs whom Ryan fought near his apartment; mission unaccomplished, they were found dead in a car outside Hoboken; furthermore, Lodo, a Mafia enforcer, has connections to Italy and even to Lucky Luciano. By phone, Ryan orders Big Man to identify sailors 'Fredo and Spanish Tom, named by Lucinda as her husband Juan's friends. Big Man identifies them as Alfredo Lias and Tomas Escalante, off the *Gastry,* and adds that Billings may have had something of international import retrieved by a skin diver from the sunken *Andrea Doria.* Informants at the docks enable Ryan to find Escalante in the Battery, but stabbed dead, with a fallen ticket for two to a "Spanish shindig up in the quarter" for tomorrow. Ryan taxis to Carmen's place. She weeps, genuinely in love with Ryan, who expresses devotion to her. They make love.

In the morning Ryan tells Carmen they will go to the shindig this evening, dance around, and locate Lias. On the street he is caught by the Etching brothers and driven to New Jersey. He disarms one, gutshoots him, pumps both for information, orders them out, drives back to Manhattan, and meets Big Man, who says someone planted drugs on the *Gastry.* Lias and Escalante took eight kilos of heroin; Juan bought it with Billings's money; Billings killed Juan before Billings was stalked and killed. Ryan orders Big Man to sweep up the thugs casing his apartment, goes to Carmen's office, notes the secretary's use of a device recording phone calls, and proceeds to Carmen's place. They go to the shindig. Someone points out Lias, but before Ryan can talk much with the terrified fellow out back, he is shot. Lias tells Ryan that Billings was the last to have the drugs but dies without identifying Lodo. Carmen has fled; so Ryan goes to his apartment. Big Man has arrested the thugs outside. Mario Sen, a Mafia killer, is inside, however; Ryan gets the drop on him and shoots him dead.

Big Man, when phoned, tells Ryan that Billings last hung out at Valley Park. Ryan used to live in an apartment there, now being torn down to make room for a housing project. Ryan figures Billings, to implicate him, planted the heroin at Ryan's there, unaware of its imminent demolition. Ryan gets hold of Carmen, safe in her apartment, and the two taxi to Valley Park. He thrills her by finding the heroin nicely hidden, sits down comfortably, and summarizes: Carmen thought he got the drugs from Billings, lured him to her by sending flowers to Billings's funeral, is Lodo, and "suckered" him. Carmen pulls an automatic and says her love for him is genuine; when he tells her he truly loved her and asks her to kill him efficiently, she shoots herself in the heart instead.

MELSE. In "Stand Up and Die!," he was a landowner ruined by old man Hart.

MENDES, BILLY. In *Bloody Sunrise,* he was killed in Panama, Tiger Mann recalls, before he could identify Tiger.

MENES, PAPA ("POP"). In *The Last Cop Out*, he is the resourceful Italian-American leader, who committed his first murder at age twelve. Now seventy-two, he heads the crime syndicate Mark Shelby wants to control. Working with Francois Verdun and others, Menes successfully engineers feuds and murders within the organization to weaken the opposition. He is cruelly forceful with Louise Belhander, the Florida prostitute, and consorts with her at his Long Island retreat, where she pulls the trigger on a .38 while sodomizing him with it.

MENES, SYLVIA. In *The Last Cop Out*, she is Papa Menes's stupid Jewish wife. Her father is a rabbi, and she is from Pennsylvania. She does not figure in the action.

MENTER, BILLY. In "Killer Mine," he is Sergeant Mack Brissom's stolid partner in police headquarters.

MERRIMAN, MONA ("MADCAP"). In *The Erection Set*, she is a New York society columnist, age sixty-one but flirtatious. She flirts with Dog Kelly at Walt Gentry's party and later.

MERTIG. In *The Big Kill*, he is the D.A.'s bespectacled aide.

MESSNER. In *Bloody Sunrise*, he was involved in action with explosives in Panama, according to Tiger Mann's recollection.

MICKEY SPILLANE'S MIKE HAMMER: THE COMIC STRIP, ed. Catherine Yronwode and Max Allan Collins (1982). Reprints of five comic strips, with texts by Spillane and art work by Ed Robbins (1919–1982). Mike is sketched with crew cut, broken nose, bulging lower lip, Kirk Douglas chin, incessantly smoking; Velda, raven-haired, svelte. "Half-Blonde": nightclub singer with strange hair, hidden by stock-watering cheaters on dead uncle's yacht, rescued by Mike; four dead, Mike shot. "The Bandaged Woman": Mike rescues hospitalized woman from dishonest physician seeking her inheritance; two dead, Mike drugged. "The Sudden Trap": Twin of debt-owing mobster's well-insured dead sister stages sudden reappearance to shock, nail brother-in-law, with Mike's help; two dead, Mike slugged. "The Child": Mike retrieves little girl from her feuding criminals' kidnappers seeking to pressure girl's politically influential, unidentified grandfather; four dead and burned up. "Christmas Story": Mike follows known thief who, with store-manager's connivance, shoplifts gifts for foundling-home kids; Mike repays store.

MICKEY SPILLANE'S MIKE HAMMER: THE COMIC STRIP, VOL. 2, ed. Max Allan Collins and Catherine Yronwode (1985). Reprints of four strips, texts largely by Spillane, art by Robbins. "Another Lonely Night": Mike witnesses murder, is used as bait by Captain Pat Chambers, to catch killers; five or so dead, Mike shot. Plot anticipates Pat's disagreement with Mike in *The Girl Hunters*. "The Dark City": mob girl stages murder to cover theft of skimmed money, hidden by brother, weak in head after Korean War; uses Mike, could kill him, but loves, spares him (thus foreshadowing *Me, Hood!* and *The Twisted Thing*); she and brother killed, one thug killed; Feds find loot; Mike slugged. One panel presents tortured girl so graphically that several newspapers cancelled comic-strip contract. "Adam and Kane": Evil old criminal's sons are Adam and Kane; Kane has daughter, kills Adam; criminal, dying, hires Mike to find Kane; he does, but Kane, wounded by often-slugged Mike, grabs father, jumps to their death into Hudson River. A minor character is Molly Lewinski, who changed her last name to Love. "Comes Murder": Mike foils gambler-counterfeiter who lures vengeful young couple into gambling ruinously but whose big-blonde double-crosses him, falls for Mike, also falls to her death; Mike slugged and shot.

Bibliography: M. Thomas Inge, *Comics as Culture* (Jackson: University Press of Mississippi, 1990); Garyn G. Roberts, *Dick Tracy and American Culture: Morality and Mythology, Text and Context* (Jefferson, N.C.: McFarland, 1993); Roy Thomas and Jon B. Knutson, "'Comics Were Great!': A Colorful Conversation with Mickey Spillane," *Alter Ego* 3, no. 11 (November 2001): 33–41.

MIDROS, STEPHEN. In *Day of the Guns,* he is a Hungarian freedom fighter who continues to work for his cause in New York.

MILCROSS, WALTER. In "Man Alone," he is a petty crook whom Patrick Regan helped once and who in return gets into Al Argenio's home and finds an amputated finger.

MILES, BINGO. In *The Last Cop Out,* he is Shatzi Heinkle's partner. The two torture William R. Hays on Francois Verdun's orders. When the two try to kill Gill Burke in a drive-by shooting, Gill shoots Bingo dead.

MILLER, JAMES. In *The By-Pass Control,* he is Doug Hamilton's junior partner, on Lexington Avenue. Tiger Mann interviews him but learns nothing of value.

MILLER, KILLER. In *The Last Cop Out,* he raped Helen Scanlon when she was fourteen. When her father, Joe Scanlon, learned of the assault, he beat up Miller so severely that he suffered brain damage and was thereafter called Silly Millie.

MILLER, PAUL. In *My Gun Is Quick. See* Bowen, Russ.

MILLER, RONALD. In *The Body Lovers,* he was in the U.S. Army with Mitch Temple and is now an engineer with Pericon Chemicals in Egypt. His sending

Temple a note has a bearing on the police investigation into the C-130 poison used to kill Helen Poston.

MILLER, THERESA ("TESSIE"). In *Survival . . . Zero!,* she is a Greenwich Village prostitute whose friendship with Beaver proves to be a useless lead in finding him.

MILLER, WENDY. In *The Long Wait. See* West, Vera.

MILLS, RENÉ. In "Killer Mine," he was one of several young criminals mysteriously murdered. He was a pimp until he tried to shake down Larry Scanlon, who killed him.

MILOS, HENRI. In *The Ship That Never Was,* he is an exile from Grandau. He lives in England and confers with Sir Harry Arnold and Teddy Benson.

MILOS, WALTER. In *The Death Dealers,* he is an assistant whom Martin Grady says he will send over to brief Tiger Mann on details of the oil industry. Casey Ballanca, however, is the expert who does so.

MINNER, ALEXIS. In *Day of the Guns,* he is a Soviet assassin taking orders from Stovetsky and masking as a U.N. clerk. Mann kills him.

MINNOW, MRS. ROBERT. In *The Long Wait,* in her fifties, she is Robert Winnow's widow. She doubts that John McBride murdered Winnow and therefore helps him.

MINNOW, ROBERT ("BOB"). In *The Long Wait,* he was corrupt Lyncastle's crusading D.A. until Lenny Servo murdered him.

MINOR, ANN. In *My Gun Is Quick,* she is a beautiful blond hostess at the Zero Zero Club, managed by Murray Candid. She was formerly a carnival stripper and a club dancer. Her friendship with Nancy Sanford leads to Mike's going to her 89th Street apartment, gaining information, praising her essential decency, and sleeping briefly with her. Her "suicide" Mike proves to be murder.

MISS MARIE. In "The Seven Year Kill," she is Cal Porter's secretary.

MIST, WILLIAM ("BILLY," "BILLY THE KID"). In *Kiss Me, Deadly,* he is a criminal associate of Al Affia and Carl Evello, among others. He dated Berga Torn. Michael Friday fingers Mist for Mike Hammer. Mist kills Affia, after which Mike chokes Mist to make him talk. The choking is too severe, and Mist dies. Mist allegedly referred Berga Torn to Dr. Martin Soberin, who changed William Mist's name on his records to "William Wierton."

MITCHI, LEW. In *The Body Lovers,* he owns the place where the bartender saw Greta Service with a rich "gook."

MOE. In "Kick It or Kill!," he is a criminal friend of Lennie Weaver. Kelly Smith kicks him to death outside Simpson's mansion.

MOE ("SHRINER"). In *The Deep,* he is one of two gunmen Hugh Peddle brings to Deep at Bennett's former apartment.

MOFFAT. In *Kiss Me, Deadly,* he is an FBI agent who answers the phone when Mike Hammer calls.

MOFFET, RITA. In "Kick It or Kill!," she is a used and discarded Simpson girl who moved from Pinewood to Sunbar.

MOFFIT, CHARLIE. In *One Lonely Night,* he was a would-be blackmailer whom Oscar Deamer murdered, in part because he was jealous of Moffit's love for Paula Riis. When Mike Hammer checks into Moffit's background, he learned that Moffit, age thirty-four, was unsuited for military service, and worked, often unreliably, at Mother Switcher's pie factory.

MONROE, SHEKKY. In *The Erection Set,* Rose Porter recalls that Monroe paid her $500 to let him feel her.

MONTGOMERY. In *The Erection Set,* Chet Linden tells Dog Kelly that if and when Dog is killed, Montgomery or Purcell may replace him.

MOONEY. In *My Gun Is Quick,* Mike Hammer and Captain Pat Chambers meet here to discuss evidence.

MOONEY, LOONEY. In *The Last Cop Out,* he was the cook when Gill Burke and Willie Armstrong were taking basic training together.

MOORE, JIMMIE. In *The Erection Set,* Stanley Cramer tells Dog Kelly that only Cameron Barrin and Jimmie Moore, both deceased, knew the combination of the new safe in the Barrin factory.

MOORE, PETER ("PETE"). In *The Death Dealers,* he is the agent sent to Selachin to rescue Teddy Tedesco.

MORGAN. In *The Deep,* Cat reminisces about the time Deep hid in Morgan's basement to avoid Frankie Carlo.

MORGAN. In "Everybody's Watching Me," he was an El Paso drug lord killed by Vetter.

MORGAN, DR. RALPH. In *Black Alley,* he is an alcoholic physician who saved Mike Hammer's life when he was wounded at the New York waterfront. Morgan takes Mike to Florida and nurses him back to health. Morgan regains his confidence, returns to New York, and is fortuitously able to aid Mike from time to time thereafter.

MORGAN, KAREN. In "The Flier." *See* Hays, Lois.

MORGAN, MRS. In "The Veiled Woman," she is Karl Terris's cleaning woman.

MORGAN ("MORG") THE RAIDER. In *The Delta Factor,* he is the adventurer-narrator, a well-educated former U.S. Army soldier during World War II. Wrongly imprisoned by Federal authorities for a $40 million heist of U.S. Treasury money in New York, Morgan will have his sentence reduced if he can rescue Victor Sable from prison in a Central American island. His pseudonym is M. A. Winters. Kimberly Stacy, an agent, marries Morgan as a cover, and helps him—as do Art Keefer, Angelo, Rosa Lee, Lieutenant Valente, and others—extricate Sable. Though macho, Morgan is celibate in this novel.

MORIARTY, P. J. In *Day of the Guns,* at his restaurant, at Sixth Avenue and 52nd Street, Tiger Mann finds Wally Gibbons having corned beef and cabbage. In *The Girl Hunters,* Mike Hammer meets Art Rickerby and later Laura Knapp, who brings Captain Pat Chambers, at Moriarty's.

MORRELI, STEPHEN. In *The Day the Sea Rolled Back,* he is the captain of the *Emory Welsch.* Disturbed when the sea level falls, he communicates by radio to land stations and other vessels.

MORRIE. In *The Last Cop Out,* he was severely criticized for awakening Papa Menes too early.

MORRIS, CONNIE. In "Return of the Hood," Ernie South names Morris as a possible source of drugs for Fly when Ryan presses South for information.

MORSE, JOE. In *The Last Cop Out,* he was a loyal worker for Mark Shelby's crime organization but was shot to death by an unknown assailant.

MORT. In *The Deep,* he turned Glover's place of business, located near where Bennett was murdered, into a dry-cleaning establishment.

MORVITCH. In *Day of the Guns,* Tiger Mann recalls that Devlin stole his papers in Yugoslavia during the war.

MOSS, GARY. In *The Girl Hunters,* Benny Joe Grissi tells Mike Hammer that "Gary Moss cleaned [i.e., battered] you one night" during Mike's seven-year drunk.

MOSSKY, EARL ("THE CREEPER"). In *The By-Pass Control,* he is a skinny, deep-voiced heroin dealer in Eau Gallie, Florida, and provides Dave Elroy with information.

MOTLEY, SONNY. In *The Snake,* he is a master criminal, imprisoned in 1932 for thirty years when his armored-car heist, planned with Simpson Torrence and Black Conley, went awry. Pretending now to be only a decrepit shoe repairman, Motley feeds Mike Hammer tidbits of information, follows him, and prepares to kill him and Velda once they locate Conley's remains and loot. Conley's skeleton kills Motley.

MOVIES AND SPILLANE. *I, the Jury* (1953) was based on Spillane's first novel (1947), of the same name. The 3-D film was written and directed by Harry Essex, starred Biff Elliott as Mike Hammer and featured Peggy Castle, Elisha Cook Jr., and Preston Foster. A 1982 reprise of *I, the Jury* starred Armand Assante. The fact that Larry Cohen, who wrote the script, was replaced as director midway through contributed to the film's lack of a consistent tone. *The Long Wait* (1954) was based on Spillane's 1951 novel of the same name and starred Peggy Castle, Charles Coburn, and Anthony Quinn. Spillane played himself as a detective in *Ring of Fear* (1954), in which a circus owner calls on his detective friend to discover the identity of a homicidal saboteur who has joined his troupe. Produced by John Wayne's movie company, *Ring of Fear* was based on a script Spillane partly rewrote. Wayne was so pleased that he gave Spillane a 1956 Jaguar XK140. *Kiss Me Deadly* (1955, title unpunctuated) was based on Spillane's 1952 novel of the same name. The film was scripted by A. I. Bezzerides, was directed by Robert Aldrich, and starred Ralph Meeker as Hammer. Critics regard this *noir* detective movie as the best one based on a Spillane book. Oddly, Bezzerides was blacklisted after hearings by the U.S. House Un-American Activities investigation of the movie industry. *My Gun Is Quick* (1957) was based on Spillane's 1950 novel of the same name. Richard Collins and Richard Powell wrote the script. Robert Bray played Hammer. The film was criticized for gratuitous violence and sex. *The Girl Hunters* (1963) was based on Spillane's 1962 novel of the same name. Robert Fellows, Roy Rowland, and Spillane wrote the script. Spillane acts as Hammer; the film costars Shirley Eaton and Lloyd Nolan, and features Spillane's friend Hy Gardner. This was the first time in movie history that a mystery writer portrayed his own creation in a full-length film. In 1969 Spillane established his own film company, Spillane-Fellows Productions, with producer Robert Fellows. *The Delta Factor* (1970), filmed by this company, was based on Spillane's 1969 novel of the same name, starred Christopher George and Yvette Mimieux, but was not widely released.

Bibliography: Julie Baumgold, "A Wild Man Proper," *Esquire* 124 (August 1995): 130, 132; Collins; Collins and Traylor; John Conquest, *Trouble Is Their Business: Private Eyes in Fiction, Film and Television, 1927-1988* (New York and London: Garland, 1990); Edward Gallafent, "Kiss Me, Deadly," pp. 240-46 in Ian Cameron, ed., *The Movie Book of Film Noir* (London: Studio Vista, 1992); Jay Robert Nash and Stanley Ralph Ross, *The Motion Picture Guide* (12 vols., Chicago: Cinebooks, 1985-1987); Chris Steinbrunner and Otto Pentzler, eds., *Encyclopedia of Mystery and Detection* (New York: Harcourt Brace Jovanovich, 1976); David Thompson, "Dead Lily [Deadlily]," *Film Comment* 33 (November-December 1997): 16-19.

MR. MUD. In *One Lonely Night*, Mike Hammer refers to a vicious Soviet agent thus.

MULLIGAN, MISS. In "The Seven Year Kill," she is the worldly-wise nurse, over sixty years old, at the Masberry Sanitarium thirty miles outside New York City. She tells Phil Rocca that Rhino Massley was an iron-lung patient but still managed to make love with Elena Harris.

MUNTZ, KITTY. In "Killer Mine," she and Rose Shaw were prostitutes whose pimp was René Mills. Kitty escaped.

MURPHY. In "Killer Mine," he is an official who gives Marta Borlig some information.

MURPHY, MRS. In "Killer Mine," she is a gossipy old woman who helps to start rumors about Lieutenant Joe Scanlon's sudden love for Marta Borlig.

MURPHY, MRS. In *The Twisted Thing*, she is a cook, age fifty-two, from Wooster. Her car is stolen, presumably by one of Dilwick's associates. The thug fights with and is defeated by Mike Hammer, who drives the car into town and abandons it.

MURPHY, RONALD. In *I, the Jury*, his estate sold a collection of old yearbooks to a Sixth Avenue book dealer. Mike Hammer discovers useful evidence against Harold Kines in some of them.

MURRAY, CAPTAIN. In *Day of the Guns*, he and young Ron Kelly are firemen whom Tiger Mann uses as decoys so that he can approach Alexis Minner's apartment.

MURRAY, ROX. In *Survival . . . Zero!*, she is a star whose show Heidi Anders tells Mike Hammer she saw soon after her compact was stolen.

MUSCO, SIG. In *The Deep,* long ago George Elcursio rewarded Deep's nerve by assigning him to do odd jobs for Musco, a manager of the criminal syndicate.

MUSIC AND SPILLANE. In 1980 Spillane wrote the script for *Oh, Mike!,* for which Cy Coleman wrote the music and which Michael Stewart produced in 1981.

Bibliography: Carol Lawson, "Broadway: Spillane's Hammer Will Solve His Next Case in a Musical," *New York Times,* November 14, 1980.

MUTT. In "Man Alone," he is a friend who helps Patrick Regan slip out of the courthouse unhounded after being acquitted of the charge of murdering Leo Marcus.

MY GUN IS QUICK **(1950).** Novel. (Characters: Barney, Cobbie Bennett, Lola Bergan, Arthur Berin-Grotin, Russ Bowen, Buck, Bucky, Byle, Murray Candid, Captain Pat Chambers, Ellison, Flo, Herman Gable, Georgie, Mike Hammer, Jimmy, Joseph Johnson, Mark Johnson, Jake Larue, Mrs. Jake Larue, Feeney Last, Joe Mast, Ann Minor, Mooney, Nat, Mrs. Porter, Ray, Nancy Sanford, Shorty, Velda, Walter Welburg.)

Mike Hammer receives $2,500 from a grateful client whose missing manuscript he found after a forty-eight-hour search. Exhausted, Mike drives to a hash joint under the El. The waiter, an ex-con called Shorty, serves him coffee. A prostitute known only as Red, with remnants of class, begs a cup from Mike. He gives her $150 and advises her to seek better work. Their chat is interrupted when a "greaseball" (later identified as Feeney Last) enters, greets her, warns her, and threatens Mike, who decks him, takes a .32 from him, calls the police, and turns him in on a weapons charge to Jake Larue, a cop he summoned and knows. His secretary, Velda, shows Mike a newspaper item that "Red" was killed in a hit-and-run accident the night after Mike met her. Hammer convinces Captain Pat Chambers, his honest homicide-detective friend, that Red was murdered. An autopsy proves her neck was broken but evidently not by any car. Mike phones Larue and learns that Last had a gun permit and is a bodyguard for Arthur Berin-Grotin. Velda tells Mike she has learned that Berin-Grotin, age eighty, is a philanthropist, but with a "sport[y]" past. Mike returns to Shorty, the hash-joint cook, and learns Red rented a room from Martha Porter around the corner. Mike bribes her to let him examine her room. It has been ransacked. He finds a greasy comb (later learned to be Last's).

Mike gets Berin-Grotin's Long Island address, drives out, and is admitted. Mr. Berin, as he calls himself, is a courteous, sad widower, whose wife, only son, and only granddaughter are deceased and who is now building a mausoleum, to commemorate his family name, in a cemetery near the local village. He says Last was recommended by a reliable firm as a bodyguard and was at the Albino Club in town with him the evening Red was killed. Last is supervising mausoleum work now. Mike drives to the cemetery, finds Last, gives him his greasy comb, and when challenged with a knife disarms him and tortures him into revealing this: Red, name unknown, stole photographs Last was using to blackmail someone. The mausoleum is decorated with a family crest.

Back at the office by 5:00 P.M., Mike learns from Pat that the hit-and-run driver's father persuaded the clean young man to turn himself in. At the morgue, Mike notes that Red's hand lacks an unusual ring he saw on it. Home again, he receives a letter she wrote him, thanking him for his friendship, saying she has done only one good thing in her life, and adding she may need him later. Mike locates a pimp named Cobbie Bennett near Canal Street, queries him about Red, and squeezes him for the address of the call house where she once worked. He goes there, only to learn it recently burned down, killing seven girls inside. At a nearby bar, he calls Pat, learns Red's name has been traced. She was Nancy Sanford. A pretty floozy hears Mike say "Nancy," tells him Nancy is dead, and won't she—Lola—do? (Between 5:00 P.M. and now, here and there, Mike has consumed a bottle of beer, a quart of beer, a glass of beer, two boilermakers, and a glass of beer, all salted with cigarettes.) Mike drives sleepy Lola Bergan out to the beach at Rockaway Point. Awake again, she tells him she worked in that call house with Nancy for a while and escaped the fire by fortuitously being hospitalized for a successful VD cure. She commends Nancy, who she also suspects was murdered. Mike and Lola make love in the sand.

Back in his apartment, Mike is roused at 1:30 P.M. by the phone. Velda says Berin wants to meets Mike in the office in an hour. The nice old fellow feels involved in Nancy's death somehow, gives Mike $1,000 to locate her family, and says that Last has quit. Mike meets Pat for a snack at Mooney's and gets him to explain about call houses: The police do what they can but can gather little evidence; call girls' "higher-ups" make the money; politicians look the other way. Over their coffee, Mike and Pat compare notes and theories and agree to cooperate.

That evening, Mike calls on Lola and learns she has suddenly landed a modeling job. Though reluctant to discuss the operations behind call girls, she tells him that Murray Candid, who runs the Zero Zero Club, is a boss. After drinks and kisses, Mike goes to the club and lies to the blonde hostess (later named Ann Minor) that he is an insurance agent seeking deceased Nancy Sanford's real name to help her beneficiaries fend off false claims. The blonde knew and liked Nancy and will ask around for the reward Mike mentions. When Candid enters, Mike tells him he is a cop from Des Moines, whose friends are coming to New York City and want a good time with some girls. He heard Candid was a supplier. Candid denies this. After a total of six drinks, Mike leaves. In the parking lot he is jumped and knocked out.

At 6:15 next morning, Mike comes to, battered, in pain, and stiff. He spots and pockets Nancy's unusual ring, dropped by one of his attackers, gets to his car, and makes his way to Lola's apartment. She puts him on the couch, cleans him up, goes to work, fetches him clean clothes from his apartment, and returns to cook him some pork chops. Meanwhile, Mike has phoned Berin, to report about the ring. Mike also phoned Pat, who tells him the hit-and-run drunk's insurance company is seeking Nancy's family "to pay off" and thus avoid a law suit, and adds that Last mailed to the police his license to carry a gun.

Mike goes to Nat, a jeweler friend, who examines Nancy's ring and pronounces it a centuries-old, European antique with a worn-off inscription. Mike proceeds to the Zero Zero Club, where Ann says she knows something of value about Nancy. Mikes phones Berin, who promises to back a substantial check for Mike to give Ann. After closing time, the two go to her Eighty-ninth Street apartment. She hates Candid and how he has his goons use girls for profit. The two make love, after which she gives Mike an old overnight bag Nancy left at the Zero Zero. It remained hidden in a storage room when the club was redecorated. It contains photos of Nancy as a happy teenager, with several young fellows, and wearing the antique ring—also baby clothes. Ah! Nancy had a baby. Who was the father? Is he the blackmailers' target?

After mulling over the evidence all night, Mike phones Berin, receives authorization for the $500 check he gave Ann, and reports details of Nancy's overnight bag. Just before noon Pat phones Mike that Last is wanted for murder on the Coast and that a Zero Zero hostess just drowned herself. Mike correctly names her as Ann Minor; contending she was murdered despite an authentic-looking suicide note, Mike gets a sample of filthy water near the death pier and has the coroner compare it to the water in the body. It proves to be bath water with a touch of soap. Returning home, Mike finds his apartment ransacked, Nancy's packet of photos gone, and evidence that the thieves also sought the ring, which he still has. Pat phones Mike this: Nancy Sanford had a stillborn baby in Chicago four years earlier, refused to name the father; Murray Candid is at headquarters being questioned about Ann.

Seizing the opportunity, Mike phones Lola and gets her to name a region where Candid might have a hangout for "some trick entertaining." Her lead sends Mike to Monica's in Greenwich Village. It is a gay bar, and a homosexual, sidling up, tells Mike that his "*dear* friend" Murray has rooms above Byle's grocery store, nearby. Mike goes there, runs into two men scattering books in search of something. A fight, with gunfire, ensues. The two leave. Mike continues the search, finds a tiny book hidden in a hollowed-out larger one, takes it, but is shot on the way out. Fortunately the bullet hit his .45, which banged into his chest.

Mike drives to Lola's apartment. She says she loves Mike but wants to deserve his love before hearing him say he loves her. When they inspect the small book Mike retained, she thinks it has a symbol indicating an assignation Murray sent her to. Mike calls Pat, who rushes over, says that Murray clammed up and that higher-ups must be paying off some cops. He analyzes the book, says he will ask experts to try to decode it, takes it, and leaves. Mike is to play dead to throw his enemies off the track. It dawns on Mike and Lola that Nancy's pictures might be valuable because of possible blackmail targets. Lola recalls this: Nancy made money photographing couples on the street, used the Quick Pix shop as an outlet, may have hocked her camera locally when she was hard up.

After breakfast, Lola trots out to check pawn shops in the hope of finding Nancy's hocked camera with her address on it. Velda relays a terrified phone call from Cobbie the pimp. Mike, though supposedly dead, buys a replacement .45, goes into Cobbie's neighborhood, and get an honest cop to reveal Cobbie's address. Mike gets to him, learns two Detroit gunnies are after him, and tells him to walk out tomorrow night at 9:30; Mike will help him leave the city permanently. A newspaper headline startles Mike: City officials are starting a crackdown on vice. Mike finds the defunct Quick Pix office, bribes the super, and locates photographs labeled "N. Sanford." He takes a box. He phones and meets Pat, and alerts him to his plan to use Cobbie as a decoy. Pat says Candid has disappeared.

Mike buys some food and reports to Lola. She failed to find the camera but senses a man is also seeking it. While they eat, they find a photograph from Nancy's collection of Berin, Last with a leer, and a young man showing fear, all standing before the Albino Club. When Mike names the scared one as Russ Bowen, a recent murder victim, Lola says he was really a pimp named Paul Miller, who supplied girls from the West Coast to the big shots' call houses. Did Nancy take these photos for blackmail? Is that why Last killed her? Mike hustles Lola to the Albino Club and spots Last there, with the guy Mike saw in the parking lot. He was looking for Nancy's ring when Mike slugged him. Mike, still playing dead, can only phone Pat, who arrives with reinforcements too late. Last has sped off. Pat tells Mike that vice raids are beginning to expose some higher-ups. Back in her apartment, Lola puts on a wedding dress, saved for a unique night. Mike can remove it only by tearing it off, which he does; uniquely delightful lovemaking follows.

Next morning the radio and papers report further vice busting. Pat phones that Candid is seen again, with a sound alibi; further, that out-of-town gunnies have been spotted. At 9:00 P.M., Cobbie nervously abandons his hideout, as ordered by Mike, who trails him. Hidden cops wait for the gunnies to make their play for Cobbie, shoot a few of them, capture the others, and never see Cobbie again. Phoning Berin's home, Mike learns the old fellow is at his suite in the Sunic House, a swank hotel. He drives there, finds Berin, is greeted hospitably, briefs him, and offers him the $500 Ann never lived to receive. While Berin mixes some drinks, Mike phones Velda at her home and learns that Lola found the pawned camera, sent Nancy's pawn ticket with her address by messenger to Mike's office. Great! Mike phones Lola, who confirms this and adds that she has the camera. Mike tells her to meet Velda and him at his office. Mike has a drink with Berin, provides the happy fellow with details, and gets to the office—only to learn with Velda that the pawn ticket is gone, together with Lola's address. Mike rushes to Lola and finds her bleeding from a stab wound. Gesturing that the assailant is near and that someone phoned, she dies. Mike chases Last into the rain-slicked street and pursues his fleeing car with his speedy one. Last crashes near a pier, fires at Mike, and dashes into a shack. Mike follows, shoots him in the hand, crushes his head into a pulp on the concrete floor, takes Nancy's pawn ticket from Last's pocket, and on it reads her address—Coney Island's Seaside Hotel. Mike gets to the place, now closed for the season, enters, and in a storage room finds her small trunk, which is crammed with a variety of evidence she was gathering to support a crackdown on city vice and corruption. Suddenly Berin is there with a naphtha lantern. Seeing Mike, he smashes the light and shoots Mike in chest and leg. Though almost paralyzed, Mike floors Berin with a shot into his hip. Spilled naphtha torches the old hotel room. A timber pins Berin down. Mike lectures him thus: Nancy was Berin's granddaughter; her pregnancy threatened family disgrace; unaided, she turned to prostitution, knew Bowen and his association with Last; saw Berin with Last; determined to break up his cushy racket. Instead of extricating Berin from the timber, Mike summons strength to hurl Nancy's trunk through a window to firemen as they approach, taunts Berin with the knowledge that he will be found a charred ruin, and shoots him dead as rescuers are about to enter.

The style of *My Gun Is Quick* is better than that of *I, the Jury.* For example, sloppy rain makes Manhattan ugly and serves as a metaphor for the often sleazy life of its inhabitants. Figures of speech in this second Hammer novel are effective. It is, however, loaded with clichés—perhaps deliberate, to suggest the narrator's quick-paced life and indifference to niceties.

N

NAKU EM ABOR. In *The Body Lovers,* he is a U.N. delegate whom Mike Hammer meets at Gerald Ute's party. Naku heads a "part Arabian complex" and knows and evidently argues with Belar Ris.

NAT. In *My Gun Is Quick,* he is a jeweler whom Mike Hammer knows and likes. Nat tells Mike that Nancy Sanford's ring is an antique centuries old. It turns out to have an inscription resembling Arthur Berin-Grotin's family crest. Mike asks Nat to remember him to Flo, Nat's wife.

NEIL. In *Vengeance Is Mine!,* he owns Neil's Joint in Greenwich Village. Though frequented by wealthy slummers, it is so smelly that several patrons, including Mike Hammer, leave it for the Bowery Inn.

NEKKO. In "The Veiled Woman," he works for Luke Ritter. During his search for Lodi Terris, Karl Terris, her husband, kills not only Ritter but then Nekko. Spillane gratuitously presents Nekko as a sobbing homosexual—with broken teeth, broken nose, gunsight-raked cheek, broken rib, pierced lung.

NELSON. In *The Big Kill,* he owns the steak house where Mike meets Ellen Scobie to discuss her filching Toady Link's file from the D.A.'s office.

NELSON. In "Me, Hood!," he owns a hangout frequented by Henry Billings.

NELSON. In *The Twisted Thing. See* Mallory, Herron.

NELSON, LEW. In *The Snake,* he and Kiley, two of Captain Pat Chambers's men, are assigned to check on Basil Levitt.

NEWBOLDER, SERGEANT. In "Return of the Hood," he is an honest policeman who is ordered to arrest Ryan on suspicion that he killed Fred Stipetto. Ryan gets Newbolder to cooperate repeatedly, instead.

NICHOLS, ALICE. In *The Twisted Thing,* she is Rudolph York's niece and lives in Wooster. She and Mike Hammer enjoy one torrid sexual encounter. She lures Myra Grange into a lesbian pose before a hidden camera, to help Rudolph stymie Myra's blackmailing endeavors.

NICK. In "Everybody's Watching Me," he is a friend of "Joe Boyle." He is beaten up in a vain effort to make him talk.

NICOLE. In *The Last Cop Out,* she is a prostitute from Phoenix. Artie Meeker once knew her.

"THE NIGHT I DIED" (1998). Short story. (Characters: Captain Pat Chambers, Dave, Mike Hammer, Earnie Haver, Jake, Joe, Ben Liter, Sid Pollack, Carmen Rich, Salvi Slocum, Ed Smith, Helen Venn, Marty Wellman, Buddy Whiteman.) Mike Hammer meets the beautiful Helen Venn at a Broadway party. Love at first sight? Forever? Ah! She says Marty Wellman, the Syndicate boss, hid $2 million and has been killed, and she is thought to know the location of the money. To protect Helen, Mike learns that Carmen Rich has taken over the Syndicate and finds him for Helen. But Helen is doublecrossing Mike. She and her partner Buddy Whiteman killed Marty and presumably have the money. She now has Buddy kill Carmen and siccs Buddy on Mike. Though wounded, Mike kills Buddy, which suits Helen. Innocently going to her for help, Mike is stabbed by Helen. This night his spirit died. Two years later, Mike finds Helen. She approaches him with her knife. He shoots her dead. "The Night I Died" was originally a radio-play manuscript which Max Allan Collins found in Spillane's home in Murrell's Inlet, South Carolina, and rewrote in story form.

Bibliography: Max Allan Collins, "Introduction," *Together We Kill: The Uncollected Stories of Mickey Spillane* (Waterville, Maine: Five Star, 2001).

NILS. In *The Last Cop Out,* he is Helga Piers's stalwart lover. When Nils saw how badly Helga was battered by Mark Shelby, he deserted her.

NOLAN, MRS. JERRY. In "Man Alone," she objects to Patrick Regan's monopolizing her husband's limited time at home.

NOLAN, SERGEANT JERRY ("JER"). In "Man Alone," he stops suspecting Patrick Regan of murdering Leo Marcus and helps him prove his innocence.

NORMAN. In "Killer Mine," he is a pawnbroker who sold a watch back to René Mills, when Mills was suddenly in the chips again.

O

O'BRIEN, CLANCY. In *Kiss Me, Deadly,* according to Bob Gellie, O'Brien bought the car the Mafia gives Mike to silence him.

O'KEEFE. In *The Erection Set,* the contact at Weller-Fabray tells Dog Kelly that O'Keefe is an active agent in Europe now, even though he has a criminal record for assault.

OLD SNARLY. In *The Erection Set,* he was an air force buddy of Dog Kelly having something to do with British Spitfires.

OLIVER, CAPTAIN. In "Killer Mine," he is Lieutenant Joe Scanlon's superior officer. He keeps pressuring Joe to solve the murder cases.

OLLIE. In *The Last Cop Out,* he, Matt Stevenson, and Woodie are assigned by Francois Verdun to guard Leon Bray. They are all gassed to death by an unknown assailant, wearing a gas mask.

OLSEN, CAPTAIN ROB. In "The Flier," he flew a search mission after Tucker Stacy's plane was missing and provides Cat Fallon with information.

O'MALLEY. In "The Gold Fever Tapes," he is a friendly doorman at the apartment where Fallon lives. O'Malley helps Fallon get clean clothes.

O'NEILL, JERRY. In *The Big Kill,* he is a young actor who adores Marsha Lee. She sets him up to kill and be killed in an alleged lovers' quarrel with Mike Hammer. But after she kills Jerry, William Decker's little boy accidentally kills her with Mike's handy .45.

***ONE LONELY NIGHT* (1951).** Novel. (Characters: Ann, Archie, Art, Lieu-
tenant Barner, Brighton, Ethel Brighton, Martha Camisole, Miss Carpenter,
Captain Pat Chambers, Bill Cowan, Lee Deamer, Oscar Deamer, George,
Henry Gladow, Mike Hammer, Linda Holbright, Harvey Robinson Jenkins,
Marty Kooperman, C. C. Lopex, Louie, Charlie Moffit, Mr. MVD, General Os-
ilov, Pete, Paula Riis, Martin Romberg, Mother Switcher, Tony, Harold Valleck,
Velda.)

Mike Hammer is so upset when a judge calls him a legalized murderer
while having to accept his self-defense argument that he goes for a walk that
snowy night to the "hump" of the George Washington Bridge. While he is
thinking glumly about his violent life, a young woman, in utter terror, rushes
up. A pudgy man approaches, tells Mike he will also die if he plays hero, and
pulls a gun. Mike shoots him disfiguringly in the face. Wrongly frightened by
Mike, the woman jumps off to her death, despite his efforts to restrain her.
He holds only her coat pocket. Inside is a curiously cut green card in a pack
of cigarettes. Mike takes the thug's possessions, including a similar card in
his otherwise empty wallet, removes his labels, rubs his fingerprints off on
nearby concrete, and kicks him into the water.

Next day Mike calls on Captain Pat Chambers, of homicide. Pat identifies
the green cards as Communist identification cards, with changes clipped to
foil spies. Pat tells Mike he is working on a case in which witnesses have
placed Lee Deamer, an incorruptible political reformer, at a murder scene.
Mike has lunch with political newsman named Marty Kooperman, who
praises Deamer and promises to aid Mike. The papers report that an uniden-
tifiable fat man, fished from the river, was the victim of a gang killing. No
woman's body has been found. Mike goes to a Communist pep rally in Union
Square, follows its leader by subway to a Brooklyn hideout, uses a green card
to gain admittance, and is welcomed as the fat man's high-up replacement.
Present is wealthy Ethel Brighton, beautiful, naive, and with "donations" she
has gathered. Mike learns that she is afraid her father will discover her activities; impressed by him, she drops him off at Times Square, where he eats
and then walks to his apartment. At 4:00 A.M. Pat orders Mike to his apartment, where he meets Lee Deamer, the quickly rising political conservative.
They drink, smoke, and talk. Lee has a vicious twin brother, Oscar Deamer,
for years in a mental institution in Nebraska, their home state. But Oscar
escaped, made it to New York, and right in front of witnesses murdered a
man named Charlie Moffit to implicate Lee. The police have hushed the event
and hidden the confused witnesses. Oscar has documents with which he is
blackmailing Lee. Mike, admiring Lee, must locate Oscar and "spirit . . . [him]
away."

The plan is for Velda to go near Oscar's East Side apartment building and
watch. Lee will follow. Mike and Pat will give him a few minutes, then grab
Oscar. But plans miscarry. Oscar rushes out, down into the subway station,
dies in front of a train, horribly mangled. Police arrive, disperse the crowd,

and remove the body. Mike visits Oscar's room but finds nothing. He meets Velda at a bar near their office. They beat up two would-be leering men. Velda says she sensed that more men than Oscar and then Lee were at the scene near the subway accident. Mike finds the Brighton family's phone number, calls Ethel, and orders her to meet him. She is scared, thinks he is testing her Communist loyalties, but relaxes when he grins easily. She drives him to her lush family log cabin near the Hudson River. They drink too much and make love before a sparkling fire.

In the morning, Mike notices his wallet has been handled. He hitches a ride into Manhattan, goes to Pat's office, and learns from Oscar's medical records, which just arrived, that he is dangerously neurotic and paranoid. Official conclusion: suicide under subway train to avoid being charged with shooting Moffit. The fat man's body had a stainless-steel tooth. Mike concludes he was a Soviet. Summoned by Lee to his office, Mike ogles his secretaries. Lee retains Mike for $1,000 and wants him to find some documents Oscar had, which could damage him. Mike has Velda check on Moffit and learns from Kooperman that Ethel's father ruined her engagement to a penniless artist by having him shipped overseas during the war, where he was reported killed. Mike dines with Ethel, begins to subvert her faith in Communism, but drives with her to another Brooklyn rally, where Mike cows General Osilov, a Soviet diplomat from Washington, D.C., who thinks Mike is a tough Moscow-sent killer. Mike impresses, flirts with, and slips his address to Linda Holbright, a plain-looking girl stationed at the door to check green cards. Ethel drops Mike off near his apartment. A car speeds by, shooting ineffectively at him. He suspects Ethel checked his wallet last night and fingered him. By phone, Velda reports that Moffit worked at a pie shop run by Mother Switcher. Kooperman, having word of the drive-by shooting, visits Mike, with other reporters, but gets the cold shoulder. Linda pops in, suddenly looks fetching, and she and Mike make love.

Next morning Mike and Velda visit Switcher and learn from fellow employees that Moffit was alternately reliable, unreliable, drunk, and womanizing. Back at their office, Mike briefs Velda on the bridge shooting of the steel-toothed man and the scared girl's suicide, and on part—only part—of his movements with Ethel. Mike's theories: Ethel blew his cover to other Soviets; they checked morgues and found the fat man's corpse; Moffit was a courier for the Soviets; Oscar killed Moffit and took the documents. Over lunch, Mike tells Pat rather little but learns that Lee is going to lecture tonight on cleaning up political graft. Mike phones Velda to have fingerprints checked from the suicide victim's cigarette pack, still in the office wastebasket.

The evening news reports an illegal duplication of secret documents at the State Department. Mike suspects Moffit and then Oscar. Mike meets Velda at the office. She is so lovely he gives her an emerald engagement ring and a few kisses. They sneak into Oscar's apartment, to look for the documents. No luck. They hear two men following them in. Much gunplay: Mike kills one (later identified by Pat as Harold Valleck), and Velda the other (Martin Romberg, whom Mike spotted at a Brooklyn meeting). Police in strategically placed vehicles hear the gunfire and approach. Escaping, Mike and Velda conclude that the documents are in Moffit's residence. Mike puts a spare barrel and firing pin on his .45 and tells Velda to fix her .32, to avoid detection.

Next morning Velda phones Mike: Pat and Lee want to see him. Pat reports the two killings, suspects Mike, and rages at him. Mike presents his .45 for a negative ballistics test. Mikes rushes to a midtown hotel, where Lee is lunching with U.N. delegates. Ethel's father is also present. Mike equivocates to prevent Lee from suspecting him of the killings at Oscar's place. Velda informs Mike he must report again to Pat, who tells him the fingerprints on the cigarette package were Mike's but also those of Paula Riis, Oscar's nurse in the mental institution. Mike tells Pat he ripped Paula's pocket, which contained the cigarettes, in a failed effort to prevent her suicide, but says nothing about shooting her fat pursuer. He theorizes thus: Paula and Oscar planned to blackmail Lee; when Oscar killed Moffit, they took some green cards from him (perhaps they already had green cards themselves); Paula, scared of Oscar's dementia, killed herself. Pat reluctantly accepts Mike's half-truths.

When Osilov and two thugs attend a court session involving arrested Communist protesters, Mike and Kooperman watch. Mike follows the Soviets to their hotel. Ethel is there. She briefly excuses herself and apparently fingers him to some men, who follow as Mike drives her toward her cabin. A second car follows both cars but is forced off the road. Mike stops, retrieves an injured FBI agent's wallet and tommy gun, and drives on. At the cabin, Ethel hopes for more love, but Mike flogs her with his belt instead. A shot rings out, wounding her in the shoulder. Mike seeks the gunman, but he has vanished. It develops that the men Ethel alerted were FBI agents and that Ethel now hates Communism. Mike calls a doctor, persuades him to hush up the incident, and leaves ahead of the ambulance. Mike picks up Velda. They toss Moffit's apartment, find no documents, but do see a photo of Paula addressed to Moffit. Conclusion: Oscar, jealous, killed Moffit. Mike asks Velda to fly to Nebraska and check Oscar's medical records.

Next day is Saturday. Mike phones the hospital and learns Ethel is better and her father is with her. Mike checks with Pat and accompanies him to the Third Avenue apartment where a has-been, drunken old actor named Harvey Robinson Jenkins has just committed suicide. Mike continues pondering death, war, violence, and his identity. A friendly policeman, when asked, says during that lonely night at the bridge a woman phoned asking a cop car to meet her there. But the car arrived too late. Mike drives to Paula's apartment, having noted the address when Pat talked to him about her. Her entire mailbox has been crowbarred out. Conclusion: Soviet agents, having found no documents at her place, took the box because Moffit mailed the documents to her there. But Paula's landlady says she collected letters for Paula. She gives all of them to Mike. He takes them to his office and hides the long-sought material—ten mazelike photostats—in his wall lamp. Drinking a little sherry, Mike phones Pat, but he is out; phones Lee's office, learns from a secretary he is in Washington, D.C.; and phones him of the good news, will see him in New York on Monday.

Mike rests in his apartment Sunday. Rainy Monday follows. News accounts praise Lee and criticize Communism. The people are striking back at last. Mike suddenly realizes he has missed his 2:00 P.M. meeting with Velda. He rushes to the office. She left a document in the lamp. He reads it happily. A message on his desk, not in Velda's handwriting, orders him to phone a certain number at 9:00 P.M. Pat gets him the location of the number—at a Times Square subway station booth. Mike stakes out the booth, phones its number, sees a thug answer, agrees by phone to exchange the photostats for Velda, follows the thug to his cab, drives after him to Astoria, and sees him enter an abandoned paint factory near the docks. Mike quietly kills two guards outside, follows the thug's tracks, and bursts in on a dreadful scene. Velda, ever silent, is hanging by her wrists and is being beaten by a rope for information. Mike uses the FBI tommy gun to kill Osilov and his two thugs, leaves the gun, torches the empty factory, takes Velda to her apartment, and summons medical attention.

Mike phones Lee, says he will explain everything quietly in the open air, and gets a friend named Archie to drive his car. The two pick up Lee and drive to the bridge "hump" where everything started. It is snowing and lonely. Archie drives off for an hour of beer over in New Jersey. Mike shows Lee the documents—microfilms of a grand secret weapon. He burns almost everything but keeps a revealing fragment, and proceeds to explain, using Velda's evidence, in part: Oscar, really Lee, escaped from the mental institution alone; Paula turned Communist, came to New York later; while Lee was away, Oscar impersonated him, spoke against Communism but planned when elected to take orders from the Kremlin, hired Jenkins to make up like Lee and be seen in public while Oscar killed blackmailer Moffit. Then Oscar killed Jenkins. Oscar, aware of his ruin, pulls a gun, but Mike takes it and drops it into the Hudson. Mike chortles that he will kill Oscar, leave his body with the micro-film bit and with a Soviet thug's wallet—this to suggest that Oscar turned patriotic, fought the Soviets, and will therefore be defined as our hero. Mike chokes Oscar to death and is soon whisked away by Archie.

One Lonely Night is one of Spillane's most popular novels but is often somewhat ludicrous. In almost any good twin–bad twin plot, the climax is predictable. Moreover, would the State Department admit its carelessness? Are Soviet agents really so thick-headed? Would Mike dull his reactions with alcohol and also miss a vital meeting with Velda? Mike's double standard vis-à-vis sex is off-putting. He can be Ethel's and then Linda's lover, all right; but Velda is to be "mine alone." When two men leer at Velda in a saloon, her decking him and Mike's mauling the man's friend offer totally gratuitous violence. Spillane often wrote too fast. In the process, here we find Mike "watching the two men," though one is "invisible." A page later we read about "squirmy worms" who intend to "rule with the whip."

O'ROARK, HELEN. In *The Big Kill,* she is an actress with Marsha Lee at the Greenwich Village theater.

ORTEGA, CARLOS. In *The Delta Factor,* he is a cruel dictator of a Central American island. He has imprisoned a valuable scientist named Victor Sable and wants his knowledge, flirts with Communists who also want it, but is outwitted when Morgan pretends to have access to $40 million in stolen money he must have laundered. When Ortega finally learns that Morgan is helping Sable escape, he and his henchmen rush to the attack. Morgan kills them all with grenades.

ORTEZ, SHARON. In 'The Flier," she is a Spanish-Irish resident of Cuba. Opposed to Fidel Castro, she is initially suspicious of Cat Fallon but ultimately saves his life by killing Andro Marcel, Juan, and their unnamed associate.

OSBORNE. In "The Veiled Woman," he is an FBI agent from whom Karl Terris tells Edward Treeglos to obtain information.

OSILOV, GENERAL. In *One Lonely Night,* he is a Russian diplomat in Washington, D.C. When Osilov attends a Communist meeting in Brooklyn, Mike Hammer convincingly acts like a Soviet agent. Mike finds Osilov torturing Velda and machine-guns him to death with two of his fellow agents.

P

PACKER, BUD. In *The Snake,* he was killed, according to Annette Lee, by Black Conley because he kidded Conley for being impotent.

PACKMAN, EDWARD ("EDDIE"). In *The Long Wait,* he is Lenny Servo's bodyguard and hit man, and owns a flashy place in Lyncastle. He stabs Inez Casey to death and knifes John McBride, who breaks both his arms.

PAGO, VINCE. In *The Snake,* he was evidently one of several persons killed by Marv Kania.

PALEY, NAT. In "Kick It or Kill!," he is a criminal associate of Lennie Weaver. When he goes for his gun in Simpson's mansion, Kelly Smith shoots him dead.

PAPA FATS. In *The Last Cop Out,* he was the target of Herm Perigino and Sal Perigino. The two missed him and were killed by Mark Shelby from ambush.

PARKER. In "Man Alone," Patrick Regan reminds Sergeant Jerry Nolan of the Parker kidnapper whom Patrick Regan investigated.

PARKS, BILLY. In *The Twisted Thing,* he is a harmless ex-con employed by Rudolph York as his chauffeur. When Rudolph's son Ruston is allegedly kidnapped, Rudolph wrongly suspects Parks and bribes Dilwick, a crooked policeman, to beat him up to seek evidence. Mike Hammer rescues Parks.

PARKS, SAM. In "The Veiled Woman." *See* Porkov, Sergi.

PARROTT, LEN. In *Survival . . . Zero!,* he owns a saloon in which Carl and Sammy asks for information about Beaver.

PASCALE. In *Kiss Me, Deadly,* he owns a Canal Street saloon above which Harvey Wallace and his wife live.

PAT. In *The Erection Set,* he is one of Stanley Cramer's cronies and, along with Jason, helps him find material concerning the antigravity device for Dog Kelly.

PATSY. In "The Gold Fever Tapes," Fallon says Patsy lives near him.

PATTERSON, LEONARD ("LENNY," "PATTIE"). In *Black Alley,* he and Howie Drago are two of Leonard Ponti's punks turned businessmen. Mike goads Patterson, slugs him in Ugo Ponti's computer office, and drives over him to escape from Ugo's upstate estate. Patterson is hospitalized in critical condition.

PATTY. In *The Big Kill,* she works with Ellen Scobie in the D.A.'s office and also rooms with Ellen. Patty helps Ellen obtain Toady Link's file from the office.

PATTY. In "Everybody's Watching Me," she owns a gin mill. "Joe Boyle" uses her telephone.

PATTY. In "The Seven Year Kill," Phil Rocca nostalgically recalls dining at Patty's years ago.

PAUL. In "Return of the Hood," he is a bellboy at the shabby hotel where Ryan holes up.

PAUNCHO, VINNY. In *The Snake,* Sonny Motley names him to Mike Hammer as a member of his old mob. Pauncho is now in a mental institution.

PEARSON, LARDBUCKET. In "Me, Hood!," he is a member of the New Jersey rackets, sent by Lodo to kill Ryan, who wounds him instead. Lardbucket is killed outside Hoboken by his bosses for failing.

PECKY. In *The By-Pass Control,* he owns a place in Eau Gallie, Florida, where Earl Mossky tells Tiger Mann and Dave Elroy drug parties are held and drugs are sold.

PEDDLE, HUGH ("HUGHIE"). In *The Deep,* he is a crooked New York City councilman. Fat and rich, he lives in his political district but has niceties in a penthouse. He takes orders from Holiday. During the finale at the Knights Owl Club, he is distressed when Helen Tate is being tortured, soon after which he is shot to death in the melee.

PEDRO. In *Day of the Guns,* he is the maître d' at the Cavalier Restaurant, where Tiger Mann sees Edith Caine while he is talking with Wally Gibbons.

PEDRO. In *The Deep,* he found Bennett's corpse and robbed it of Bennett's wallet and watch. Deep gets the truth out of Pedro. Later, Deep is afraid Roscoe Tate may have killed Pedro, who does not reappear in the action.

PEDRO ("PETE"). In "Return of the Hood," he is Izzy Goldwitz's busboy at the Cafeteria. He is beaten up by a Soviet agent, perhaps Manos Dekker, for information about Fly. Pedro, a hardworking Puerto Rican, tells Ryan what little he can about his assailant.

PEE, WALLY. In "Return of the Hood," he is a runner for Sal Upsidion.

PEELER, HARRY. In "Me, Hood,!" he is a truck driver who accidentally ran over and killed Juan Gonzales, who was deliberately thrown in front of the truck. A likable family man, Peeler is not suspected of homicide.

PEE WEE. In *The Twisted Thing,* he lives in a shack near the shore where Mike Hammer discovers evidence of Myra Grange's disappearance.

PEGGY. In *The Erection Set,* she was employed in a liquor store where Alfred Barrin bought scotch to bribe the police with.

PELHAM, JULIE. In *The Body Lovers,* she is a New York prostitute who agrees to accompany a driver and be a guest at Belar Ris's party. She becomes frightened, escapes, and is briefly aided by Velda. Julie is caught and is killed by Ris along with the driver.

PELLONI, STEPHEN. In *The Death Dealers,* he owns a club featuring belly dancers. Virgil Adams places men to watch it in case Malcolm Turos goes there. This lead is not mentioned again.

PENNER, DEL. In *The Snake,* he is a gunman who replaced Kid Hand when the Kid was killed. Penner was hired, supposedly by Dickerson, to kill Mike Hammer. Penner forces Velda to phone Mike and thus meets Mike.

PENSA, ARTURO. In *The Death Dealers. See* Turos, Malcolm.

PENTA. In *The Killing Man,* this is the name assigned by federal authorities to the unidentified, internationally sought murderer. It is the name signed on the note left by the killer of Anthony DiCica in Mike's office. *See* Bradley, Bennett.

PEPPY. In *The Last Cop Out,* it was his rude little tavern that Mark Shelby frequented before the crime organization grew to its present opulence.

PERCY, ED. In "The Affair with the Dragon Lady," he was the tail gunner aboard the Dragon Lady.

PERCY, STEVE. In *The Day the Sea Rolled Back,* he is a radioman on Ara Island.

PERIGINO, HERM. In *The Last Cop Out,* he and Sal Perigino were assigned to kill Papa Fats, failed, and were killed by Mark Shelby. The pair may have been brothers.

PERIGINO, SAL. In *The Last Cop Out,* he and Herm Perigino missed Papa Fats and were killed by Mark Shelby.

PETE. In *The By-Pass Control,* he is one of Captain Hardecker's policemen.

PETE. In *One Lonely Night,* he is an aging reporter who offers Mike Hammer his moral support by smiling in court when the judge calls Mike a "legalized murderer."

PETERS, BANJIE. In *Survival . . . Zero!,* he informs Little Joe about the red-vested pickpocket, who turns out to be Beaver.

PETERS, MARLENE. In "The Gold Fever Tapes," she is a prostitute to whom Squeaky Williams promised marriage. She is sad when Squeaky is killed. When Charlie Watts and other policemen try to interrogate her, Fallon, aware they have no warrant, makes them stop bothering her.

PETERSON. In *The Erection Set. See* Bell, Arnold.

PETERSON. In *The Last Cop Out,* he is the policeman assigned to investigate the murder of William R. Hays.

PETERSON. In "The Seven Year Kill," Mannie Waller tells Phil Rocca he remembers when Rocca, as a reporter, wrote about "the Peterson snatch."

PETERSON. In *Survival . . . Zero!,* he is a policeman under Captain Pat Chambers. Peterson fruitlessly checked into sales of .38 weapons after a .38 slug was found in Lipton Sullivan's room.

PETE-THE-DOG ("PETE"). In "Me Hood!," he sells newspapers in Ryan's neighborhood and provides Ryan essential information. In "Return of the Hood," he provides Ryan vital information, enabling him to rescue Karen Sinclair.

PETE THE MEAT. In *The Last Cop Out,* he is the photographer Mark Shelby is aware he could hire to take pictures that would compromise Shelby's wife if she ever made trouble.

PETROCINNI, VICTOR ("ROLLER," "VIC"). In *The Last Cop Out,* he is one of Mark Shelby's criminal associates. His neat murder increases Shelby's anxiety.

PHIL. In *The Death Dealers,* he is a circus entertainer whom Tiger Mann knows and to whose hotel room near "the Garden" Tiger takes Lily Tornay to question her.

PHILBERT. In *The Long Wait,* he owns a variety store in which photostating work is done.

PHILIPS, ARNOLD. In *The Snake,* he was evidently Marv Kania's fellow murderer on the West Coast and in St. Louis.

"THE PICKPOCKET" (1954). Short story. (Characters: Barney, Bill, Buster, Detective Coggins, Marty, Sally, Willie.) One day Willie, a reformed pickpocket now happily married to Sally and with a little boy, witnesses Marty, a criminal he used to know, drive away after shooting someone. Marty sends Buster to Willie's home to scare him into silence. Willie jumps on him, but Buster pushes him back and waves a big .45. Willie gloats that his slick fingers removed the magazine. Sally conks Buster with a sugar bowl. Willie phones Detective Coggins, who used to harass Willie for his past, but now quickly arrives and begins to treat Willie right.

PIEL, MOE. In *The Last Cop Out,* he is a killer friend of Herman Shanke. Piel, who murdered a witness in the Lindstrom case, drives a truck to pick up weaponry for Herman from Bingo Miles and Shatzi Heinkle in New York. They kill Piel and booby-trap the weaponry.

PIERCE, DR. In *The Twisted Thing,* he is a physician who Mike Hammer discovers didn't treat a thug Mike wounded.

PIERS, HELGA. In *The Last Cop Out,* she is Mark Shelby's busty Swedish girlfriend. She and Nils, her lover, plan to rob Shelby eventually; but he beats her viciously, and Nils deserts her. Gill Burke finds Shelby's incriminating microfilm in a candle in her room.

PIETRI, MARCUS. In *The By-Pass Control,* he is an enemy Tiger Mann recalls having killed. Tiger found evidence on him that the Soviets were offering a low sum for Virgil Adams's death.

PIMPLES. In *The Long Wait,* he is a cocky young punk working for Lenny Servo. Pimples's efforts to guard John McBride backfire, and McBride shoots him to death.

PITKIN, MOSS. In *The Last Cop Out,* he is a criminal from St. Louis. Papa Menes has Pitkin beaten up when he tries to raid Menes's dry-cleaning establishments.

POE, GEORGE. In "The Affair with the Dragon Lady," he was a crewmember aboard the Dragon Lady.

POLACK IZZIE. In "Killer Mine," Lieutenant Joe Scanlon recalls fighting unsuccessfully with him for Marta Borlig's attention when the three were children.

POLLACK, SID. In "The Night I Died," he is a ratty reporter who tells Mike Hammer that Carmen Rich took over the Syndicate from Marty Wellman.

PONTI, ANGELO. In *Black Alley,* he was the Sicilian don of a powerful New York Mafia family. His son is Lorenzo Ponti. Mike's friend Marcos Dooley worked for Angelo, who died peacefully, "ninety-some," in Brooklyn.

PONTI, AZI. In *Black Alley,* he was one of Lorenzo Ponti's sons, the other being Ugo Ponti. Azi typifies the impatient members of younger generations of Mafia families. Azi planned to kill his father. When Azi shot Mike twice during the waterfront fracas, Mike shot him dead and later boldly tells Lorenzo so. Andy Reevo is named as Azi's associate.

PONTI, LORENZO. In *Black Alley,* he is Angelo Ponti's son and Ugo Ponti's brother. Born on Ellis Island and hence a U.S. citizen, Lorenzo is now in his eighties. Mike annoyed Lorenzo earlier by verifying his ownership of four buildings on Fifth Avenue. When Ugo learned Azi plotted to kill their father, Ugo didn't warn him, knowing he wouldn't be believed. Mike boldly meets with Lorenzo, shortly before Ugo murders Lorenzo.

PONTI, MRS. LORENZO. In *Black Alley,* she is mentioned as the legal owner of Lorenzo Ponti's estate in the Adirondacks.

PONTI, UGO ("BULLETPROOF," "PONTI THE YOUNGER"). In *Black Alley,* he is Angelo Ponti's grandson, Lorenzo Ponti's son, and the deceased

Azi Ponti's brother. He knew that Azi Ponti and Andy Reevo, a henchman, planned to kill Lorenzo but said nothing, knowing he wouldn't be believed. When Ugo sees Mike at Marcos Dooley's funeral, he suspects Mike knows where Dooley hid $59 billion, follows him, shoots him in his bulletproof vest, but is shot by Mike, captured, and delivered to the authorities.

POPS. In "Killer Mine," he owns the deli where René Mills bought food for himself and Larry Scanlon.

PORKOV, SERGI. In "The Veiled Woman," he is a Communist agent, in his early forties. Calling himself Sam Parks, he seeks information on cosmic energy from Karl Terris. He works with Ann Fullerton, who falls in love with Karl and kills Porkov.

PORTER, CAL. In "The Seven Year Kill," he was the attorney who prosecuted Phil Rocca on a bum rap. Porter is now New York City's D.A. and reluctantly helps Rocca nail Rhino Massley.

PORTER, MARTHA. In *My Gun Is Quick,* she was recently Nancy Sanford's landlady, near Shorty's hash joint. Mike Hammer observes she is fat and in her late fifties.

PORTER, ROSE. In *The Erection Set,* she is a pleasant prostitute, age twenty-eight. She attaches herself mostly to Lee Shay, and is used by Dog Kelly to try to entrap Alfred Barrin and Dennison Barrin. She succeeds with the latter. Lee will marry Rose.

POSTON, HELEN. In *The Body Lovers,* she was an attractive blond schoolteacher from Nebraska. Wanting a good time, she bought a car and headed out of town. Greta Service knew her in New York. Helen was one of the girls Belar Ris was responsible for torturing to death, evidently by slow-acting C-130 poison.

POTTER, BIBBY. In *The Erection Set,* he is the philandering assistant director of Cable Howard Productions, a movie company.

POTTER, SYLVIA. In *The Erection Set,* she is the unfaithful wife of Bibby Potter, of Cable Howard Productions. She will force her husband to give her stud of a lover a part in a movie, or she will divorce him and get half his estate.

POXIE. In *Survival . . . Zero!,* he is a pimp whom Little Joe says Beaver beat up for infringing on his turf in his sideline as a pickpocket.

PRICE, SERGEANT. In *The Twisted Thing,* he is an honest, tough state trooper, who aids Mike Hammer, mostly by not interfering with Mike's extralegal maneuvers in tracking down Ruston York's alleged kidnappers.

PRINCE, FLORIO. In *The Last Cop Out,* he remembers that Herman Shanke became permanently opposed to Papa Menes when Menes had Herman beaten up and exiled from New York.

PRINCE, MATT. In *The Body Lovers,* he helped Theodore Gates develop his photographs.

PROCTOR, TED. In *The Last Cop Out,* he tried to pawn the gun given him by Mark Shelby. When Jimmie Corrigan, the policeman, saw Proctor waving the gun, he suspected a robbery and shot Proctor dead.

PROVETSKY, MARGIE. In "Kick It or Kill!," Kelly Smith recalls that years ago in New York she called Lennie Weaver "Pigface."

PULLEN, HARVEY. In *Kiss Me, Deadly,* while at his bar in the area of 30th Street, Mike Hammer learns he is being set up to be killed at Long John's.

PURCELL. In *The Erection Set,* Chet Linden tells Dog Kelly that if Dog is killed, Purcell or Montgomery may replace him.

PUTTICHE, MEL. In *The Erection Set,* Dog Kelly remembers that he and Mel used to climb a tree, look through windows, and watch the action at Lucy Longstreet's brothel.

Q

QUICK, BENNY. In "Kick It or Kill!," he is a criminal working for Simpson. He spots Kelly Smith and identifies him as Al Braddock, a federal agent. He hides in Smith's hotel room, shoots Smith in the arm, and is shot dead.

R

RAAB, BILL. In *Black Alley,* he is the helpful security guard at Mike's apartment building.

RADIO AND SPILLANE. "The Mickey Spillane Mystery: That Hammer Guy" was a 1953 radio series. Starring Larry Haines and also Ted De Corsia as Hammer, the show received poor ratings. Spillane wrote "The Night I Died" as a radio play. Max Allan Collins found the manuscript, revised it in short-story form, and published it in 1998.

Bibliography: Collins and Traylor; Alex McNeil, *Total Television: The Comprehensive Guide to Programming from 1948 to the Present,* 4th ed. (New York: Penguin, 1996).

RAINEY. In *Vengeance Is Mine!,* he is a crooked fight promoter. He is ordered to scare Emil Perry into lying about Chester Wheeler. Mike Hammer traces him to his Long Island boxing arena, threatens him, and when rebuked shoots him in the leg. Rainey is later murdered.

RALPH. In *Vengeance Is Mine!* Connie Wales tells Mike Hammer that when word circulated at the Bowery Inn that Rainey had been murdered, Ralph drove her home.

RAMSEY, FELIX. In "The Flier," he obtains demolition bombs from Cable-Hurley Supplies Company for Cat Fallon's use.

RANDOLPH, HAL. In *Day of the Guns,* he works with Thomas Watford and has connections in Washington, D.C. In *Bloody Sunrise,* Hal Randolph heads a team of agents ordered to protect Gabin Martrel, a Soviet defector. Randolph resents Tiger Mann's interference, which, however, proves essential. In *The Death Dealers,* Randolph is part of the official committee welcoming Teish El Abin to New York. Randolph tries unsuccessfully to interfere with Tiger's dual mission of guarding Vey Locca, Teish's fiancée, and discomfiting Malcolm Turos, the Soviet killer. In *The By-Pass Control,* Randolph finds Tiger at the murder scene of Doug Hamilton and Vito Salvi and again becomes an obstructionist. When Tiger is ever-closer to finding Louis Agrounsky, Randolph wants to pull him off the case.

RANDOLPH, MRS. HAL. In *Bloody Sunrise,* she is the federal officer's wife. Charlie Corbinet warns Hal Randolph to cooperate with Tiger Mann—or else Corbinet promises to tell his wife about something unsavory involving Hal in Detroit.

RASMUSSEN. In "The Veiled Woman," he is a federal official who attends Karl Terris's hearing.

RATH, PARNELL. In *The Death Dealers,* he is a convicted murderer recently released from prison and under Malcolm Turos's command. When Rath, pretending to be a television repairman, fails to poison Teish El Abin, Turos deftly kills him with a seemingly inept neck blow.

RAVENAL, DENNIS. In *The Last Cop Out,* he was the East Side subchief of Mark Shelby's crime group, shot dead by an unknown intruder.

RAY. In *The Girl Hunters,* he was one of Mike Hammer's remembered war buddies.

RAY. In "Killer Mine," he runs a place where Lieutenant Joe Scanlon and Marta Borlig have coffee once.

RAY. In *My Gun Is Quick,* this is the name a criminal shouts to ask Mike Hammer if he, Ray, is there. Mike answers affirmatively and is thus exposed. There was no Ray.

RAYBURN. In "Kick It or Kill!," she was Bob Rayburn's daughter. She was lured, used, and discarded by Simpson, after which she turned silent and required hospitalization.

RAYBURN, BOB. In "Kick It or Kill!," he is a Pinewood resident whose daughter Simpson ruined.

RAYMOND. In *The Delta Factor,* Art Keefer tells Morgan and Kimberly Stacy to report to Raymond's place, to be flown to the Central American island.

RAYMOND. In *Vengeance Is Mine!,* he is a rich young fellow who takes his date to the Bowery Inn for thrills.

RAYMOND, NICHOLAS ("NICK"; original name: Raymondo). In *Kiss Me, Deadly,* he was an old flame of Berga Torn. She participated in drug smuggling from Italy with him in 1940. Raymond, age forty-two, was killed in a Mafia-arranged automobile accident. Mike finds Raymond's drugs and smuggling apparatus in Raymond's City Athletic Club locker.

RAZZTAZZ ("RAZZ"). In "Me, Hood!," he is a crippled man often near Ryan's apartment. He gives Ryan information, once at the expense of a beating by Lou Steckler.

READING. In "The Gold Fever Tapes," using his rare-book business as a cover, he is the mastermind behind the theft of 800 pounds of gold, which he plans to ship to Europe disguised as his safe, painted black. He is responsible for the murders of Squeaky Williams and Henry Borden. Fallon solves all of his crimes.

RED. In *My Gun Is Quick. See* Sanford, Nancy.

RED DOG WALLY. In "Kick It or Kill!," according to Artie, he has "a bookie stall on Forty-ninth" in New York City and provided evidence about Lennie Weaver to Artie.

REED, DEL. In "The Flier," he is a state's attorney in Florida, works with Lieutenant Trussky in investigating Tucker Stacy's activities and death, but is of little help to Cat Fallon.

REED, SAM. In "The Bastard Bannerman," he runs "a horse parlor" in Chicago and provides Cat Cay Bannerman information about Syndicate ambitions in Culver City.

REEDEY, DR. BURKE. In *The Killing Man,* he served in Vietnam and is Mike's friend. Mike appeals to him to care for Velda after she has been slugged. Reedey's nurse, Meg, helps out.

REESE, AL. In "Killer Mine," he is the leading criminal in Lieutenant Joe Scanlon's old neighborhood. He has political connections. Joe humiliates him in front of his henchmen. Reese, ambitious to share Larry Scanlon's heist proceeds, tries to lure Larry to Paula Lees's apartment. Larry arrives ahead of Reese and kills him.

REESE, BERT. In *The Snake,* he is a friend of Joey Adams. Joey's wife, Cindy Adams, got information from Reese about Sally Devon Torrence.

REESE, TIM. In "Return of the Hood," he worked with Karen Sinclair to map Soviet underwater missile pads. He gave the microfilm of Soviet charts to her before he was killed, evidently by Manos Dekker.

REEVES, HYMIE. In "Man Alone," he is mentioned as a marijuana dealer.

REEVES, JUNO. In *Vengeance Is Mine!,* she is captivatingly, sinuously beautiful, though always fully clad. She hires pretty girls to be photographed by Anton Lipsek, her associate from their time together in France during the Nazi occupation, and to lure men to Clyde Williams's Bowery Inn. Her downfall comes when one of her victims is Chester Wheeler, whose murder leads Mike Hammer to expose her not only as a multiple murderer but also as a transvestite. When "she" goes for a weapon, Mike kills him. Mike is curiously mistaken when he describes Juno as having "laughing, youthful breasts."

REEVES, MORRIE. In *The Deep,* he is a killer from Illinois, imported with Lew James from Philadelphia to kill Deep. When the two arrive in New York City, Reeves registers in their hotel as George Wagner, the brother of Charles Wagner (i.e., James). Sullivan, the beat cop, shoots Reeves dead outside Deep's residence.

REEVES, VAN. In "Man Alone," he is a policeman in the records section. He gives Patrick Regan information about Mildred Swiss.

REEVO, ANDY. In *Black Alley,* he is mentioned as a Ponti family hood from New Jersey. He and Azi Ponti, whom Mike killed, planned to kill Lorenzo Ponti, Azi's father. Mike tells Ugo Ponti, Azi's brother, that Reevo is also dead.

REGAN, PATRICK ("PAT"). In "Man Alone," he is the narrator, a good, tough bachelor policeman wrongly accused of murder. Regan falls in love with Madaline Stumper, solves the nonkilling of Leo Marcus, and kills both Marcus and Al Argenio, the crooked policeman in cahoots with Marcus. In the light of the magnificent heroism of Todd Beamer and others aboard Flight 93 immediately after the attacks on New York's World Trade Center, September 11, 2001, Regan's command to Steve McCall, "[L]et's roll," has an unanticipated, dreadful relevance.

REGGIE. In *The Day the Sea Rolled Back,* Jake Skiddo recalls the fact that Reggie's father found some Spanish cannon underwater fifty years ago.

REIMS, VIRGINIA R. In *I, the Jury,* Captain Pat Chambers names her as a drug addict now in rehab.

RELLS, EDNA. In "Man Alone," she is Popeye Lewis's long-time lover. Both are painters. Patrick Regan watches her show off nude while painting a nude of herself.

REMY. In *The Last Cop Out,* he is a member of Mark Shelby's criminal group and heads an army of investigators.

RENNER, SOL. In *The Body Lovers,* he writes ads for women's trade magazines. When Mike meets him at a Greenwich Village bar, Sol tells Mike he knew Greta Service.

RENO. In *Survival . . . Zero!,* his is a place where, according to Tim Slatterly, Velda may be found at one point.

RENZO, MARK. In "Everybody's Watching Me," he is a drug lord, age thirty-one, operating out of his Hideaway Club, in cahoots with Gulley and in opposition to Phil Carboy. He tortures "Joe Boyle" and is abusive to Helen Troy. Boyle outwits him, identifies himself as Vetter, and kills him.

"RETURN OF THE HOOD" (1964). Short story. (Characters: Alex, Carlos Amega, Lennie Ames, Andy, Tony Bay, Benny, Carney, Maxine Choo, Billy Cole, Cortez, Treetop Coulter, Lewis Coyne, Manos Dekker, Fly, Mort Gilfern, Izzy Goldwitz, Joey Gomp, Bill Grady, Moe Green, Sy Green, Buck Harris, Carl Hoover, Happy Jenson, Matt Kawolski, Martino, Rudy Max, Connie Morse, Sergeant Newbolder, Paul, Pedro, Wally Pee, Pete-the-Dog, Tim Reese, Ryan, Schmidt, Cliff Shaffer, Karen Sinclair, Millie Slaker, Ernie South, Ike South, Steve, Fred Stipetto, Primo Stipetto, Vincent Stipetto, Junior Swan, Tarbush, Sal Upsidion, Chuck Vinson, Walter Weir, Doe Wenzel, Lisa Williams.)

Ryan, once he finishes dinner, is about to be arrested by Schmidt and Sergeant Newbolder, two cops, in the Cafeteria, for killing Vincent Stipetto, which he didn't do. A woman enters, sits opposite him, says she is Karen Sinclair, a government agent, slips him a capsule looking like heroin but hiding a microfilm, goes out again, and is wounded on the street. Ryan escapes out back but is sapped by Fly, who takes him to a room, ties him up, gloats that Ryan is a junkie because of the capsule he found on him, and tells Lisa Williams to guard him while he summons Vincent's brother Primo Stipetto, to come torture Ryan to death. Lisa owes Ryan a favor and unties him. Fly returns to the door shouting that Primo is coming in five minutes. Ryan smashes Fly horribly, cannot locate Karen's capsule on him, bruises Lisa to make her look innocent, and rushes out to phone Newbolder about Karen's mission. Ryan asks Pete-the-Dog, at his news stand, to check, and reads a newspaper account about the shootout, his being wanted, and Karen (called an FCC secretary) recovering at Bellevue Hospital.

Ryan gets a secret room at a shabby off-Broadway hotel, through Lennie Ames, a clerk there who owes him a favor. Ames's fellow clerk is a mousy homosexual. Ryan rests, ponders, and visits Bill Grady, an army buddy and now a canny newsman. They are allowed to see Karen briefly. She whispers that the capsule contained powdered sugar. When Grady phones a source at police headquarters, he learns that the bullets hitting Karen didn't come from any Stipetto or any police gun. At Chuck Vinson's saloon, Ryan gets a message through Pete-the-Dog that Ernie South supplies Fly with heroin. Ryan finds South, who when threatened says only that Primo is covering Fly's sources. Back at the Cafeteria, Ryan learns that a man seeking both Fly and Ryan beat up Pedro, the busboy, without learning anything. Ryan phones Newbolder at his home, reports about Fly, and learns that Karen has been kidnapped from Bellevue.

Needing substantial help, Ryan calls in Shaffer, part of "a Fed team" he once helped. They meet at a diner, and Shaffer says Karen microfilmed maps showing where the Soviets, aided by Manos Dekker, an international criminal, has deployed underwater missile pads off American coasts. He shows Ryan photos of Manos, reactivates Ryan as an official agent, and orders the cops to stop seeking Ryan. Still evading Stipetto's gang, Ryan finds Lisa, drunk after being sexually abused by Walter Weir, a Stipetto hood from Miami, and learns from her that Fly has gone to Tarbush's Coffee Shop, a hangout for Ernie South, seeking heroin. Leaving Lisa, Ryan sees Weir outside, conks him, loads him in Weir's car, and drives to Tarbush's place. Ryan finds Fly there, murdered. Karen's capsule isn't on Fly's body, well searched, evidently by Manos, who did not take Fly's heroin packets.

Back at his hotel, Ryan mails Fly's heroin to Newbolder and phones Pete-the-Dog, who tells him his sources say that some Stipetto men have put Fly's corpse back in his own pad. Pete's leads send Ryan to the printing shop of Mort Gilfern, a Communist sympathizer. Ryan sneaks into the shop, where he finds two Russians guarding half-naked Karen. Ryan kills both, then captures a third, rushing in from outside. Ryan forces him to say Manos went to retrieve "the thing" and then conks him with hideous force. Ryan phones Shaffer to get to the shop, hails a cab, and puts Karen in his hotel bed to recuperate.

Ryan taxis to Fly's hovel and finds beside his corpse that of Martino, another Stipetto thug, stabbed to death. Ryan finds the capsule under a socketed lamp bulb. Primo Stipetto enters, with Ernie South. Stipetto slugs Ryan and ties him up, to torture for killing his brother Penny. But Lisa enters with a gun, accuses Primo of killing both Fly and Martino and adds that Snow, Penny's drug-turf rival, killed Penny and put the blame on Ryan. Snow gut-shoots Lisa. Primo kills Snow. Primo, about to kill Ryan anyway, is shot dead by Lisa, who, dying, asks for a goodbye kiss from Ryan. Newbolder and others arrive in squad cars. Ryan gets Newbolder to phone Shaffer, who orders Ryan's release. Ryan rushes to his hotel, but Karen is gone. Manos phones Ryan, who agrees to exchange capsule for Karen, will await for directions to be phoned later, but hears an extra phone click. He rushes to the night desk, where the homosexual is on duty. Ryan forces him to confess he is working for Manos, who is in that homosexual's room. Ryan marches him there and shoves him in first. Manos shoots, killing the clerk. Ryan kills Manos, delivers the capsule to Karen, also there, and they kiss and contemplate a long future together. "Return of the Hood" was republished as "The Big Bang" (1965).

RICE. In *The Delta Factor,* he is a CIA man from Washington, D.C, who questions Morgan with other federal agents.

RICH, CARMEN. In "The Night I Died," he allegedly takes over the Syndicate when Marty Wellman is killed. When Mike Hammer finds Carmen, Buddy Whiteman kills him for Helen Venn.

RICHARD, PRICE. In *Day of the Guns,* he was a British intelligence agent. He told Charlie Corbinet that Rondine Lund dropped from sight during the war after the invasion. Richard died three years ago.

RICHMOND. In *Black Alley,* he is the owner of a funeral parlor where Marcos Dooley paid for his funeral and cremation.

RICKERBY, ART. In *The Girl Hunters,* he is a calm, deadly, bespectacled FBI agent, was Richie Cole's supervisor, and cooperates unofficially with Mike Hammer to find Cole's murderer. When Mike pins down Gorlin as the killer, Mike phones Rickerby to tell him where Gorlin is. In gratitude, Rickerby gives Mike a federal badge and extraordinary powers. To try to upset Rickerby, Mike calls him "Rickeyback" and "Rickety." In *The Snake,* Rickerby intervenes to keep city authorities off Mike's back.

RIERDON. In *The Last Cop Out,* he was killed by Papa Menes in Pennsylvania long ago.

RIIS, PAULA. In *One Lonely Night,* she was Oscar Deamer's nurse, age thirty-four, in the Nebraska mental institution. After he escaped, she followed, and was or became a Communist sympathizer. She liked Charlie Moffit, a would-be blackmailer; so Oscar killed him. A Soviet gunman pursued her to the George Washington Bridge. Mike Hammer killed him but looked so ferocious himself that Paula thought he was going to kill her, so she jumped off the bridge to her death.

RILEY, BUDDY. In "I'll Die Tomorrow," he was a war veteran with a bullet hole in his right ear, then a criminal. Rudolph Lees was paid to kill him and shot him into the water, but did not finish him off. Riley survived, prospered as a criminal, hires Lees to kill him, but tricks and kills him instead. While dying, Lees identifies his old buddy by his ear wound.

RILEY, TIM. In *The Body Lovers,* he is an alcoholic sports writer who obtains carbon copies of Mitch Temple's columns for Mike Hammer to read.

RIS, BELAR. In *The Body Lovers,* he is a post–World War II citizen of an unstable, newly independent Third World country. Rich through illegal black-market and arms deals, Ris represents his country as a U.N. delegate. He is intent on having Naku Em Abor's "part-Arab complex" accepted. Privately, Ris uses Ali Duval, a smuggler, and Dulcie McInnes, a fashion-magazine editor, to deliver beautiful young women to his embassy on Long Island for spectacular torture and murder scenes for depraved U.N. guests. Mike Hammer is captured there, outwits his enemies, and blows up the place.

RITTER, LUKE. In "The Veiled Woman," he works with Sergi Porkov. Karl Terris kills Ritter and his associate, Nekko, in Ritter's office.

RIVERA, GUY. In "Man Alone," he is a cabbie who drove Patrick Regan to Leo Marcus's home the night Regan supposedly shot Marcus to death.

ROBERTS. In *The Big Kill,* he is the former D.A. When Mike phones him, he tells Mike that, yes, he did see an envelope, which was empty, sent to his office by Charlie Fallon ten years ago.

ROBERTS. In *Bloody Sunrise,* this is the name of a woman registered in the Shrevesport Hotel. Tiger Mann wonders if she could be Sonia Dutko, but she proves to be too ugly.

ROBERTS, MR. In *The Delta Factor,* Angelo pretends he is paging Mr. Roberts at the Regis Hotel when he wants to approach Morgan with a message.

ROBERTS, MRS. In *The Big Kill,* she is the ex-D.A.'s wife and answers the phone when Ellen Scobie phones their residence.

ROCCA, PHIL. In "The Seven Year Kill," he was a New York City reporter, framed by Rhino Massley and prosecuted by Cal Porter. After spending seven years in prison, Rocca becomes an alcoholic bum for three years. He reforms when Terry Massley enters his life. He falls in love with her, and she with him, even while he is seeking evidence through meeting a sequence of people to nail Rhino, her criminal father. Phil Rocca's name is perhaps only coincidentally close to that of Paul ("The Waiter") Ricca (1897–1972), Chicago criminal boss, who testified before Estes Kefauver's Senate Crime Investigating Committee (1950, 1951).

Bibliography: Sifakis.

ROCCO. In "Everybody's Watching Me," he is one of Phil Carboy's henchmen.

ROMA, SAL. In *The Last Cop Out,* he supplies gunmen from his territory when the Big Board needs them.

ROMBERG, MARTIN. In *One Lonely Night,* he is a Communist agent. Mike Hammer encounters him at the Communist meeting in Brooklyn. When Romberg and an agent later identified as Harold Valleck pursue Mike and Velda to Oscar Deamer's apartment, Mike kills Romberg and then Velda kills Valleck.

ROMERO, CAPTAIN. In *The Delta Factor,* he is a corrupt officer in the Rose Castle. Morgan pretends to be supplying him with heroin. When Romero gets suspicious and draws his gun, Morgan kills him.

ROMERO, MRS. In *Bloody Sunrise. See* Lighter, Ann.

RON. In *Bloody Sunrise,* he works at Stanton's bar. Tiger Mann asks Charlie Corbinet to leave him a photograph in care of Ron.

RON. In *The Death Dealers,* he is a tough ex-pugilist and is now a doorman at Edith Caine's apartment building. Tiger Mann asks him to grab Malcolm Turos if he can. Ron is unable to do so. In *The By-Pass Control,* Ron, unnamed here, helps Tiger exit Edith's apartment, is wounded, and by pretending to be a corpse taken away by ambulance makes Tiger's enemies think Tiger is dead. Spillane satirizes modern mangling of English by having Ron use "like" badly here.

RONDINE. In *Bloody Sunrise. See* Caine, Edith.

RONDO, LUIS. In *The Delta Factor,* he is Kimberly Stacy's contact in or near the Regis Hotel. He supplies her with information, agrees to get Morgan a Queenaire plane, and flies Morgan, Kimberly, Victor Sable, and Joey Holley to safety.

RONDO, SEÑORA. In *The Delta Factor,* she was Luis's wife and is said to have died of cancer a year earlier.

RONNIE. In "Killer Mine," he is Sigmund Jones's nephew and works at Jones's candy store.

ROONEY. In "The Seven Year Kill," Phil Rocca nostalgically recalls dining at Rooney's years ago.

ROONEY, ED. In *Kiss Me, Deadly,* Leopold Kawolsky was a bartender at Rooney's saloon.

ROSA LEE. In *The Delta Factor,* she is a singer at the Orino Bar. No more than twenty-five, she is an agent whose cooperation with Morgan Art Keefer arranges. She helps Morgan send messages by a secret radio in her home, where she is murdered, presumably by Sal Dekker.

ROSARIO. In "The Seven Year Kill," Phil Rocca meets Dan Litvak at Rosario's.

ROSE. In *The Last Cop Out,* she was a loyal worker for Mark Shelby in a newly assigned territory but was mysteriously killed.

ROSIE. In *The Body Lovers,* she is a low-life Bronx prostitute so hopeless that she lets even Orslo Bucher consort with her.

ROSS, MRS. In *The Big Kill,* she is Marsha Lee's "ponderous nurse." Spillane gratuitously equips her with a mustache that Mike Hammer notices.

ROSSER, KLIM. In *Bloody Sunrise,* he used Monger poison to kill a witness in Madrid. Anderson of Newark Central tells Tiger Mann that Monger poison was unsuccessfully tried on Gabin Martrel.

ROSSI, SERGEANT NICK. In "Killer Mine," he is the desk officer in police headquarters out of which Lieutenant Joe Scanlon is assigned when he starts to solve the murder cases.

ROTH, MANNY. In *The Last Cop Out,* he saw Helen Scanlon with Gill Burke in a restaurant and loyally reported the fact to Francois Verdun. When Helen explains dishonestly, Verdun has Roth beaten up.

ROTH, MRS. MANNY. In *The Last Cop Out,* she is a cleaning woman in Francois Verdun's office. She warned her husband not to talk to Verdun about Helen Scanlon.

RUBIN. In *The Death Dealers,* he is Leo Rubin's son, age eleven. He tells Tiger Mann that the man who bought the old suit was driving Yamu Gorkey's 1963 Chevy.

RUBIN, LEO. In *The Death Dealers,* he is an East Side tailor who also sells old clothes. He tells Tiger Mann about the man who bought a suit for a fellow in a car. Tiger concludes that the purchaser was Malcolm Turos and the recipient was Teish El Abin.

RUBIN, MRS. LEO. In *The Death Dealers,* she is the tailor's wife. He rudely silences her.

RUBY. In "The Seven Year Kill," Phil Rocca encounters Mannie Waller at Ruby's East Side steak house. Later, Ruby guards Waller, but Rocca shoots Ruby dead.

RUDINOFF, SERGEI. In "Kick It or Kill!," he is a recently arrived Soviet diplomat. He is involved in a Cuba-China-Russia drug-smuggling ring. He attends a Simpson orgy. Kelly Smith finds him there, shoots him dead, and takes his briefcase for evidence.

RUSSELL. In *Day of the Guns,* when the company called the Russell-Perkins hired Charlie Corbinet, he had lots of money at his disposal.

RYAN ("IRISH"). In "Me, Hood!," he, the narrator, defines himself as a hood. He says he attended college for two years and "was a war hero." Big Man, head of a crooked police squad, hires Ryan to find Lodo and crack his drug ring. This results in Ryan's narrowly escaping death, falling in love with Carmen Smith, and discovering that she is Lodo. In "Return of the Hood," Karen Sinclair obtains a microfilm of Soviet underwater missile pad sites. At this time, Primo Stipetto is gunning for Ryan, incorrectly believing Ryan killed Primo's brother Fred. Ryan clears himself and rescues Karen from Soviet master-criminal Manos Dekker. Ryan is connected to the deaths of Fly, two unnamed Soviet agents, Martino, Ernie South, Lisa Williams, an unnamed homosexual hotel clerk, and Manos. To Cliff Shaffer, a federal agent, Ryan presents his hood code: "I can chisel the chiselers and don't have to pay any respect to the phony politicians who run us into the ground for their own egotistical satisfaction."

S

SABIN, RUSSO. In *The Delta Factor,* he is a ruthless, oily Director of Police operating under Carlos Ortega's control. His lust for Lisa Gordot distracts him from close attention to Morgan. When Rabin and Ortega get wise and pursue Morgan, he kills them both with a grenade.

SABLE, VICTOR. In *The Delta Factor,* he is a brilliant American scientist, in his fifties, and possessing knowledge wanted by both the United States and the Soviets. Carlos Ortega holds him in his Rose Castle and has hooked him on heroin. Morgan rescues him.

SABRE, BOB. In *The Body Lovers,* he is a friend, perhaps in Los Angeles, whom Velda phones for information about Maxine Delaney. Sabre says Maxine failed to become a model in Chicago.

SACHS, MRS. BENNIE. In *The Erection Set,* she is at home when Dog Kelly visits her husband, Sergeant Bennie Sachs.

SACHS, SERGEANT BENNIE. In *The Erection Set,* he is an honest policeman working in and near Linton. Cross McMillan tried ineffectively to have Sachs arrest Dog Kelly at the beach. Sachs tells Dog Kelly he caught Alfred Barrin with a girl in a wrecked car.

SADIE. In *The Last Cop Out,* she was to have been Clough's date at the theater until he had to leave town. She might be his wife.

SADIE. In "The Veiled Woman." *See* Fullerton, Ann.

SALISBURY, RICHARD. In *The Body Lovers,* he is a New York journalist having a Washington, D.C., "beat." When naming Salisbury, as well as Salisbury's fellow journalist Norman Harrison, Spillane must have been aware of Harrison Salisbury (1908–1993), the famous *New York Times* writer. Shortly before *The Body Lovers* was published, Harrison Salisbury was filing dispatches from China and then Vietnam that Spillane would have regarded as naively optimistic.

SALLY. In "The Pickpocket," she is Willie's generous, loving wife and the mother of Bill, their little boy.

SALVI, VITO. In *The By-Pass Control,* he is a vicious Soviet agent who tortured and killed Doug Hamilton and two federal agents in search of information about the by-pass control. Then Tiger Mann found and fought him, gets a little information from him, and shoots him dead.

SALVO, MRS. PETEY. In "The Bastard Bannerman," she is Cat Cay Bannerman's friend Petey's "busty doll" of a wife, and the mother of their many children.

SALVO, PETEY ("WOPPO"). In "The Bastard Bannerman," he was Cat Cay Bannerman's high-school buddy in Culver City. Petey, a tough bouncer at the Cherokee Club, helps Cat, mainly by subduing Popeye Gage and Cal Matteau.

SAM ("BIG SAM"). In *I, the Jury,* he is a big, tough black friend of Hammer's. He runs the Hi-Ho Club, where Hammer meets Bobo Hopper and has a fight with two feisty black fellows, before and after which he gains information from Bobo. The fight is gratuitous, present only to please a certain level of Spillane's readership. In it, Mike Hammer breaks one man's wrist and smashes the other man's teeth.

SAMMY. In *Black Alley,* he is one of Lorenzo Ponti's estate guards.

SAMMY. In *Kiss Me, Deadly,* he works in a garage near Mike Hammer's apartment and loans Mike a car.

SAMMY. In *Survival . . . Zero!,* he and Carl are two of Woodring Ballinger's thugs. Sammy likes but is loathed by Heidi Anders. Stanley, William Dorn's hired killer, stabs Sammy to death.

SANDERS, GUY. In "The Bastard Bannerman," he is an ex-convict wrongly accused of killing Chuck Maloney.

SANDY. In "Me, Hood!," he is an old caretaker at the Valley Park housing development.

SANFORD, NANCY. In *My Gun Is Quick,* she is Arthur Berin-Grotin's granddaughter. When she had a baby (stillborn in Chicago, four years earlier) and Berin-Grotin abandoned her, she fell into prostitution, associated with Feeney Last and Russ Bowen on the West Coast, and came to New York City. She saw Berin-Grotin and Last together, photographed them, and planned to use this picture and other photographs to expose city vice and corruption. Mike Hammer happens to meet her at Shorty's hash joint. When she is killed, Mike determines to uncover the truth, and does. Her ring has an inscription resembling Berin-Grotin's coat of arms. Mike calls her Red.

SANTINO, MARTY. In *The Killing Man,* he is a hit man who impersonates a hospital orderly when he and Nolo Abberniche try to kidnap Velda. He is shot to death by the police summoned by Captain Pat Chambers, who also kills Abberniche.

SATWORTHY, PETER CLAUDE. In "The Flier," he is an old fisherman who retrieved part of the wreckage from Tucker Stacy's plane. He provides Cat Fallon proof that the plane was dynamited in midair.

SAUNDERS, BLACKIE. In *The Erection Set,* he is a gunman Chet Linden brings from Trenton, New Jersey, to frighten Dog Kelly. When Saunders attacks Dog at Lucy Longstreet's brothel, Dog decks him and ties him up.

SAXTON. In *The Delta Factor,* it is mentioned that he was killed in a duel over Lisa Gordot.

SCADO, TURNER. In "Me, Hood!," a gunman from Elizabeth, New Jersey, he seeks to kill, fails, and is therefore killed by his bosses near Hoboken.

SCALA, ENRICO. In *The Last Cop Out. See* Holland, Stanley.

SCANLON. In "Killer Mine," he was the father of Lieutenant Joe Scanlon, Larry Scanlon, and nine other children. A World War I veteran, he was accidentally shot to death by a policeman who thought the bottle he was carrying was a weapon.

SCANLON, HELEN. In *The Last Cop Out,* she is the deceased Joe Scanlon's beautiful daughter, age thirty. When she honestly testified in Lennie Scobie's case, the police blackballed her and stopped her budding career as an actress. She became Francois Verdun's receptionist. She distrusts Gill Burke at first, never is certain he is not an avenging murderer, but vigorously loves, helps, and will undoubtedly marry him.

SCANLON, JOE. In *The Last Cop Out,* he was the father, a deceased cop, of Helen Scanlon. The mob planted money in his home and caused his disgrace. Gill Burke knew and admired him.

SCANLON, JOE ("BIG PIG," "PIG"). In "Killer Mine," he is a New York police lieutenant. He grew up in a slummy neighborhood, bettered himself, went to college for two years, became a policeman, and was in World War II. Joe is assigned to his old neighborhood to investigate the murders of Doug Kitchen, René Mills, Hymie Shapiro, and Noisy Stuccio. He renews friendship with Marta Borlig, goes after Al Reese and his criminal associates, and confronts and kills Larry Scanlon, his own long-lost twin brother.

SCANLON, LARRY ("CHIEF CRAZY HORSE"). In "Killer Mine," he is Lieutenant Joe Scanlon's twin brother. His slummy New York neighborhood helped turn him evil. He was declared missing in action in World War II, assumed a dead soldier's identity, got into blackmarketeering and other crimes, robbed the criminals who held up an armored car in Canada, returned to the Scanlon family's old neighborhood, and murdered local criminals who sought to shake him down. Larry finally meets Joe, who kills him.

SCANLON, MRS. JOE. In *The Last Cop Out,* she was the devoted wife of an endangered cop. Her fatal illness burdened her family financially.

SCHMIDT. In "Return of the Hood," he is Sergeant Newbolder's partner.

SCHMIDT, ERIK. In *The Last Cop Out,* he is a gun expert, has his own shop, and is consulted by Francois Verdun.

SCHMIDT, KURT. In *The Erection Set,* Dog Kelly recalls that Schmidt last year offered $500,000 to anyone who would kill Dog.

SCHNEIDER, SERGEANT AL. In *The Last Cop Out,* he is in charge of police records and reluctantly helps Gill Burke.

SCHNEIDER, TOM-TOM. In *Survival . . . Zero!,* he was a policy-racket hood. He was murdered the same night Lipton Sullivan was murdered. Schneider's killers are cornered and killed in Detroit. Schneider's death is unconnected with Sullivan's.

SCHULBURGER. In *The Snake,* he was evidently the victim of a contract killing by Marv Kania.

SCHWARTZ, ANNIE. In "Man Alone," she rents a room in Brooklyn to Helen the Melons.

SCHWARTZ, MOE. In *The Deep,* from his store long ago Deep and Cat stole a couch. Cat still has it.

SCIPIO. In "Man Alone," Al Argenio is on the so-called Scipio case out on Long Island when Patrick Regan tells Walter Milcross to search Argenio's home for possible evidence.

SCOBIE. In *The Big Kill,* he is mentioned as a Texas oil man. He raises race-horses and has argued with his daughter, Ellen Scobie.

SCOBIE, ELLEN ("TEXAS"). In *The Big Kill,* she works for the D.A. and Captain Pat Chambers. She flirts with Mike and shows him how to make money betting on the "nags," her ability to do so having been acquired from her father, a racehorse owner. Ellen helps him get Toady Link's file from the D.A.'s office, and would love him forever but for his being more interested in violence than in settling down. The two settle for one torrid night.

SCOBIE, LENNIE. In *The Last Cop Out,* this cheap gunman was drunk and with Helen Scanlon at the time a murder was committed. Her honest testimony got him off.

SCOTCH, PETIE. In *The Deep,* Deep recalls that long ago Scotch killed Bunny Krepto in the Knights Owl Club.

SCOTTORIGGIO, JOSEPH R. (1918–1946). New York City Republican Party activist. He was fatally beaten on Election Day, perhaps on orders from Michael Coppola (1904-1966) because of Scottoriggio's opposition to the crime family headed by Gaetano Luchese (1899-1967). In *Kiss Me, Deadly,* Mike names Scottoriggio to Captain Pat Chambers as a person whose murder remains unsolved.

Bibliography: Sifakis.

"THE SCREEN TEST OF MIKE HAMMER" (1955). (Characters: Carmen, Gus, Mike Hammer, Helen.) A bum warns Mike Hammer: Carmen, a killer, is loose and is threatening to shoot everybody on the street; the police, having blocked the street, are using Helen for bait. Carmen hates her. Mike tells the bum to leave, waits. Helen rushes up, expresses fear of Carmen. Mike says she just killed Carmen, whose body is right here. Mike chokes Helen. Spillane wrote this five-minute script as a screen test for actors trying out to star in the movie version of *I, the Jury.*

Bibliography: Max Allan Collins, ed., *Mickey Spillane, Tomorrow I Die* (New York: Mysterious Press, 1984).

SEARS, ARTHUR. In "The Bastard Bannerman." *See* Colby, Vance.

SEBULL, FATS. In "Me, Hood!," he is a friend Ryan sees at Pat Shane's restaurant. Fats tells Ryan that Carmen Smith is a superb card player.

SELIGA. In *Day of the Guns,* while reminiscing, Tiger Mann and Wally Gibbons discuss Seliga, who was evidently killed by the Communists during the war.

SELKIRK. In "Man Alone," he and Monty Selkirk, of the law firm Selkirk and Selkirk, successfully defended Patrick Regan when he was tried for Leo Marcus's murder. The elder Selkirk told George Lucas that Helen the Melon's stocks are junk.

SELKIRK, MONTY. In "Man Alone," he and the elder Selkirk got Patrick Regan off on the murder charge.

SELWICK, BURTON. In *Day of the Guns,* he is an Oxford graduate, a businessman age fifty-plus, and now a British adviser at the U.N. His wife is in England. Selwick, now ill, associates with Rondine Lund and her friend Gretchen Lark, who is painting his portrait. She dopes him with sodium pentothal to obtain governmental secrets from him. Incapacitated, he is with Gretchen when Rondine and Mann burst in at the climax. In *Bloody Sunrise,* Tiger Mann and Edith Caine stash Sonia Dutko in Selwick's unused summer house in Connecticut. Spaad Helo follows Tiger there.

SELWICK, MRS. BURTON. In *Day of the Guns,* she is in England and wants her husband, who is ill, to be replaced and returned home. Gretchen Lark is allegedly drawing his portrait for her.

SEN, MARIO. In "Me, Hood!," he is "a tap man for the Mafia," assigned to kill Ryan. Ryan braces him, conks him, and robs him. When Sen seeks to ambush Ryan in Ryan's apartment, Ryan kills him.

SERVICE, GRETA. In *The Body Lovers,* she is the sister of Harry Service, whom Mike Hammer helped send to prison. Harry asks Mike to find Greta. Mike discovers that Greta, though beautiful and with "ink-black hair," is a failed model. To help Harry financially, she volunteers to perform in a show for Belar Ris, a sadist. Mike rescues her.

SERVICE, HARRY. In *The Body Lovers,* he has been jailed in upstate New York on an armed-robbery charge. Mike contributed to his conviction. Prison has helped Harry reform. He asks Mike to find his sister, Greta, who has promised to help him financially if and when he is paroled. Harry's telling Mike that Greta knew Helen Poston, a murder victim, contributes to Mike's nailing Belar Ris.

SERVO, LIEUTENANT. In *The Long Wait,* he controls most saloons and gambling joints in Lyncastle. He was bankrolled by Havis Gardiner. Servo uses, abuses, and discards attractive girlfriends, including Troy Avalard, Gracie Harlan, Carol Shay, and Vera West. Servo's ill-fated criminal associates include Havis Gardiner, Larry, Lobin, Edward Packman, Pimples, and Tucker. John McBride, Servo's nemesis, calls him "a stinking pig . . . , a son of a bitch of a cheap con man."

"THE SEVEN YEAR KILL" (1964). Short story. (Characters: Aldridge, Best, Carey, Coleman, Joe Coon, Crosetti, Garcia, Gates, Gifford, Leo Grant, Gomez, Hal, Elena Harris, Hines, Dr. Thomas Hoyt, Joe, Johnny, Jolly, John Lacy, Buster Lafarge, Leavy, Dan Litvak, Kum Frog, Jeanne McDonald, Miss Marie, Mrs. Rhino Massley, Rhino Massley, Terry Massley, Terry Massley, Mermak, Miss Mulligan, Patty, Peterson, Cal Porter, Phil Rocca, Rooney, Rosario, Ruby, Anthony Smith, Joe Stack, Vinnie, Mannie Waller.)

Phil Rocca, a reporter whose story exposing New York criminals was squelched, was framed by Syndicate czar Rhino Massley, was prosecuted by Cal Porter (recently made the D.A.), served seven years in prison, and for three years since then has been an alcoholic bum. Rhino's long-estranged, taciturn wife recently died in Los Angeles. Their daughter, called Ann Lowry but answering to the name Terry, comes to New York with her mother's documents and a letter to Terry from her father seeking reconciliation. Pursued by hoods, she hides in Phil's tenement pad and elsewhere. Phil will be glad to find Rhino—to kill him. Phil is beaten up to no avail by thugs on orders from Mannie Waller, now Syndicate boss, who seeks Terry, because her inherited papers may expose him. Terry, voluptuous, and Phil, reformed by her admiration, fall in love. Rhino, an iron-lung patient with polio, was treated in a sanitarium outside New York City, moved with Elena Harris, his gorgeous nurse, to Phoenix, and according to newspaper accounts died there. But perhaps not. Phil tells Terry that Rhino was his revenge target but now isn't; they search her mother's documents, even her wallet, but see nothing useful. Phil briefs Dan Litvak, a canny newsman, accepts money from Terry, and flies to Phoenix. He locates Rhino's old ranch, now a polio research center by his bequest, disarms Buster Lafarge, the ex-mobster grounds-keeper there, and forces him to dig up Rhino's grave out back. The coffin is empty. Gunmen, sent by Mannie, swarm them, kill Lafarge, but miss Phil. Retaining Lafarge's .45, Phil is saved by police, who were alerted by Joe Stack, a tough reporter privy to Phil's mission. Phil returns to New York, confers with Porter and Litvak, and theorizes thus: Rhino faked his death, fled with lovely Elena, known to be in Rio de Janeiro; Rhino ran out of money, has returned to grab Terry's papers, blackmail Mannie with them. Phil finds a note from Terry; she is in his old pad. He goes there, only to encounter Mannie and some goons, is slugged, but is rescued by a squad led by Porter. A neighbor tells Phil that Terry is in a room past a certain filthy alley. He finds Rhino, now maniacal, torturing Terry in search of his documents. Rhino incapacitates Phil and bellows that his only child is Terry, a long-missing son. Phil still has Lafarge's .45 and disintegrates Rhino's head with multiple bullets. Phil suddenly realizes that the documents will be found in storage, receipts for which they saw in Terry's mother's wallet. Phil embraces Terry, says that the faceless corpse was just another hood and that her father, dead long since, she never knew.

SEVERN, DAVE. In *Bloody Sunrise,* he is a political legman for the newspaper employing Wally Gibbons. Tiger Mann gets information from Severn in return for alerting him to possible scoops.

"SEX IS MY VENGEANCE" (c. 1954). Short story. (Characters: None named). The narrator, a writer, is interviewing an attractive prostitute in a New York City bar. Others often ask her how she got into prostitution. He intrigues her by asking why. She explains that she was made pregnant in high school by a lad whose family covered it up and had her sent to a reform school. When her alcoholic father learned about it, he beat her up, then urged her to sell herself for money he then filched, and tried to rape her himself. Her battered mother was too scared to do anything. The young woman, who kept her son and is raising him well, got involved with a drug addict turned pimp, loved him, helped him, and missed him when he went to jail. She gradually rose in the ranks of high-class prostitutes. For protection, she has little volumes naming her male visitors, of various types she graphically describes. She has come to relish lucrative sex herself and is now using it as revenge against a society in which, she philosophizes, her profession has a hypocritically tolerated place.

SHAEFER, BONNIE ANN. In "Kick It or Kill!," she and her sister, Grace, have been lured by Simpson into drugs, prostitution, and dirty dancing. In addition, they have mink coats and have a lot of money.

SHAEFER, GRACE. In "Kick It or Kill!," she and her sister, Bonnie Ann, have joined Simpson's criminal group for money.

SHAFFER, CLIFF. In "Return of the Hood," Ryan successfully calls on this reluctantly cooperative federal agent for information and assistance. Shaffer briefs Ryan concerning Karen Sinclair and also orders the police to discontinue harassing Ryan.

SHANE, PAT ("PATSY"). In "Me, Hood!," he runs a restaurant which Ryan frequents. Pat relays rumors about Lodo to Ryan.

SHANKE, HERMAN ("HERM," "HERMAN THE GERMAN"). In *The Last Cop Out,* he is an experienced criminal, in charge of Miami mobs. Ever since

Papa Menes had Shanke severely beaten and exiled from Manhattan, he has sought to kill and replace Menes as syndicate boss. He orders weaponry from New York but is blown up when it arrives in Miami, booby-trapped by Menes's men.

SHAPIRO, HYMIE. In "Killer Mine," he was killed by Larry Scanlon, along with Doug Kitchen, René Mills, and Noisy Stuccio.

SHAPIRO, MORRIE. In *The Erection Set,* when Veda Barrin lost heavily once while gambling, Shapiro cancelled her chits.

SHAW, ROSE. In "Killer Mine," she was René Mills's prostitute, along with Kitty Muntz. She began at age seventeen in Miami, got "clapped up" there briefly, and moved to New York at age twenty-one. Lieutenant Joe Scanlon gets information from her about Mills and in return promises to ask a photographer he knows to try her as a model.

SHAY, ART. In "Me, Hood!," he is an able journalist who got in trouble in Germany in 1945, became a knowledgeable newsman in New York City, and bought Papa Manny's three-floor brownstone near Second Avenue. An alcoholic, he grows careless and is murdered.

SHAY, CAROL. In *The Long Wait,* she is Lenny Servo's beautiful, hard-drinking receptionist, age twenty-six. Hating him, she protects herself by professing to be stupid.

SHAY, LEE. In *The Erection Set,* he is one of Dog Kelly's army buddies. He now helps with publicity for S. C. Cable, the movie producer. Lee's prostitute friend is Rose Porter. Dog uses Lee's apartment on East 55th Street, gets Lee almost killed once, and generally terrifies him.

SHEELY, TIM. In "I'll Die Tomorrow," he was one of Rudolph Lees's victims, from Detroit.

SHEEN, BILL. In *The Killing Man,* he was a beat cop who can vouch for Mike Hammer's alibi on the Saturday morning when Anthony DiCica was murdered in Mike's office.

SHELBY, MARK (real name: Marcus Aurilieus Fabius Shelvan). In *The Last Cop Out,* he is the well-educated Manhattan criminal, one-quarter Jewish, living in Trenton, New Jersey. He is ambitious to unseat crime-boss Papa Menes. He is unhappily married, consorts sexually with Helga Piers, and has hidden invaluable crime records on a microfilm in a candle in her apartment. He "made his bones" by ambushing Herm Perigino and Sal Perigino, killed

Berkowitz and Manute the photographers, seeks to kill Turley the pawn-broker, but is killed by Captain Bill Long. Spillane says Shelby displays a Phi Beta Kappa key ostentatiously. (Candace Amory will do the same in *The Killing Man.*)

SHELBY, MRS. MARK. In *The Last Cop Out,* she is the crime-boss's wife, who prefers playing bridge in Trenton to much else. Shelby regards her as flat, flabby, and whining.

SHERMAN, CHARLES. In *I, the Jury,* he is Harmon Wilder's assistant. The two are heroin addicts, supplied by Charlotte Manning.

SHEY, SARIM. In *The Death Dealers,* he is Teish El Abin's traitorous adviser. Sarim, Oxford educated and pro-Communist, conspires with the Soviets to prevent AmPet, the American oil company, from doing business with Teish. Malcolm Turos, a murderous Communist agent, works with Sarim to abduct Teish and then kills Sarim.

SHIGLEY. In *The By-Pass Control,* it is over his place on 56th Street off Seventh Avenue that Martin Grady maintains an apartment. To it he sends Tiger Mann and Edith Caine there.

SHIPP, DR. LEONARD. In "Man Alone," he is the dentist who tells Patrick Regan he made Leo Marcus two sets of dentures.

***THE SHIP THAT NEVER WAS* (1982).** Novel for juveniles. (Characters: Sir Harry Arnold, Teddy Benson, Aktur Cilon, Larry Damar, Vincent Damar, Georg, Ashford Hampton, Helena, Herman, Jon, Embor Linero, Herbert Mackley, Margo, Henri Milos, Kevin Smith, Vali Steptur, Princess Tila, Josh Toomey, Timothy Toomey, King Tynere, Mary Verne.)

Larry Damar and Josh Toomey, both about twelve, are sailing their *Sea Eagle* when they spot and rescue an old sailor named Vali Steptur, dehydrated in a longboat from H.M.S. *Tiger,* a British jinx ship that disappeared from history in 1791. The boys and their fathers, Vincent Damar and Timothy Toomey, all living on Peolle Island in the Caribbean, release the longboat to a knowledgeable British naval archivist, and learn through a Miami linguist that Steptur speaks the language of Grandau, a small European country whose royalty and loyalists were expelled by a sequence of vicious dictators long, long ago. From Steptur's graphic sign language and a map he draws, the boys learn that those exiles boarded the deserted *Tiger* at sea, let her drift and went by her longboat to Montique Island, far southeast in the Caribbean. Larry and Josh head there in the *Sea Eagle.* Their fathers will follow when the engine of the *Blue Tuna II,* Vincent's vessel, is repaired. Once on Montique, the boys are wondered at and befriended by Princess Tila, age twelve, its current ruler. Meanwhile, two assassins employed by the current Grandau dictator kill the linguist, learn where Montique is, go there by ketch, and rendezvous with a submarine crew, who plan a bombardment of the unarmed islanders to prevent Tila's return to Grandau to re-establish the monarchy. Larry and Josh find the *Tiger,* washed into a remote hidden cave the natives knew nothing about. She is shipshape still and with tons of gunpowder. Just as the submariners start firing on the island, the boys set the *Tiger* loose. She drifts into the submarine, explodes, and eliminates all the would-be evildoers. The boys, in due time, plan to visit Tila, Grandau's newly enthroned princess.

The conclusion of *The Ship That Never Was* seems to imply that Larry and Josh might visit the grateful princess in Grandau one day. If so, Spillane never wrote the sequel. At one point, he promised four more short novels for juveniles. To date, none has appeared. The intriguing title of *The Ship That Never Was* becomes apt when at the end everyone realizes that the true fate of the *Tiger* could never be told because it would never be believed.

SHORTY. In *My Gun Is Quick,* he is an ex-convict running an all-night hash joint. Mike Hammer chances to encounter Nancy Sanford and Feeney Last there.

SHU, TEDDY. In *The Last Cop Out,* he is a Chicago criminal. Shortly after he calls Papa Menes from his penthouse to report Francois Verdun's arrival in New York, Shu is shot dead.

SIDERMAN, JOE. In *Survival . . . Zero!,* Lipton Sullivan worked loyally for Siderman's wholesale grocery business. While checking on Sullivan's death, Mike Hammer learns this.

SILBY, CARMEN. In *I, the Jury,* he is a drug addict now in rehab, according to Captain Pat Chambers.

SILVERMAN. In "Stand Up and Die!," he is mentioned as having a ravine near the land rich in uranium deposits.

SILVESTER, PHIL. In *The Body Lovers,* he is a photographer who took pictures of Greta Service and another model for a brochure. The second girl is identified as a murder victim.

SIMON, FRED. In *The Erection Set,* he is Lucella Barrin Simon's ex-husband. He had polo ponies and race cars, which Lucella sold for the fine life in Europe before he bought a Mexican divorce and married an old woman.

SIMON, LUCELLA BARRIN. In *The Erection Set,* she is one of Dog Kelly's cousins. She and her ex-husband, Fred Simon, dribbled their money away having the high life abroad. Now she is divorced and sad.

SIMON, MRS. FRED. In *The Erection Set,* she is Fred Simon's second wife, who is old.

SIMPSON. In "Kick It or Kill!," he owns a mansion outside Pinewood, surrounds himself with gunmen, spreads money around town, gets girls hooked on heroin, and forces them into prostitution and dirty dancing to delight drug-dealing guests. Kelly Smith finds the obese fellow in his office and blows his head off with a shotgun taken from one of his guards.

SINCLAIR, KAREN. In "Return of the Hood," she is a Federal counter-intelligence agent. She gives Ryan a microfilm of Soviet missile pad charts, is wounded, hospitalized, and then kidnapped by Manos Dekker. Ryan rescues her.

SINCLAIR, MARTY. In "The Bastard Bannerman," he lives in New York City and by phone provides Cat Cay Bannerman with information.

SINGLETON, JEAN. In *The Body Lovers,* he or she is mentioned as a journalist specializing in foreign news.

SINKWICH, TINY. In "The Affair with the Dragon Lady," he was the right waist gunner aboard the Dragon Lady.

SKIDDO, JAKE. In *The Day the Sea Rolled Back,* he and Petey Betts rent Oliver Creighton's dune buggy to explore the sea bed.

SKIPPY. In *Survival . . . Zero!,* she is a red-headed prostitute who lives across the street from Lipton Sullivan.

SKUBAL, GENERAL RUDOLPH ("RUDY," "SKUBE"). In *The Killing Man,* he is an old army officer who was experienced in covert operations in Germany during and after World War II. Discharged in 1949, he was employed by the CIA and is adept in combating Middle Eastern terrorism. He trained Harry Bern and Gary Fells and tried to recruit Mike Hammer, who appeals to him for information about Bern, Fells, and Penta. Mike casts a lustful eye on Edwina West, Skubal's "secretary" in his Long Island mini-fortress. Skubal, whose name has to be related to "screwball," is surrounded by computers, as in a sci-fi movie.

SLADE, ROBERTA. In *The Body Lovers,* she is a prostitute whom Lorenzo Jones pimps for, beats up, and cheats financially. Mike Hammer finds Roberta sipping martinis at a bar. He interviews her. She leads him to Jones. Mike pummels him, takes $3,000 from his wallet, and gives it to Roberta to share with some of the other girls in Jones's "stable." Mike's conversation with Roberta, a highlight of the novel, relates to Spillane's "Sex Is My Vengeance."

SLAKER, MILLIE. In "Return of the Hood," she tells Pete-the-Dog about the ambulance Karen Sinclair was abducted in.

SLATEMAN. In *Black Alley*, he is the caretaker at Slipped Disk Harris's place. He is friendly when Mike Hammer and Velda talk with him. Ugo Ponti slugged him and threw him down a cistern. Mike rescues him.

SLATTERLY, TIM. In *Survival . . . Zero!*, he works at a newsstand and tells Mike Hammer about seeing Velda.

SLOAN. In *The Death Dealers*, he owns an East Side bar above which Yamu Gorkey lives.

SLOCUM, SALVI. In "The Night I Died," he was one of Helen Venn's boyfriends.

SLOPPY JOE. In *The Twisted Thing*, Mike Hammer assigns this name to a waiter at a diner in Sidon.

SMALL. In "Man Alone," Patrick Regan reminds Sergeant Jerry Nolan of the Small-Greenblatt spy case, involving secret police work Regan managed.

SMALL, VINCENT ("VINCE"). In *The By-Pass Control*, he teaches philosophy at Brownwell College, near Eau Gallie, Florida. He and his friend Claude Boster know Louis Agrounsky and provide Tiger Mann useful information.

SMALLHOUSE, SUGAR. In *Kiss Me, Deadly*, he and Charlie Max are hired from Miami to kill Mike Hammer. When Mike encounters the two at Long John's bar, he chokes Smallhouse into unconsciousness. He and Max are machine-gunned to death while in police custody.

SMILEY, RICHARD. In *The Killing Man*, for twenty years he owned an old garage, often left it to bet on the ponies, and seemed to have considerable money. He let Jason McIntyre clean the garage. Harry Bern and Gary Fells seize Mike, take him there, and try unsuccessfully to learn about Penta from him. Later, either Bern or Fells kills Smiley.

SMITH. In *Bloody Sunrise*, he and Jones are two able, taciturn men under Hal Randolph's command. Tiger Mann badmouths them both. Randolph obviously misnames both agents.

SMITH. In *Day of the Guns*, he and Gorbatcher are named in connection with Tiger Mann's fake fire-inspection ploy.

SMITH. In "The Flier," he is a government internal bureau man, superior to Del Reed and working with Jones. When Smith sticks close to Cat Fallon, he is shot dead by Andro Marcel.

SMITH. In "Killer Mine," Lieutenant Joe Scanlon and Marta Borlig have some beer at his place.

SMITH, ANTHONY. In "The Seven Year Kill," Mannie Waller tells Phil Rocca he remembers when Rocca, as a reporter, "laid out Anthony Smith's bunch after the war."

SMITH, CARMEN. In "Me, Hood!," she was a slick gambler's daughter. She was nine when her father was killed. She shot the killer. Disguising her criminal operations (as Lodo, Mafia enforcer) by being a vice president for Peter F. Haynes III, she commits several murders in an effort to repossess eight kilos of stolen heroin that Ryan also seeks. Earnestly loving her, Ryan calls her "baby," "chicken," "kid," "kitten," "sugar," and "sweetie," and tells her he wouldn't shoot her if he could. Uniquely loving Ryan in return, she commits suicide when she could have shot him and escaped.

SMITH, DOLLY. In *The Big Kill. See* Lucas, Georgia.

SMITH, ED. In "The Night I Died," he was one of Helen Venn's boyfriends.

SMITH, HARRY. In *The Death Dealers. See* Harry.

SMITH, KELLY. In "Kick It or Kill!," he is a federal agent. While vacationing in Pinewood, outside New York City, and recovering from a gunshot wound, he stumbles into a drug-smuggling, criminal, orgiastic ring led by Simpson. On his way to killing Simpson and his Soviet associate, Sergei Rudinoff, Smith kills Harry Adrano, Calvin Bock, Carter Lansing, Moe, Nat Paley, Benny Quick, and four unnamed Simpson gunnies, and watches Ruth Gleason kill Lennie Weaver. Smith and Dari Dahl, the Pinewood hotel proprietress, also fall in love. Smith's real name is Al Braddock.

SMITH, KEVIN. In *The Ship That Never Was,* he is Sir Harry Arnold's aide.

SMITH, LEW. In "I'll Die Tomorrow," he was one of Rudolph Lees's victims. Lees stabbed him to death with an icepick in a theater.

SMITH, PHILLIP. In *The Killing Man,* he is an FBI agent assigned to work under Frank Carmody. He soon disappears from the action.

SMITHWICK. In *Day of the Guns,* he is slated to replace Burton Selwick at the U.N.

***THE SNAKE* (1964).** Novel. (Characters: Cindy Adams, Joey Adams, Angelo, Dr. Beckhaus, Nicholas Beckhaus, Frankie Boyle, Harmony Brothers, Sherman Buff, Carlysle, Lieutenant Joe Cavello, Captain Pat Chambers, Charlie, Black Conley, Pauline Coulter, Devon, Sue Devon, Dickerson, Nat Drutman, Willie Fingers, Charles Force, Hy Gardner, George, Gleason, Arnold Goodwin, Francis Gorman, Inspector Spencer Grebb, Howie Green, Lew Green, Mike Hammer, Kid Hand, Harry the Fox, Jersey Toby, Marv Kania, Kiley, Geraldine King, Thomas Kline, Pete Ladero, Annette Lee, Basil Levitt, Connie Lewis, Mrs. Quincy Malek, Quincy Malek, Marge, Sonny Motley, Lew Nelson, Bud Packer, Vince Pago, Vinny Pauncho, Del Penner, Arnold Philips, Bert Reese, Art Rickerby, Schulburger, Carl Sullivan, Guido Sunchi, Teddy, Tillson, Sally Devon Torrence, Velda, Tippy Wells.)

Mike Hammer, having saved Velda from The Dragon (*see The Girl Hunters*), finds her safe, sound, and kissable after seven years. They no sooner embrace than a gunman enters her apartment, demands "the kid," but is mortally wounded when two rival gunmen enter and shots explode. The first gunman (Basil Levitt) and one other (Kid Hand) die, but the third (Marv Kania), escapes, horribly gutshot by Mike. Velda explains: Sue Devon, "the kid," is upstairs. Though twenty-one and lovely, she is slight. Mike sends Velda and Sue to hide with Velda's friend, Connie Lewis. Soon arriving are Captain Pat Chambers and Art Rickerby, the FBI agent to whom Mike delivered The Dragon and who gave Mike a badge and extraordinary powers. Pat and Mike patch up their differences.

Mike meets Velda and Sue, who reveals this: Simpson Torrence married her widowed mother (Sally Devon Torrence), now deceased; Torrence adopted Sue; Sue thinks he killed her mother and is trying to have Sue killed; Sue left his home. Mike checks with newsman Hy Gardner and learns that Torrence, formerly a D.A., seeks to be New York governor. Mike tells Hy the killers' target was Sue, not Velda, as the public believes. Mike goes to Pat, who reveals this: Levitt was small-time; Hand was a bookie, worked for Tillson and, after Tillson's murder, for his mysterious replacement, known as Mr. Dickerson.

Mike drives a rented Ford to Torrence's mansion. Geraldine King, his gorgeous political-party secretary, introduces Torrence, who tells Mike this: Sally, his showgirl wife, became an alcoholic in the Catskills, was tended there by Annette Lee, died drunk; Sue wrongly blames him; he has no vicious enemies, no girlfriends. When Mike tells Sue is safe but fears him, Torrence pays Mike $5,000 to uncover the truth. At an off-Broadway bar, Mike finds Jersey Toby, a knowledgeable pimp, who offers this: Hand was the "right-hand boy" of Dickerson, who has "firepower" and a new gunny named Del Penner; Kania is a hit man from "St. Loo," who Mike should hope is dead—or else.

Vera is waiting, naked and sexy, when Mike returns. All business, however, he orders Vera to find and "con" Penner while he checks on Levitt. A storekeeper who sold Levitt cigarettes tells Mike she heard Levitt phone to demand more money for a job. In Levitt's apartment looking into Vera's hideout, Mike finds a rifle and concludes Levitt cased Velda four days hoping to spot Sue with her and shoot Sue; when Mike entered, Levitt figured Mike also sought Sue and attacked.

Mike goes to Joey Adams, entertainer, and his wife, Cindy, columnist, and asks them to research Sally. Mike returns to Sue, who says "a snake" killed her mother. He persuades her to return to Torrence. Geraldine provides her a limousine. Mike goes to his office and is shot at but missed, presumably by Kania. Mike phones details about Kania to Pat, then answers a coded phone message from Velda about trouble. He goes where Velda specified and is grabbed by two thugs and taken to Penner. He has Velda and is Hand's replacement. Mike warns Penner, who refuses to discuss Dickerson, his boss, and releases Mike and Vera. They proceed to Teddy's restaurant, where Hy, Joe, and Cindy report the following: Sally was a prostitute with racketeers; Torrence, then the D.A., got charges against her dismissed and married her. Hy has old clippings about threats to Torrence. Back in two hotel rooms, Mike again puts off sex-hungry Velda and digests the clippings: Sonny Motley, out of prison and now seventy-two, repairs shoes; Sherman Buff is an imprisoned two-time loser; Arnold Goodwin was paroled after a rape conviction; Nicholas Beckhaus, jailed for shooting a cop, was paroled.

In the morning, although Velda parades naked before him, Mike wants only to be briefed: Buff is happily married, has a good job; Beckhaus was brain-damaged in prison; Goodwin is missing. So they visit Motley, who explains: Motley and Black Conley, in 1932, robbed an armored car; Torrence, tipped off, blocked the heist; Motley, abandoned by Conley, wounded him; Conley disappeared with $3 million; Motley served thirty years, while Torrence gained fame. Mike asks Velda to check on Levitt and Hand, and taxis to see Torrence, who expresses doubt that Sally's background could be grounds for blackmail now. Mike goes to the adjacent Torrence summer house and finds Sue rummaging through her mother's old papers. She shows Mike a photograph of her mother and a strange man, then leaps on Mike with a kiss hotter than Geraldine's, which he also just relished.

Mike reports to Inspector Spencer Grebb, Pat's new boss, and Charles Force, their new D.A. Both dislike Mike, who insults them and identifies Kania, whose photograph Pat produces. Alone, Pat tells Mike this: An informant reported Levitt's boast of being close to big money; new hoods are in town and Syndicate men seem smug; Pat knows nothing about any Dickerson. Mike fills Pat in and asks him to grab up Kania and check on Goodwin. Mike meets Joey, who takes him to aged Annette Lee. She mutters this: Torrence was kind to Sally; Sally talked about the snake but died of drink; Conley, one of Sally's pursuers, made off with $3 million. Mike sends Velda to check on Penner and get Conley's rapsheet from Pat. Meanwhile, Mike theorizes: Conley was jealous enough that Sally had Sue by another man to want Sue dead, still has his $3 million, has re-entered the caper as Dickerson. Velda arrives with information, including a photo of Conley, who was the man in Sally's photo Sue showed Mike. Velda says she's rented an apartment with a double bed. Mike finds Motley having a beer. Motley says this: Motley and Conley vied for Sally's affections; Conley doublecrossed him, took the $3 million, perhaps trucked it into the Catskills, but must be dead since "he couldn't live without the broads and now is too old."

Mike encounters Jersey Toby at the Automat and forces him to reveal that Marge, one of his prostitutes, serviced a vicious killer from Chicago who is in New York to team up with the Syndicate. Mike phones Pete Ladero, Hy's associate, to bring the Motley-Conley file. It includes one reporter's comment that Sally testified she wanted "to get the snake" who queered the heist. Mike phones Pat, who says Goodwin recently died in a car crash outside Saratoga, further, that Torrence and Force successfully defended Levitt in separate criminal cases. Answering a frantic call from Geraldine, Mike rushes to the Torrence mansion and learns not only that Sue told Torrence her mother hid a note implicating him in what would soon become her demise, but also that Sue, while burning some of her mother's old papers, destroyed the summer house. Torrence, reportedly in Albany, is in the clear. Mike comforts Sue, sedated and hugging her favorite teddy bear. Geraldine offers Mike a drink, then her stripped-down self, but after only one ripe-lipped kiss falls asleep. Mike proceeds to his apartment, finds Velda slugged, and Kania with a gun. Before Kania can quite shoot the two, he laughs so hard he drops dead, of a horribly festering gutshot. Mike and Velda must get some sleep at once.

Pat brings Grebb and Force, both angry, next morning. Mike criticizes both. Velda, recovering, says Annette Lee wants to see Mike again. He taxis to her and learns this: Conley was impotent; Torrence never slept with Sally; Sally conspired in the Motley-Conley heist; Conley hired Howie Green, bootlegger turned real-estate agent, now deceased, to locate some Catskills hideout property. Returning to Pat, Mike learns Grebb was, though a rookie, an arresting cop after the heist. Half-liking Grebb now, Mike shares his belief that Conley is alive, in his eighties. Pat gets a relayed phone call: Levitt's picture, shown in Brooklyn by a cop to Thomas Kline, a bar owner, resulted in Kline's murder. Pat and Mike visit the scene. Alerted by seeing Torrence's campaign poster nearby and fearing for Geraldine's and Sue's safety, Mike phones Geraldine to get Sue and herself to Velda's apartment; phones Velda to go ask Torrence's campaign staffers his itinerary yesterday; and tells Pat this: Torrence probably hired Levitt to kill Sue, suspected of having evidence that could stymie his career; Torrence suspected Kline saw Torrence with Levitt and therefore killed Kline. Pat and Mike weave slowly through traffic to Torrence's mansion, find him shot dead and Sue's teddy bear scorched and with a protruding letter, which Mike hastily pockets. Evading cops and reporters, Pat drops Mike at Velda's. Geraldine and Sue are there. News of Torrence's death gives Geraldine a sense of freedom, oddly. Velda phones: Torrence was absent two hours from his headquarters yesterday. Mike stashes Geraldine and Sue in another hotel. Sue's teddy-hidden letter proves to be from her mother, revealing this: Torrence is "The Snake"; he masterminded the heist, foiled it to advance his career, wrongly exiled Sally, wants to kill you, Sue. Mike summarizes: Torrence cared more for advancement than money, found Sally drunk, let her die in the snow, adopted Sue as a cover, hired too-talkative Levitt to kill her; Conley, a bigger snake, is alive, with the money. Velda arrives. Mike clears everything with Rickerby, who promises to continue Mike's untouchable status. Mike's and Velda's long-delayed sexual consummation is interrupted by Pat at the door. He reports progress in his men's checking on the old land-sales records of Quincy Malek, Green's partner.

Mike must see Motley again. A taximan shows them Motley's Harlem hovel. Motley is glad to learn Torrence is dead, says Conley killed Malek after getting a Catskills hideout somewhere, says Malek once rented to a pair of old sisters, wants no trouble, would, golly, appreciate seeing Velda naked. Mike and Velda depart, alert Pat to those sisters' lead, learn from him that the Syndicate is cooperating with newly arrived "enforcers." Mike finds Malek's widow's phone number. He and Velda go there, learn someone paid her to loan out Malek's old records, which a delivery boy picked up and later returned, and sells them to Mike for $500. He and Velda work until the next afternoon on them, find Conley bought property in Ulster County, upstate, go there, but find only a vermin-riddled shack. They build a leafy "love nest," start the consummation process yet again, until Mike spots a rusted old taxi in some far-off brush. They hasten there, find Conley's skeleton, finger still on the trigger of the rifle he used to head-shoot the cabbie also dead therein, and the $3 million in canvas sacks. Conley made it there but died of the chest wound Motley inflicted when doublecrossed during the post-heist chase. Motley suddenly appears, armed, peppy, and gloating thus: He knew about Conley, planned soon to bribe his way into the Syndicate; Mike threatened his scheme; he hired Kania, who failed to kill Mike; he followed Mike and Velda, whom he lasciviously orders to undress and then be shot along with Mike. Mike taunts him that he better check for the money first. When Sonny opens the taxi door, Conley's skeleton wiggles, his rifle discharges, and Sonny falls dead of a chest shot. Mike and Velda are surely primed to return to their love nest for the night.

Reviewers rightly fastened on the deus-ex-machina conclusion of *The Snake*. Even more surprising is Mike's attitude toward Velda. He tells the willing lovely, "You're only a broad and I do what I want," then, "I never ask. I take." He calls intercourse "the big now," but when cometh now?

SNYDER, ARNIE. In *The Day the Sea Rolled Back,* people on Ara Island recall that Bud Jimson boasted to Arnie Snyder about knowing the location of the *San Simon.*

SNYDER, DR. LARRY. In *The Girl Hunters,* he is a physician whom Captain Pat Chambers gloatingly asks to comment on Mike Hammer in his alcoholic phase. Snyder does so, but then hospitalizes Mike and marvels at his sudden recovery.

SOBEL, LENNY. In *The Deep,* he is a significant figure in the New York City criminal syndicate. His main bodyguards are Al and Harold. Helen Tate has consorted with Sobel for the purpose, she tells Deep, of gaining information. Years ago, Deep shot Sobel in the buttocks and does so again, at Bimmy's tavern. When Sobel brings Deep to Holiday, Sobel's boss behind the scenes, Deep, though battered by Sobel, escapes, and later disables Sobel, by then drunk and boastful, by dislocating his shoulder.

SOBERIN, DR. MARTIN. In *Kiss Me, Deadly,* he masterminds the criminal actions of Al Affia, Carl Evello, William Mist, and others. Dr. Soberin, who has an office near Central Park, examined Berga Torn and placed her in a sanitarium. Mist allegedly referred Berga to Soberin, who on his records changed William Mist's name to "William Wierton." Soberin is the tolerant lover of Berga's fire-mutilated friend who takes the name Lily Carver, after the real Lily is drowned. Mike Hammer discovers Soberin's machinations, disarms him, breaks some of his fingers, and shoots him to death. "Lily" attacks Mike, but he burns her to death.

SOKOLOV. In *The By-Pass Control,* Tiger Man says that Sokolov and Botenko were involved in a 1964 Soviet trial.

SOLITO, VANCE. In *Survival . . . Zero!,* he is a small-time criminal who, along with his friend Jimmy Healey, Mike Hammer recognizes on the elevator in the hotel where Beaver lived and was murdered.

SOLOMON, MEYER. In *Survival . . . Zero!,* he is a bailbondsman who tries to help Mike Hammer locate pickpockets.

SOLOMON, SID. In "Me, Hood!," he is Diego Flores's numbers boss.

SOPHIA. In "The Gold Fever Tapes," she is a hotel hooker Arthur Littleworth knew more than a little. Fallon gets her to talk. In this part of the story, Spillane uses repulsively racy language.

SOUTH, ERNIE. In "Return of the Hood," after he got out of Sing Sing, he killed Fred Stipetto over a drug-turf argument. South supplies Fly with heroin. Ryan forces South to give him what amounts to limited information. On learning that South killed Fred Stipetto, his brother Primo Stipetto kills South.

SOUTH, IKE. In "Return of the Hood," Fly tells Lisa Williams he needs drugs from Ike South. Fly may mean to say "Ernie" South.

SPACER, GEORGE. In *The Last Cop Out,* he is one of Papa Menes's underlings. Spacer and his partner, Carl Ames, are reluctant to awaken Menes early to give him news.

SPANISH JOHN. In *The Deep,* he was shot years ago, Deep recalls, by Bennett with a zip gun. Roscoe Tate aims the same old gun at Deep during the Knights Owl Club finale.

SPENCER, ANN. In "The Seven Year Kill." *See* Massley, Terry (the female).

SPUD. In "Man Alone," he is an old waiter at the Climax. He identifies Mildred Swiss for Patrick Regan and tells him she served Regan the drugged drink.

STACEY, MRS. In "Everybody's Watching Me," she is the bribed landlady of "Joe Boyle."

STACK, JOE. In "The Seven Year Kill," he is the Phoenix police reporter who aids Phil Rocca with information and timely reinforcements.

STACKLER, MARTY. In *The Last Cop Out,* he and his cousin Mack Ferro are ordered by Richard Case to capture Shatzi Heinkle. Instead, Shatzi stabs all three to death but, shot by Mack, also dies.

STACY, KIMBERLY ("KIM"). In *The Delta Factor,* she is an experienced, gorgeous federal agent, ordered to marry Morgan and accompany him on the mission to a Central American island to rescue Victor Sable. She suspects Morgan of having stolen $40 million but cooperates with him. Kimberly is slugged by Sal Dekker and would be shot by him but for Morgan's shooting Dekker first. Made aware of Morgan's innocence, Kim signals her everfeminine loyalty to him by making a delta figure with her fingers, as he parachutes out of her agent Luis Rondo's airplane. On the island, Morgan and Kim are known as Mr. and Mrs. M. A. Winters.

STACY, TUCKER ("TUCK"). In "The Flier," he was an air force buddy of Cat Fallon. He built up an airport complex in Celada, Florida, made a lot of money, got involved in anti-Castro flights over Cuba, and crashed in the Caribbean. He left his estate to Fallon, who determines the cause of Stacy's death, which was murder. (At one point, Tucker is called "Tuckey.")

STAMPH, HARRY. In "The Affair with the Dragon Lady," he helped rescue the downed F-100 pilot.

STANDISH. In *Day of the Guns,* he is an agent working with Toomey and Wilson to help Mann.

"STAND UP AND DIE!" (1958). Short story. (Characters: Heller Beansy, Belchey, Chigger Bolidy, Billy Bussy, Mrs. Cahill, Trumble Cahill, Bud Cooper, Donan Cooper, Oliver Cooper, Dukes, Grady, Hart, Caroline Hart, Clemson Hart, George Hart, Macbruder, Melse, Silverman, Mitch Valler.) Mitch Valler, the narrator, is a tough ex-P-51 pilot with experience in World War II and the Korean conflict. While he is flying a load of Maine lobsters in a C-47 over an isolated, mountainous area probably in the southern part of the United States, an engine fails. Just before the plane crashes, he parachutes to safety and practically lands in the arms of gorgeous Caroline Hart. The two kiss and instantly feel just meant for each other, even though she is engaged to an enormous hillbilly brute named Billy Bussy. Mitch learns that old Hart, having discovered uranium in nearby hills, killed or drove off illiterate landowning neighbors, filed land claims, and intends to reap a vast profit. Despite threats and confrontations, Mitch thwarts the Harts' machinations. Aided by a kid named Trumble Cahill, Mitch finally evades a booby-trapped fence, lures all opposition to explosive death, and walks to safety hand in hand with Caroline. "Stand Up and Die!" has intriguing fable elements: Hero, marvelously armed and able, drops from sky; must rescue fair-haired damsel from evil family and ogre-like lover, is aided by small boy; peasants, cruel because ignorant, in amphitheater-like enclosure in mountain-girdled valley, isolated from outside world, mistake Geiger counters for weapons and dynamite blasts for earthquakes; lovers exit through magic gate. The narrative starts in medias res, jerks back and forth in time, and remains semi-inexplicable—deliberately or through stylistic infelicities. The story contains an early usage of Spillane's common phrase for death—"the long road."

STANLEY. In *Survival . . . Zero!,* he is William Dorn's hired killer. His stabbing Lipton Sullivan to death starts Mike Hammer on a long investigation. After Stanley kills Woodring Ballinger, Carl, Sammy, and Beaver, Mike finds him with Dorn and stabs him dead.

STAN THE PENCIL. In "Man Alone," he is a bookie operating partly out of the Climax. Patrick Regan squeezes him for information about Ray Hilquist, Leo Marcus, and Mildred Twiss. Spillane satirizes Stan by having him overuse the currently popular "like" in scared talk.

STANTON. In *Bloody Sunrise,* he owns a bar on Broadway which Tiger Mann uses as a delivery point and as a place to meet friends.

STANTON. In *Vengeance Is Mine!,* his studio is mentioned as one left by Marion Lester when she went to Anton Lipsek's establishment.

STANTON, HENRY. In *The By-Pass Control,* he is the Belt-Aire Electronics plant manager whom Tiger Mann intimidates into allowing him the run of the place.

STAPLES, SAM ("BAD BEAR"). In "Killer Mine," he was one of the kids playing with Lieutenant Joe Scanlon and his chums when they were youngsters.

STARSON, VICTOR. In *The Killing Man,* it is said that Starson is slated to replace Bennett Bradley in the State Department and continue searching for Penta.

STASH. In *The Erection Set,* Dog Kelly remembers that he and Stash fell from a tree while they were watching action in Lucy Longstreet's brothel.

STASHU. In *The Deep,* he is the head waiter at the Signature, a restaurant Lenny Sobel owns.

STATTO. In *The Last Cop Out,* this is the name of the family that owns a warehouse in Brooklyn. Gill Burke surmises that Shatzi Heinkle is being taken there by Marty Stackler, who used to work there.

STAZOW, COUNT. In *The Erection Set,* the agent at the Weller-Fabray haberdashery says they'll not make this boorish fellow a suit.

STECKLER, LOU. In "Me, Hood!," he works with Stan and Stash Etching, was arrested for assaulting Razztazz and for carrying an illegal firearm.

STEELE, MARTY. In *The Delta Factor,* he is an Australian farmer whom Sal Dekker murdered and whose identify he then took.

STEGMAN, MISCHELLE. In "Killer Mine," when Lieutenant Joe Scanlon was a child he saw Stegman mug Jew Jenkins and was a courageous witness to the event.

STEIGER, MORT. In "Kick It or Kill!," he rents Kelly Smith a boat and tells him about Simpson.

STEIN, ANNIE. In *The Girl Hunters,* she owns a flophouse, called the Harbor Hotel, where Bayliss Henry tells Mike Hammer he can find Red Markham. Mike, Henry, and Hy Gardner talk to Red there.

STEPHAN. In "The Veiled Woman." He is one of Ann Fullerton's thugs. Karl Terris kills him.

STEPHANO. In "The Affair with the Dragon Lady," he and his brother helped rescue the downed F-100 pilot.

STEPTUR, VALI. In *The Ship That Never Was,* he escapes by a *Tiger* longboat from Montique Island with proofs of Princess Tali's authenticity, is rescued by Larry Damar and Josh Toomey near Peolle Island, and reveals details about his island to the boys and their fathers.

STERLING, PETE. In *I, the Jury. See* Hammer, Mike.

STEUBEL, LOU. In *The Delta Factor,* he was a criminal whose sister was abused by Whitey Tass. When Lou sought an advantage over Tass because of the incident, Tass killed him.

STEVE. In "Me, Hood!," he and Sandy are caretakers at the Valley Park housing project. Sandy tells Ryan that Steve is nearby but drunk.

STEVE. In "Return of the Hood," Ernie South tells Ryan that Fly lives in a basement near Steve's Diner.

STEVE. In *Survival . . . Zero!,* he owns a bar and grill near Columbus Avenue and 110th Street. Mike Hammer goes there looking for Beaver.

STEVENS, CARLOS. In *The Deep,* Deep recalls that Carlos Stevens knifed a "skinny kid" from a rival gang years ago. The kid was raiding the Knights Owl Club "arsenal."

STEVENS, CONRAD. In *I, the Jury,* according to Captain Pat Chambers, he is a drug addict now in rehab. Hammer recalls that he "spent a stretch in the big house [i.e., prison]."

STEVENSON, MATT. In *The Last Cop Out,* he, Ollie, and Woodie are assigned by Francois Verdun to guard Leon Bray. They are all gassed to death by an unknown assailant.

STILES. In "The Gold Fever Tapes," he is a partner with MacIntosh. The two let Henry Borden use equipment in their Brooklyn casting factory to make a safe for Reading out of gold.

STIPETTO, FRED ("PENNY"). In "Return of the Hood," Ryan is falsely accused of killing Fred Stipetto. Ryan merely beat him up for hurting Rudy Max, Ryan's friend. Ernie South killed Fred in a rivalry over drug turf.

STIPETTO, PRIMO ("BIG STEP," "STEP"). In "Return of the Hood," he is the Stipetto family head. When he thinks Ryan killed his brother Fred Stipetto, Primo goes gunning for Ryan. Learning that Ernie South, Fred's drug-supplying rival, killed Fred, Primo kills South.

STIPETTO, VINCENT ("LITTLE STEP"). In "Return of the Hood," he is Primo Stipetto's younger brother and Fred Stipetto's older brother. Vincent is killed during the gunfight outside the Cafeteria, when Karen Sinclair is wounded.

STOEFFLER, GENERAL. In *The Girl Hunters,* Senator Leo Knapp was on his staff, according to Laura Knapp, Leo's widow.

STONE, MRS. In *Survival . . . Zero!,* she owns the building where Mike Hammer finds Woodring Ballinger, Carl, and Sammy murdered.

STONEY. In *The Erection Set,* he and Juke are two of Stanley Cramer's cronies. The three play cards and try to help Dog Kelly.

STOVETSKY. In *Day of the Guns,* he is presumably a high-ranking Soviet agent at the U.N.

STRAUSS. In *The Erection Set,* he and Betterton in London are agents that Dog Kelly tells the manager at Weller-Fabray to telephone for instructions.

STRAUSS. In "Killer Mine," he owned a store near where Polack Izzie lived.

STREBHOUSE, HENRY. In *I, the Jury,* when Captain Pat Chambers mentions Strebhouse as a drug addict now in rehab, Mike Hammer recalls that the man spent time in prison earlier.

STRICKLAND, AUGIE. In *The Girl Hunters,* he repaid a debt he owed to Mike Hammer by giving Nat Drutman money to pay for Mike's phone bills while Mike was on his seven-year drunk.

STUCCIO, NOISY. In "Killer Mine," he was a pimp operating with René Mills over Sigmund Jones's store. Noisy and Mills roomed together until Mills mysteriously came into money. Larry Scanlon killed Noisy and Mills, among others.

STUCKER. In "Man Alone," Popeye Lewis tells Patrick Regan that Stucker is the dummy owner of the Climax, secretly owned by Leo Marcus.

STUMPER, MADALINE ("MAD," "MISS MAD"). In "Man Alone," she grew up knowing Patrick Regan. She became the owner of the Sturvesent Agency, a Madison Avenue call-girl and modeling agency. She used her money to support an alcoholic father, an invalid mother, and seven siblings. Mad helps Regan, is kidnapped by Al Argenio, but is rescued by Regan. After Regan and Mad make love, she fears her past disqualifies her from marriage, to which he says, "It's now and later that counts. Not the before part."

SUGAR BOY. In *The Girl Hunters,* he is the bouncer at Benny Joe Grissi's saloon. Sugar Boy and Mike Hammer have a brawl, then turn friendly.

SULLIVAN ("SULLY"). In *The Deep,* he is an experienced, ever-suspicious beat cop in the neighborhood where Deep and the others grew up. Sullivan once pounded Deep with handcuffs. Deep saves Sullivan's life by warning him that Morrie Reeves is about to attack. Sullivan shoots Reeves in the forehead.

SULLIVAN, CARL. In *The Snake,* he was the person in whose name Black Conley purchased his Catskills hideaway.

SULLIVAN, LIPTON ("LIPPY"). In *Survival . . . Zero!,* he was a schoolmate of Mike Hammer's long ago. He earned a medal during World War II, then lived in a small apartment on West 42nd Street, and worked for a grocer. His providing a bed in his room for Beaver, a pickpocket, led to his being mistaken for Beaver and being murdered. This starts Mike's investigation.

SUMMERS, HENNY. In *The Deep,* he is the old janitor, now age sixty-five, still at the Knights Owl Club after twenty-five years. He and Deep reminisce.

SUNCHI, GUIDO. In *The Snake,* Sonny Motley names him to Mike Hammer as a deceased member of his Motley's mob.

SURVIVAL . . . ZERO! (1970). Novel. (Characters: Dr. Vance Allen, Heidi Anders, Aspen, Johnny Baines, Woodring Ballinger, Barney, Beaver, Larry Beers, Mrs. Sammy Brent, Sammy Brent, Petie Canero, Carl, Carmine, Captain Pat Chambers, Lou Chello, Sid Cohen, Sergeant Corbett, Wilber Craft, Mrs. Robert Crane, Robert Crane, Eddie Dandy, Mrs. Eddie Dandy, Dr. Delaney, William Dorn, Finero, Teddy Finlay, Gabin, Hy Gardner, George, Gostovich, Irving Grove, Mrs. Irving Grove, Mike Hammer, Jimmy Healey, Henaghan, Bunny Henderson, Mumpy Henley, Mrs. Spud Henry, Spud Henry, Denny Hill, Chipper Hodges, Matt Hollings, Jackie, Jenkins, Jim, Josie, Sigmund Katz, Joseph Kudak, Leo, Lindy, Little Jore, Louise, Mrs. Luden, Maria, Theresa Miller, Rox Murray, Len Parrott, Banjie Peters, Peterson, Roxie, Reno, Sammy, Tom-Tom Schneider, Joe Siderman, Skippy, Tim Slatterly, Vance Solito, Meyer Solomon, Stanley, Steve, Mrs. Stone, Lipton Sullivan, Gomez Swan, Renée Talmage, Reginald Thomas, Raul Toulé, Austin Towers, Caesar Mario Tulley, Velda, Anton Virelli, Coo-Coo Weist, Welch, Wiley, Dewey Wong, Janie Wong, Sergeant Woods, Sal Wooster.)

Mike Hammer answers a call from Lipton ("Lippy") Sullivan, an old friend, rushes to his fleabag apartment, and finds him dying of torture stabbings. He says only he didn't know his assailant and there was no reason for the attack. Mike calls Captain Pat Chambers of homicide, who takes over. He meets Velda at the Blue Ribbon, drops her by cab at her place, and goes to his own. The morning newspapers report the murder of Tom-Tom Schneider, a big-time hood, but ignore Lippy's. Mike learns from Pat that the police found two stilluntraced sets of fingerprints, and that Jenkins and Wiley, a pair of detectives, are investigating Lippy's murder. Mike returns to Lippy's rooms, let in by the superintendent, and notices Lippy's new couch gone, finds it in the super's room, searches under its zippers, and orders the super to return whatever he removed. Mike locates Jenkins and Wiley having coffee, and learns that Lippy had a bank account of $2,700. Did someone attack him for possible cash? Mike checks with the wholesale grocer for whom Lippy worked and learns he bought extra food a few weeks earlier. Was he helping a needy roommate? At the Automat, Mike bumps into Eddie Dandy, a television reporter, and learns this: Dandy was at a hospital investigating the covered-up death of someone who twitched in the subway; while there, Dandy saw Robert Crane of the State Department and Matt Hollings, the latter in charge of the disposal of a shipment of nerve gas. Is the twitcher's death connected with those of Lippy and Schneider? Mike rummages through garbage outside Lippy's apartment building and finds a shoebox loaded with wallets. Was Lippy a pickpocket? While Mike showers in Velda's apartment, she goes through the shoebox and makes two finds—a diamond-studded compact inscribed by Bunny to Heidi Anders, actress friend of Bunny Henderson, wealthy jet-setter, and the identifiable wallet of Woodring ("Woody") Ballinger, big-spending racketeer.

Pat tells Mike that William Dorn, Irving Grove, and Reginald Thomas have also been identified as persons whose wallets Lippy stole. Pat lets Mike return the various wallets and request donations to the Police Athletic League as rewards. Pat bridles when Mike asks about the subway fatality but confidentially reveals that it may have been caused by a germ-warfare agent. Mike rushes into Ballinger's Fifth Avenue office, a fancy front for his crimes, and orders him to have his goons identify the "dips" (i.e., pickpockets) operating in the theater district. Posing as a cop, Mike interviews Heidi in her Lexington Avenue place, and she agrees a dip took her compact, which she missed only much later. She gives him a drink and offers him more than a hot kiss, but after fingering nothing but her hip huggers he agrees to get the compact from the police and bring it to her later. Telling Velda to interview Lippy's neighbors for information, Mike goes to Irving Grove, at his Broadway men's shop. Grove cannot recall who lifted his wallet. While wolfing a bite at the Blue Ribbon, Mike sees Dandy on TV. He is accusing the government of a cover-up concerning the subway death, which he says was possibly caused by a germ weapon.

Mike and Pat rush to a government office on Madison Avenue and meet with Crane and some D.A. assistants. Crane, who hates Mike, accuses him of leaking to Dandy; but Mike, backed by Pat, silences him and gets him to reveal government secrets. In 1946 a Soviet agent was under orders to attack several American cities with weapons of mass destruction. A second agent was alone privy to telling him when. But the political situation is now changed; the Chinese are turning against the Russians, who therefore want to call off the attack. The trouble is, the second agent is dead and the attack is still viable. The officials bring in Dandy and persuade him to retract his true story on television. In exchange, he will be given the ultimate scoop. Pat releases the stolen items to Mike. He finds Ballinger dining at Finero's Steak House, with two fancy girls and four goons, named Larry Beers, Carl, Gomez Swan, and Sammy. Mike gives Ballinger his wallet and proceeds to Heidi's apartment. She is invitingly unclothed; Mike, however, discovers that her compact contains heroin in a secret compartment, lectures her graphically about her likely premature death, and leaves.

When told about his wallet, Dorn invites Mike to lunch. Before getting to a fancy French restaurant, Mike learns from Dandy that Dorn is an executive officer in electronics and chemical companies. Dorn is handsome and smooth, accepts his wallet graciously, and introduces him to his lovely accountant, Miss Renée Talmage, who is fascinated by Mike when he is revealed as that famous private investigator. He tells her about Lippy. Dorn boasts about the usefulness of his companies to the American military establishment. Back in his office, Mike gets a message from Velda to phone their friend Sammy Brent, who sells theater tickets. Sammy says Lippy was one of his useful ticket scalpers. Mike recalls the address of a furniture company on an envelope in Lippy's garbage, calls the outfit, and learns Lippy bought his couch two weeks earlier. Conclusion? Lippy, always generous, needed an extra bed to let a down-and-out man stay with him, learned he was a dip, and kicked him out. The dip returned, tortured Lippy for something—perhaps some loot—and killed him. When asked, a bailbondsman names several recently arrested dips; Johnny Baines seems Lippy's likely roomer.

Velda phones to tell Mike someone is in Lippy's apartment. Mike rushes there, is shot at, fights back, but is knocked unconscious as Velda charges in, firing. At police headquarters, Mike, with Velda along, gives a statement about the attack, then tells Pat he believes Lippy argued with a dip he housed and was killed by someone who thought Lippy had the wallets the other dip took. Velda is sad that Mike confides in her only to a degree. He checks Lippy's neighbors and learns one of Mike's attackers was bald and another wore heel taps. He observes enormous troop movements through the streets. The government is desperately looking for weapons of mass destruction. Mike thinks New York City might be better if it were depopulated. Checking his phone machine, Mike learns Renée wants to meet him at Dewey Wong's restaurant, goes there, fingers her panties, and takes her to his apartment. He declines her nude advances, undresses to answer her query about his manhood, says he calls the shots in this man's world, and tells her she wants information not him. She departs, smiling.

Next morning Mike has coffee with Dandy, voices his philosophy of not worrying, and chats with him about Ballinger, who, he learns, is an uptown racketeer. Velda leaves a taped message that Little Joe, an informant, said Lippy was seen with a tall, skinny hustler. Pat tells Mike this: American and

Soviet officials alike are worried and are cooperating to stop any chemical-biological attack; the authorities are tailing Dandy. Mike chances to find Heidi at Finero's, is pleased she is trying to stay off drugs, and tells Ballington's goons, Carl and Sammy, who are slavering over her, that he is looking for Larry Beers. Mike phones Renée, has a drink with her at a bar, and at her request takes her on a tour of seamy New York. He meets Caesar Mario Tulley, a friendly panhandler, who, when asked, says he saw a tall, skinny hustler, notable for sporting a red vest. Renée invites Mike to attend a business meeting this evening involving her boss, Dorn, and some political and commercial types. Arriving there, Mike quips curtly about capitalism with Joseph Kudak, a Russian friend of Dorn's. Nearby is a well-guarded, Soviet-hosted party, where Mike sees Teddy Finlay, whose boss is Crane of the State Department and who tells him Dandy is now in protective custody. Mike takes Renée to his office for possible messages. His instincts suddenly alert him to danger, and he takes evasive action. An assailant shoots at him but kills Beers, creases Renée's skull with a bullet, and escapes. Danger: Ballinger's thugs heard and then destroyed Velda's recorded messages. Mike takes Renée to a doctor and then to her apartment, tries unsuccessfully to locate Velda and Ballinger, but gets leads to the red-vested dip. Mike summons Pat to his office to handle Beers's corpse there. Pat says a canister, with bacterial weaponry inside, was found in an upstate water reservoir with evidence as to other cannisters timed to go off in six days.

Exhausted, Mike sleeps until afternoon. Little Joe tells him he conned a cop into identifying the red-vested dip as Beaver, and even gave him a photo of him. Mike turns on his office radio and hears about cooperation between the United States and Russia, and about Schneider's killers being trapped, with hostages, in Detroit. Mike has copies of Beaver's photos made and gives Pat several to circulate. Mike visits Heidi, drug-free, naked, and eager. Right off, she tells him Sammy, momentarily busy, wants a date with her and will phone soon. He does; she hears three toots and an order for Sammy to hang up. Mike knows such toots indicate construction blasting. Mike phones his answering machine, which contains a request to see Dorn at his apartment. Finlay and some noisy Soviets are there. Mike tells Dorn of Renée's injury. Dorn asks Mike to check on her; so Mike grabs a taxi for her apartment. She seems better and is also naked. He phones Henaghan, a public-department official, to ask where blasting is occurring in Manhattan. Mike's office recording machine has a message: Velda has followed Ballinger and his gunmen, who are following the red-vested dip to 92nd Street. Mike shows Beaver's photo to Renée. She treats Mike to a vibrator massage. Time passes. Henaghan phones back, enabling Mike to narrow Sammy's location to Columbus Avenue and 110th Street. Conclusion: Sammy and others have surrounded Beaver there. Suddenly, Renée seems faint; so Mike calls her maid to report at once and also phones Dorn's secretary, learns of an evening meeting he must conduct, and says Renée cannot attend an evening meeting Dorn is planning.

Journalists report leaks about possible germ warfare. Mike finds Dandy, and they discuss possible worldwide destruction. Mike asks Dandy to phone Pat to concentrate the search for Beaver at Columbus Avenue and 110th Street. Mike follows leads from a sequence of informers. He forces Austin Towers to locate Tulley and a friend, both unconscious from marijuana supplied by Austin, and gives Austin an hour to prepare them to talk; checks a quiet construction site; and learns Sammy and Carl, plus others, are in a deserted building nearby. He storms up the stairs, hears gunfire, and is knocked unconscious by Sammy's dead body falling on him. Velda, faithfully staking out the place, revives him, and they also discover Carl, Ballinger, and the unnamed bald man—all murdered. Beaver, leaving a bit of torn red vest, escaped through the window. So Ballinger sought Beaver. But who sought Ballinger?

Leaving Velda to await the approaching cops, Mike returns to Tulley and his friend, who says Beaver lives at the Stanton Hotel. Mike rushes there by cab and finds Beaver tortured, just like Lippy, and dead. Although Beaver's room has been ransacked, Mike finds a sheet of onionskin hidden in his red vest. It is a map locating all the bacteria-loaded cannisters. Mike calls Dandy, who comes, vomits when he sees Beaver, and tells Mike that the Russians have revealed not only the failure of their plans but also the fact that vaccine for protection of chosen survivors has proved ineffective. Dandy is aware of the scoop Mike hands him in connection with the onionskin. Mike phones Pat that the world is safe. Mike sneaks into Dorn's apartment, raps his maid unconscious, and hears Dorn rebuke a killer named Stanley for not finding the onionskin taken from Dorn's wallet. Ordered to bring drinks, Stanley, the multiple murderer, stumbles into Mike, who kills him, then shoots his tardily arriving associate to death, and bursts in on Dorn—and his guilty cohorts, Renée and a Soviet agent named Kudak, whom he also kills. Now aware that Renée gave Dorn a copy of Beaver's photo, leading to that would-be blackmailer's murder, Mike sums up the nefariousness of both Dorn and Renée and chortles that the vaccine they took to protect them from the deadly weapon will wear off. Before Mike can bring them to America's slow justice, they bite cyanide capsules and die.

Although Spillane does not explicate the title *Survival . . . Zero!* in his text, it is clear that germ warfare could virtually destroy the world. This Armageddon suggestion may be a function of Spillane's Jehovah's Witness visions. The novel contains the most vulgar diction of any Spillane novel to its date (later, *The Erection Set* will outdo *Survival . . . Zero!*). In addition to milder words already employed (for example, "balls," "crap," and "shit"), the following appear: "Beaver," "buy tail," "get laid," "her period," "horny," "hosed," "piddle," and "snatch." To underline the grittiness of the novel, Spillane also uses the word "hell" thirty-five times, has rain spew over Manhattan too often, and images the city as an octopus and its efforts at renovation as "cancerous" ruins on ruins. Once again, he criticizes the stupidity of federal officials, liberal U.N. giveaway programs to ingrate countries, and liberal young long-hairs.

Bibliography: Collins and Traylor.

SWAN, GOMEZ. In *Survival . . . Zero!,* he had a criminal gang in which Larry Beers was a *pistolero* when Beers was a teenager.

SWAN, JOE. In *Day of the Guns,* he aids Tiger Mann by being an informer. Swan's wife was a heroin addict who murdered her supplier for giving her an overdose.

SWAN, JUNIOR. In "Return of the Hood," Ryan scares Ernie South into talking by reminding him of the time Ryan permanently crippled Swan's hands.

SWEIBER, MAX. In *Day of the Guns,* he is a hood from Chicago, sent with Tommy Williams to kill Tiger Mann, who kills both of them.

SWISS, MILDRED ("MILLIE"). In "Man Alone," she was a European-born redheaded beauty in her late twenties. She associated with Ray Hilquist.

SWITCHER, MOTHER. In *One Lonely Night,* he is not a woman. He runs the pie factory where Charlie Moffit worked until he was murdered.

T

TABOR, MISS. In *The Body Lovers,* she is Dulcie McInnes's receptionist. Mike whispers something, not revealed, in her ear that, according to Dulcie, terrified her.

TAG. In *The Erection Set,* he was an air force buddy of Dog Kelly having something to do with British Spitfires.

TAGGART. In *The Last Cop Out,* he was one of Mark Shelby's men, recently murdered.

TALBOT. In *Day of the Guns,* he is a British embassy employee with minor functions. Rondine Lund (really Edith Caine) knows him. In *The Death Dealers,* Talbot is a British agent at the U.N. Described as Oxford educated, he knows Teish El Abin from a mission in Selachin and is invited to Teish's party. In *The By-Pass Control,* Virgil Adams informs Tiger by phone that Talbot and Edith have gone to Washington, D.C.

TALBOT, H. In *Bloody Sunrise. See* Mann, Tiger.

TALMAGE, RENÉE. In *Survival . . . Zero!,* she is William Dorn's beautiful coconspirator, in her thirties. She attracts and misleads Mike Hammer, treats him at one point to a vibrator massage, but, confronted with the truth, kills herself with a cyanide capsule.

TARBOK, MEL. In *The Erection Set,* Dog Kelly recalls that fifteen years ago this agent had Box number 655 in a post office.

TARBUSH. In "Return of the Hood," he was imprisoned in Elmira "for pushing Bennies on the teenage set." Freed, he owns Tarbush's Coffee Shop, where Fly seeks Ernie South for heroin.

TASS, WHITEY. In *The Delta Factor,* he is a powerful New York criminal. When Gorman Yard worked for him and tried to cheat him, Tass had Yard imprisoned and later killed. Aware that Bernice Case and Joey Jolley are aiding Morgan, Tass has Bernice killed, pursues Jolley to the island where Morgan is busy rescuing Victor Sable, and tries to kill Jolley. Sal Dekker kills Tass instead.

TATE, HELEN ("IRISH"). In *The Deep,* she was Deep's old love and is now a Broadway actress. She is called Roscoe Tate's half-sister but is not. Helen and Deep grew up together in the old neighborhood. When he returns, he learns that she consorted with Bennett, recently murdered, and then with Lenny Sobel. Helen, in turn, suspects Deep of still being a criminal. Helen is hurt caring for Tally Lee. At the Knights Owl Club, Deep saves her from being killed by Roscoe.

TATE, ROSCOE. In *The Deep,* he grew up in the same criminal neighborhood as did Bennett, Deep and Helen Tate, among others. He and Helen call themselves half-siblings, but in reality Roscoe was Helen's father's stepson. Roscoe has become an admired journalist who despises Deep. In reality, Roscoe is frustratedly in love with Helen, is a murderer, and would shoot Deep to death, in Helen's presence, in the Knights Owl Club, but for the fact that Deep kills him and thus saves her.

TAYLOR, DARCY. In *The Erection Set,* he is one of the guests at Walt Gentry's party and is evidently connected with the movie industry.

TAYLOR, MOLLIE. In "The Veiled Woman," Karl Terris mentions her as Ann Fullerton's friend when Karl calls Ann's mother for information. Mollie is fictitious.

TED. In *The Girl Hunters,* he is the owner of a water hole frequented in the afternoon by reporters, including Bayliss Henry.

TEDDY. In *Black Alley,* he is one of Lorenzo Ponti's guards, stationed on the grounds of Ponti's estate.

TEDDY. In *The Body Lovers,* he is the owner of a lower Manhattan restaurant or bar where Mike Hammer meets Hy Gardner.

TEDDY. In *The Snake,* he owns "a lush restaurant" where Mike Hammer meets Cindy Adams, Joey Adams, and Hy Gardner to receive information on Sally Devon Torrence.

TEDDY THE LUNGER. In *The Deep,* Deep recalls defeating Teddy in a fight with ice picks years ago in the Knights Owl Club.

TEDESCO, TEDDY. In *The Death Dealers,* he is an American agent sent into Selachin. He is currently in danger. Peter Moore is dispatched to rescue him. Tiger Mann persuades Teish El Abin to order their rescue and release.

TEEN, ED. In *The Big Kill,* he is the dapper, suave mastermind behind the city's racketeers. Lou Grindle is his main underling. Johnny and Martin are two of his gunnies. He is being blackmailed by Marsha Lee and Toady Link, until he is killed. Teen's empire will collapse once the authorities are aware that Grindle, Johnny, and Martin are dead and that Georgia Lucas is about to reveal being forced to help cause Charlie Fallon's death.

TEISH EL ABIN. In *The Death Dealers,* he is the childless king of Selachin, a suddenly oil-rich country near Saudi Arabia. In his early sixties and evidently impotent, he is engaged to Vey Locca and wants Tiger Mann to impregnate her to generate a royal heir. His coming to New York and Washington to obtain a government loan to permit deep oil drilling challenges Tiger and his cohorts. Sarim Shey, Teish's traitorous adviser, conspires with Malcolm Turos, a Soviet agent. Tiger foils their machinations.

TELEVISION AND SPILLANE. *Mickey Spillane's Mike Hammer* was a seventy-eight-episode series in 1958–1959 starring Darren McGavin as Hammer. *Mickey Spillane's Margin for Murder* was a 1981 TV film based on characters created by Spillane, including some from *I, the Jury,* and starring Kevin Dobson as Hammer. *Mickey Spillane's Murder Me, Murder You* was a 1983 TV film again based on Spillane characters (some from *Vengeance Is Mine!*) and starring Stacy Keach as Hammer. *Mickey Spillane's Mike Hammer* was a durable TV series, airing, with interruptions, in 1984–1987. Spillane successfully demanded that his Hammer must carry a .45 (not a sissy .38) and have beautiful women all about him, and that the series must be shot in New York City. Production was interrupted when Keach was arrested in April 1984 for possession of cocaine in England and served a prison sentence there. *Mickey Spillane's More Than Murder* (1984), *The Return of Mickey Spillane's Mike Hammer* (1986), and *Mike Hammer, Murder Takes All* (1989), were made-for-TV movies and again starred Keach, as did *The New Mike Hammer* (1986–1987, twenty-two episodes) and *Mike Hammer, Private Eye* (1997–1998, twenty-six episodes). *The Return of Mickey Spillane's Mike Hammer* (1986), *Come Die with Me* (1994) and *Deader Than Ever* (1996) starred Rob Estes as Hammer. Spillane made guest appearances on "The Buick [Milton] Berle Show" (1954), "Person to Person" (1954), "The Ford Show" (1956), "The Match Game" (1956), "Art Linkletter's House Party" (1968), "The Mike Douglas Show" (1970), "Columbo: Publish or Perish" (1974), "Tomorrow" (1978), and "Late Night with Conan O'Brien" (1995), and in the 1970s and 1980s in numberless ads for Lifebuoy soap and Miller beer, the latter with the actress Lee Meredith, whom he regularly called "the doll."

Bibliography: Collins; Collins and Traylor; Leslie Halliwell, *Halliwell's Who's Who in the Movies,* ed. John Walker, 13th ed. (New York: Harper/Perennial, 1997); David M. Inman, *Performers' Television Credits, 1948–2000,* 3 vols. (Jefferson, N.C.: Mc-Farland & Company, 2001); Alex McNeil, *Total Television: The Comprehensive Guide to Programming from 1948 to the Present,* 4th ed. (New York: Penguin, 1996).

TEMPLE, LILY. In *The Delta Factor,* she is a prostitute with whom Bernice Case is friendly. Did Spillane name Temple as he did because of Temple Drake in *Sanctuary* (1931) by William Faulkner?

TEMPLE, MITCH. In *The Body Lovers,* he is a columnist for *The News.* He writes about Broadway events, politics, and the Mafia. His digging into a possible connection between the murders of Maxine Delaney and Helen Poston results in his being stabbed to death by Orslo Bucher. Temple's friends, Biff and Al Casey, help Mike Hammer make sense of Temple's investigation.

TERRIS, KARL. In "The Veiled Woman," in Africa while seeking uranium deposits, this multimillionaire, the narrator, met and married Lodi (*see* Terris, Lodi), a descendant of a race from Mars and Venus. Communist agents, led by Ann Fullerton and Sergi Porkov, suspect them of having a cosmic-energy machine. He kills several enemies. Porkov kills Lodi. Ann, falling for Terris, kills Porkov, makes love with Terris, who kills Ann. Terris calls himself Alan Carney when calling Ann's mother for information. Spillane has Terris, while rebuking Ann, voice red-blooded Americans' Cold War definition of Soviet-style "people's democracy": "Slave labor, purges, secret police, rigged trials, mass executions."

TERRIS, LODI. In "The Veiled Woman," she is a Martian-Venusian African, entirely gorgeous but all green, hence veiled, and sometimes radioactive. At age twenty, she married Karl Terris, came with him to New York, appears before a federal commission, and is killed by Communist-agent Sergi Porkov.

THELMA. In *The Deep,* she works for Wilson Batten in his office.

THERESA. In "I'll Die Tomorrow," Rudolph Lees paid her to let him sexually torture her. He planned to play with big Joan and Theresa together later.

THOMAS, REGINALD. In *Survival . . . Zero!,* Beaver stole his wallet, along with those of others.

THOMPSON, PAPPY. In "The Affair with the Dragon Lady," he was a general under whose command the Dragon Lady crew flew during the war. He barks orders helping them rescue the downed F-100 pilot.

THOMPSON, WHITEY. In "The Flier," he is an army buddy whom Joe Conway tells Cat Fallon he will ask to check old photograph albums to try to locate Verdo and Cristy. (Thompson's nickname is also spelled "Whity" once.)

THORPE. In *The Erection Set*, this was the last name of the female comptroller at the Barrin factory, now deceased.

THURBER, RICHARD ("RICH"). In "Tomorrow I Die," he is an ex-movie actor. The hero is mistaken for him and is called Rich by Carol LaFont, who falls in love with him (and he with her). Rich is taken hostage by Auger and his fellow bank robbers but foils their plans. The upshot is that the police presumably kill all but Trigger, whom Auger left to guard Rich and the other hostages. Rich, a killer at heart, murders Trigger.

TICE, VERN. In "The Affair with the Dragon Lady," he was the narrator's copilot aboard the Dragon Lady.

TILA, PRINCESS. In *The Ship That Never Was*, she is the naive ruler of descendants of exiles from Grandau, all of whom live on Montique Island. Larry Damar and Josh Toomey rescue her from Aktur Cilon, Embor Linero, and the crew of the Grandau submarine.

TILLMAN. In *The Body Lovers*, he and Kraus hired Mike to look into an accident at the Capeheart Building.

TILLSON. In *The Death Dealers*, he owns a garage where Virgil Adams promises to have a car ready should Tiger Mann need it. Tiger evidently didn't.

TILLSON. In *The Snake*, he was a bookie who, when killed a year earlier, was replaced by Kid Hand.

TILLSON. In "Tomorrow I Die," he is mentioned as a Forestry Service employee. He does not appear in the story.

TILLSON, CUBBY. In *The Erection Set*, he tried to kid Cross McMillan about Cross's wife Sheila, for which McMillan beat him up.

TIMELY, MRS. GUSTAVE ("GUSSIE"). In *The Delta Factor*, she is the widowed landlady who rented rooms in her house on the West Side of Manhattan in the Forties to strange characters such as Bernice Case, Sal Dekker, Melvin

Gross, Morgan, Mario Tullius, and Gorman Yard. Morgan later obtains information from her.

TIMOTHY ("TIM"). In *The Day the Sea Rolled Back,* he is a native of Ara Island, Josh's father, and the friend of Vincent Damar and Larry Damar. In *The Ship That Never Was,* Timothy's full name, Timothy Toomey, is given.

TOBANO. In *The Erection Set,* he is a hospital clerk who notifies his brother, Sergeant Vince Tobano, about injuries suffered by Bridey-the-Greek and Markham.

TOBANO, SERGEANT VINCE. In *The Erection Set,* he is an honest policeman who questions Dog Kelly about Bridey-the-Greek and Markham, after Dog tortured the two, and after Tobano's brother, a hospital clerk, alerted Vince. Dog later delivers the casket of heroin to Vince.

TODD, HIRAM. In *The Erection Set,* he owns and operates a run-down old club in Linton. Formerly big and strong, he is wasted by cancer. He helps Dog Kelly.

TODD, TONY. In *Kiss Me, Deadly. See* Affia, Al.

"TOGETHER WE KILL" (1953). Short story. (Characters: Claire, Francis, Gloria, Helen, Henri, Jean, Joe, Guy Kimball.) Joe, the narrator, parachuted into France during World War II to blow up a key bridge. By chance met Claire, a young French partisan, who led him to the bridge. They made moonlit love and promised to try to meet at a certain bistro off Broadway on the ninth of every month after the war. He destroyed his target, was picked up by plane, and escaped. Seven years later, Joe, a skilled bachelor engineer in New York, is offered work in Bolivia but has to be married. Claire, now a famous Broadway star, has probably forgotten their rendezvous plans. Joe drifts into the bistro anyway, meets her, and wedding bells will soon sound.

TOHEY, JAMIE. In "Me, Hood!," he keeps his laundry carts near Ryan's apartment.

TOLLY. In *The Big Kill,* she is one of Cookie Harkin's girlfriends. She modeled for a painter; when he started selling nude photos of her, she started blackmailing him. Although she has a Bronx boyfriend, she offers her sexy self to Mike Hammer, who declines.

TOM. In *The Death Dealers,* he is an ex-Selachin native, now a Brooklyn resident. Jack Brant gets him to help Tiger Mann. Tom's friends are Dick and Harry.

TOM LEE FOY. In *The Death Dealers,* he sells litchi nuts near Flood's Warehouse, according to George Tung, in conversation with Tiger Mann.

TOMMY. In "Everybody's Watching Me," he is one of Mark Renzo's thugs, killed during the drug bust.

"TOMORROW I DIE" (1956). Short story. (Characters: Allen, Auger, Bernie, Carmen, George, Harold, Carol LaFont, Sheriff LaFont, Leo, Richard Thurber, Tillson, Trigger, Miss Whalen.) The narrator gets off a train for some beer at a bar in a hot little desert town. Carol LaFont, there with Sheriff LaFont, her father, mistakes him for Richard Thurber, ex–movie star. Four thugs enter. Their leader is fat, conceited Auger; the others are Allen, Trigger, and Leo. They slug the sheriff, kill the bartender, and wait. Bernie, their pal, walks in with George, LaFont's deputy. Leo slugs George. Carmen, another thug, is to lure Harold, the mayor, Carol's fiancé. But Harold is away. The gang plans to rob the local bank. They put Carol, Harold, George, "Rich Thurber," and the others as hostages in two cars, the lead one being the sheriff's. They execute the robbery, and both cars speed out of town. LaFont drives onto a remote country road and raises such dust that the trailing car, with Bernie, Carmen, Carol, and George, skids onto the shoulder. Thrown clear, Carol is uninjured, but George is badly hurt. LaFont backs into the other car, and Bernie and Carmen tumble down a gully, with the loot. LaFont says a lonely man has a cabin nearby. Auger takes everyone remaining to an old man's cabin nearby. In the morning, Auger tells Rich and Carol to take the old man's Jeep to the gully, retrieve the loot, and return. Any mishap, and gun-happy Trigger gets to shoot the hostages. Carol and Rich, by now fond of each other, follow Auger's orders. When they are returning, they are spotted by a police plane, and Harold leads some squad cars to the scene. Harold callously tells Carol his men must rush the cabin, regardless of casualties. Rich and Carol sense that Harold has headlines and consequent political advancement in mind. Rich misleads the police as to the cabin's location. Harold remains with Carol and Rich, who slugs him, leaves him on the road, and drives with Carol near the cabin. Rich hides the money and prepares a note for Auger saying where. The two enter. Rich is frisked for big weapons he might have taken from Bernie and Carmen but didn't. Telling Trigger to shoot the hostages, Auger, with Allen, goes for the loot. Trigger, toying with his weapon, boasts too long. The police open fire on Auger and the others down the road. Rich pulls a .32 from a sleeve holster and kills Trigger.

TONY. In *The Deep,* he is one of Lenny Sobel's gunmen. When Deep escapes their clutches, Tony is grateful that Deep merely knocks him unconscious and lets him live.

TONY. In "Killer Mine," he and Fat Mary, probably his wife, operate Tony's Pizza. They both give Lieutenant Joe Scanlon useful information.

TONY. In *The Killing Man,* the Italian woman who runs a coffee shop and tells Mike Hammer about Richard Smiley, her neighbor, and also mentions Tony, who may be her husband, son, lover, or whatever.

TONY. In *One Lonely Night,* he is the bartender at the place where Velda and Mike Hammer meet. When two drunks leer at Velda, she decks one and Mike batters the other.

TOOMEY. In *Day of the Guns,* he is a tough agent who represents Martin Grady and aids Tiger Mann significantly. While occupying Mann's hotel room in Mann's place, Toomey is murdered by Vidor Churis.

TOOMEY, JOSH. In *The Ship That Never Was,* he and Larry Damar rescue Vali Steptur, sail to Montique Island, and save Princess Tali and all of her subjects from her would-be Grandau killers. In *The Day the Sea Rolled Back,* Josh's last name is not given. (*See* Josh.)

TOOMEY, TIMOTHY ("TIM"). In *The Ship That Never Was,* he and his friend Vincent Damar follow their sons, Josh Toomey and Larry Damar, to Montique Island too late to help them rescue Princess Tali and her subjects.

TOPPETT. In *The Delta Factor,* he is gossipy Ma Toppett's husband. While Morgan talks to her, Toppett is busy snoring in front of his television set.

TOPPETT, MA. In *The Delta Factor,* she is a gossipy neighbor of Mrs. Gustave ("Gussie") Timely. Ma enjoys watching her neighbors and tells Morgan about Gorman Yard.

TORN, BERGA. In *Kiss Me, Deadly,* she is an attractive Swiss-Italian girl, smuggled with Nicholas Raymond, was Carl Evello's mistress, was confined to a sanitarium by Dr. Martin Soberin, and was about to reveal information about the Mafia when she was enabled to escape and begin hitchhiking. Mike gives her a lift, but she is soon murdered. Mike realizes that her cryptic message to him is about stomachs, has her autopsied, and recovers a key in her stomach leading to Raymond's City Athletic Club locker.

TORNAY, LILY. In *The Death Dealers,* she is an agent working for Interpol and the State Department. She is assigned to tail Tiger Mann, who warns her of her danger, but takes her clothes so she cannot leave her room in the Taft Hotel. This results in Malcolm Turos's finding and killing her. Tiger seems not to mind greatly, because he plans to avenge her death.

TORRENCE, SALLY DEVON. In *The Snake,* she was a showgirl and "a shack job" for mobsters, married a man named Devon, and had a child, Sue Devon, by him. After Devon died, Simpson Torrence got her off a drug charge and later married her. While being cared for by her friend Annette Lee, Sally died of acute alcoholism in the Catskills. She left a letter for Sue implicating Torrence in a heist he engineered with Black Conley and Sonny Motley.

TORRENCE, SIMPSON ("SIM"). In *The Snake,* he is a former New York D.A., the husband of deceased Sally Devon Torrence, and the father by adoption of her daughter, Sue Devon. Torrence is campaigning to be governor of New York. Torrence hires Mike Hammer to find who is trying to kill Sue. Mike's investigation leads him to learn that Torrence is "the snake" who masterminded the heist by Black Conley and Sonny Motley of an armored car back in 1932. Torrence foiled the heist for political advancement. Conley disappeared with the loot. Motley, out of prison after thirty years, determines upon revenge, in the course of which Torrence is shot dead.

TORRES, JUAN. In *The Killing Man,* he is named as the big drug dealer for whom Anthony DiCica worked beginning about 1960.

TOSCIO. In *Kiss Me, Deadly,* he owns a restaurant where Velda says she met Eddie Connely to gain information.

TOULÉ, RAUL. In *Survival . . . Zero!,* Mike Hammer finds Jenkins and Wiley in Toulé's basement coffee shop.

TOWERS, AUSTIN. In *Survival . . . Zero!,* he is a marijuana dealer. Mike Hammer forces him to take him to Caesar Mario Tulley, one of Towers's customers.

"TOYS FOR THE MAN-CHILD" (1975). Short story. (Characters: None named.) Spillane hesitantly visits a toyshop, fears he will be the only adult, but meets another man who also loves "pre-plastic" toys. Spillane admits having a little boat he sails in the bath tub but won't let his "kid" commandeer. He also fondly recalls his long-gone climbing monkeys, rubber-band guns, and mock tanks made from thread spools.

TRAUB, CHARLIE. In "The Flier," he was Tucker Stacy's loyal chief mechanic. After Stacy's death, Traub works loyally for Cat Fallon.

TRAVERS, LIEUTENANT. In "The Bastard Bannerman," he is an honest Culver City police officer who helps Cat Cay Bannerman and is on hand when Cat turns Vance Colby over to him.

TREEGLOS, EDWARD ("EDDIE"). In "The Veiled Woman," he is an investigator who helps Karl Terris when Terris's wife Lodi is kidnapped.

TRENT. In "Killer Mine," he owns a candy store near which Ralph Callahan lives.

TRENT. In *The Last Cop Out,* he is a policeman who shows Gill Burke and Sergeant Al Schneider the grisly color photo of William R. Hays, horribly mutilated.

TRIGGER. In "Tomorrow I Die," he is a gun-happy member of Auger's bank-robbing gang. Auger distresses him by calling him Jason. Richard Thurber, one of Auger's hostages, hints that Trigger is homosexual. When Trigger gets boastfully careless, Thurber kills him.

TRIVAGO, CARMEN. In *Kiss Me, Deadly,* he is a dapper hotel manager. Mike rushes to see him, once he learns that Trivago knew Nicholas Raymond. Mike pommels Trivago into telling him about Raymond.

TROTTER, JEAN. In *Vengeance Is Mine!,* she is a model working for Juno Reeves. Chester Wheeler had a date with her, recognized her as a friend of his daughter, and got blackmailed and then murdered. To escape, Jean said she was eloping. Instead, she was murdered. Connie Wales tells Mike Hammer that Jean changed her name. He determines she was originally Julia Travesky.

TROY, HELEN. In "Everybody's Watching Me," she is a beautiful young woman, almost thirty years old, victimized by Mark Renzo, and ashamed of her past—that is, until she falls in love with "Joe Boyle" and he encourages her to regain her self-respect. They check into a hotel registered as Mr. and Mrs. Valiscivitch. This Helen [of] Troy must be beautiful.

TRUSKY, LIEUTENANT. In "The Flier," he is a big, congenial police officer in Celada. He and Del Reed, a state's attorney in Florida, try to investigate Tucker Stacy's activities, but it remains for Stacy's friend Cat Fallon to solve Stacy's murder.

TUCKER. In *The Big Kill,* this is the name of the bar where Cookie Harkins meets Mike Hammer.

TUCKER ("TUCK"). In *The Long Wait,* he is a cruel, crooked cop under Captain Lindsey and takes orders from Havis Gardiner, the bank president. Tucker mistreats John McBride. When McBride sees him outside Gardiner's window about to shoot McBride, he shoots Tucker dead.

TUCKER, RAY. In *The Body Lovers,* he is the taxi driver who tells Mike he followed the speeding car in which Greta Service was a passenger but lost her.

TULLEY, CAESAR MARIO. In *Survival . . . Zero!,* he is a professional panhandler. Austin Towers takes Mike Hammer to Tulley and a friend of Tulley's. The friend tells Mike where Beaver has a room.

TULLIUS, MARIO. In *The Delta Factor,* he was one of Mrs. Gustave ("Gussie") Timely's tenants. She tells Morgan that Tullius died of pneumonia.

TUNG, GEORGE. In *The Death Dealers,* he is a Chinese laundryman who tells Tiger Mann that James Harvey and Tom Lee Foy both sell litchi nuts.

TUNNEY. In *The Killing Man,* he does guard duty with Eddie outside Lewis Ferguson's cabin. Penta kills both men. (Mike Hammer's delay while talking with Velda may have cost Eddie and Tunney their lives.)

TUREZ, MAJOR. In *The Delta Factor,* he is Carlos Ortega's tall, stiff assistant.

TURK, THE. In *The Erection Set,* he is a European drug dealer and sends poor Bridey-the-Greek and Markham to New York to kill Dog Kelly. When Le Fleur's men wound The Turk, he blows the whistle on Le Fleur, who is arrested but soon murdered.

TURLEY. In *The Last Cop Out,* he runs the pawnshop where Jimmie Corrigan shot Ted Proctor. When Gill Burke and Captain Bill go there, Mark Shelby shoots from ambush at Gill but, when Gill ducks, kills Turley.

TUROS, MALCOLM. In *The Death Dealers,* he is a Soviet KGB assassin. Tiger Mann tangled with him in Brazil, shot him in the neck, and permanently damaged his voice. Turos is assigned to capture Teish El Abin and also eliminate Tiger. Turos almost kills Edith Caine, does kill his colleague Parnell Rath and Lily Tornay, and captures Teish. Tiger rescues Teish and kills Turos. In Brazil, Turos called himself Arturo Pensa.

***THE TWISTED THING* (1966).** Novel. (Characters: Andy, Mrs. Baxter, Carmen, Captain Pat Chambers, Dr. Clark, Miss Cook, Roxy Coulter, Bill Cuddy, Dillon, Dilwick, Charlie Drew, George, Martha Ghent, Rhoda Ghent, Richard Ghent, Richard Ghent Jr., Arthur Graham, William Graham, Myra Grange, Dr. Griffin, Hammer, Mike Hammer, Harvey, Henry, Janie, Herron Mallory, Mrs. Herron Mallory, Charlotte Manning, Mary, Mrs. Margaret Murphy, Alice Nichols, Billy Parks, Pee Wee, Dr. Pierce, Sergeant Price, Sloppy Joe, Mrs. Rudolph York, Rudolph York, Ruston York.)

Billy Parks, a decent little ex-con arrested in Sidon, a town outside New York City, uses his one phone call to appeal to Mike Hammer for help. Mike drives to Sidon and finds Billy being battered by Dilwick, a vicious cop. Mike challenges Dilwick, slugs him, and orders Parks released to Rudolph York, a rich, widowed scientist, for whom Parks chauffeurs. Barging into the York estate, Mike learns that Ruston York, Rudolph's son, age fourteen and a brilliant, home-educated lad, has been snatched; further, that Rudolph fingered Parks as the suspect and paid Dilwick $10,000 to torture him secretly for information. Mike rebukes Rudolph and his live-in family members, demands another $10,000 from Rudolph to seek young Ruston, and boasts of his past successes as a no-holds-barred private detective. Billy returns, re-employed. Mike asks about Rudolph's servants, and especially eyes "Miss Malcom," Ruston's governess, whom Mike recognizes as Roxy Coulter, ex-stripper (but also a nurse).

Mike quizzes Roxy about Ruston, whom she calls brilliant and whom she has helped for two years. She says Rudolph recently suffered damaging radiation burns. Mike inspects Ruston's room, notes his pajama set is missing its bottoms, returns to the living room, and meets the following: Rudolph's icy sister Martha Ghent, her henpecked husband Richard Ghent, their half-"pansy" son Richard Ghent Jr., and Rhoda Ghent, their daughter; and Archer Graham and William Graham, Rudolph's nephews, and Alice Nichols, Rudolph's sexy niece. Questioning everyone, Mike learns that Myra Grange, Rudolph's laboratory helper, left work and was in her town apartment at the time of the kidnapping. Mike goes to a local gas station. The attendant says he saw Myra's car the night of the kidnapping and gives Mike her address. Mike forces himself in there. Myra insists she was not out driving that night. Mike stops at a honky-tonk near Sidon, sees the bartender swabbing his bar with Ruston's pajama bottoms, and learns he got them from a clam digger named Bill Cuddy, who lives in a beach shack. Mike goes there and rouses the drunken Cuddy, who shows him a shack near which he found the pajamas. Mike checks around, finds naked Ruston, comforts the brave, likable kid, hides him when they hear noises, is then attacked by two men, wounds one and rips another's mouth, but is kicked unconscious.

Ruston shakes Mike awake and tells him this: The attackers fled looking for him; he doubled back to Mike; he had been slugged in his room, put on a boat, heard one assailant named as Mallory, was brought to the shack by a drunk, threw his pajamas out the window to alert any possible passerby, and was left alone tied and naked. Mike drives him to his father. Ruston goes to bed. Rudolph gives Mike a check for $10,000. When Mike says someone named Mallory is involved, Rudolph says "the dirty, man-eating bitch has sold me out," vainly seeks papers in a secret place by his fireplace wall, takes some medicine, and persuades Mike to be Ruston's bodyguard on the quiet, because the boy is on the verge of a scientific breakthrough. Mike goes to a guest room. Alice is there and undresses provocatively. Mike tells her he is too tired; she leaves; he falls asleep and dreams of Alice, whose undulations contrast with Myra's mannish moves. Sudden conclusion: Myra is a lesbian. Mike dresses, seeks but cannot find Rudolph, notes Rudolph's .32 is missing, and drives past Henry, Rudolph's sleepy gatekeeper, to Myra's apartment—only to find Rudolph murdered by a meat cleaver in his head.

Mike phones Sergeant Price of the state police. Mike notices that someone searched absent Myra's room and that Rudolph's gun is missing. Dilwick, notified by Price, enters with a coroner and Price, who praises Mike and suppresses Dilwick's rage. Explaining details, Mike agrees to work with Price, returns to the Yorks, and talks with several people. Roxy explains she was in her room. Mike tenderly breaks the news to Ruston, who is distraught, hugs Mike, and is comforted when Mike calls him brave.

Mike informs the family members of the murder. They react variously. Alice is sarcastic. Martha wonders about Myra. Mike rouses Parks, who explains that he was in his room and while there heard three people, including Mike, leave. Intending to sleep briefly, Mike asks Harvey, the helpful butler, to awaken him when the police arrive. But when they come, Dilwick orders Harvey to let Mike keep on sleeping. Suddenly Mike hears Ruston playing the piano magnificently, and learns this from him: Price and Dilwick have taken statements from family members; Myra's empty car was found in the water; she is presumed washed away; Parks and Roxy retrieved Rudolph's car, at Myra's; Price wants to see Mike. At Price's office, Mike learns that Myra's body may be swept out to sea and that Dilwick, though thuggish, is sharp and has men watching her place. Mike evades them, gets into Myra's apartment, and finds documents hidden behind a baseboard. Going to a diner for a hamburger, he checks the crumbly papers and finds stock certificates and Rudolph's will naming Myra sole beneficiary.

Driving to the estate, Mike pockets the will and puts the certificates in the glove compartment. He visits Roxy and learns this: Mallory is a name unknown to her; Rudolph liked Rhoda, then liked Alice more, said Myra would handle his estate. Roxy dances before Mike; they kiss, but consummation is stymied when Ruston, who is in the adjacent room, asks for a drink of water please. Parks tells Mike he knows no Mallory either. Mike visits Rudolph's laboratory and sees Richard Ghent Jr. rifling Rudolph's files, taking a document but leaving a will in which Rudolph favored Ruston and Alice, and scurrying out. Two men beat up Richard outside and flee when Mike pursues and shoots. Another shot rings out. Parks yells that Roxy is shot. Mike finds her wounded in the shoulder and Ruston in shock. Mike recovers a .32 slug. From Rudolph's gun? He summons a doctor and squeezes Richard into saying he took only a document (with an unknown attachment) that he signed for Rudolph confessing he stole some money from Rudolph; his assailants took it from him. The doctor sedates Roxy and Ruston. Mike gets Parks to guard Ruston all night.

Mike phones details to Price's office, gets Alice's town address in Wooster, learns Myra's hat was found floating by the inlet, and checks with somnolent Henry, undoubtedly given sleeping pills in place of aspirin, to prevent his watching the gate. Mike visits Alice and soon enjoys bedding down with her. As Mike walks out later, he is slugged, taken for a ride in a bumpy car, dragged into some woods, and asked by a masked man where it is. Where what is?,

Mike answers. They scuffle, and the stranger runs away. Mike drives the thug's stolen car into Wooster, retrieves his own car near Alice's place, and concludes: Richard Jr.'s attackers took something from him but then dropped it when Mike shot at them; they thought Mike had it. Mike searches their getaway path, finds and pockets a dew-sealed envelope, returns to the York estate, finds Roxy better, and tells Parks to walk with Ruston outside. Mike opens the envelope, finds secretly snapped pornographic photos in which a knowing Alice compromises Myra. Ah! Myra blackmailed Rudolph about something, until he got Alice to do this to silence her. What could Myra have on Rudolph? Mike checks Rudolph's fireplace and finds a compartment, empty except for a torn New York *Globe* newspaper clipping dated October 9, fourteen years ago, just when Ruston was born.

A leggy worker (later identified as Miss Cook) in the town library helps Mike find the identical *Globe* issue, gets scared by his questions, thinks he regards her as a lesbian, and admits Myra was in the library recently. A pharmacist verifies the pills Mike took from Henry are sleeping pills. Mike bursts in on Alice, confronts her with the incriminating photos, finds William Graham in her bedroom, recognizes him as the one who took him for a ride, pommels him, and makes Alice admit she promised a share of Rudolph's bequest to William and his brother Arthur if they retrieved the photos. Mike drives to New York City, gets Captain Pat Chambers to meet him at the big public library, and the two find the appropriate newspaper account: Herron Mallory accused Rudolph York of having Mallory's baby boy switched in the hospital for York's dead baby boy; the nurse, Rita Cambell, in a written statement denied the event; Mallory, a petty criminal, dropped charges. Mike wonders if Mallory waited fourteen years, snatched Ruston to shake Rudolph down, bungled the crime, followed Rudolph to Myra's place, and killed him there. Chambers lets Mike read Mallory's rap sheet, which merely teases his puzzled mind.

Mike visits Price, in his office with Dilwick, who accuses Mike of breaking into Myra's apartment. Mike boasts of doing so and produces Rudolph's two wills. Dilwick hits Mike, whom Price then restrains. Reading the wills, Dilwick concludes this: Mike and Alice told Rudolph that Myra was Rudolph's blackmailer; when Rudolph attacked her, she killed him; Mike killed Myra, and he and Alice will split Alice's bequest. Mike guffaws at Dilwick, who, however—Mike fears—could get the Graham brothers to implicate him. Dilwick leaves. Mike tells Price that Ruston is the mysterious Mallory's son and that Myra must be found. At the library, Mike learns that Miss Cook is missing, finds her address, and with her worried landlady's permission checks the girl's room. All is tidy; she is gone, but he finds a torrid love letter to the girl from Myra, in the nurse Rita Cambell's handwriting. Price lets Mike check photos of Myra's half-submerged car, and Mike has a hunch. After phoning the York estate to learn that Ruston, Roxy, and Parks are safe, he drives to Myra's crash sight, finds evidence her car was forced off the road into the water, strips to his underwear, and drifts as she would to the north shore, presses through briars festooned with bits of her dress to a shack, and finds it empty. A codger nearby tells him a slob (answering to Dilwick's description) was there. Ah! Dilwick has Myra under wraps.

Mike returns via a bridge, dresses in his car, gets to a phone and calls Price, learns Myra is still missing, has breakfast, and locates Dilwick and follows him to the latter's all-night girlfriend. Next morning he buys a bottle of milk from a vendor, follows Dilwick again, and is led at night into the country. A car from behind, with two of Dilwick's crooked cops inside, passes and cuts him off. A fight ensues. Mike shoots one dead; the other kicks him unconscious but runs off. Recovering, Mike drives near the York estate, hides his car, phones Price from a neighboring bungalow, and gets him to back off a while. Mike sleeps in a haystack, and at night makes his way past Dilwick's guards into Roxy's bedroom. She and Ruston are there. Dilwick has Parks downstairs, unhurt. Ruston bravely agrees to play decoy to track the killer, but suddenly Mike decides he doesn't need any decoy. He sneaks out and though shot at escapes to his hidden car, and sleeps in it.

Next noon Mike drives into Sidon, checks physicians to see who might have treated any of his assailants, and spots at the door the thug whose mouth he tore. Mike follows that man's car out of town, forces the fellow off the road, commandeers his .38, tortures his stitched mouth, and learns this: Nelson, a casino owner, is his boss; he knows no one named Mallory. When Price arrives, Mike tells him about Nelson, then finds the casino himself. He fights his way into Nelson's office, and calls the rat-faced fellow Mallory. Asked where Myra—that is, Rita Cambell—is, Mallory loses some teeth fighting Mike, and says this: Myra is in his nearby boathouse; he knows no Miss Cook; he admits Ruston is his son and Ruston's kidnapping was revenge on Rudolph, whom Mallory didn't kill. Mallory's men approach, and Mike forces Mallory to the boathouse, where both Myra and Miss Cook are tied. Dilwick, who brought Miss Cook there, enters. Mike wounds him, but Dilwick shoots Mike's .45 out of his hand. Mallory bawls out Dilwick for "bleeding" him. Dilwick kills Mallory with Mike's gun, intends as a dutiful cop to kill Mike, but Mike pulls the hidden .38 and kills Dilwick. Price and his men enter. Mike briefs him and is allowed further free time.

Mike drives to the York estate past Henry and past Harvey, and accosts Roxy, Ruston, and Parks, who hugs him in dramatic relief. Telling Roxy and Parks he'll explain tomorrow and sending them to bed, he turns to Ruston, who plays the piano beautifully, then suddenly says, "So you found me out, Mr. Hammer." Certainly. Mike explains: Grahams and Ghents sought bequests, worried about the two wills; Myra shook down Rudolph; Rudolph counterblackmailed by having Alice photographed playing lesbian with her; Ruston saw Roxy and Mike kissing, shot at Roxy, whom he—boy genius with maturing sex drive—loves; only Ruston named Mallory as on the boat; Ruston sent Mallory the newspaper clipping; Parks heard Ruston leave the night of the kidnapping; Ruston, age fourteen, figured on a light sentence if ever caught. When Mike pulls his .45, Ruston explains he removed its clip during a hug, covers Mike with his father's .32, and explains: Rudolph, whom he secretly reviled, educated him to be a monster, with prodigious intelligence and knowledge but therefore hopelessly unattractive—"a thing, a twisted thing." He toys with the idea of shooting Mike but, instead, blows out his own brains.

In 1948, after *I, the Jury* was published, Spillane sent Dutton a manuscript titled "For Whom the Gods Would Destroy." Rejected as having an outlandish plot, despite Spillane's claim that the teenaged criminal's personality was based on fact, the narrative became *The Twisted Thing* and enjoyed many fine reviews. Spillane's use of names gets confusing, with two Bills, four Ghents, two Grahams, a Grange, a Price, a Pierce, and three characters changing their names. But Mike's calling Ruston "Lancelot," a character out of Sir Thomas Malory's *Morte d'Arthur,* is an onomastic coup, since Ruston is really Herron Mallory's son and one Graham is an Arthur. *The Twisted Thing* is notable for lightning action but also a greater load of clichés than normal in a Hammer narrative.

Bibliography: Collins and Traylor.

TYNERE, KING. In *The Ship That Never Was,* he was the deposed king of Grandau. His descendant, Princess Tali, rescued by Larry Damar and Josh Toomey, returns to rule.

u

UPGATE, SLIM. In "The Flier," he is a highly influential friend whom Cat Fallon calls on to recommend him to George Clinton of Celada. Clinton then helps Fallon.

UPSIDION, SAL. In "Return of the Hood," he is a numbers boss for whom Wally Pee is a runner.

UTE, GERALD. In *The Body Lovers,* he is a rich, widowered businessman, age sixty-two. Hy Gardner takes Mike to a party thrown by Ute at his townhouse at Fifth Avenue opposite Central Park. Mike learns there that Dulcie McInnes acts as Ute's hostess. Ten years earlier, Ute donated property at Bradbury, on Long Island, for use as embassies for U.N. legations. Belar Ris, a corrupt U.N. delegate, owns one.

UTE, MRS. GERALD. In *The Body Lovers,* she was Ute's wife. She urged him to move from Chicago to New York for its superior social life, was the first to invite Proctor Group models to their parties, but died a year after their move.

V

VALENTE. In *The Delta Factor,* he is Lieutenant Valente's brother, works at Carlos Ortega's switchboard, and warns the lieutenant that Ortega and others are about to attack Morgan at the Rose Castle.

VALENTE, LIEUTENANT. In *The Delta Factor,* he is a corrupt officer assigned under Captain Romero at the Rose Castle. After Morgan kills Romero and Juan Fucilla, he persuades Valente to aid him, be slugged, and emerge after Morgan's escape as a valiant, if unsuccessful, national hero. Valente agrees.

VALENTINE, CINDY. In "I'll Die Tomorrow," Rudolph Lees was hired to kill her before the district attorney could have her investigated. Lees remembers Cindy as his sixteenth victim. He gained entrance to her apartment by offering jewelry. When she undressed before him in gratitude, he first got the idea of sadistically treating women.

VALISCIVITCH. In "Everybody's Watching Me." *See* Vetter.

VALISCIVITCH, MRS. In "Everybody's Watching Me." *See* Troy, Helen.

VALLECK, HAROLD. In *One Lonely Night,* he is an associate of Martin Romberg. Both are Soviet agents. When they follow Mike Hammer and Velda to Oscar Deamer's apartment, Mike kills Romberg and Velda kills Valleck.

VALLER, MITCH. In "Stand Up and Die!," he is a veteran combat pilot of World War II and the Korean conflict. While trying to deliver a load of Maine lobsters by air, he loses an engine and must parachute to safety. He falls in love with Caroline Hart; frustrates her father's and brothers' efforts to profit by seizing land rich in uranium; beats up Billy Bussy, who has laid claims to Caroline; and avoids being hanged by the Harts and Bussy. When the evil men seek to blow Mitch up, he evades them and they all blow up. Mitch and Caroline walk away together.

VANCE. In *Day of the Guns,* while talking with Charlie Corbinet, Mann mentions that Vance was killed by the enemy in Los Angeles.

VANCE, SERGEANT HAL. In "Kick It or Kill!," he is Captain Cox's swaggering but ineffective assistant.

"THE VEILED WOMAN" (1952). Short story. (Characters: Maurice Anton, Winston Blake, Caldwell, Millard Cavendish, Demarest, Ann Fullerton, Eric Fullerton, Mrs. Eric Fullerton, Granger, Gregory, Senator McGill, Mather, Mrs. Mather, Max, Mrs. Morgan, Nekko, Osborne, Sergi Porkov, Rasmussen, Luke Ritter, Stephan, Mollie Taylor, Karl Terris, Lodi Terris, Edward Treeglos.)

Multimillionaire Karl Terris, narrator, and his beautiful, veiled African wife, Lodi Terris, are thought to have a cosmic-energy machine. Russian spies enter their home in Clinton Township, Catskill County, north of New York City, to gain his secret. Terris kills one; their leader, Ann Fullerton, a "college pink," and two remaining thugs—Gregory and Stephan—drug Terris, kidnap Lodi. Terris learns Ann's identity by checking old yearbooks, phones her parents, learns she worked for deceased Maurice Anton and Sergi Porkov, New York importers, but supposedly died in a warehouse fire. Terris tracks Luke Ritter, Porkov's associate, to his office; is slugged unconscious; comes to; after much talk kills both Ritter, by gun, and Nekko, his homosexual guard, by blows. Terris answers Ritter's phone, mimics his voice, learns Lodi is held at the burned warehouse by Ann and Max. Terris goes there, finds Lodi. Gregory and Stephan enter with guns, but Terris outwits them and shoots the three men dead. Government men appear, collar Terris and veiled Lodi for questioning next morning by high-ranking officials. Terris confirms or admits this: He photographed by air African regions rich in uranium deposits; his plane crashed, destroying the pictures; he and Lodi married, chartered a tramp steamer, voyaged to the United States; two passengers later using their cabin died of radiation exposure; Terris knows about harnessing cosmic energy, knowledge of which would cause worldwide death and destruction. When officials want this power for defense, Terris says other nations, including Communist ones, would gain it, and the world would end. Lodi beseeches Terris to reveal this: When his plane crashed, he was saved by descendants of superior beings from Mars via Venus, now living in a vast underground city in Africa. Their unique power, from cosmic radiation, energizes the place and even gives them longevity following brief, controlled personal exposures. Terris got homesick, took Lodi—recently reradiated—to his estate, was attacked by Communists. When the officials are skeptical, Terris removes Lodi's veil and clothing. She is one gorgeous green. Released, the Terrises drive to their estate, only to be confronted by Porkov and Ann. To pressure Terris into revealing his secret, Porkov shoots Lodi dead. Before Terris can attack him, Ann shoots Porkov dead, says she adores macho Terris. He and Ann make furnace-hot love. Ann showers, then asks to share her life with Terris, who shoots her dead, then wonders what the authorities will think now. (So does the nonplussed reader.) In this exceedingly gory story, Spillane extends himself to describe filth in Manhattan streets.

VELDA. In *I, the Jury,* she has been Mike Hammer's beautiful, loyal, helpful secretary for three years. She is tough and carries a .32., likes him greatly, and is distressed when she sees lipstick on him. She would accept his proposal of marriage, which he spoofingly delivers and then withdraws.

In *My Gun Is Quick,* Velda faithfully manages Mike's office and relays messages by phone to him from time to time. His (and perhaps Spillane's) attitude toward women is suggested by Mike's calling Velda "baby," "chick," and "kiddo."

In *Vengeance Is Mine!,* Velda aids Mike, first by flying to Columbus, Ohio, to check into Chester Wheeler's background, and second by flirting with Clyde Williams and thus gaining information about his illegal operations. Mike, who finds Velda wonderfully attractive, narrowly saves her from being raped.

In *One Lonely Night,* Velda and Mike kiss a few times and become tentatively engaged. When Lee Deamer hires Mike to investigate his being blackmailed by his twin brother, Oscar Deamer, Velda helps Mike, notably by flying to Nebraska to check into Oscar's medical records. Velda is kidnapped by three Soviet agents and tortured to induce her to reveal the location of microfilmed State Department documents. She resists, and Mike bursts in and kills all three. In *The Girl Hunters,* Mike, remembering Velda, recalls the gory episode with relish.

In *The Big Kill,* Velda is on a case taking her to Miami. When she phones Mike that it is wrapped up, he orders her to follow up in Cuba. This because Mike, even though he "felt like a heel," is sexually attracted to Marsha Lee.

In *Kiss Me, Deadly,* Velda obtains information about the Mafia from Ed Connely, pretends to be Candy Lewis, and dates Congressman Geyfey and Al Affia, slugs Affia, but is caught by William Mist and taken to Dr. Martin Soberin's office. Mike rescues her.

In *The Girl Hunters,* Velda never appears. Seven years ago, Mike assigned her to guard jewelry belonging to the wife of Rudolph Civac (in reality, Gerald Erlich, ex-Nazi). Velda disappeared, behind the Iron Curtain. Mike learns she was an O.S.I. agent during the war, spied successfully, and was being pursued by Gorlin, an ex–Nazi killer. Richie Cole, who when dying tells Mike that Velda is alive, helped get her back to America. Mike kills Gorlin and will soon see Velda again. In *The Snake,* Mike rejoices that Velda, who "was . . . during those years behind the Iron Curtain in the biggest chase scene civilization had ever known," helped cause many Communist deaths in Moscow, East Berlin, South America, and indeed "across the face of the globe . . . in uncountable numbers."

In *The Snake,* when Mike finds Velda at last, she is in the process of keeping Sue Devon from being killed. Gunfire erupts at Velda's apartment door, after which Mike is so busy following leads generated by Sue's suspicion that Torrence killed her mother, Sally Devon Torrence, that Mike's and Velda's physical consummation of their love for one another gets put off until novel's end.

In *The Twisted Thing* Velda neither appears nor is mentioned.

In *The Body Lovers,* Velda assists Mike by obtaining background information concerning Maxine Delaney and Helen Poston. Velda infiltrates the activities of Belar Ris at his mansion in Bradbury, on Long Island, befriends Julie Pelham briefly there, and rescues Mike and Greta Service from terrible danger there.

In *Survival . . . Zero!,* Velda tries to locate the red-vested pickpocket, ultimately identified as Beaver. She half-scoffs at Mike's statement that he may legalize their relationship by marriage.

In *The Killing Man,* Velda, Mike's "doll," "honey," and "kitten," takes a phone message from Penta, who calls himself Bruce Lewison and who then storms into Mike's office, slugs Velda, and kills Anthony DiCica. Velda is almost helpless in the hospital, on a gurney, and at the cabin which Lewis Ferguson owns and to which Mike takes her for safety. There Mike saves her from Penta's clutches.

In *Black Alley,* Velda waits confidently for Mike's return from seeming death. When he finds himself on the trail of $89 billion in missing Mafia money, she helps him, comforts him when he gets dizzy, goes with him to Slipped Disk Harris's cave despite her fear of bats, and survives with him when Ugo Ponti tries to kill them in their motel. Velda is ecstatic when her "boss" gives her a diamond engagement ring and she can at last anticipate marriage, after decades of faithful waiting.

***VENGEANCE IS MINE!* (1950).** Novel. (Characters: Andrew, Artie, Roy Carmichael, Petey Cassandro, Captain Patrick Chambers, Ed Cooper, Lillian Corbett, Flynn, George, Joe Gill, George Hamilton, Mike Hammer, Homer, Joseph, Kate, Ted Lee, Marion Lester, Anton Lipsek, Rita Loring, Martin, Marshall, Neil, Emil Perry, Rainey, Ralph, Raymond, Juno Reeves, Stanton, Jean Trotter, Velda, Connie Wales, Chester Wheeler, Clyde Williams.)

Mike Hammer first met Chester Wheeler, a fellow veteran, in Cincinnati, Ohio, in 1945, just after the war. Five years later and in New York City on a buying trip—he owned a department store in Columbus—he bumped into Mike again. They exchanged war stories, drank too much, and wound up in Wheeler's hotel room. Mike comes to there and is questioned by cops about

Wheeler's apparent suicide with Mike's .45 in the room. Dragged to headquarters, Mike, though vouched for by Captain Pat Chambers, must surrender his gun and private-eye license to an overbearing D.A. Mike gets his secretary, Velda, already licensed, to become their agency detective while he clears his name, and, if possible, Wheeler's. He thinks Wheeler was murdered.

Mike pretends he lost his watch in the hotel room, is allowed in, and finds a bullet hole in the bed he used. From a saloon he phones Joe Gill, a detective who owes him a favor, has him backtrack Wheeler. Pat tells Mike he has learned Wheeler met with a business friend named Emil Perry, who said Wheeler was depressed and mentioned suicide. Mike finds Perry's Bronx address, drives to it, but does not ring—because he sees Emil, his fingers flashing with fine jewelry, being scared by a thug named Rainey, whose reputation as a crooked fight promoter Mike knows well. Mike drives to the Greenwood Hotel, a dump in the Eighties, to meet Gill. Gill reports that Wheeler requested—and got—$5,000 wired to him from Columbus, and also attended a fashion show in New York, drank excessively, and may have taken a model, from the Anton Lipsek Agency, on a date afterwards.

Next day Mike finds Anton's place on Thirty-third Street. After photographing a gorgeous model named Connie Wales for business advertisements, Anton, when asked, amiably turns to Juno Reeves, his gorgeous associate who booked the fashion show attended by Wheeler. Juno agrees to ask various girls if they remember Wheeler. Connie, a wild sexpot, entices Mike to take her for several beers, then gets him to her Sixty-second Street apartment, where they have coffee, eggs, and cocktails. He explains his Wheeler mission. When he wonders at her interest, she slugs him, rips off her clothes, accepts a hard slap from him in return, and they tangle in rough sex.

Mike takes Connie to a Chinese dinner. She gets him to a dirty bar, where they join five rich, thrill-seeking men she knows. They are Andrew, Homer, Joseph, Martin, and Raymond. These five, and their dates, and Mike and Connie go to the Bowery Inn, a tourist trap that sports drinking, lewd dancers, and a hidden gambling den. Perhaps Wheeler went there with a model. Mike recognizes the owner, Robert Hobart Williams, who calls himself Clyde. Mike, who calls him Dink and Dinky, shot him a while ago in the leg while he was driving a killer's car. The two trade insults. Mike fights his way past a thug, enters the den, and sees Anton and Juno. Mike reassures potentially jealous Connie that, though stunned by Juno's incredible beauty, he dislikes her. Juno tells him that a model named Marion Lester got drunk with Wheeler, who decently left her in her room at the Chadwick Hotel. As Mike and Connie, who say she is "sloshed," leave, he sees Velda buttering up Clyde at his bar.

In the office next morning, Velda says she flew to Columbus; learned that Wheeler was happily married, with a son and a daughter, was successful in business with a good credit rating; returned, went to the Bowery Inn, and thus met, and immensely pleased, Clyde. Mike finds Marion Lester in her room, regards her as attractive and sweet, and learns that Wheeler didn't misbehave with her, although she admits she was drunk. Mike drives to Emil Perry's place; barges past his African American maid; says he will treat Perry worse than Rainey could; says Rainey told Perry to lie to the police about Wheeler's talk of suicide. When Perry faints, Mike leaves. As snow falls on Manhattan, Mike parks in a lot, taxis to Juno's office, and they go (Mike at the wheel of her Cadillac) to lunch at a "fag joint" she innocently recommended. A lesbian gives Juno the eye. Juno says Clyde gathered signed photographs of models, hung them in his inn, and thus lured wealthy tourists. They take her Caddy to her Riverside Drive apartment for one drink. He resists her goddesslike beauty, explaining her golden hair makes him think of Charlotte Manning, whom he loved but shot dead. While walking along Broadway and then into Thirty-third, he is shot at but missed, twice. Mike finds Velda in their office. She is so stunningly dressed, for a working date with Clyde, that Mike kisses her and, when she leaves, turns glum at seemingly losing out. He arms himself with a hidden .25 automatic, summons Pat, and tells him that Rainey scared Perry into lying and that Dink calls himself Clyde, who Pat says is now influential among higher-ups in the city. Mike drives to Connie's place; learns that Juno rescued Anton in France, where he collaborated with Nazis, and got him to New York; learns Connie regards Marion as snooty; tells her to lure a moneyed date to Clyde's Bowery Inn and listen about possible payoffs to city officials. Mike takes Connie for a seafood dinner, then turns her loose. He phones Gill and asks him to check into Perry's business reputation. He goes to the office of Ed Cooper, sports editor at the *Globe,* and learns Rainey is promoting some fights tonight at his Glenwood arena, out on Long Island. Mike drives there, makes his way into Rainey's office, where he is counting crooked-fight loot, and accuses him of shooting at him back on Broadway. Mike disarms Rainey, shoots him in the thigh with Rainey's own .32, warns him not to bother Perry again, shoots Rainey's skinny thug, Artie, when he enters, and departs.

Next morning Gill phones Mike that Perry withdrew $20,000 from his bank and obviously is being blackmailed. Mike gets to Perry's home, finds it empty and deserted, puts ashes of burned papers into an envelope, and returns to his office, where he is arrested, taken to the D.A.'s office, charged with shooting Rainey (now murdered), but released when Pat comes and lies that he and Mike played cards all night. Alone with Mike, Pat adds not only that two Detroit gunmen have been brought in but that the D.A. is under pressure to clean up the city. He gives Pat the ashes. (They turn out to be burned photos.)

A note from Velda in the office tells Mike to call Connie. He drives to her place, and she tells him this: She went to the Bowery Inn, which was filled with talk of Rainey's murder and Mike's being sought; Anton was there, drunk and harassing girls; Clyde showed up late. Professing love for Mike, Connie suddenly strips; but, manfully resisting, he goes to his apartment for a .30 Luger, only to be jumped there, in the dark, by an unknown wiry person. They fight. Mike tears off part of the old suit of his assailant, who escapes as

Mike knocks himself out in a fall. Awakening, he sees the D.A. and some assistants over him, summoned by a neighbor. Without a warrant, the D.A., whom Mike calls a "yellow-bellied little bastard" and a "crummy turd," gets nowhere and takes his leave. Pat, also present, stays to brainstorm with Mike, adding that Robert Hobart Williams (Clyde) has just purchased Rainey's sports area. Mike holsters his Luger, finds Velda at her place, just leaving for a date with eager Clyde, phones Connie, who is out, and then Juno, who invites him over. They dine, drink, and dance; and he tells her about Wheeler, Rainey, and Clyde, resists her unearthy attractions, leaves, and checks into a hotel.

About 9:00 the next evening Mike awakens, phones Velda, and learns that Clyde is so wild about her that he wants not only to seduce her but to make her his partner in hinted-at crimes. Mike meets Pat at a secret hangout. Pat warns him that the D.A. checked and knows Pat lied to cover for Mike. A witness saw Mike at Rainey's Glenwood arena, and the D.A. wants Mike arrested. Pat is on his way to a suicide off the Brooklyn Bridge. Mike goes along; hears a barge captain say he saw the girl thrown in the water; recognizes the girl as Jean Trotter, one of Anton's models who, according to Connie, quit to get married; gives Pat a photo of Jean from a bunch he has from the studio. Mike goes to Connie's place. Although nude and enticing, she reveals only this of importance: Jean changed her name from Julia Travesky when modeling. By phone, Mike warns Velda to avoid Clyde, but she says Wheeler's widow told her Wheeler said he met Jean, his daughter's former schoolmate, in New York. Mike concludes this: Wheeler went out with Jean that fatal night; Marion, instead, lied that Wheeler was with her.

While Pat chases leads to Jean's murderer, Mike seeks Marion and finds her dead in her apartment of a broken neck. After tersely phoning the police, he rushes to Anton's apartment, goes on a door-breaking rampage, rushes past expensive paintings by Old Masters, and finds a beautiful bedroom with a camera pointing through a painting. Wheeler must have been there with Jean and gotten blackmailed. Anton enters, sees the mess, and escapes. Mike drives after Anton's car, which fatally crashes. Mike finds evidence on Anton's body that Clyde sent Anton money. So Clyde is the brains of the racket? Mike gets to Clyde's apartment, finds him hovering over Velda, holds his Luger on Clyde in the nick of time, recites evidence of his crimes, but is disarmed by Clyde's henchman from behind. Clyde sits Mike on a chair, preparing to mistreat Velda and then kill Mike. But Velda pulls a tiny automatic from her shoulder and shoots the henchman. Clyde escapes. Suspecting he has gone to Anton's for incriminating photos, Mike follows—only to find Connie there, her neck also fatally wrenched.

Now Mike thinks he knows all. He drives to Juno's place, demands to know who masterminded all those murders, says he mistakenly suspected Anton and then Clyde, threatens to shoot Juno, but cannot—because he remembers Charlotte. Juno, fearfully wiry, suddenly slugs Mike; they fight; he pulls off her dress. Knowing the truth now, Mike says Juno killed Wheeler (who would have exposed the truth), Rainey (who got greedy), Jean and then Marion (who knew the truth), and Connie (who also got killed). Mike gives Juno a chance to go for a gun, then shoots him dead—yes, he was a man.

Notable in *Vengeance* is the fast pace of action. For example, in a single day, Mike is briefed by Velda in office, interviews Marion, drives to Bronx to scare Perry, taxis to Juno's office, lunches with her in Greenwich Village, takes her to her Riverside apartment, walks to Broadway and Thirty-third, is shot at twice, meets Velda in office, chats with Pat there, visits Connie's place, dines out with her, phones Gill, goes to the *Globe* office, drives through snow to Long Island, catches a boxing bout, finds Rainey's office, warns then shoots him, shoots Artie, and leaves—the while enjoying at least eight drinks and many cigarettes. The next day is equally crowded. Notable is a slight increase in off-color language, although subsequent advances in action fiction and on television make pale Spillane's use of "balls," "butt," crap," "cripes," "goddamn," "nuts," "tail," and "turd" in now-remote 1950.

VENN, HELEN. In "The Night I Died," she is a beautiful, duplicitous criminal. Mike Hammer falls in love with her and promises to protect her from the Syndicate. In truth, she and Buddy Whiteman killed Marty Wellman, and she sought Carmen Rich, who took over Syndicate leadership. When Mike finds Carmen, Helen has Buddy kill him. Wounded by Buddy, Mike kills him, and seeks help from Helen, who stabs him. Two years later, Mike finds and kills Helen.

VENUS. In *The Long Wait,* she is a madam recommended by Jack to John McBride, who learns she was once on stage, married to a cop, and shot him to death. She gives McBride information and sleeps memorably with him. McBride calls her a "lovely zombie."

VERDO. In "The Flier," "Verdo and Cristy" was a code signal Cat Fallon and Tucker Stacy used.

VERDUN, FRANCOIS ("FRANK," "FRANKIE"). In *The Last Cop Out,* he is an experienced, sadistic killer. A homosexual, he regards murder as orgasmic. Mark Shelby recruits him to come to Manhattan. Verdun hires Helen Scanlon as his receptionist. He orders tortures and murders in an effort to find out who is killing Shelby's men. Shatzi Heinkle mutilates and fatally stabs Verdun and cuts out his navel before he dies. When Louise Belhander, once raped by Verdun, learns that Papa Menes associates with Verdun, she determines to kill Menes.

VERNE, MARY. In *The Ship That Never Was,* she is mentioned as a girl Josh Toomey likes.

VERNIE. In *The Body Lovers,* he is a Los Angeles contact whom Velda phones for information about Maxine Delaney.

VERNON. In *The Deep,* it was with his Chicago "mob" that George Elcursio associated before coming to New York City.

VETTER. In "Everybody's Watching Me," posing as Joe Boyle and using his legendary reputation as a killer, Vetter works eighteen months pushing carts laden with scrap metal, learns about the drug operations of Phil Carboy, Gulley, Mark Renzo, and Sergeant Detective Gonzales, and outwits them all. Vetter rescues Helen Troy, and the two fall in love. They check into a hotel as Mr. and Mrs. Valiscivitch.

VIC. In *The Last Cop Out,* he was Mark Shelby's faithful worker in a newly assigned territory but was mysteriously killed.

VICKERS, EILEEN. In *I, the Jury,* she was a college student from Poughkeepsie, New York, was corrupted by Harold Kines, had an abortion, and was forced into prostitution. Her father, R. H. Vickers, abandoned her. Hammer finds her in Miss June's brothel. She is sorry when Hammer tells her of the murder of Jack Williams, who knew her earlier. In her late twenties and calling herself Mary Wright, Eileen is murdered by Charlotte Manning.

VICKERS, R. H. In *I, the Jury,* he is Eileen Vickers's father. When she got into trouble in college, he called her sinful and refused to help her.

VIGARO ("VIG"). In *The Last Cop Out,* he owns a motorboat shop in Miami. Herman Shanke ships a load of weapons to it, but it soon blows up.

VILECK, JOHN. In *The Big Kill,* he is the big, rough superintendent of the apartment where William Decker lived. Vileck and a gentle priest, who happens to be with him, tell Mike that Decker was a fine man, missed his deceased wife, and tried to work to support their little boy.

VINCE. In *The Delta Factor,* Art Keefer warns Morgan that Vince, their colleague, just reported that Morgan's movement toward the Central American island is known. Kimberly Stacy calmly says she planted the information.

VINNIE. In "Man Alone," he runs a restaurant where Sergeant Jerry Nolan regularly enjoys a Saturday lunch of "wop clam chowder." Patrick Regan meets Nolan there.

VINNIE. In "The Seven Year Kill," he loans Phil Rocca a jacket.

VINSON, CHUCK. In "Return of the Hood," he owns a saloon where Ryan has a beer before stalking and finding Ernie South.

VIRELLI, ANTON. In *Survival . . . Zero!,* he is a bookie. Velda phones Mike Hammer that she saw the pickpocket near 92nd Street and Broadway, where Virelli operates.

VON SELTER, GENERAL. In *Day of the Guns,* while reminiscing to himself, Tiger Mann recalls tricking this man.

VOORHIES. In *The Erection Set,* Dog Kelly recalls that Bridey-the-Greek killed Voorhies with an icepick.

W

WAGNER, CHARLES. In *The Deep. See* James, Lew.

WAGNER, GEORGE. In *The Deep. See* Reeves, Morrie.

WALD, MISS. In *The Body Lovers,* she is a receptionist on the floor of the building in which Theodore Gates has his office.

WALES, CONNIE. In *Vengeance Is Mine!,* she is a beautiful, gamy model, likes Mike Hammer warmly, discovers that a gift for Jean Trotter's marriage is unnecessary because the girl never eloped, and is murdered for her pains.

WALKER, ED. In *The Body Lovers,* he is a young lawyer working under the new D.A. Walker tells Mike that Belar Ris is part owner of the *Pinella,* the ship off which the C-130 poison that killed Helen Poston was stolen.

WALKER, SERGEANT. In *The Long Wait,* he answers the phone when John McBride phones Captain Lindsey.

WALLACE, DENNIS. In *The Girl Hunters,* he packed Velda in a crate to remove her from the *Vanessa,* according to Red Markham. When Mike Hammer and Hy Gardner get to Wallace, they find him tortured and murdered (by Gorlin).

WALLACE, HARVEY. In *Kiss Me, Deadly,* he drove the truck that killed Leopold Kawolsky in a Mafia-engineered "accident." His conscience troubled him until Mike explained matters. Wallace and his wife live over Pascale's saloon.

WALLACE, MRS. HARVEY. In *Kiss Me, Deadly,* she is the innocent truck driver's wife.

WALLER, MANNIE. In "The Seven Year Kill," he is the fat New York City crime kingpin, ever since Rhino Massley's supposed death. When he hears that Rhino is returning in search of documents to blackmail him with, Waller seeks him through Terry Massley and Phil Rocca. Waller's numerous goons injure Rocca, who, however, is responsible for Waller's arrest.

WATFORD, THOMAS ("TOMMY"). In *Day of the Guns,* he is a Manhattan import-export expert who controls politicians, whereas Martin Grady and Mann use money more amorally. Tiger Mann irritates Watford by defying him at every turn. In *Bloody Sunrise,* Tiger again operates in ways to discomfit Watford.

WATSON, HOMER. In *Black Alley,* he is a competent, patient Treasury agent, whose specialty is sniffing out money hidden from federal tax collectors. For ten years he has been on the trail of Mafia money supposedly hidden by the Ponti family. Watson attends the funeral of Marcos Dooley, his primary suspect, and tries to keep up with Mike while that resourceful man also looks for the money.

WATTS, CHARLIE. In "The Gold Fever Tapes," he is a police captain who enjoys needling Fallon after he gets out of prison. Watts is unaware that Fallon is still a policeman now operating undercover to find 800 pounds of stolen gold.

WATTS, RAYMOND ("RAY"). In *Bloody Sunrise,* he operates an agency, headquartered in Los Angeles, to find missing persons. Tiger Mann phones him to check on Sonia Dutko. Watts assigns William Copely, his New York agent, to do so, and Copely is murdered.

WAX. In *The By-Pass Control,* he owns a fish house in Leesville, North Carolina, which Louis Agrounsky frequented.

WEAL, FERRIS. In *The Erection Set,* he is a drug-enforcement agent, now aged, whom Dog Kelly remembers working with in 1948. Weal enjoys making it difficult for Dog Kelly to find him twenty-some years later. When Dog does so, Ferris gives Dog the casket of missing heroin.

WEAVER, LENNIE ("LEN," "PIGFACE"). In "Kick It or Kill!," he is a New York City criminal working for Simpson in Pinewood. He got Ruth Gleason hooked on heroin, abused her, and has discarded her. When he refuses to give her more drugs, she kills him with a pointed stick in the belly.

WEBBER. In "Everybody's Watching Me," he works for Mark Renzo and told him he saw Helen Troy at Gulley's pier.

WEIR, WALTER ("PIGEON"). In "Return of the Hood," he is a Miami hood imported by Primo Stipetto to assault Lisa Williams sexually. Ryan finds Weir, knocks him unconscious, loads him into his own car with Florida plates, and rams Weir's knife "up to the hilt in his tail," as a warning against further sodomizing.

WEIST, COO-COO. In *Survival . . . Zero!,* he is named by Meyer Solomon as an eighty-year-old pickpocket.

WELBURG, WALTER. In *My Gun Is Quick,* he is a criminal Mike Hammer beats up when he finds Welburg seeking Nancy Sanford's ring, dropped in the parking lot near Murray Candid's Zero Zero Club.

WELCH. In *Survival . . . Zero!,* he owns a bar frequented by the superintendent of the apartment building in which Lipton Sullivan lived.

WELCH THE DUTCHMAN. In "Man Alone," he is a vicious policeman who Patrick Regan recalls enjoyed killing people "in the line of duty."

WELKES, RICHARD. In *The Killing Man,* he is the owner, living in Miami Beach, of the Mercedes fitted with New York license plates and driven by Harry Bern and Gary Fells in New York City.

WELLMAN, MARTY. In "The Night I Died," he was the Syndicate boss whom Helen Venn and Buddy Wellman killed.

WELLS. In "The Bastard Bannerman." *See* Bannerman, Cat Cay.

WELLS. In *Bloody Sunrise,* according to Clement Fletcher, Wells and Chobeay told him about uranium strikes near Vera Cruz.

WELLS, HELEN. In *Bloody Sunrise. See* Dutko, Sonia.

WELLS, TIPPY. In *The Snake,* Sonny Motley names him to Mike Hammer as a member of his old mob. Wells is dead, Motley adds.

WEMBER, DR. ANTHONY. In "The Bastard Bannerman," he is the police surgeon who admits that any kitchen knife, not necessarily a stiletto, could have killed Chuck Maloney.

WENZEL, DOE. In "Return of the Hood," Lisa Williams tells Ryan she remembers his protecting her from Wenzel, at the expense of being shot himself.

WEST, EDWINA. In *The Killing Man,* she is a well-trained CIA agent, age forty-eight, assigned to General Rudolph Skubal as his "secretary" and found by Mike to be lusciously attractive. All they can do is kiss hotly. He promises her a more satisfactory encounter later.

WEST, VERA. In *The Long Wait,* she was John McBride's girlfriend (and wife), thought he stole from the bank, and turned to Lenny Servo for help. When McBride returns to Lyncastle with amnesia, Vera, calling herself Wendy Miller and employed as a singer at Louie Dinero's steakhouse, goes slow in identifying herself. But she helps him, sleeps with him, and finally reveals her true identity. Spillane strains credulity by having Vera, a blonde, dye her hair roots black and her hair ends blonde, to deceive McBride.

WHALEN, MISS. In "Tomorrow I Die," Auger, the leading bank robber, names her in connection with a reference to the mayor. Perhaps Miss Whalen, who does not appear in the story, is the mayor's secretary.

WHEELER. In *The Death Dealers,* he and his wife entered Edith Caine's apartment building, according to Ron, the doorman.

WHEELER, CHESTER ("CHET"). In *Vengeance Is Mine!,* he was a captain in the air force and a veteran when Mike Hammer met him in 1945. Five years later, Wheeler owns a successful department store in Columbus, Ohio, comes to New York City to attend a fashion meeting, and dates Jean Trotter, a model his daughter knew in high school. He is blackmailed and murdered. Mike Hammer solves his murder and several subsequent ones resulting from it.

WHEELER, MRS. In *The Death Dealers,* she accompanied her husband as they entered Edith Caine's apartment, according to the doorman, Ron.

WHITE. In *Day of the Guns,* Mann recalls saving White, along with Connors, in Poland during the war.

WHITE. In "Kick It or Kill!," he owns a restaurant, where Kelly Smith has supper after arriving in Pinewood.

WHITEMAN, BUDDY. In "The Night I Died," he and Helen Venn killed Marty Wellman, the Syndicate boss.

WHITMAN ("WHIT"). In *The Long Wait,* he is Alan Logan's New York friend who tells Logan about Gracie Harlan's identity.

WICKHOFF, LOUIS. In *The Death Dealers,* he is the boss of the waiters at the Stacy Hotel. Tiger Mann gets him to hire Lennie Byrnes as a waiter and

Harry as a cook specializing in Middle Eastern dishes, including items featuring sheep's eyes.

WIERTON, WILLIAM. In *Kiss Me, Deadly. See* Mist, William.

WILDER, GUS. In "Killer Mine," he was a criminal wanted by the Gordon-Carbito mob to prevent his testifying against them. He is incorrectly suspected of robbing the men who pulled off the Canadian armored-car heist. Instead, he jumped bail in Toledo, phoned his stepbrother Henry Wilder in New York for money, failed to receive it, and committed suicide.

WILDER, HARMON. In *I, the Jury,* he was a successful criminal lawyer, went into private practice, and handles investments for Esther and Mary Bellemy. Charlotte Manning supplies heroin to Wilder, and his friend Charles Sherman. Mike Hammer saw Wilder at Miss June's brothel, and sees him later with Sherman, at the Bellemys' dinner party.

WILDER, HENRY. In "Killer Mine," he is Gus Wilder's bachelor stepbrother, is about fifty years old, and runs a dry-cleaning shop. He helps Lieutenant Joe Scanlon find Rose Shaw and also confirms the time Gus phoned Henry to appeal, unsuccessfully, for money.

WILEY. In *Survival . . . Zero!,* he and Jenkins are detectives assigned to investigate Lipton Sullivan's murder.

WILKENSON, GEORGE P. In "The Bastard Bannerman," he was Cat Cay Bannerman's grandfather's attorney, prepared and held his will, and tells Cat about the possibility of his inheriting millions. It is fortunate that Wilkenson, age ninety-three, is alive after Cat's disappearance from Culver City for twenty-five years.

WILLIAMS, CLYDE (real name: Robert Hobart Williams; nicknames: "Dink," "Dinky"). In *Vengeance Is Mine!,* he is a longtime criminal. Mike Hammer shot him in the leg a while back; so they dislike each other. Mike discovers that he runs the Bowery Inn, a tourist trap for the rich unwary. Williams's undoing comes when he tries to seduce Velda, sicced on him by Mike. Although Mike suspects him of multiple murders, he was in cahoots with Anton Lipsek and Juno Reeves, both more guilty than he. Clyde remains alive.

WILLIAMS, JACK. In *I, the Jury,* he saved Hammer's life in combat during World War II by blocking a Japanese soldier's bayonet thrust, and lost an arm doing so. Once a cop, he found work as an insurance-company investigator. Before the war, Jack met Myrna Devlin, a junkie, helped her go cold turkey, and was engaged to her when he was murdered. Hammer vows to kill his killer, and does.

WILLIAMS, LISA. In "Return of the Hood," she was a rising musical star, until Primo Stipetto, who used and thought he owned her, caught her with other men and beat her viciously. Although this destroyed her beautiful face, Primo continued with his sexual demands. Ryan gained Lisa's gratitude once by rescuing her from a gunman. Lisa, now a hopeless alcoholic, saves Ryan from Fly, a drug addict associating with Stipetto. Stipetto and Ernie South, another criminal, catch up with Ryan; but Lisa rescues him again, this time at the cost of her life.

WILLIAMS, SQUEAKY. In "The Gold Fever Tapes," when he got out of prison, he became an expert at handling radios and other sound equipment. Sadly, he chanced to record a conversation about a theft of gold. His attempting to engage in blackmail got him murdered on Reading's order.

WILLIAMS, TOMMY ("CHUM"). In *Day of the Guns,* he is a hood from Chicago, sent with Max Sweiber to kill Tiger Mann. Tiger kills them both.

WILLIAMS, TONY. In *The By-Pass Control,* he is an agent from whom Tiger Mann does not want help. He tells Martin Grady he prefers Don Lavois. Williams thus escapes Lavois's fate, being murdered by Niger Hoppes.

WILLIE. In "The Pickpocket," he is a reformed pickpocket. Willie sees Marty after he shot somebody. When Marty sends Buster to scare Willie, he disarms Buster and phones Detective Coggins. Thereafter, Coggins treats Willie amiably.

WILLIE-THE-ACTOR. In *Black Alley,* he is a high-voiced alcoholic Mike Hammer hires to get on the phone to Ugo Ponti and pretend he has spotted someone trying to break into his computer office.

WILLIS. In *The Erection Set,* he is Leyland Ross Hunter's limousine driver.

WILLIS, BING. In *Bloody Sunrise,* he used to frequent Stanton's bar, Tiger Mann recalls, until he died two years earlier.

WILSON. In *Day of the Guns,* he is an agent who works with Toomey and Standish to help Tiger Mann.

WILSON, FRANK. In *Day of the Guns. See* Mann, Tiger.

WILSON, GEORGE. In *The Long Wait,* he was John McBride's look-alike fellow construction worker. A wanted murderer, he exchanged identities with McBride after an accident gave McBride amnesia. He later died trying to rescue McBride from another accident.

WILSON, RAY. In *The Killing Man*, he is a police officer experienced in intelligence and three weeks short of retirement. He helps Captain Pat Chambers and Mike Hammer, not least when he breaks a code enabling him to pinpoint the location of the cocaine-filled trailer.

WINKLER, MRS. In "Me, Hood!," when Ryan is in his half-demolished old Valley Park apartment, he recalls that she gave him a drop-leaf table, still there.

WINTERS, M. A. In *The Delta Factor. See* Morgan the Raider.

WINTERS, MRS. M. A. In *The Delta Factor. See* Stacy, Kimberly.

WONG, DEWEY. In *Survival . . . Zero!,* he owns a restaurant on East 58th Street. Captain Pat Chambers takes Mike Hammer and Eddie Dandy to dinner there. Later Renée Talmage meets Mike there. Dewey's wife is Janie Wong.

WONG, JANIE. *Survival . . . Zero!,* she is Dewey Wong's beautiful wife.

WOODIE. In *The Last Cop Out,* he, Ollie, and Matt Stevenson are assigned by Francois Verdun to guard Leon Bray. They are all gassed to death by an unknown assailant.

WOODRING. In *The Erection Set,* when Dog Kelly asks Chet Linden to buy Barrin stock, Linden gets some from young Woodring.

WOODS, SERGEANT. In *Survival . . . Zero!,* he works under Captain Pat Chambers and answers the phone once when Mike Hammer phones for Pat.

WOODY. In "Kick It or Kill!," he is a Pinewood policeman and, at Captain Cox's order, takes Kelly Smith's fingerprints.

WOOLART, GAVIN. In *The Delta Factor,* he is an able State Department agent who assigns Morgan the difficult job of rescuing Victor Sable, provides his false name (M. A. Winters) and funds, and promises a reduced prison sentence if Morgan is successful.

WOOSTER, SAL. In *Survival . . . Zero!,* Caesar Mario Tulley tells Mike Hammer that Sal saw Beaver pick the pockets of two people.

WOPE, HARRY. In "Killer Mine," he was saved by Lieutenant Joe Scanlon's father during their army service in France in World War I. Out of gratitude, Wope gives Joe information about Al Reese.

WRIGHT, MARY. In *I, the Jury. See* Vickers, Eileen.

WYNDOT, JERRY. In *The Long Wait,* he is the milkman who delivers to Wendy Miller (*see* West, Vera).

Y

YARD, GORMAN. In *The Delta Factor,* he was a petty criminal and a black-marketeer during World War II. He tried to cheat Whitey Tass later. Joey Jolley asked Mrs. Gustav Timely to rent him a room. He was jailed in Elmira, New York, after a hit-and-run accident in Syracuse. Tass ordered Yard killed in prison.

YORK, MRS. RUDOLPH. In *The Twisted Thing,* she died giving birth in New York to her husband's son, who also died.

YORK, RUDOLPH. In *The Twisted Thing,* he is a gifted, rich scientist. When his wife died in childbirth in New York, he caused Herron Mallory's infant son, born at the same time, to be switched as his and called him Ruston York. For fourteen years, Rudolph educated Ruston. Mallory and Rita Cambell, who as a nurse connived in the switch and who calls herself Myra Grange, plan to blackmail Rudolph. Ruston stages his own kidnapping and subsequently murders Rudolph, whom he loathes.

YORK, RUSTON. In *The Twisted Thing,* he is Herron Mallory's brainy son, switched at birth in New York to be Rudolph York's son. For fourteen years, Rudolph so home-schools Ruston that the precocious lad becomes "a twisted thing," stages his own kidnapping, murders Rudolph, and when caught by Mike Hammer commits suicide. Initially regarding the bright kid as brave, Mike nicknames him "Lancelot."

General Bibliography

Abbott, Megan E. *The Street Was Mine: White Masculinity in Hardboiled Fiction and Film Noir.* New York: Palgrave Macmillan, 2002.

Baker, Robert A., and Michael T. Nietzel. *Private Eyes: One Hundred and One Knights: A Survey of American Detective Fiction 1922-1984.* Bowling Green, Ohio: Bowling Green State University Popular Press, 1985.

Banks, Jeff R. "Anti-Professionalism in the Works of Mickey Spillane." *Notes on Contemporary Literature* 3 (1973): 6-8.

Carlson, Michael. "Mickey Spillane." *Crime Time,* August 6, 2001, pp. 1-15.

——. "Spillane and the Critics." *Armchair Detective* 12 (Fall 1979): 300-307.

Cawelti, John G. *Adventure, Mystery, and Romance: Formula Stories as Art and Popular Culture.* Chicago and London: University of Chicago Press, 1976.

——. "The Spillane Phenomenon." *Journal of Popular Culture* 3 (Summer 1969): 9-22.

DeAndrea, William L. *Encyclopedia Mysteriosa: A Comprehensive Guide to the Art of Detection in Print, Film, Radio, and Television.* New York: Prentice Hall General Reference, 1994.

Dietze, Gabriele. "Gender Topography of the Fifties: Mickey Spillane and the Post-World-War-II Masculinity Crises." *Amerikastudien: American Studies* 43 (1998): 645-56.

Evans, Odette L'Henry. "Towards a Semiotic Reading," pp. 100-14 in *American Crime Fiction: Studies in the Genre,* ed. Brian Docherty. New York: St. Martins Press.

Haut, Woody. *Pulp Culture: Hardboiled Fiction and the Cold War.* New York: Serpent's Tail, 1995.

Johnston, Richard W. "Death's Fair-Haired Boy." *Life,* 32 (June 23, 1952): 79-80, 82, 85-86, 92, 95.

La Farge, Christopher. "Mickey Spillane and His Bloody Hammer," pp. 176-85 in *Mass Culture: The Popular Arts in America,* ed. Bernard Rosenberg and David Manning White. Glencoe, Ill.: Free Press, 1957.

Landrum, Larry. *American Mystery and Detective Novels: A Reference Guide.* Westport, Conn.: Greenwood Press, 1999.

Landrum, Larry N., Pat Browne, and Ray B. Browne, eds. *Dimensions of Detective Fiction.* Bowling Green, Ohio: Bowling Green University Popular Press, 1976.

McCann, Sean. *Gumshoe America: Hard-Boiled Crime Fiction and the Rise and Fall of New Deal Liberalism.* Durham & London: Duke University Press, 2000.

Niebuhr, Gary Warren. *A Reader's Guide to the Private Eye Novel.* Boston: G. K. Hall, 1993.

"1947 Fifty Years Ago: Sex, Violence, and Motorcycles." *American Heritage* 48 (July–August 1997): 98–99.

Porter, Dennis. *The Pursuit of Crime: Art and Ideology in Detective Fiction.* New Haven and London: Yale University Press, 1981.

Rolo, Charles J. "[Georges] Simenon and Spillane: The Metaphysics of Murder for the Millions," pp. 165–75 in *Mass Culture: The Popular Arts in America,* ed. Bernard Rosenberg and David Manning White. Glencoe, Ill.: Free Press, 1957.

Ruehlmann, William. *Saint with a Gun: The Unlawful American Private Eye.* New York: New York University Press, 1974.

Silet, Charles L. P. "The First Angry White Male: Mickey Spillane's Mike Hammer." *Armchair Detective* 29 (Spring 1996): 194–99.

Van Dover, J. Kenneth. *Murder in the Millions: Erle Stanley Gardner, Mickey Spillane, Ian Fleming.* New York: Frederick Unger, 1984.

Waugh, Hillary. *Guide to Mystery & Mystery Writers.* Cincinnati: Writer's Digest Books, 1991.

Index

About the Author

ROBERT L. GALE is Professor Emeritus of English at the University of Pittsburgh. His previous books include *A Dashiell Hammett Companion* (2000), *An Ambrose Bierce Companion* (2001), *A Lafcadio Hearn Companion* (2002), and *A Ross Macdonald Companion* (2002), all available from Greenwood Press.

DATE DUE			

IHUMW   810
         .9
         SP4G

GALE, ROBERT L.
   A MICKEY SPILLANE
COMPANION

IHUMW   810
         .9
         SP4G

HOUSTON PUBLIC LIBRARY
CENTRAL LIBRARY

JUL 04